THE LAND OF ISRAEL:
JEWISH PERSPECTIVES

UNIVERSITY OF NOTRE DAME
CENTER FOR THE STUDY OF
JUDAISM AND CHRISTIANITY
IN ANTIQUITY

Number 6

The Land of Israel:
Jewish Perspectives

LAWRENCE A. HOFFMAN, EDITOR

UNIVERSITY OF NOTRE DAME PRESS
NOTRE DAME, INDIANA 46556

Library of Congress Cataloging-in-Publication Data

The Land of Israel.

(Studies in Judaism and Christianity in antiquity ;
no. 6)
    Bibliography: p.
    1. Palestine in Judaism. 2. Judaism—Doctrines.
I. Hoffman, Lawrence A., 1942–   . II. Series:
University of Notre Dame. Center for the Study
of Judaism and Christianity in Antiquity (Series) ;
no. 6.
BM729.P3L36   1986   296.3   86-40241
ISBN 0-268-01280-6

Manufactured in the United States of America

Contents

PART IV: THE LAND OF ISRAEL
IN THE MODERN PERIOD

Acknowledgments

This book has been long in coming. It began ten years ago, when the Theology Department of the University of Notre Dame sponsored two series of lectures on Jewish themes: first (in 1976), "Prayer in Judaism"; and a year later (1977), "The Land of Israel in Jewish Thought." In both cases, it was hoped that the papers would be collected and published. The available manuscripts on "Prayer," however, proved insufficient to fill an entire volume, so I was invited by Charles Primus to include the talk I had given in that first series—it dealt with liturgical traditions hailing from the Land—in the volume he was editing emanating from the second one. Again, however, as so often happens with scholarly colloquia, for many good reasons, the book did not materialize.

When I expressed my interest in taking over the project, Jim Langford, who directs the University of Notre Dame Press, was most encouraging, to the point of telling me that the Press considered the subject of the Land of Israel of such enormous importance that even if it took several years, he was able to guarantee publication. Only rarely are editors blessed with this kind of enthusiastic support for their work, and without it, this book would never have come into being.

Profound thanks are due, then, first, to Charles Primus, for his vision which I inherited, and to Jim Langford, for sharing that vision, and for sustaining it with his confidence in my ability to see it realized.

This was in 1980, however, and by then the only available essays that still fit the volume as it was newly conceptualized were those of Joseph Gutmann and Charles Primus himself. Since the Land of Israel is not an independent field of academic specialization within the somewhat arbitrary classification of disciplines into which university departments sort themselves, I approached colleagues in related fields of expertise. A translation of Shalom Rosenberg's classic Hebrew essay, originally published in *Cathedra*, was an obvious choice; and just before he died, Uriel Tal (*zichrono livrakhah*) was quick to send me a manuscript that he had already prom-

vii

ised for a memorial volume dedicated to the late Professor Jacob L. Talmon, but which he felt demanded inclusion here as well. Harry Orlinsky too graciously consented to rework an essay he had already promised for a Hebrew publication. All other chapters are newly composed in their entirety for this work. They derive from colleagues in the United States and in Israel who shared with me the recognition that Judaism's essence cannot be fathomed without due acknowledgment of the Land of Israel's critical centrality.

As the chronology here indicates, the scholarship of this book's contributors is matched only by their patience. But the book is finally here, and I hope they find that patience rewarded in the end. To them all goes my heartfelt gratitude! Acknowledgments go also to *Cathedra* and to the Israel Academy of Sciences and Humanities and to the Magnes Press, Hebrew University, for permission to republish Uriel Tal's essay.

The University of Notre Dame is remarkable also for its staff. Andrea Midgett has worked diligently to assure adequate publicity for this volume, and Margaret Gloster is responsible for the beautiful cover. Richard Allen has been unusually attentive to the thousand and one editorial concerns that arise with a book containing so much diverse, and often, technical material. More than merely edit, though that would have been enough, Richard has demonstrated commitment to the very idea of the book as a whole, and to the accurate expression of each and every idea of its several contributors.

For my part, I would be remiss if I were not to say that it is my own conviction of the Land of Israel's unique religious importance to Jews and to Judaism that drove me on through the various complexities of this book's preparation. I would dedicate my own labor here to Joel, Robert, and Shira — they will know what I mean — and to all others who, like them, love the Land.

I gladly cite a section from the Grace After Meals that may stand as a mark of that love:

> Thanks be to God who has bequeathed to our forebears a beautiful, good, and spacious land. . . . Blessed is the Eternal One, for the Land. . . ."

LAWRENCE A. HOFFMAN

Key to Transliteration

In this book, transliteration from the Hebrew generally follows the guide to Hebrew transliteration established by Werner Weinberg in 1964.* It seeks to be more functional than the competing scientific alternatives in general scholarly use. The latter are more precise, in that they permit a completely isomorphic coding of Hebrew characters into assigned English equivalents; but they then require decoding by the reader, before either pronunciation or translation can occur.

Weinberg's system, on the other hand, avoids the arbitrary use of diacritical marks as signs, thus permitting immediate phonetic recognition of the Hebrew original. Without the need to master a complex interposing transliteration code (which is itself neither Hebrew nor English, but a third "language" that only looks like English), readers who know Hebrew can reconstruct the original far more readily, and those who do not, will find, at least, that their reading speed is not retarded by the necessity to interrupt their comprehension of a sentence's message in order to bypass strange clusters of unfamiliar marks that seem to defy even pronunciation.

The only regular ambiguities are those inherent in the phonetic code on which the system is based. Thus, *kaf* and *kuf* both appear as "k"; *sin* and *samech* as "s"; and so on. *Ayin* and *alef* are alike disregarded, as not phonemically relevant, except in the middle of a word where they may be indicated by an apostrophe for better enunciation of that word, as in the holiday of Tish'ah Be'av. Silent *sheva* is not represented, and vocal *sheva* occurs as "e." The *dagesh* is rarely represented, except where common usage demands it (as in *Shabbat*) and prefixes are generally written together with the word they introduce (*hashabbat*). As the two previous examples indicate, proper nouns may be capitalized when written alone, but not when introduced by a prefix (so as to avoid the anomaly of capital letters in the middle

---

*Werner Weinberg, *Guide to Hebrew Transliteration according to Israeli Pronunciation* (1964: reprint. ed., New York: Union of American Hebrew Congregations, 1977).

of a word). Commonly found English variations from the system (like *Eretz [Yisra'el]* itself, which ought, by these rules, to occur as *Erets*) are not subjugated to the system's dictates, but reproduced as they are usually found by readers elsewhere, again in order to facilitate comprehension, even at the expense of scientific precision.

The system employed in this book deviates from the above principles only in its differentiation of *chet* ("ch") from *khaf* ("kh"). Also, in one instance —a citation from an Aramaic manuscript—where there was a need for scientific precision, a more appropriate notation that left no room for ambiguity was substituted.

Introduction:
Land of Blessing and "Blessings of the Land"

LAWRENCE A. HOFFMAN

1

Few concepts rival that of the Land of Israel for uniqueness in Jewish thought and practice. Yet remarkably little research has been done in exploring the scope and parameters of this seminal idea and the ways in which it interrelates with other categories in the system of religious thought and action we call Judaism. The Land of Israel remains a fertile field for research.

To be sure, the field has not gone completely untended. Several essays of magnitude and even full-length monographs and books are available on the subject. But none seeks precisely to do what this collection of essays does, at least not with the same scope, and not in the same detail. Every work is dependent on its predecessors, however, and a word should be said at the outset about some of the pioneering efforts with which this volume claims to be continuous.

On the one hand, we find works motivated in part by the centrality of the Land as an agenda item in current Christian-Jewish dialogue: Arthur Hertzberg's "Judaism and the Land of Israel," for example, which was prepared expressly for a conference with representatives of the World Council of Churches, only two years after the significant 1967 Six-Day Arab-Israeli War that catapulted the Land into a major dialogue desideratum for Jews and Christians;[1] or Walter Brueggemann's *The Land*, published fully ten years later, where the author expressly calls for renewed Jewish-Christian dialogue in which the Land-centeredness of the former is taken for granted;[2] or W. P. Eckert's excellent collection entitled *Jüdisches Volk – gelobtes Land* (1970), whose editor notes, "Der 6-Tage-Krieg brachte an den Tag . . . das Verhältnis zwischen Christen und Juden neu zu verstehen"[3] so that his book will serve "einige Fronten im Gespräch zwischen Juden und Christen deutlich machen."[4]

1

But we have also the work of W. D. Davies, *The Gospel and the Land,*
which appeared in 1974.[5] Unlike the abovementioned entries, Davies' mag-
num opus is but one more in his series of similar scholarly works stretching back beyond the 1967 war, so can hardly be viewed as being initiated
solely by that event's influence. As in his prior work, Davies' general task
is motivated by the desire to place Christianity within a first-century Jewish context within the Land;[6] and thus, to see Judaism and Christianity as
integrally related from the beginning, in the sense that a thoroughgoing
knowledge of Christian origins is assumed to require an equally insightful
familiarity with the Jewish milieu in which they occurred.[7]

What unites all these cases (Hertzberg, Brueggemann, Eckert, and
Davies) is the fact that the motivation behind them is in large part something other than satisfaction of one's academic curiosity regarding the nature of Judaism alone. For all but Davies, it is the contemporary interface
between Jewish and Christian consciousness that determines what scholars
discuss. (Would we even have the essays without the Six-Day War and the
resulting realization that partners-in-dialogue must come to terms with the
role of the Land in the Jewish psyche?) For Davies, even if we minimize
the influence of the 1967 war, the goal remains an understanding of Judaism so as to maximize comprehension of the background out of which
Christianity arose. Neither agenda vitiates the validity and significance of
these scholars' findings, certainly, and there can be no question of casting
aspersions on their legitimate appreciation of and empathy for Judaism as
a religious system complete and significant in its own right. But there is
often a resultant problem, nevertheless: the fact that discussion is initiated,
and its terms set, by considerations that are external to Jewish tradition itself; and—as Davies argues at the outset of his work—the categories of discussion that arise from an external setting of the agenda are not necessarily
the most apt criteria for proceeding to understand a phenomenon which
surely deserves a set of ordering concepts arrived at through a direct confrontation between the scholar and the phenomenon in question, without
regard for how that phenomenon sheds light on other topics of debate.

Davies himself illustrates the need for this intrinsic confrontation, in
his polemic against understanding Judaism with the religious categories borrowed from Christianity. He is at pains to avoid Christian preconceptions
of licit religious categories of understanding. And correctly so. But here we
face a second, albeit related, difficulty. If Judaism is not to be comprehended
from the perspective of religion as Christianity defines the term, how is it
to be approached? The normal alternative, in large part well illustrated by

Davies himself, is the generous citing of Jewish text which, presumably, lays bare the Jewish authors' own recorded perspective as they themselves willed it to posterity, what we can call their indigenous or "native" mind-set. But is the citing of text alone sufficient? Let us liken the patient researcher in ancient texts to an anthropologist weighing the evidence of field informants, and then returning home to catalogue the results of the interviews. In both cases we have a body of data collected with due care for their authenticity from the perspective of the culture being surveyed. But the anthropologist who limits him/herself to a recapitulation of the data quickly discovers that what is missing is precisely the most important thing of all: the key to the cultural patterning of experience that all informants take for granted to the point that they have not even bothered to share it with their interlocutor, or, for that matter, even with themselves, since it operates as a pregiven gestalt into which their explanations for phenomena are molded from the beginning. Thus, Clifford Geertz reminds us that

> the thing to ask [about events or statements in a culture under investigation] is not what their ontological status is. . . . The thing to ask is what their import is: what it is . . . that in their occurrence and through their agency, is getting said.[8]

"What is getting said" is the connective tissue that unifies discrete behavioral or speech acts into an interlocking web of significance to the native actors or speakers; the pattern that renders their culture the unique entity that it is. In Geertz's analysis, the raw data of evidence must be grasped according to the categorical scheme of those giving it, until it all coheres as a sort of systemic "construction" (Geertz's word) of discrete data entries. Native informants already have such a construction in mind, else how could they frame propositions in the first place? But we interlopers on their cultural turf still lack comprehension as long as we do not take one more step: compose our own insistent patterning of what they say into a second-order construction of their universe, a "construction of their construction," to be exact. It is precisely this constructing of a second-order construction in an effort to get at "what is being said" that is lacking in most reporting efforts on what Judaism says about itself.

What constructive technique do we use, then? Clearly, if we could transport ourselves through time and space to be actual inhabitors of another culture, in this case, Jewish Palestine of the first century, we would need no technique at all, beyond an elementary grasp of the given gestalt into which we were socialized along with everyone else. We should then

know both more and less than we do now: more, in that we should ourselves be able to make pronouncements on the Land of Israel as a significant entity, and then leave it to later, retrospective, seers to look back on
our words to decide how we put words into sentences to say something
meaningful; but less too, since the very objectivity of those who come later
is what gives them—that is, *us*, in reality—the perspective from which to
see how little it is that native informants actually understand consciously
of their own constructive categories. Though the Land would be very real
to us, and though we should be able to say a great deal about it, we still
might not be able to express to others exactly what it means, or how it
coheres systemically with other cultural categories of thought. We would
be in possession of the first-order construction of experience, but not of
the superordinate second order that an outside scholar brings to things. Now
we, as outside scholars, wish to mine Jewish tradition's evidence on the Land
as cultural vehicle of meaning, and we ask how, given the fact that we are
not members of the society under scrutiny, we may do so. Clearly, this is
the situation with which we began, in that it was, in retrospect, a Christian "construction of a construction" that was attempted by many who knew
full well that native evidence from Mishnah or Gemara will never *in and
of itself* yield a full picture of the cultural reality which those books take
for granted. That the construction from the categorical framework of Christianity skewed the pattern should not lead us to imagine that we can do
without any pattern at all.

Faced with the same problem elsewhere, social scientists have opted
for their own religiously "neutral" pattern, a collection of heuristic concepts
that seem to describe cultural phenomena in question, ideas like Eliade's
sacred space and time, Van Gennep's rites of passage, Turner's liminality and
communitas, and many more.[9] Undoubtedly, notions like these too skew
the picture somewhat. Though, for example, first-century Jews certainly
thought about the sacrality of their Land—in their own parlance, its *kedushah*—it is questionable indeed whether they subscribed to a religiously "neutral" doctrine of sacred space, or even if they did (but didn't know it), whether
they would have explained their fascination with their Land by pointing
us toward a generic category of spatial sacrality of which their own case
was but an example as species is to genus, or a single case to a class; or
whether biblical Hebrews who certainly conceived of the Land as covenanted (see Orlinsky's essay, below) would have explained the Land *precisely*
in terms equivalent to *our modern*, westernized conceptualization of legal
contract; surely neither Spinoza nor Mendelssohn would have described their

work as treatments on the subject of demystification and resymbolization of religious concepts. Yet in the essays that follow, we use such conceptual tools as these nonetheless, because far more than subverting the evidence of Jewish texts, these external conceptualizations and analogies illuminate it. The goal of the essays presented here is not only to examine evidence hitherto unearthed but to present it with enough sweep and depth that it takes on shape; and that shape is regularly presented by the authors of the several studies in this book with a self-conscious attempt to see it first as native informants would have — that is, to listen intently to their evidence given through the texts they bequeathed us; and then, to generate conceptual aids to second-order constructions of their evidence: whether the notion of Land as legal covenant (as Orlinsky characterizes the biblical paradigm); or Land as immovable vs. movable sacred space (as Primus understands one stratum, at least, of second-century rabbinic debate); or the demystification and resymbolization of Land in modern thought (as Eisen describes developments after Spinoza and Mendelssohn) — to cite but three examples.

Another way of thinking about the challenge is to discuss it from the perspective of emic versus etic description, an opposition popularized by Kenneth Pike[10] and refined or otherwise debated by others since. As Marvin Harris describes it,

> Emic operations have as their hallmark the elevation of the native informant to the status of ultimate judge of the adequacy of the observer's descriptions and analyses. The test of the adequacy of emic analyses is their ability to generate statements the native accepts as real, meaningful or appropriate. In carrying out research in the emic mode, the observer attempts to acquire a knowledge of the categories and rules one must know in order to think and act as a native.[11]

"Emic" and "etic" are terms derived from the lexicon of linguistics, where phon*etic* denotes the objective existence of sounds, without regard for the social fact of a given speech community's ability to distinguish among them, whereas phon*emic* means the *significant* differences in sounds, as people in fact discriminate them. If the study of culture should proceed along emic lines, the goal would be an elucidation of cultural categories as individual peoples actually think of them, precisely what is intended here. Harris cites Pike expressly to argue with his preference for emic study, so he would surely object to a similar intent behind this book. As part of his campaign to substitute a discussion of etic categories — particularly, what he calls the infrastructural biopsychological constants of production and reproduction[12]

—for emic ones, he warns us against Mary Black's insistence that "emics are concerned *both* with the conscious content of elicited responses and with the unconscious structures that may be found to underlie surface content."[13] Harris's reproach to the contrary, this book is largely an emic study as Black describes it, in which the authors listen to native speakers describing the Land of Israel, and then posit structures of thought—sometimes, structures of history—that may be said to underlie the surface syntax of their statements. More than that: the very idea that the Land deserves its own spotlight in this way betrays a decision to listen very carefully to the native accents through the ages; for if we do, it soon appears that Jews talked about the Land of Israel—its produce, its boundaries, its laws and its lore—as much as they discussed anything else. It was evidently an emic category of thought with wide ramifications for much that Jews said, did, hoped, and feared. It is those ramifications that we hope this book explores.

But before turning to those essays, a word about a subject otherwise absent from them is in order. I mean the extent to which the ritual life of the Jew demonstrates the emic importance of the Land of Israel in the Jewish scheme of things.

2

A recent comprehensive application of social-scientific principles to historical analysis is Wayne Meeks' *The First Urban Christians*,[14] in which Meeks summarizes the role of ritual as it is understood by growing numbers of researchers, which Meeks traces back to Durkheim's functionalism:

> Many of the scholars who adopt this perspective would say that ritual communicates the fundamental beliefs and values of a society or a group . . . what the society holds to be of primary importance.
>
> For Emile Durkheim . . . the relation of ritual to language was more intrinsic. Ritual did not merely encode ideas that could be expressed otherwise; rather, it *created* the essential categories of human thought. For Durkheim, ritual solved the Kantian problem of the origin of the necessary concepts. . . . Thus Mary Douglas . . . treats "ritual forms like speech forms as transmitters of culture," but insists that they create as well as reflect social reality. . . . Other communications-oriented students of ritual take a similar position with more or less important variations. Berger and Luckman, for example, describe "the

social construction of reality," and Clifford Geertz proposes that "sacred symbols" serve to synthesize "world view" and "ethos" of a community.[15]

Certainly the authors included in these pages have demonstrated the role of Land as a motivating and ordering concept in all ages of Jewish thought. We should ask here, albeit briefly, as space permits, whether the ritual life of Jews indeed presents the Land of Israel as a pivotal category according to which other ideas and actions are measured.

We begin with one of the earliest rituals known to us, the confession of the farmer as ordained by Deut. 26. According to the Mishnah,[16] the practice was still extant in at least the earliest ages to which Mishnaic memory reached, and probably as late as the first century C.E. This ritualized recitation retained sufficient popularity that later still it was enshrined in yet another ritual, the Passover seder, albeit in a novel midrashic manner,[17] according to which the literal recitation of the Deuteronomic passage in question was outfitted with rabbinic commentary and included in the annual Passover rite along with its newly created embellishment. Our interest here, however, is the rite before its metamorphosis at the hand of the rabbis responsible for Haggadah and midrash, that is, the rite as described in the Bible:

(1) When you enter the land that the Lord your God is giving you as a heritage, and you occupy it and settle it, (2) you shall take some of every first fruit of the soil, which you harvest from the land that the Lord your God is giving you, put it in a basket and go to the place where the Lord your God will choose to establish His name. (3) You shall go to the priest in charge at that time and say to him, "I acknowledge this day before the Lord your God that I have entered the land which the Lord swore to our fathers to give us." (4) The priest shall take the basket from your hand and set it down in front of the altar of the Lord your God. (5) You shall then recite as follows, before the Lord your God: "My father was a fugitive [old JPS translation: wandering] Aramean. He went down to Egypt with meagre numbers and sojourned there; but there he became a great and very populous nation. (6) The Egyptians dealt harshly with us and oppressed us: they imposed heavy labor upon us. (7) We cried to the Lord, the God of our fathers, and the Lord heard our plea and saw our plight, our misery, and our oppression. (8) The Lord freed us from Egypt by a mighty hand, by an outstretched arm and awesome power, and by signs and

portents. (9) He brought us to this place and gave us this land, a land flowing with milk and honey. (10) Wherefore, I now bring the first fruits of the soil which You, O Lord, have given me."[18]

Much could be said to demonstrate the centrality of the Land of Israel as an emic category that pervades the ritualistic arena of Jewish practice, but no single citation so well illustrates the thesis as this one, which, in addition, has the merit of being so early as well. For purposes of discussion, I shall refer to it as early Israel's Sacred Myth.

The central feature of the myth—and what I will call its Mythic Theme—is the contrast between its beginning and end, the former presenting the "problem," and the latter, the "solution." The myth presents Israel first as wanderers, seeking a place to settle; they end up as settlers in the Promised Land that "flows with milk and honey." They began history independently—a fugitive Aramean; no mention of divine providence here—but finish their tale as God's people, for it is God who "heard our plea and saw our plight" (v. 7), "freed us from Egypt" (v. 8) and "brought us to this place and gave us this land" (v. 9). There are notable elements missing from this ritualized accounting of Jewish origins—notably, standing at Sinai(!)—so the essential problematic of Israel's history (according to this myth) is not the dichotomy between Israel without, and then Israel with, the divine gift of Torah. No, the dominant theme to which the biblical pilgrim gave voice was the role of landedness. Israel began its career unlanded; it ended with land. Land, not Torah, is the essential gift from God that our pilgrim remembers. However much it may be that later, rabbinic, society transferred the emphasis to Torah, even borrowing on the description of Wisdom from the Book of Proverbs (3:18) to call it a "tree of life to those who hold it fast,"[19] the real wellspring of sustenance for this earlier society of whom Deuteronomy 26 speaks, was the Land, flowing with milk and honey to a once-wandering people, a Land whose first fruits were appropriately to be offered back to God who gave it.

The obvious question flowing from this observation is whether, having redefined the covenant in terms of Torah and Sinai, rabbinic tradition also devalued the symbolic role of the Land. More than a few historians of Judaism have held that it did; Solomon Zeitlin, for example, dedicated considerable effort to describing how the three pilgrimage festivals were transformed from "national or agricultural aspects given in the Pentateuch to purely religious connotations."[20] To be more specific, in the case before us, the ritualized recitation of Deut. 26:5–10, it is glaringly transparent that the later Passover Haggadah ritual was outfitted only as far as verse 8, which affirmed how "The Lord freed us from Egypt by a mighty hand, by an outstretched arm and awesome power, and by signs and portents." We know of no standard seder rite that incorporates also verse 9, with its climactic claim, "He brought us to this place and gave us this land, a land flowing with milk and honey," not to mention the next verse (10) which concludes, "Wherefore, I now bring the first fruits of the soil which You, O Lord, have given me." The latter omission occasions no surprise, since the recitation had been moved to a new ritual locus, the seder, instead of the first-fruit offering, and, in any event, in all probability the latter had come to an end altogether with the demise of the cult. But there is no a priori reason to have removed also verse 9, which had been the whole point of the story, the desired contrast to the sorry state of wandering with which the farmer's profession of sacred history had commenced. E. D. Goldschmidt, drawing on the pioneering work of David Hoffmann who had uncovered what he took to be long-lost tannaitic strata of parallel text to our Haggadah midrash, announced:

> There is no doubt [sic!] that when the Temple was still standing the midrash contained also the next verse, "God brought us to this place, and gave us this Land, a land flowing with milk and honey." [But] they eliminated this verse when the Temple was destroyed.[21]

Is Goldschmidt correct? Was the Land the central focus only as long as the Temple stood and its agriculturally related sacrifices still offered? Do we explain the missing verses as a calculated emendation to accommodate changing less Land-centered ideology? Maybe. But there is certainly no evidence for such a conclusion, and we are justified in seeking alternative reconstructions.

Another way of seeing the whole issue is to discriminate at the outset between theological concepts, which are necessarily honed to fine perfection for the purposes of clarity, and liturgical or ritual metaphor (sometimes metonymy) that is deliberately maintained in a syntactic framework that defies specificity. Since the same linguistic sign is used for both cases, we are apt to confuse them and assume that what is true of a word in one context (theological debate) is true of it in the other context as well (ritual performance). Thus, to cite but one example, since theologically the concept of messianic redemption is conceptually distinct from that of rebuilding Jerusalem, one might easily conclude that liturgically too a parallel precise differentiation of denotation ought to prevail. But one look at liturgy demonstrates just the opposite. The fourteenth and the fifteenth benedictions of the standard *Tefillah*, for example, request the upbuilding of Jerusalem and the coming of a Davidic savior, respectively. But we know that the old Palestinian form of the *Tefillah* as displayed by the Genizah fragments mix the two ideas together in one single blessing. On the other hand, the various blessing-parallels on the theme (themes?) in question sometimes mix references to David and to Jerusalem, and sometimes do not.[22] In other words, unlike philosophers or theologians, worshippers did not take particular care to retain conceptual purity in liturgical syntax. If anything, words there are not even concepts *per se*, but symbols, with a multivocality capable of calling up a host of associations, such that the words Jerusalem and David might even be used interchangeably without any alteration in the worshipper's consciousness.

I am suggesting just the opposite of the familiar notion of symbolic condensation.[23] Condensation is the quality of symbols to condense within themselves a host of alternative meanings, so that people may explain a given symbol by more than one *significatum*, all of which are equally correct. In such a case we have a single symbol with multiple meanings. I suggest now that it is equally possible to have multiple symbols pointing to a single *significatum*. Hence the failure of the symbol "Land" to appear in a Haggadah ritual should not be taken to imply a committed turning away from Land as a hitherto central concept in Judaism. It is equally likely that we have a shifting of symbolic *terms* from Land to Exodus, but no radical about-face in religious *thinking*. In one ritual context, the first-fruits ceremony, we find explicit statement of Land; in another, the seder, we find explicit emphasis on Exodus. The symbolic word chosen—"Land" or "Exodus"—varies with the intent of the festive occasion, but the central Sacred Myth of a people moving from a state of wandering and need to one of settlement and sustenance has not been altered. Nor has the Land been displaced as a central tenet of Jewish faith. When the seder celebrants of the first century recited Deuteronomy and the midrash thereto, they were equally as certain of the Land's pivotal importance in their covenant with God as the farmer delivering first fruits had been.

In part, the evidence for this claim comes from a second ritual arena, the diverse blessings surrounding the consumption of food. These benedictions come into being in the very centuries that the Haggadah and its midrashic version of Deuteronomy 26 do. Not only is the role of the Land not denied in them, but, in fact, one cannot comprehend the logic behind their existence without conceding the Land's continued reality as a formative principle in the categorization of experience that marked rabbinic Judaism.

The Bible, of course, knows no rabbinic blessings. In biblical narratives, people generally eat and drink with neither preparatory nor concluding benedictions. They may show thanks to God in any number of ways, mostly by offering the proper sacrifices, but also by expressing freely their own individual sense of gratitude for favors received, and, in one case (1 Sam. 9:13), awaiting a blessing demanded by a sacrifice. By rabbinic times, however, a series of prescribed liturgical acts other than the sacrificial system becomes common. Though psalms and biblical citations are not uncommon, rabbinic worship is typified more by its invention of a unique prose formula which we recognize today as the blessing.

Blessings before and after food were particularly popular, partly, no doubt, because of the cultural model of Greco-Roman tableship cults,[24] so that by the conclusion of the Tannaitic age much of the corpus of literature detailing prayer requirements could be given over to discussions of food benedictions. The Mishnah's tractate on blessings, for example, allots two chapters to the *Shema* and its blessings (1–2): two chapters to the *Tefillah* (4–5); one chapter to circumstances that exempt one from *Shema* and/or *Tefillah* (3); one chapter for occasional blessings—on seeing miraculous sights, and sites of the miraculous, for example (9); but fully three chapters on food and meal regulations: one chapter on introductory benedictions (6); one chapter on Grace after Meals (7); and one chapter on tableship customs about which the Hillelites and the Shammaites differed (8). Clearly food rituals were critical enough to Pharisaic and subsequent Tannaitic Judaism, that whereas the Hillelite-Shammaite debates in general are recollected only singly and in passing elsewhere in the Mishnah, an entire chapter of their debates on tableship rules was recalled for inclusion here; and of all regularized prayer, synagogue and home, food blessings accounted for one-third of the material handed down. The Tosefta, if anything, is even more decisive in this regard.

The theological stance behind food blessings is fairly clearly stated in the Tosefta, and repeated thereafter in midrash and aggadah elsewhere.

> One should eat nothing before saying a blessing, as it is written, "The earth is the Lord's and the fullness thereof" (Ps. 24:1). One who makes enjoyable use of this world without blessing is guilty of sacrilege.[25]

Or, as the Babli restates this basic idea,

It is written [in one place], "The earth is the Lord's and the fullness thereof" (Ps. 24:1) [and, in another,] "He has given the earth to human beings" (Ps. 115:16). [But] there is no contradiction [between the two verses]. The first verse reflects the situation before we say a blessing, whereas the second verse is after the blessing has been said.[26]

As Lieberman summarizes, the world is modeled after the cult, so that eating without a benediction is tantamount to eating *Hekdesh,* sanctified property.[27]

The blessings provided in the Mishnah, however, are by and large not just for food in general. Their wording varies from food to food. Foods are discriminated according to a variety of classification systems, but the most far-ranging, obvious, and central one is derived from a consideration of the botanic origin of the food in question, that is, the "delivery system" (so to speak) by which the earth in general yields each specific form of produce, whether via trees, ground, or vines. As logical as this scheme may appear to those who use it automatically, it is not the only system conceivable; we might imagine an alternative based in food color, shape, or weight; or a simple dichotomous system differentiating cooked from raw; or, following the basic binary dyad of kosher foods, two separate sets of blessings, one for milk and another for meat, with some variation prescribed for mediating cases like fish and fowl. Cultural taxonomy schemes are arbitrary, in the sense that they are arrived at not because the world is objectively structured so that one and only one system is possible; the system is adopted so as to say something about the nature of the reality being named. So we ought to pause long enough to ask what is getting said (to revert to Geertz's challenge, for a moment) by the system of blessing divisions that Judaism did, in fact, select: why should the contents of blessings depend on whether food comes from trees, the ground, or vines?

At the very least, it is evident that the emphasis on how food reaches us from its natural habitat of the earth is fully in keeping with the theology we noted in the Tosefta (and elsewhere) above: in that those sources characterize blessings as a sort of delivery system by which food in its naturally sanctified state of nature is removed from that natural habitat not only physically but conceptually, so that it may be transformed for use by ordinary human beings. No wonder these blessings pay careful heed to the specificity of the natural habitat of each food in question.

The sixth chapter of Tractate Berakhot is allotted to food benedictions: appropriately, then, the Mishnah begins it by laying down its basic rule:

(a) What blessings does one say for fruit [*perot*]?

(b) Over fruit of the tree [*perot ha'ilan*] one says [Blessed art Thou . . .] who creates the fruit of the tree [*borei peri ha'ets*];

>(b1) except for wine, for which one says, ". . . who creates fruit of the vine [*borei peri hagafen*]."

(c) For fruit of the earth [*perot ha'aretz*] one says ". . . who creates fruit of the soil [*borei peri ha'adamah*]";

>(c1) except for bread [*pat*] for which one says ". . . who brings forth bread from the earth [*hamotzi lechem min ha'arets*].

(d) For vegetables [*yerakot*], one says ". . . who creates the fruit of the soil." Rabbi Judah says, ". . . who creates kinds of greenery [*borei minei desha'im*]."

The basic category of food, then, is *perot*, but the word means more than fruit, in the sense of apples, oranges, and dates. It includes all of the earth's produce, including grains that go into bread (C1) and vegetables (C). (Section D does not mean to introduce a new category called "vegetables" that has not been considered as yet. The form of the mishnah indicates that after the rhetorical question of introduction [A], we get a twofold all-inclusive answer patterned into two equivalent semantic units, i.e.: "For fruit of the X one says Y [B and C] except for P for which one says Q [B1 and C1]." D is tacked onto this basic Mishnah because of a debate with Judah that was preserved and that seemed to belong here; it is not original in this place, and is not patterned like B and C. It does not answer A's query about *perot* at all. But in the process of answering its real unstated question, "How do Judah and the majority of Rabbis differ on the blessings over vegetables," it cites blessings, so seems to belong here.)

We can go even further. We tend to think of the Rabbis' concern with the proper blessings over *perot*—let us call it fruit, for simplicity's sake—as a subcategory of their larger interest in blessings over food in general: as if they first decided that people should bless whatever they eat, and then turned to fruit as a subcategory of things that are edible; the conceptual framework would then be the act of eating, the end of the action chain that begins with harnessing nature's bounty and ends with the act of ingestion by which it is used as food. But from the perspective of pure logic, it is equally likely that they began by concentrating on the beginning of that action chain, not its end, with the earth's harvest being no subcategory of an original larger idea of edible substances in general, but the original germinal idea itself. Rather than linking the need for blessings to everything we eat, and then specifying fruit of the earth as a particular type thereof, the Rabbis may well have begun with fruit of the earth itself as deserving a blessing; and then, only secondarily, did they *expand* that notion to include blessings for things other than fruit of the earth as well (like chickens and eggs). Certainly chapter 6 here in no way addresses the issue of discriminating edible substances in general. It deals instead, almost wholly, with fruit in this larger sense of its being the earth's produce, and introduces its only exception—locusts—as part of a list of examples (sour wine or unripe fruit) that one might eat, but probably would not (6:3). In any case, if they are consumed, they are to be prefaced with a benediction that is consistent with the others, in that it explains their origin, even as it implicitly excludes the notion that they derive from the earth (". . . by whose word all things exist"). The Mishnah is nowhere concerned with differentiating among kinds of main courses—red meat, fowl, fish, and so on—as it would be, if its prime category were food in general and fruit of the earth (*perot*) but one subcategory thereof. As we see from the Mishnah's introductory question (A), its central, not subsidiary, interest is fruit, because (unlike moderns) the rabbis' interest was not just eating in general, but eating the "fruit of the earth" in particular, *perot*—as they called it—that the earth produces and so, is holy, like God's earth, and requires blessings before being released as food.

Since the determining principle uniting diverse *perot* into one category of food that requires blessings was that they all come from the earth, they were categorized in terms of blessing content according to the means by which the earth presents them to human beings for food: either trees or soil, with wine and bread being special subcategories within these two. And then, as the idea was generalized to other substances as well, a new blessing "by whose word all things exist," was introduced for non-fruit edibles. But here too, it is the earth or non-earth origin of the food that receives official recognition, since the Mishnah tells us explicitly (3:2) that this latter blessing is for "all things that do not grow from the earth." The Rabbis' concern that the blessing in question explicate the delivery system remains intact.

A purely structuralist analysis such as the kind favored and popularized by Claude Lévi-Strauss or Edmund Leach would require our finding some organizing principle whereby wine and bread (the exceptions, B1 and C1) differ in their innate qualities of growth or harvest, such that they received their own blessings. (It would not be enough, for example, to say that vineyards are sufficiently different from trees as to constitute a separate case. So are bushes, but berries do not attract special attention with respect to how they grow.) A structuralist analysis, however, is not my goal. That these foods received their own blessings is evident from the fact that they have them, but the reason for their being selected out for their own unique treatment is beyond the scope of the argument here. It may even be that although the blessings in question designate food according to its manner of growth, it was not on account of their manner of growth that they were all *originally chosen*. Rabbis may have been led to select them for any reason at all, but—and this is what interests us here—having done so, the benediction they framed seized on the means by which the food in question reaches us. It may be that wine and bread received special attention because of their special significance to Roman tableship rites: wine becoming ubiquitous in its symbolic associations in the various cults and clubs; bread being withheld beyond the hors d'oeuvre stage of the banquets, so as to be served at the main course, as a symbolic substance of the meal itself.[28] All I wish to establish here is the fact that once it was decided that they should receive such blessings, it was again the *provenance* of the food involved that determined their content. Thus, the blessing over wine stipulates that it comes from the vine. As for bread, we find ". . . who brings forth bread from the earth," a formula that generalizes the lesson that we saw above from Psalm 21: "The earth is the Lord's . . . ," but its food is relegated to humans by means of their blessings. Thus the bread we eat is food that is brought forth, in a general way, not from vines, or the ground or an orchard, but still, from God's own earth.[29]

To be sure, there are many exceptions to this categorization according to how food reaches us from the earth. Both Mishnah and Tosefta discuss whole cases of exceptions—food that is about to change state, for example;[30] and some Rabbis admit optional formulas even for the foods listed above—Rabbi Judah, for instance, whose opinion about vegetables we encountered in the addendum to the mishnah quoted above, or Rabbi Meir who allows people to say, "Blessed is God who created (name of food); how beautiful it is!"[31] But in general, foods receive benedictions that emphasize their manner of growth, their particular earthly provenance. That benedictory taxonomy has its own message, its own "what is being said" that deserves our attention, because it will help us see how important the Land of Israel still was in the rabbinic mentality.

What is striking is the consistency in the message of the blessing system, and the message of the theology behind saying blessings over food in the first place. As we saw, the latter, clearly attested in the Tosefta, holds that the earth's produce is sacred, beyond human consumption. Blessings achieve the primal function of freeing that produce from its sacred state.

Blessings themselves, we now see, were applied, in the first instance, not to food in general, but to *perot*, "fruit" of the earth; and blessings differ from one another by virtue of the means by which the *perot* in question become available to us for food. Thus, the blessings for basic foods reflected the theology of human consumption: all food comes from God, usually from God's earth, but is released through blessing. So at the time of eating, one should concentrate on the specific origin of the particular "food from the earth" in question, whether the ground, or the trees, or vines, or (in the case of bread, which represented the meal in general) the earth itself.

With this background, we can return to the Land. As much as one can imagine the natural habitat in which foods grow being important enough to a farmer as to generate blessings according to whether things grow on trees or in the ground or on vines, there is no botanical logic whatever that would lead us to predict that the Rabbis would have differentiated food also on the basis of whether it grew in the Land or outside of it. But that is exactly what they did. For them, the Land of Israel was no mere human-made demarcation of a segment of the earth's surface. It was a natural geographic phenomenon, equally as inherent to the earth's structure as trees and vines, so that its produce deserved its own classificatory blessings.

The determination of Land foods—the seven species, as they were known[32]—is derived from Deuteronomy 8:7–8:

> The Lord your God is bringing you into a good land . . . a land of wheat and barley, of vines, figs, and pomegranates, a land of olive oil and honey.

On the basis of this description, certain grains and produce were demarcated as deriving from the Land of Israel, and, therefore, deserving their own blessing: ". . . who creates species of foods." In this way, the Land was categorized beyond nationhood, beyond social systems in general, and was assumed instead to be a phenomenon of natural geography, with, of course religious and metaphysical significance to the people entrusted with inhabiting it and with tending its fields and eating its food.

Special attention to foods grown in the Land can be found also in the benedictory classification system governing the Grace after Meals. The usual form of Grace is a chain of four benedictions, introduced by an invitation known as *Zimmun*, and sometimes described itself as a blessing, even though it lacks formal benedictory prose style. The four actual blessings in question are known as *Hazan* ("Sustenance," or, literally, [God] "who sustains"), *Ha'aretz* ("the Land"), *Yerushalayim* ([the upbuilding of] "Jerusalem"), and *Hatov Vehameitiv* ([the One] who "is good and does good"). Tradition ascribes the first three to biblical personalities: Abraham, who must have composed the first when he fed the visiting angels (or, according to another version, Moses did so for the manna); Joshua, who is said to have composed a blessing for the Land when he conquered it, and David and Solomon, together, who demonstrated their concern for Jerusalem in an appropriate blessing for its welfare. The last blessing is said to be of more recent origin, a composition reflecting the Hadrianic persecutions. When Hadrian finally relented and allowed the burial of bodies from the Bar Kokhba revolt, the inhabitants of Judea were said to have begun thanking God for being good and doing good, in that it was God who influenced the imperial decision.[33] Scholars see the origin of the Grace in the tableship ritual to which we have already referred.[34]

However, there are actually two other forms of Grace as well. The first is a simple blessing thanking God for "creating different creatures with their needs . . .";[35] and the second is a blessing known as *Berakhah achat me'en shalosh,* or "one benediction expressive of three," the three being the first "biblically-based" staples of the normal long Grace.[36] Of interest to us here is the fact that this *Berakhah achat* is demanded for the Land foods of Deuteronomy 8. Thus we see that Land foods are singled out for attention not only by their introductory blessing but by their unique concluding one as well. The blessing is explicit in its adulation of the Land:

> Blessed art Thou . . . for the lovely, good, and spacious Land in which You delighted, bequeathing it to our forefathers, to eat of its fruit and to be satisfied with its goodness. . . . Blessed art Thou for the Land and for its produce.[37]

The longer Grace too selects out Land foods for special notice. Logically, we would have no reason to expect a separate benediction for the Land, since one would think that thanks for food in general would suffice for everything. But even here, Jewish ritual is faithful to its category structure, whereby the Land of Israel merits separate attention, its species of produce holding a separate place in the hierarchy of food. Thus, immediately after thanking God for sustaining the world of creatures in general (via the first blessing, *Hazan*), the second blessing (*Ha'aretz*) asserts:

> We thank You . . . for bequeathing to our forefathers a lovely, good, and spacious Land. You took us out of Egypt delivering us from slavery; for the covenant you stamped in our flesh, for the Torah which

you taught us, for the laws of which You informed us; for life, grace, and mercy with which you have favored us . . . as it is written, "When you have eaten your fill, give thanks to the Lord your God for the good land which He has given you." Blessed art Thou, for the Land and for sustenance.

Clearly, this blessing alone is rich in matters of interest. The reference to the covenant (circumcision) has been interpreted as a polemic against nascent Christianity, which denied the need for circumcision, against the backdrop of the second-century devastation of the Land.[38] The symbolic complex of Exodus-Torah-Land is also evident here; reference to one leads easily to the others. But the germane issue before us is simply demonstrating through food legislation that Land theology remained what it had been in biblical days when the farmer bringing first fruits professed his Sacred Myth of Israel's origins before God's representative, the priest. Specific reference to the Land was lacking in the recasting of that profession in the Passover seder, but the food blessings have shown how that absence should not be taken to mean a deliberate attempt to underplay the Land's importance. On the contrary, every meal was accompanied by conscious recognition of the Land of Israel's particularity.

The same theology that governed Deuteronomy 26 is evident also in Deuteronomy 8, to which the second blessing of the Grace (*Ha'aretz* — the Land) refers as prooftext. There, 8:1 explicitly promises that the reward of the commandments is "that you may thrive and increase and be able to occupy the Land which the Lord promised on oath to your fathers." Exactly as in the farmer's profession, 8:2–3 establishes the binary opposition of wandering without a Land, in this case, however, not the patriarchal nomadism, but the desert trek on the way to the Land, when "God made you travel in the wilderness . . . [and] subjected you to the hardship of hunger." But (8:7) now "the Lord your God is bringing you into a good land" with its own unique species of food (8:8) that demands its own thanks to God (8:10).

3

Judaism is not the sole religion to have a Sacred Myth; even civil religion seems to require a subjective arranging of historical events into a pattern that justifies and explains one's religious ethos.[39] Myth-making may be a necessary part of a religion's attitude to its past. But taken as a whole, the past is endless and constantly growing, so that the myth as a whole eludes comprehension in all its entirety. Part of the American myth, for example, is Abraham Lincoln's rise to office from simple beginnings and his subsequent "martyrdom." Another chapter in the myth is the Boston Tea Party, nearly a century before. Insofar as a myth purports to be historical, it is necessarily diachronic, a series of story entries that explain a people's mission but do not lose their character of being past events that at best demonstrate meaning for the present, without, however, being that present.

The myth of wandering-to-Landedness, and of covenanting with God over the Land of Israel, is of a different nature. It is similar to the Christian story of Jesus' passion and resurrection. In both cases, we see Sacred Myths that purport to be transhistorical, synchronic in the sense that they are timeless, available to people in all ages for their participation. Religious rites of both faiths retell and recelebrate their timeless truths that lie at the heart of what their adherents are about. Specific chapters in their respective mythic histories may come and go in the consciousness of different generations, but Christians are constantly reminded in their rituals of their participation in the central Christian mystery, just as Jews are in theirs. We need a way to demarcate the ever-repeated central truth of the Sacred Myth from the various chapters of specific detail that individual ages contribute. Their contributions are not shaped freely; they are conditioned by their prior comprehension of the single timeless truth that ever after establishes a blueprint for their own telling of their own lives' meaning. That repeated truth, easily memorized and internalized as the pregiven summary for the story line that new generations will add, constitutes a mythic fulcrum which balances all the rest. The lesson it provides for successive generations, as these latter view their history, is the Mythic Theme.

The details of the mythic fulcrum too are open to the vagaries of each generation's ability to fathom it. For the Christian, Jesus' death and resurrection appeared sometimes as an overwhelming representation of suffering; at other times, as a relatively stoic celebration of conquering the grave. For Jews too, the tale of "wandering – Egypt – redemption – Torah – Landedness" was perceived with new emphases in different periods and places.

Here, the Jewish case differed significantly in that it was rooted in a particular Land, whereas the Christian Myth was not. One is reminded of anthropological studies of other peoples who formulate their Mythic Theme in a similar dependence on a geographic given that they endow with metaphysical significance: the Mbuti fascination with the forest that envelopes them physically and spiritually, for example, so that:

> the forest permeates their whole life. [They] talk, shout, sing to the forest, addressing it as "Father," "Mother," or both, referring to its goodness and its ability to "cure" or to "make good" . . . it is the same word.[40]

One could multiply examples of the forest's all-pervasive reality in Mbuti life, or think similarly of other peoples, desert dwellers, for example, for whom the desert is the linchpin to their view of self, the source of a Mythic Theme in which "desertness" determines the specific content of the fulcral account, and, ever after, the patterning of later entries to the Sacred Myth. But the point should be clear enough. Jews too have addressed the Land in song and speech; proclaimed that "the atmosphere of the Land of Israel makes one wise,"[41] and so on. How does a people keep faith with itself when its Mythic Theme is dependent on a geographic locale, whereas it has become a world people?

That question dominates the essays in this volume. Each is by a scholar in a different field; each author has been asked to consider the role of the Land of Israel in the testimony of the documents with which he or she is familiar. One by one, these essays listen to the evidence of their "native informants"; structure them according to some pattern, so as to understand "what is being said"; and add to our knowledge of Judaism's Sacred Myth, by giving us a comprehensive survey of the *Land of Israel: Jewish Perspectives*.

Notes

1. Arthur Hertzberg, "Judaism and the Land of Israel," *Judaism* 19 (1970): 423–34; and expanded in idem, *Being Jewish in America: The Modern Experience* (New York, 1959), pp. 246–68. See also German version in Eckert, n. 3 below.

2. Brueggemann, *The Land*, p. 190.

3. W. P. Eckert, ed., *Jüdisches Volk – gelobtes Land* (Munich, 1970), p. 9.

4. Ibid., p. 11.

5. W. D. Davies, *The Gospel and the Land* (Berkeley, 1974).

6. See, for example, his *Paul and Rabbinic Judaism* (1948).

7. See, for example, E. P. Sanders' comments on Davies and his scholarly tradition, in *Paul and Palestinian Judaism: A Comparison of Patterns of Religion* (Philadelphia, 1977), pp. 1–12, 33–75.

8. Clifford Geertz, *The Interpretation of Cultures* (New York, 1970), p. 10.

9. Cf. Mircea Eliade, *The Sacred and the Profane* (New York, 1959); A. van Gennep, *The Rites of Passage* (London, 1960); Victor Turner, *The Forest of Symbols: Aspects of Ndembu Ritual* (Ithaca, 1967), pp. 93–111; and idem, *The Ritual Process* (Chicago, 1969), pp. 94–165.

10. Kenneth Pike, *Language in Relation to a Unified Theory of the Structure of Human Behavior* (The Hague, 1967).

11. Marvin Harris, *Cultural Determinism: The Struggle for a Science of Culture* (New York, 1979), Vintage paperback edition, p. 32.

12. See Ibid., pp. 55–58.

13. Ibid., p. 37.

14. Wayne Meeks, *The First Urban Christians: The Social World of the Apostle Paul* (New Haven, 1983). Citations here are to the Yale University Press paperback edition.

15. Ibid., pp. 141–142.

16. M. Bik., Ch. 3.

17. We do not know for sure when it entered the Passover Haggadah. As far back as 1943, Finkelstein tried to show that it belonged to the earliest stratum and was, therefore, the oldest midrash extant (!) owing its origin to a desire by Jews living under the Ptolemaic regime to deflect anti-Egyptian sentiment on Passover eve to the rival Seleucid dynasty. See Louis Finkelstein, "The Oldest Midrash: Pre-Rabbinic Ideals and Teachings in the Passover Haggadah," *HTR* 31 (1943): 291–317. His position is largely eschewed now, particularly in the light of the critique issued by E. D. Goldschmidt, who preferred a very late dating, post-talmudic in fact, for the midrashic elaboration of the biblical narrative. (E. D. Goldschmidt, *Haggadah Shel Pesach Vetoldoteha* [Jerusalem, 1960], pp. 30–48.) For more recent discussions of the text in question, which, however, are not probative with regard to the dating of the midrash to which the text refers, see David Halivni, "Comments on the Four Question" (Hebrew), in Jakob J. Petuchowski and Ezra Fleischer, eds., *Studies in Aggadah, Targum, and Jewish Liturgy in Memory of Joseph Heinemann* (Jerusalem, 1981), pp. 69–70; and Baruch M. Bokser, *The Origins of the Seder: The Passover Rite and Early Rabbinic Judaism* (Berkeley, 1984), pp. 71–72.

18. Deut. 26:1–10.

19. Liturgy surrounding the reading of Torah; see Philip Birnbaum, *Daily and Sabbath Prayer Book* (New York, 1949), p. 389. Liturgical usage of this symbolic expression for Torah seems not to be present in Amram (see E. D. Goldschmidt, *Seder Rav Amram Gaon* [Jerusalem, 1971], Pt. 1, #100). It may be an old Palestinian custom, since most of our early Torah ritual derives from Palestine. *Massechet Sofrim* does not display it, but that source is hardly a complete catalogue of customs; and the genizah fragments rarely cite this section of the service in any detail. Cf. short discussion of usage in Ismar Elbogen, *Der Jüdische Gottesdienst in seiner Geschichtlichen Entwicklung* (1913: reprinted Hildesheim, 1962), p. 201.

20. See, for example, his summary statement in Solomon Zeitlin, *The Rise and Fall of the Judaean State*, vol. 3, pp. 283–84.

21. E. D. Goldschmidt, *Haggadah Shel Pesach Vetoldoteha*, p. 39.

22. This insight is central to the new form-critical research pioneered by Heinemann, who illustrated his approach particularly with Jerusalem-David benedictions. See his chart of alternatives in his *Prayer in the Talmud: Forms and Patterns* (Richard Sarason, trans., Berlin, 1977), pp. 70–76; and idem, "Birkat Boneh Yerushalayim Begilguleha," in *Sefer Chaim Schermann*, Shraga Abramson, Aaron Mirsky, eds. (Jerusalem, 1970), pp. 93–101.

23. See Victor Turner's discussion, following on Sapir, in *The Forest of Symbols*, p. 28.

24. For exemplary accounts, see, for example, Ramsay MacMullen, *Paganism in the Roman Empire* (New Haven, 1981), pp. 36–40; the Jewish dependence on tableship sociality has been emphasized particularly by Jacob Neusner in his many works. For a recent treatment, see Baruch M. Bokser, *The Origins of the Seder*. Pioneer studies, still very valuable, are S. Stein, "The Influence of Symposia Literature on the Literary Form of the Pesah Haggadah," *JJS* 7 (1957): 13–44; Gordon J. Bahr, "The Seder of Passover and the Eucharist Words," *Novem Testamentum* 12 (1970): 181–202; and Joseph Heinemann, "Birkath Hazimmun and Havurah Meals," *Journal of Jewish Studies* 13 (1962): 23–29.

25. T. Ber. 4:1. See full discussion of this and parallel texts in Baruch M. Bokser, "*Ma'al* and Blessings over Food: Rabbinic Transformation of Cultic Terminology and Alternative Modes of Piety," *JBL* 100 (1981): 558–70.

26. Ber. 35a.

27. Saul Lieberman, "*Tosefta* to Berakhot" p. 18, n. 1. See Bokser, "*Ma'al* and Blessings over Food."

28. Thus, M. Pes., which describes the seder, tells us that after the hors d'oeuvres were brought, people would "dip with lettuce until they got to the main course, at which time someone would set before them the *matzah* [i.e.: the bread], *chazeret* [the vegetable], *charoset* and two cooked dishes [that constitute the main course]" (Pes. 10:2). The Hebrew for "main course" is *parperet hapat*. *Parperet* alone stands either for hors d'oeuvre or dessert; but *parperet hapat*, that is, "the helping at which bread is served" means only main course. See Bahr, "The Seder of Passover."

29. For the further symbolic significance of bread, see Lawrence A. Hoffman, "A Symbol of Salvation in the Passover Haggadah," *Worship* 53 (1979): 519–37.

30. T. Ber. 4:3.

31. T. Ber. 4:5.

32. See, for example, Ber. 1:4, Bik. 1:3.

33. Sotah 10b, Ber. 48b.

34. See esp. Joseph Heinemann, "Birkath Hazimmun and Havurah Meals."

35. Ber. 37a.

36. M. Ber. 6:8; Ber. 37a.

37. The wording varies depending on what the actual produce is, again emphasizing its origin: vines, trees, or the ground.

38. See Sidney B. Hoenig, "Circumcision: the Covenant of Abraham," *JQR* 53 (1962): 322–334. He cites only some of the evidence, however. Cf. Justin's "Dialogue with Trypho," Chap. 16 (trans. Thomas B. Falls, *The Fathers of the Church* [New York, 1948], p. 172); Irenaeus' "Against Heresies," 3:12:11; Tertullian's "An Answer to the Jews," in Alexander Roberts and James Donaldson, eds., *Ante Nicene Fathers* III (New York, 1896), p. 154.

39. The classic account, including the example of Lincoln, is Robert N. Bellah, "Civil Religion in America," in *Daedalus* of 1966, and reprinted several times since. See, for example, Bellah's collection of essays, *Beyond Belief: Essays on Religion in a Post-Traditional World* (New York, 1970), pp. 168–91.

40. Colin M. Turnbull, *The Human Cycle* (New York, 1983), p. 30.

41. B. B. 158b.

PART I

*The Land of Israel
in the Biblical and
Hellenistic Periods*

The Biblical Concept of the Land of Israel: Cornerstone of the Covenant between God and Israel*

Harry M. Orlinsky

[Editor's note: Dr. Harry M. Orlinsky, Professor of Bible at the Hebrew Union College—Jewish Institute of Religion in New York, has long been one of the foremost interpreters of biblical thought. Central to his perspective has been the thesis that "the Bible is more than a collection of individual books that contain or deal with, among other things, history, saga, prayers, wisdom, ritual, chronicles, literature, autobiographies, laws and collections of laws; it is a lawbook, a work which in its totality derives from and constitutes the expression of law." It is a lawbook, moreover, dedicated to the explication of the contract, or covenant, between God and Israel. In this essay, Orlinsky pursues this general theme, but from the perspective of elucidating the role of the Land of Israel in that contractual relationship, as the Bible itself expresses it. His treatment is rich in citations—the accounts of the patriarchal covenant, the Deuteronomic recapitulation of the covenant's terms, and the prophetic harangues and consolation, for example—all of which introduce the Land as no mere appendage to the biblical authors' concerns, but as a pivotal concept inherent in the very notion of covenant itself. Central to Orlinsky's argument is his philological analysis of the Bible's language which he reveals as typified by the conscious use of technical terminology related specifically to its foremost concern with contractual law, but easily misunderstood by modern readers who see only the nontechnical denotation of the same words as they occur in other, more general, contexts: the root *ntn*, for example, which, in the context of God's "giving" the Land to Israel, means not just "to give" but "to assign, deed, transfer, convey," an interpretation that receives substantiation from Aramaic real estate documents of the Jewish community at Yeb/Elephantine in Egypt (from the sixth century B.C.E.). As befits a discussion of contractual obligation, Orlinsky underscores the biblical preference for a court setting, as presupposed by passages from Deuteronomy, Joshua, and the later prophets. Throughout, he presents the Land as not simply one central idea among many that the Bible offers us, but another facet of *the* primary motif without which, he says, the entire biblical corpus cannot be comprehended accurately: "the Land as covenant" itself.]

1

The role of the Land in the Bible, as of every concept or event discussed by the biblical writers, can be comprehended only if the essence of the Bible itself is first fully understood.

The Bible is more than a collection of individual books that contain or deal with, among other things, history, saga, prayers, wisdom, ritual, chronicles, literature, (auto)biographies, individual laws and collections of laws; it is a lawbook, a work which in its totality derives from and constitutes the expression of law.

The law, without which there would be no Bible, is the contract— covenant is the popular, in effect the theological term—that God and Israel entered into, voluntarily and as equals (see n. 4 below). This contract stated that the two parties agreed to remain loyal to one another forever, to the exclusion of all other parties: Israel would worship no other deity, and God would choose no other people to protect and to prosper. In accordance with legal procedure, both parties confirm, usually by a vow or a sacrifice, their exclusive contractual obligation to one another.

This legal concept and contract, *in action,* is what the Bible is basically about. For from beginning to end, the Bible presents only the careers of God and Israel on earth in their contractual relationship, the acting out of their contract in the most concrete form possible. The careers of everything and everyone else—non-Israelite nations, heavenly bodies, natural phenomena, animal life—all are but incidental in the biblical comprehension of the universe; for even Genesis 1–11, in outlining the emergence of the nations of the world in general, served basically to describe the debut of Israel in particular.[1]

The first eleven chapters in the Book of Genesis are devoted to the earliest history of the universe and its multifarious occupants—God's creation and ordering of the world, His destruction of much of it, and His subsequent restoration of it in the form that the inhabitants of the Near East in ancient times knew it—from Adam and Eve and their progeny to Noah and his household and their progeny. This series of worldwide events resulted in a contract between God and the whole world. When God accepted Noah's sacrifice after the Flood (Gen. 8:21, "The Lord smelled the pleasing odor"),

> . . . the Lord said to Himself: Never again will I doom the ground
> because of man . . . nor will I ever again destroy every living being . . .
>   (22) So long as the earth endures,

> Seedtime and harvest,
> Cold and heat,
> Summer and winter,
> Day and night,
> Shall not cease.[2]

Or as the parallel version[3] worded it (Gen. 9:8ff.):

> And God said to Noah and to his children with him: (9) I herewith establish My covenant with you and your offspring to come, (10) and with every living thing that is with you . . . on earth. (11) I will maintain My covenant with you . . . never again shall there be a flood to destroy the earth.

Henceforth the whole world — all human and animal life, all heavenly bodies, all natural phenomena — would have to abide by the universal (or Noahide, or natural) laws that God had introduced (see further n. 13 below).

2

With the appearance of Abra(ha)m son of Terah on the scene, this universal covenant was supplemented by a more limited and specific but no less everlasting contract, one that involved God on the one hand and Abraham and his household and heirs on the other. As put by the biblical writer (Gen. 12:1–4):

> (1) The Lord said to Abram: Go forth [lekh-lekha] from your native land and from your father's house to the land that I will show you.
>   (2) I will make you a great nation, / And I will bless you; I will make your name great, / And you shall be a blessing:
>   (3) I will bless those who bless you, / And curse those who curse you; All the families of the earth / Shall bless themselves by you.
> (4) And Abram went forth [vayelekh] as the Lord had spoken to him . . .
> (5) When they arrived in the land of Canaan . . . (7) The Lord appeared to Abram and said, "I will assign [eten] this land to your heirs [lezarakha]." And he built an altar there to the Lord. . . .

Thus Abraham agreed to God's proposition, and they entered into a contract with one another. If God had not made this binding offer to Abram, or if Israel's progenitor, after due consideration, had decided not to accept it, there would have been no contract, and consequently no Bible and no Land of Israel. No force and no threat—no kind of pressure—induced either party to offer or to accept this contract.[4]

This contract was renewed between God and Abraham's son Isaac. As recorded in Gen. 26:2–4, the Lord appeared to Isaac in Gerar, in the territory of King Abimelech of the Philistines, and said:

> (2) . . . Do not go down to Egypt; abide in the land [*shekhon ba'arets*] which I point out to you. (3) . . . I will be with you and bless you; to you and your heirs [*ki lekha ulezarakha*] I will assign [*eten*] all these lands [or regions, territory; *aratsot*], fulfilling the oath that I swore [*et hashevu'ah asher nishbati*] to your father Abraham. (4) I will make your heirs as numerous as the stars of heaven, and I will assign to your heirs [*venatati lezarakha*] all these lands, so that all the nations of the earth shall bless themselves by your heirs.

Isaac accepted this proposition; as the text has it, succinctly:

> (6) So Isaac stayed [*vayeshev*] in Gerar.

Isaac's son Jacob is said to have had the same experience with God and the covenant that his father and grandfather did; Gen. 35:9ff. offers one of several statements to this effect:

> (9) God appeared again to Jacob, on his arrival from Paddan-aram, and He blessed him. (10) God said to him:
> You whose name is Jacob,
> You shall not be called Jacob any more;
> But Israel shall be your name. . . .
> (12) The land that I assigned
> to Abraham and Isaac,
> To you I herewith assign it;
> And to your heirs to come
> I assign the land.

And so Jacob too entered into the covenant with God, a contract sealed by the erection of a sacred stele accompanied by a libation offering:

> (13) God parted from him at the spot where He had spoken to him. (14) And Jacob set up a pillar at the site where He had spoken to him, a pillar of stone, and he offered a libation on it and poured oil upon it. (15) And Jacob gave the site, where God had spoken to him, the name Bethel.

Essentially the same statement is made, e.g., in Gen. 28:13ff., when God appeared in a dream to Jacob, who was on his way from Beersheba to Haran, and said to Him:

> I am the Lord, the God of your (grand)father Abraham and the God of Isaac: the land on which you are lying, to you I will assign it and to your heirs [ha'arets . . . lekha etnena ulezarekha]. (15) I will protect you wherever you go and will bring you back to this land. I will not leave you until I have done what I have promised you.

This is supplemented by Jacob's plea to God, made on the way back from Haran to Canaan and in dread of the confrontation with his brother Esau (Gen. 32:10ff.):

> (10) Then Jacob said: O God of my (grand)father Abraham and God of my father Isaac, O Lord, who said to me, "Return to your native land and I will deal bountifully with you." . . . (12) Deliver me, I pray, from the hand of my brother, from the hand of Esau. . . .

But before proceeding further, several matters of syntactical-literary and especially of technical terminology must be noted.

(a) In the Hebrew, the syntactical position of *ve'et ha'arets* as of *lekha*, in 35:12 — and similarly, e.g., of *ha'arets . . . lekha* indicates an emphasis that translation hardly brings out. Or note how the same word is used in 12:1 and 4 both for God's proposal to Abram and for Abram's acceptance of the proposal: *lekh-lekha . . . vayelekh* ("Go . . . And he went ["goed"!]); similarly, it is synonyms that are so employed in 26:2–4: God said to Isaac: "Abide in the land" of Gerar [*shekhon ba'arets*] and "So Isaac stayed in Gerar [*vayeshev . . . bigerar*]" — though it may be that the precise nuance of *shkhn* here (and sometimes elsewhere) eludes us.

(b) In the course of examining and translating the numerous passages quoted or referred to in this study, I came to believe that the root *ntn* in these contexts had the force not simply of "give" but of "assign, deed, transfer, convey," that it was used as a legal, real estate term to indicate transfer of ownership of or title to a piece of property. It was with more than passing interest, then, that I noted the use of the corresponding term *yhv* in the Aramaic real estate documents of the Jewish community at Yeb/Elephantine in Egypt (from the sixth century B.C.E. on), e.g., in *The Brooklyn Museum Aramaic Papyri* edited by E. G. Kraeling (1953). Numerous examples of *yhv* are to be found in these documents for our statement about its biblical equivalent *ntn*; but we shall content ourselves here with citing but a few of them that we subsequently noted also, e.g., in Y. Muffs, *Studies in the Aramaic Legal Papyri from Elephantine* (1973) and in H. Z. Szubin and B. Porten, "Testamentary Succession at Elephantine," *BASOR* 252 (1983): 35–46.

I note at random such a passage as lines 10ff. in Papyrus 3 (Kraeling, p. 154), "(Line 7: Now these are the boundaries of that house which we sold to you [*byt' zk zy 'nḥn zbn lk* . . .]) . . . The two of us, we have sold and deeded/assigned/transferred/conveyed to you [*kl 2 'nḥn zbn wyhbn lk*] and relinquished title to it [*wrḥqn mnh*] from this day forever (*mn ywm' znh w'd 'lmn*) . . ."; see on this passage, Muffs, 30f. and n. 2, and Szubin and Porten, p. 38. Or compare the use of *yhv* as a technical term, "deed, assign," etc., in Papyrus 4, where Kraeling, e.g. (p. 169, lines 2, 4, 6, 9), has missed the point by rendering mechanically "give." Or compare Papyrus 9, lines 16–17, where *yhbth* in association with *rḥmn* (on which see immediately below) denotes a *quid pro quo* exchange (not as Kraeling, p. 237, simply "give [. . . in affection]"): the father transfers title to his house to his daughter in exchange for her taking full care of him in his old age until his death.

In his article, "Promises to the Patriarchs," *IDB, Supplementary Volume*, 1976: 690a–693b, 3c, "Promise of the Land" (692a), C. Westermann has noted the technical use of *ntn* in the "promise [and] formula for the legal transfer of land (cf. Gen. 48:22) . . . 13:14–17 . . ."

A fresh study of *natan* in the Bible will doubtlessly bring to light numerous other passages where technical use was made of it. Thus *tittenu* . . . *tittenu* . . . *tittenu* in Num. 35:13–14, where the Israelites are commanded to provide "cities of refuge," should be rendered "(The towns that) you assign [so the *NJV*] . . . (Three cities) shall be assigned (beyond the Jordan and the other three) shall be assigned . . . ," where traditional "give" has missed the point; similarly 36:2, where in connection with the claim of the daughters of Zelophehad, the family heads said to Moses, "(The Lord said to my lord) to assign the land (to the Israelites as shares by lot . . . and) to assign (the share of our kinsman Zelophehad to his daughters)," and where the NJV has correctly rendered both instances of *la-tet* "to assign," as against traditional-mechanical "to give." Or see the use of *natan* in connection with ritual law in which specific parts of a sacrifice are permanently "assigned" (not simply "given") to members of the sacerdotal community, e.g., Lev. 6:10, "I have assigned [*natatti*] it (as their portion from My offerings by fire)" and 17:11 "(For the life of the flesh is in the blood,) and I have assigned it [so NJV, for *netativ*] (to you for making expiation. . .)."

(c) In their above-cited study of "Testamentary Succession at Elephantine," Szubin and Porten have noted that "theoretically, the term 'your seed/sons after you' [cf., e.g., *lezarakha acharekha* in Gen. 17:7–8] entitles all the legitimate heirs to inherit. The parent, however, might single out a particular heir for special consideration, occasionally even to the exclusion of others." In passages such as ours, *zera* is to be treated as a technical term, favorite or even sole heir. In addition, of special significance in this connection is the technical use of the word *ahab*, where not simply "to love" but "to favor" is intended, i.e., where anyone, especially a parent, designates one as the exclusive or major heir. Thus, first-born Ishmael is an heir (*zera*) no less than Isaac, and is—unlike his younger brother, who is their mother Sarah's favorite—the favorite of his father Abraham; but it is Isaac, on command of God, who is designated the major heir (Gen. 21:10–13):

> (10) [Sarah] said to Abraham, "Cast out that slave-woman and her son, for the son of that slave-woman shall not share in the inheritance with my son Isaac." (11) The matter distressed Abraham greatly, for it concerned a son of his. (12) But God said to Abraham, "Do not be distressed over the boy or your slave-woman; whatever Sarah tells you, do as she says, for it is through Isaac that heirs [*zera*] shall be continued [lit. called] for you. (13) As for the son of the slave-woman, of him too I will make a nation, for he is an heir of yours [*zarakha*]."

Among other passages cited by Szubin and Porten (pp. 36ff.) is Gen. 22:2:

> (1) (. . . God put Abraham to the test . . .) (2) He said, "Take your son, your only one, whom you love, Isaac [*kakh na et binkha et yechidkha asher ahavta et-yitschak*] and go to the land [or region] of Moriah. . . ."

Clearly this literal rendering is hardly acceptable, for Isaac was not Abraham's only son and Ishmael was certainly loved by his father no less than Isaac was. Actually, the term *ahab* here, as Szubin and Porten have argued (p. 37b), indicates the favored one, "The one designated as sole heir." Similarly, when God is said in Mal. 1:2–3 to have declared,

> After all . . . Esau is Jacob's brother [*halo ach esav leya'akov*]; yet *va'ohav* Jacob (3) but Esau *saneti* . . . ,

the terms *ahav* and *sane* denote here not "love" and "hate" but forensic "favor" and "reject" (so NJV).

What emerges clearly from the few but typical passages quoted about the patriarchs, and reinforced independently by the recognition of key words employed in these passages as technical legal terms,[5] is one central, basic fact and the thrust of this study—that the cornerstone, the essense of the exclusive contract into which God and each of Israel's three progenitors voluntarily entered, is the "Land" [ha'arets]! Were it not for the Land that God promised on oath to Abraham and to Isaac and to Jacob and to their heirs forever, there would be no covenant. For be it noted that everything in the contract, all the blessings—economic, territorial, political, increase in population, and the like—all these would be forthcoming from God to Israel not in Abraham's native land in Mesopotamia, nor in Aram-naharaim/ Paddan-aram, nor in Egypt, but in the Promised Land.

Thus the various versions of God's or Abraham's blessings of Isaac and Ishmael, and of God's or Isaac's blessings of Jacob and Esau—blessings in which all parties are to have numerous descendants and abundant prosperity—are marked by one major and most significant fact, namely, that Isaac and Jacob are to receive the land of Canaan whereas Ishmael and Esau must be content with another region. In Gen. 15:1ff.—the biblical order of the data is followed here for the sake of convenience only, and they are drawn from Gen. 15–17, 27–28, and 36–37—we are told:

> (1) Some time later, the word of the Lord came to Abram in a vision. . . . (7) He said to him, "I am the Lord who brought you out from Ur of the Chaldeans to assign to you this land as a possession [latet lekha et ha'arets hazot lerishtah]." . . . (18) On that day the Lord made a covenant [karat . . . berit] with Abram: To your heirs I assign this land [lezarakha natati et ha'arets hazot], from the river of Egypt to the great river, the Euphrates River. . . .[6]

In 16:10ff., after Hagar, slave of Sarai, had fled into the wilderness from the harsh treatment at the hands of her mistress,

> (10) The angel of the Lord said to her,
>   "I will greatly increase your offspring,
>   And they shall be too many to count."
>   (11) . . . "Behold you are with child
>   And are about to bear a son;
>   You shall call him Ishmael. . . .
>   (12) He shall be a wild ass of a man,
>   His hand against everyone
>   And everyone's hand against him;

> And over against (or in defiance of) all his kinsmen
>   he shall abide."

Isaac blesses both Jacob and Esau with prosperity, but in distinctly different locales. In blessing Jacob, Isaac declares (Gen. 27:28–29):

> (28) May God give you
> Of the dew of heaven and the fat of the earth,
> Abundance of new grain and wine.
> (29) Let peoples serve you,
> And nations bow to you;
> Be master over your brothers,
> And let your mother's sons bow to you.
> Cursed be they who curse you,
> Blessed they who bless you.

As for Esau (vv. 39–40),

> His father Isaac answered, saying to him,
>   "See, your abode shall enjoy the fat of the earth
>   And the dew of the heaven above.[7]
>   (40) Yet by your sword you shall live,
>   and you shall serve your brother;
>   But when you are restive,
>   You shall break his yoke from your neck."

However, when Rebekah and Isaac send Jacob off to Paddan-aram, Isaac blessed him and instructed him (28:1ff.),

> "You shall not take a wife from among the Canaanite women. (2) Up, go to Paddan-aram . . . and take a wife there from among the daughters of Laban, your mother's brother. (3) May El Shaddai bless you, make you fertile and numerous. . . . (4) May He grant you the blessing of Abraham, to you and your offspring, that you may possess the land where you are sojourning, which God assigned to Abraham."

Esau, on the other hand, spited his father (v. 9): "Esau went to Ishmael and took to wife, in addition to the wives he had, Mahalath the daughter of Ishmael. . . ." And his abode was "the land of Seir, the country of Edom" (32:4). The author of Gen. 36 put it this way:

> (6) Esau took . . . all the members of his household . . . and all the possessions that he had acquired in Canaan, and went to another land

because of (or, away from) his brother Jacob. (7) For their possessions
were too many for them to dwell together, and the land where they
sojourned could not support them because of their livestock. (8) So
Esau settled in the hill country of Seir—Esau being Edom. (9) This,
then, is the line of Esau. . . .

By contrast, the chapter immediately following (Gen. 37) begins with:

Now Jacob was settled in the land where his father had sojourned,
the land of Canaan, (2) This, then, is the line of Jacob. . . .⁸

Gen. 17:15–22 offers as clear a summing up of the matter as one could
wish. After Hagar bore Ishmael,

(15) God said to Abraham, "As for your wife Sarai . . . her name shall
be Sarah. (16) I will bless her; indeed, I will give you a son by her . . .
(19) . . . and you shall name him Isaac; and I will maintain My covenant with him as everlasting covenant for his heirs to come [*vahaki-
moti et beriti ito liverit olam lezaro acharav*]. (20) As for Ishmael, I have
heeded you. I hereby bless him, I will make him fertile and exceed-
ingly numerous. (21) But My covenant I will maintain with Isaac. . . ."

There are other aspects in the saga of the patriarchs that a more detailed study of the role of the Land in the covenant between God and Israel
would have to consider. Thus, e.g., the change of name—and name-giving
in the Bible is an event of significance—is associated with the Land. When
God changed Abram's name to Abraham (Gen. 17:1–8), the covenant is
the central item involved, and Canaan as an "everlasting holding" (see n. 8)
is the climax of the statement. When God tells Abraham to name his wife
Sarah instead of Sarai (vv. 15–21), the dialogue closes with God's assurance,
"But My covenant I will maintain with Isaac." Or when God informs Jacob
that He has renamed him Israel (35:9–12), the Land is, again, the climax
in the contractual blessing involved. And see below (and n. 14) on the name
YHWH.

However the episode in Gen. 14 is to be comprehended in its present
context—the still very enigmatic battle of "four kings against five" and involving King Chedorlaomer of Elam and Abram the Hebrew—the redactor
had it followed immediately by an account which once again constituted
an assurance and a reassurance from God to Abraham in the matter of the
Land. After telling Abraham that just as the stars are too numerous to be
counted "So shall your offspring be" (15:5), God continues immediately with
"I am the Lord who brought you out from Ur of the Chaldeans to assign

this land to you as a possession" (v. 7). And when Abram asked, "O Lord God, how can I be sure (lit., how shall I know) that I am to possess it?", God initiated a sacrifice that sealed the contract (vv. 9ff.) and

> (18) On that day the Lord made a covenant with Abram: To your heirs I assign this land, from the river of Egypt to the great river, the Euphrates River. . . .

The account of the transaction involving the burial place of the patriarchs and matriarchs too presupposes the special status of the Land. The main point in the tale of the transfer of a small piece of Ephron the Hittite's property to Abraham (Gen. 23) is that the property was accepted by Abraham, not as a gift (as offered by Ephron), but as a legal and binding acquisition, paid for in the amount of "four hundred shekels of silver at the going merchants' rate . . . in the presence of the Hittites" (vv. 14–20). This transaction is specifically mentioned later on, at the end of Jacob's last will and testament to his twelve sons (Gen. 49:29ff.), when he instructed them: "Bury me in . . . the cave which is in the field . . . that Abraham bought from Ephron the Hittite as a burial holding (asher kanah . . . la'achuzat kaver) . . . the field and the cave in it, bought from the Hittites."[9]

With the death of the last of the patriarchs, the covenant with God ceases to be individual, and becomes national, i.e., it is the descendants of the patriarchs, as a nation—in accordance with God's initial and oft-repeated promise—who become the covenanted partner; while He was the "God of Abraham, of Isaac, and of Jacob," He never became the God of Moses,[10] or of David,[11] or of Elijah, or of Amos, or of any other individual,[12] but only of Israel [elohei yisra'el].[13]

When God first spoke to Moses out of the bush that was ablaze but not consumed (Ex. 3:6ff.), "He said: I am the God of your ancestor(s), the God of Abraham, the God of Isaac, and the God of Jacob . . . , (7) I have marked well the plight of My people in Egypt. . . . (8) I have come down to rescue them from the Egyptians and to bring them out of that land to a good and spacious land, a land flowing with milk and honey, the region of the Canaanites. . . ."

Again, when God revealed Himself for the first time by the name YHWH, He said to Moses (Ex. 6:2ff.):

> (2) . . . I am the Lord. (3) I appeared to Abraham, Isaac, and Jacob as El Shaddai, but I did not make Myself known to them by My name [YHWH]. (4) I also established My covenant with them, to as-

sign to them the land of Canaan, the land in which they lived as sojourners. . . . (6) Say, therefore, to the Israelite people: I am the Lord.
I will free you from the labors of the Egyptians and deliver you from
their bondage. . . . (7) And I will take you to be My people, and I
will be your God. . . . (8) I will bring you into the land which I swore
(lit. raised My hand) to assign to Abraham, Isaac and Jacob, and I
will assign it to you for a possession [morashah], I am the Lord.[14]

From the Exodus on, including the theophany at Mount Sinai (whatever be its date of composition and redaction) and all the laws that were
associated with it, the emphasis is on the getting to and into the Promised
Land and on the kind of society to be set up there. The laws promulgated
in Ex. 21ff., the making of the Tabernacle and its paraphernalia (Ex. 25ff.),
the ritual-priestly laws (much of Leviticus and Numbers), the primary purpose of the book of Deuteronomy—regardless of their historical setting and
date of composition—all these, for their authors, compilers, and redactors,
pertained to the structure and quality of the community of Israel after God
had fulfilled His vow to settle them in the Land in which their ancestors
had lived as sojourners.

Thus one of the Ten Commandments to the Israelites reads (Ex. 20:12;
cf. Deut. 5:16), "Honor your father and your mother, that you may long
endure on the land that the Lord your God is assigning to you." Deuteronomy ends the parallel chapter with the admonition (5:29–30), "Be careful . . . (30) follow only the path that the Lord your God has enjoined upon
you . . . that you may long endure in the land you are to possess [asher
tirashu]."

Such statements abound in Deuteronomy; see, for example, 4:40, "Observe His laws and commandments . . . that it may go well with you and
your children after you, and that you may long remain in the land that
the Lord your God is assigning to you for all time [noten lekha kol hayamim].
Or 8:1ff., "You shall faithfully observe all the Instruction that I enjoin upon
you today, that you may thrive and increase, and enter and possess the land
which the Lord promised on oath [nishba] to your ancestors. . . . (7) For
the Lord your God is bringing you into a good land, a land with streams
and springs and lakes . . . (8) a land of wheat and barley, of vines, figs, and
pomegranates . . . (9) a land where you will lack nothing; a land whose
rocks are iron and from whose hills you can mine copper. (10) When you
have eaten your fill, give thanks to the Lord your God for the good land
which He has assigned to you." Or cf. 11:8–21, again for the glorification

and idealization of the land, ending with the formula, "to the end that you and your children may endure in the land that the Lord promised on oath [*nishba*] to your ancestors to assign to them, as long as there is a heaven over the earth [*kimei hashamayim al ha'arets*]."

With all the rhetoric that characterizes the Book of Deuteronomy, the bottom line throughout is the fulfillment of the contract with the patriarchs to give their descendants the Land. So that when the hortatory speech in Deut. 9 begins with, "Hear, O Israel! You are about to go in to dispossess nations greater and more populous than you. . . . (3) Know this day that none other than the Lord your God is crossing at your head . . . ," and continues with (v. 4), "Say not to yourselves, 'The Lord has let us enter because of our virtues (lit. just deeds)'; it is rather"—the climax of this speech declares (v. 5)—"because of the wickedness of those nations that the Lord is dispossessing them before you, and in order to fulfill the oath that the Lord made to your ancestors, Abraham, Isaac, and Jacob."

A variation of this version is offered in Deut. 7:6ff., when God commands the Israelites to annihilate the pagan inhabitants of Canaan and their religious structures and paraphernalia and their way of life:

> (6) For you are a people consecrated to the Lord your God: of all the peoples on earth the Lord your God chose you to be His treasure people. (7) It is not because you are the most numerous of peoples that the Lord set His heart on you and chose you—indeed, you are the smallest of peoples; (8) but it was because the Lord loved you and kept the oath He made to your ancestors. . . . (12) And if you obey these rules and observe them faithfully, the Lord your God will maintain for you the steadfast covenant [lit. the covenant and the faithfulness; see S. R. Driver, *ICC on Deuteronomy*, at 7:9 on p. 101, on *"The faithful God"*] that He made on oath with your ancestors; (13) He will love you and bless you and multiply you; He will bless the issue of your womb and the produce of your soil, your new grain and wine and oil, the calving of your herd and the lambing of your flock, in the land that He swore to your ancestors to assign to you. . . .

Cheating in buying and selling goods, using dishonestly larger and smaller weights and measures, is forbidden; but note the reason why: "You must have," Deut. 25:15 commands, "completely honest weights and . . . measures, if you are to endure long on the soil that the Lord your God is assigning to you."[15]

Since the greatest reward offered Israel in the covenant with God is
peace and prosperity in their own land, so the greatest punishment for violating the covenant is the loss of the land, exile; drought, epidemic, locust,
even invasion by and loss of sovereignty to a more powerful nation—these
were in comparison relatively minor penalties to suffer. Passages such as
Deut. 4:25ff. and 30:15–20 have this to say:

> (25) Should you, when you . . . are long established in the land, act
> wickedly and make yourselves a sculptured image in any likeness . . .
> (26) I call heaven and earth to witness against you this day that you
> shall soon perish from the land which you are crossing the Jordan to
> take possession of; you shall not long endure in it, but be utterly wiped
> out. (27) The Lord will scatter you among the peoples, and only a
> scant few of you shall be left among the nations to which the Lord
> will drive you. . . . (29) But if you search there for the Lord your
> God . . . with all your mind and being [traditionally, heart and soul]
> . . . (31) . . . the Lord your God will not fail you nor will He let you
> perish; He will not forget the covenant which He made under oath
> with your ancestors.

Thus God would never sever His contract with Israel and would, after due
punishment, resume their contractual relationship and restore her to the
Land.

In chap. 30, following the dramatic events involving the awesome
curses and blessings (27:11ff.), the thrust is, once again,

> (19) I call heaven and earth to witness against you this day: I have
> set before you life and death, blessing and curse. Choose life . . . (20)
> by loving the Lord your God. . . . For thereby you shall have life and
> shall long endure upon the soil that the Lord your God swore to
> Abraham, Isaac, and Jacob to assign to them.

And this constitutes also the climax, a most fitting one, to the great Song
of Moses (chap. 32):

> (45) And when Moses finished reciting all these words to all Israel,
> (46) he said to them: Take to heart all the words with which I have
> warned you this day. Enjoin them upon your children, that they may
> observe faithfully all the terms of this Teaching. (47) For this is not
> a trifling thing for you: it is your very life; through it you shall long
> endure on the land which you are crossing the Jordan to possess.

The Israelite occupation of Canaan, then, constituted and fulfilled not just an element, even an important one, but the very heart of the covenant between God and each of the three patriarchs and, finally and for all time,[16] the Israelite nation. God's blessings, even the full worship of God (e.g., sacrifices along with prayer), are associated with and are possible in the Land of Israel alone.[17] But, alas, this has hardly been recognized in the scholarly study of the Bible.

Thus in Harper's popular *Bible Dictionary* (ed. M. S. and J. L. Miller, 1952; 8th ed., 1973, "revised by eminent authorities"), there is no mention of "the land" in the article "Covenant" (p. 116);[18] nor does "the Land" fare any better in Mendenhall's article "Covenant" in the scholarly *IDB* (see n. 4 above). In his comprehensive book on *The Land* (1977), W. Brueggemann offers the reader virtually everything that the Hebrew Bible (and the New Testament) has to say about the subject; but his main interests and his concept of "The Land as Gift" (the subtitle of the book is *Place as Gift, Promise, and Challenge in Biblical Faith*) tend to obscure the main point of our study. And such more recent projects as *Encyclopedia Mikra'it* would have done better had they utilized the article on "Covenant" by K. Kohler in the old *Jewish Encyclopedia* (IV [1903] 318a–320b). On the other hand, attention may be drawn to two recent studies of merit, in addition to Brueggemann's: the first is an article by W. Rendtorff, "Das Land Israel im Wandel der alttestamentlichen Geschichte," pp. 153–68 in *Jüdisches Volk – gelobtes Land*, ed. W. Eckert, N. P. Levinson, and H. Stöhr (1970). Rendtorff's studies must be read as a whole, so as to understand his comprehension of "Old Testament Theology" and thus also of the role of the Land so far as biblical Israel is concerned. See, e.g., his essay "Towards a New Christian Reading of the Hebrew Bible," *Immanuel* 15 (Winter 1982/83), 13–21. The second is *Das Land Israel in biblischer Zeit*, Jerusalem-Symposium 1981 der Hebraischen Universität und der Georg-August-Universität (= *Göttinger Theologische Arbeiten*, Band 25), ed. Georg Strecker (1983).[19]

3

In his widely used college and seminary textbook, *Understanding the Old Testament* (1957; frequently reprinted), B. W. Anderson wrote (Chap. 3, "The Promised Land," p. 62 [= p. 68 in his *The Living World of the Old Testament*, 1971]),

. . . This theme [viz., Yahweh's gift of the land] is colored by Israelite nationalism. . . . But it is noteworthy that even the great prophets, who vigorously attacked Israel's proud nationalism, did not surrender the conviction that the gift of the land was the supreme sign of Yahweh's benevolence and grace toward his people. Amos (2:10), Hosea (chapter 2), and Jeremiah (3:19) all emphasized the gift of land. . . .

In Israel's experience the conquest of Canaan . . . occurred within the providence of God. Therefore, the land was not a possession to boast about, but a gift to be received with humility and gratitude (Josh. 24:13).

This statement hardly does justice to the overall biblical statements with regard to the Land and Israel. The pejorative use of the terms "colored" and "proud" and "boast about" in connection with Israel's "nationalism" hardly derives from the biblical view of the covenant between God and Israel; if that contractual relationship doesn't make for a most natural and legitimate nationalism, then the monotheism that the covenant constitutes and from which Israel's nationalism derives ("I will be your God, and you shall be My people") isn't legitimate either. But nowhere would anyone apply such terms as "colored" and "proud" and "boast about" pejoratively to monotheism! The reason is clear enough: whereas the monotheism of the Hebrew Bible—the very heart of the New Testament and Christianity, and of Islam—is perfectly acceptable, the Israelite nationalism of the Bible and its consequences so far as the Land is concerned is not. Furthermore, in accordance with the covenant between God and each of the patriarchs and with the people Israel, which both parties to the contract vowed to fulfill, God gave Israel the land of Canaan. This is not a gift, "something that is given voluntarily and without compensation, a present" (*The American Heritage Dictionary of the English Language*, 1969); the Hebrew Bible regarded the covenant as a case of *quid pro quo*, an altogether legal and binding exchange of obligations and rewards for each of the two contracting parties. If God became Israel's Deity and no other people's, and if He gave to Israel, and to no other people, the land of Canaan, Israel in turn had to accept and worship God alone and no other deity, powerful and attractive as so many of the deities flourishing at the time appeared. This solemn agreement on the part of God and Israel was no gift, with no strings attached—no more on the part of God than on the part of the patriarchs or Israel; on the contrary, it was a normal and valid case of give and take common to every kind of contract into which two parties voluntarily enter, with strings very much attached thereto. But let us go directly to the four passages cited by Anderson.

(a) Joshua 24 begins with the statement that:

> Joshua assembled all the tribes of Israel at Shechem. He summoned Israel's elders and commanders, magistrates and officers, and they presented themselves before the Lord.

From this verse alone, it is evident that the writer has put what he will proceed to record in a legal, court setting, viz., he has the two parties of the covenant and of the dispute arising from it confronting each other—the phrase *vayityatsvu lifnei ha'elohim* points to that; one can compare here, e.g., Job 1:6 and 2:1, when the divine beings entered and took up position before (or beside) God, with the adversary (or prosecutor) among them [*vayavo'u benei ha'elohim lehityatsev al-YHWH vayavo gam hasatan betokham*]. The text in Joshua then proceeds at once to recount all that God had done for His covenanted partner Israel, from Abraham in Ur to his "patriarchal" descendants in Canaan, to the Eisodus and Sojourn in Egypt, followed at long last by the Exodus and the Forty-year Wilderness Wandering, now culminating in the Conquest of Canaan; as put in v. 13 (cf., e.g., Deut. 9:1ff. and 7:6ff. quoted above, or 8:11ff.):

> I have assigned to you a land for which you did not labor, and towns which you did not build, and you have settled in them; you are enjoying vineyards and olive groves which you did not plant.

In short, God had carried out His part of the contract.

Verses 14ff., beginning with the very first word, the particle *ve'ata* used forensically, continue to point up the legal character of the chapter: whereas God had kept the contract, you, Israel,

> Therefore, revere the Lord and serve Him with undivided loyalty [or true integrity, *betamim uve'emet*] . . .

The response of the people is a vigorous "Yes!":

> (16) Far be it from us to forsake the Lord and serve other gods! (17) For it was the Lord our God who brought us and our ancestors up from the land of Egypt. . . . (18) And then the Lord drove out before us all the peoples . . . that inhabited the country. . . . (25) On that day at Shechem, Joshua made a covenant for the people. . . .

Thus the entire chapter clearly denotes the Land not as a benevolent gift from God to Israel but as a contractual obligation for both of them.

(b) In Jer. 3:19ff., God is said by Jeremiah to have levelled an accusation against His people:

> I had resolved to adopt you as My child [lit., how I would put you among the sons/children] and give you [or, and I gave you] a desirable land — the fairest heritage of all the nations; and I thought you would surely call me "Father" and never cease to be loyal to Me [lit. and would not turn from following Me]. (20) Instead, you have broken faith [or dealt treacherously, *begadtem bi*] with Me, as a woman breaks faith with a paramour [cf. 3:3, lit., companion; trad., her husband], O House of Israel — declares the Lord.

Here too, then, there is no concept of "gift" but a totally complete contract of the kind that husband and wife enter into; Israel was disloyal to God and broke her contract with Him (the legal term *begadtem*), after God had fulfilled His part of the contract by assigning to her the "pleasant land" and "goodliest/most beauteous heritage of the nations." Indeed, in the immediately preceding v. 18, mention is made of a restoration of both the Southern Kingdom of Judah and the Northern Kingdom of Israel,

> In those days . . . they shall come together from the north [viz. Mesopotamia] to the land I assigned to your ancestors as a heritage.

Here the legal term *nachalah*, in the phrase *asher hinchalti et avoteikhem* (cf. *nachalat tsevi* in v. 19) denotes not a gift but the legal transfer of property.

Even more. Israel is accused of violating her contract with God in terms of a woman who has violated her contractual marriage vow to her husband; yet God is so bound to Israel that He is willing to break the law and take Israel back as His own! As put in 3:1–18:

> (1) To wit: If a man divorces his wife, and she leaves him and marries another man, can he ever go back to her? Would not such a land be defiled? You have whored with many lovers; can you return to Me? — says the Lord. . . . (14) Turn back, rebellious children — declares the Lord. For I am your lord [or master; Hebrew of uncertain meaning]; I will take you . . . and bring you to Zion. . . .

(c) Precisely the same legal significance is to be found in Hosea 2:20:

(4) Accuse your mother, accuse her [*rivu be'imkhem rivu*],[20]
For she is not My wife
And I am not her husband. . . .

where the New Jewish Version of *The Prophets* (1978) has a note that reads: "The Lord addresses Hosea and his fellow North Israelites, see 1:9 [and 2:25]. The mother is the nation; her children the individual North Israelites."

(10) She did not acknowledge
That it was I who gave her
The new grain and wine and oil. . . .

That is, that God had fulfilled His part of the contract by giving His people the Land and its bounty (cf., e.g., Josh. 24:13 quoted in §(a) above). Yet withal,

(20) In that day . . . I will banish [lit., break] bow, sword, and war from the land, and I will let them lie down in safety.
(21) And I will espouse you forever:
I will espouse you with equity and justice,
With devotion and compassion;
(22) I will espouse you with faithfulness —
And you shall acknowledge the Lord . . .
(25) And I will sow her [viz. Israel] in the land
      as My own [*uzratiha li ba'arets*]:
I will take Lo-ruchamah back in favor,
I will say to Lo-ami, "You are My people,"
And he will say, "[You are] my God."

(d) In Amos 2:10ff. the prophet accuses Israel bluntly, in the name of God:

I, I brought you up from the land of Egypt
And led you through the wilderness forty years
To possess the land of the Amorites! . . . .
(11) . . . Is that not so, O people of Israel?
            — says the Lord.
(12) But you . . .

In fine, God had kept His part of the pact with Israel, but Israel had not; in their contractual relationship, Israel had not delivered her *quid* in return for God's *quo*.

4

For the biblical writers, God's vow to the Patriarchs and to the Israelites in bondage in Egypt having culminated in Israel's settlement in the land of Canaan, the main concern became the explanation of Israel's economic, political, social, and military ups and downs—always in relation to, even in proportion to her observance or lack of observance of the covenant.[21] Central to that view was the Land. In the predominantly agricultural and only secondarily commercial community, which also constituted geographically a land bridge between Asia and Africa, the usual punishment for violation of the covenant was seen as drought, locust, harassment, invasion, and even subjugation by other peoples; the most extreme form of punishment, however, was banishment from the Land, exile and captivity. Passages to this effect abound, provided—apart from the Pentateuch—by the authors of such historical books as Joshua, Judges, Samuel, Kings, Ezra-Nehemiah, and Chronicles on the one hand, and God's spokesmen, the prophets, on the other. We shall limit ourselves here to but a few such passages, typical ones; deriving as they do from Hosea and Amos to Second Isaiah and Ezra, they cover a period of some three centuries, the period which saw such momentous events as the Fall of both the Northern Kingdom of Israel and the Southern Kingdom of Judah and the Restoration of the latter.

Hosea proclaims, 9:1–5:

(1) Rejoice not, O Israel, / As other peoples exult; For you have strayed / Away from your God. . . . (3) [You] shall not be able to remain / In the land of the Lord [be'erets YHWH]. But Ephraim shall go back to Egypt / and shall [have to] eat unclean food in Assyria. (4) It shall be for them like the food of mourners / all who partake of which are defiled. They will offer no libations of wine to the Lord, / And no sacrifices of theirs will be pleasing [i.e., acceptable] to Him; But their food will be only for their hunger, / It shall not come into the House of the Lord [as sacrifices]. (5) What will you then do about feast days, / About the festivals of the Lord?

And Amos proclaims, 7:17 (to Amaziah, priest of Bethel):

(17) This, I swear, is what the Lord said: Your wife shall play the harlot in the town, your sons and daughters shall fall by the sword, and your land shall be divided up with a measuring line. And you yourself shall die on unclean soil; for Israel shall be exiled from its soil.

However, subsequent to the catastrophe of destruction and exile as punishment for breaking the covenant, restoration to (and of) the Home-land is the ultimate reward. So that the same Hosea who uttered "Rejoice not, O Israel"—or even a later writer—will declare (11:8–11):

> (8) How can I give you up, O Ephraim? / How surrender you, O Israel? . . . I have had a change of heart, / All My tenderness is stirred. (9) I will not act on My wrath, / Will not turn to destroy Ephraim — For I am God, not man. . . . (10) The Lord will roar like a lion, / And they shall march behind Him; When he roars, His children shall come / Fluttering out of the west: (11) They shall flutter from Egypt like sparrows, / From the land of Assyria like doves; And I will settle them again in their homes—declares the Lord.

And the book of Amos ends with this proclamation (9:11–15):

> (11) In that day, I will set up again the fallen booth of David . . . (14) I will restore My people Israel: / They shall rebuild ruined cities and inhabit them; They shall plant vineyards and drink their wine, / They shall till gardens and eat their fruits. (15) I will plant them upon their soil, / Nevermore to be uprooted / From the soil I have given them — said the Lord your God.

Ezekiel provides an excellent example of what the Land meant to the people. Never before had the people and its Land suffered such humiliation, subjugation, and devastation as when the Babylonian army came, saw, and conquered (587–86 B.C.E.). To the prophet, for aliens to defile God's holy Land and Temple was the ultimate horror; in turn, and in accordance with the already age-old biblical comprehension of history, to have merited such extreme punishment, the people must have violated the covenant as never before. And so Ezekiel found sin everywhere in the Judean community. The modern authors of biblical history who do not comprehend this basic theological aspect of biblical thought, are content to rehash the biblical text and to prate about inner decay and immorality—as though Chaldean imperialism and military superiority depended upon Judah's lack of righteousness — ignoring the similar fate of other countries that succumbed to the Chaldean army, countries that had no covenant with Israel's God. In fact, however, one gets the impression that Ezekiel had walked about in his native country with what we might nowadays call a sinometer, measuring the presence of sin, its quantity and quality, in every nook and cranny of the Land. A few examples out of very many may be quoted here.

Ezekiel 5: 5ff.:

> (5) Thus said the Lord God: I set this Jerusalem in the midst of nations, with countries round about her. (6) But she rebelled against My rules and My laws, acting more wickedly than the nations and the countries round about her. . . . (9) On account of all your abominations . . . (17) I will let loose against you famine and wild beasts and they shall bereave you, pestilence and bloodshed. . . .

Ezekiel 6: 3ff.:

> (3) . . . I will bring a sword against you and destroy your shrines. (4) Your altars shall be wrecked and your incense stands smashed, and I will hurl down your slain in front of your fetishes. . . . (8) Yet I will leave a remnant . . . among the nations. . . . (9) And those of you that escape will remember Me . . . And they shall loathe themselves for all the evil they committed and for all their abominable deeds. (10) Then they shall realize that it was not without cause that I the Lord resolved to bring this evil upon them.

Or Ezekiel 7: 2ff.:

> . . . Thus said the Lord God to the land of Israel: Doom! Doom is coming upon the four corners of the land. (3) . . . I will let loose My anger against you and . . . (27) I will treat them in accordance with their own ways and judge them according to their deserts. And they shall know that I am the Lord.[21]

But as asserted, e.g., in 6: 8 ff. cited above, and in accordance with the view of his predecessors, Ezekiel understood the covenant as endless, so that God and Israel would in time resume their contractual relationship in the Land of Israel. In the justly famous Vision of the Valley of Dry Bones (chap. 37), perhaps the most electrifying passage in the entire Bible, Ezekiel describes graphically how God will breathe life once again into the scattered heaps of bleached bones lying in the valley, and how after

> (10) . . . they came to life and stood up on their feet, a vast multitude, (11) He said to me: O mortal, these bones are the whole House of Israel. They say, "Our bones are dried up, our hope is gone; we are doomed." (12) Prophesy, therefore, and say to them: Thus said the Lord God: I am going to open your graves and lift you out of your graves, O My people, and bring you to the land of Israel. . . . (25)

They shall remain in the land which I gave to My servant Jacob and in which your ancestors dwelt; they and their children and their children's children shall dwell there forever. (26) I will make a covenant of friendship [shalom] with them — it shall be an everlasting covenant with them — and . . . I will be their God and they shall be My people.[22]

The declarations of Second Isaiah, he of the Exile, begin on a passionate note with the announcement and assurance that God is planning the imminent liberation and restoration of His covenanted people from their exile in Babylonia to their homeland (40:1ff.):

> (1) Comfort, oh comfort My people,
> Says your God.
> (2) Speak tenderly to Jerusalem,
> And declare to her
> That her term of service is over,
> That her iniquity is expiated;
> For she has received at the hand of the Lord
> Double for all her sins. . . .

Or as put in 44:23ff.:

> (23) Shout, O heavens, for the Lord has acted;
> Shout aloud, O depths of the earth!
> Shout for joy, O mountains,
> O forests with all your trees!
> For the Lord has redeemed Jacob,
> Has glorified Himself through Israel.
> (24) Thus said the Lord, your Redeemer . . .
> It is I, the Lord, who made everything . . .
> (26) . . . who say of Jerusalem, "It shall be inhabited,"
> And of the towns of Judah, "They shall be rebuilt;
> And I will restore their ruined places."

Indeed, this exodus from Babylonian bondage to their own Land is likened to the Exodus from their Bondage in Egypt — except that the new exodus will be more leisurely and the trek from Babylonia to Judah will be much more pleasant than the Forty-year Wandering through the Wilderness to reach Canaan, "for," the prophet declares (52:12),

> You will not depart in haste [bechipazon],
> Nor will you leave in flight;

For the Lord is marching before you,
The God of Israel is your rear guard,

Here, the use of the term *chipazon* at once recalls its two other occurrences
(Ex. 12:11 and Deut. 16:3), both in connection with the Exodus.[24] As for
the long, overland trek across the Fertile Crescent, God declares through
the prophet (42:16):

I will lead the blind
By a road they did not know,
And I will make them walk
By paths they never knew.
I will turn darkness before them to light,
Rough places into level ground.
These are the promises—
I will keep them without fail.

With vivid imagery, he declares (49:7ff.):

(7) Thus said the Lord,
(8) . . . I created you and appointed you
A covenant people,
Restoring the land,
Alloting anew the desolate holdings [*lehanchil nechalot shomemot*]. . . .
(10) They shall not hunger or thirst,
Hot wind and sun shall not strike them,
For He who loves them will lead them,
He will guide them to springs of water. . . .
(22) Thus said the Lord God:
I will raise My hand to nations
And lift up My ensign to peoples;
And they shall bring your sons in their bosoms,
And carry your daughters on their backs.
(23) Kings shall tend your children,
Their queens shall serve you as nurses.
They shall bow to you, face to the ground,
And lick the dust of your feet.
And you shall know that I am the Lord—
Those that trust in Me shall not be shamed.[25]

Zechariah, among the last of the prophets, is associated with a similar exhortation (2: 14ff.—the famous *haftarah* that begins with *rani vesimchi bat tsiyon,* designated most appropriately for the Sabbath of Hanukkah):

> (14) Shout for joy, Fair Zion! For lo, I come; and I will dwell in your midst—declares the Lord. (15) . . . Then you will know that I was sent to you by the Lord of Hosts. (16) The Lord will allot Judah to Himself as His portion (*venachal YHWH . . . chelko*) in the Holy Land, and He will choose Jerusalem once more. (17) Be silent, all flesh, before the Lord! For He is roused from His holy habitation.

Finally, we cite the famous Edict of Liberation that was issued about 538 B.C.E. by the Persian Government of Cyrus II; it constituted the triumph and vindication of the covenant between God and Israel, namely, the return to the Land. Ezra 1: 1ff. (cf. 6.1ff., Darius) has recorded it thus:

> (1) In the first year of King Cyrus of Persia, when the word of the Lord spoken by Jeremiah [Jer. 29: 10] was fulfilled, the Lord roused the spirit of King Cyrus of Persia to issue a proclamation throughout his realm by word of mouth and in writing as follows:
> (2) Thus said King Cyrus of Persia: The Lord God of Heaven has given me all the kingdoms of the earth and has charged me with building Him a House in Jerusalem, which is in Judah. (3) Anyone of you of all His people—may his God be with him —let him go up to Jerusalem that is in Judah and build the House of the Lord God of Israel; and let all who stay behind . . . assist . . . with silver, gold, goods, and livestock, beside the freewill offering to the House of God that is in Jerusalem . . .
> (7) King Cyrus of Persia released the vessels of the House of the Lord which Nebuchadnezzar had taken away from Jerusalem and had put in the house of his god . . . (11) in all, 5,400 gold and silver vessels. Sheshbazzar brought all these back when the exiles came back from Babylon to Jerusalem.

And so, 2: 70 states:

> The priests, the Levites, and some of the people, and the singers, gatekeepers, and the temple servants took up residence in their towns and all the rest of Israel in their towns.

The point of the biblical version of the Edict is that God's sacred abode in Judah had to be rebuilt and His covenanted people re-established in the Land, with full authority over the Temple in the hands of the Judeans themselves. And after a number of ups and downs, in part the result of the upheavals within the Persian Government and Empire, the Judean population had grown to the point where the rebuilding of the ruined city and Temple became feasible, and was achieved.[26]

There is so much more that a study of the Land in connection with God's covenant with Israel ought to involve. Thus, e.g., there is the aspect of holiness that was associated in the Bible with the Land, and the exclusive status of Jerusalem as the only Holy City—a status that Jerusalem never lost among the Jewish people but which it did come to share with other cities in Judaism's two major daughter religions, Christianity and Islam.[27] To the biblical writers, the holiness of the Land derived immediately and directly from the holiness of God Himself, that is to say, God is holy and His presence [*kavod*, trad., "glory"] and abode are holy, and they generate holiness; and so the Land (as His people) is holy and must be maintained unmarred and undefiled by wrongdoing. A few passages out of very many will indicate this.

Isaiah is aware of course that God is the Master of the Universe and that the whole world is filled with His presence; yet he also recognizes that God chose the Land that He had promised to the patriarchs and their heirs, as His territorial base on earth; and Mount Zion in Jerusalem as the site of His Temple, His abode in the Land. As the prophet put it in 2:2ff. (the prophet Micah also, 4:1ff.):

> (2) In the days to come,
> The Mount of the Lord's House
> Shall stand firm above the mountains
> And tower above the hills;
> And all the nations
> Shall gaze on it with joy.
> (3) And the many peoples shall go and say:
> "Come! Let us go up the Mountain of the Lord,
> To the House of the God of Jacob,
> That He may instruct us in His ways,
> And that we may walk in His paths."
> For instruction shall come forth from Zion,
> The word of the Lord from Jerusalem.

And in 6:1ff. the prophet reported that he beheld the seraphs standing in attendance on the Lord in His Temple,

> (3) And one would call to the other,
> "Holy, holy, holy!
> The Lord of Hosts!
> His presence [*kevodo*] fills all the earth!"

It is precisely because Jerusalem-Zion and the Land of Israel constitute God's abode that the author of Lamentations in inconsolable grief over the Babylonian destruction of Judean sovereignty and the defilement of God's temple, was constrained to cry out (2:1ff.):

> (1) Alas!
> The Lord in His wrath
> Has shamed Fair Zion,
> Has cast down from heaven to earth
> The majesty of Israel.
> He did not remember His footstool [viz. the Temple]
> On His day of wrath.
> (2) The Lord has laid waste without pity
> All the habitations of Jacob;
> He has razed in His anger
> Fair Judah's strongholds.
> He has brought low in dishonor
> The kingdom and its leaders.

It is only in the period before the Israelites took possession of Canaan that a site outside the Promised Land can be described as holy. In Ex. 3:1ff. (on which Josh. 5:15 is patterned; the place involved was at Jericho), Moses is commanded by (an angel of) God in the wilderness at Horeb ("the mountain of God") not to approach the bush that was all aflame but not consumed:

> (4) "Moses! Moses! . . . (5) Do not come closer. Remove your sandals from your feet, for the place on which you stand is holy ground [*admat-kodesh hu*]."

Indeed, so holy is the Land, that sacrifices may not be offered to God outside the Land, and the food there is unclean:

Hosea 9:3:

They shall not be able to remain
In the land of the Lord [*be'eretz YHWH*].
But Ephraim shall return to Egypt
And shall [have to] eat unclean food [*tame yokhelu*] in Assyria.

Amos 7:17:

. . . the Lord said . . .
And your land [*ve'admatkha*] shall be divided up with a
    measuring line.
And you yourself shall die on unclean soil [*al-adamah teme'ah*];
For Israel shall be exiled from its soil.

And Ezek. 4:13:

The Lord said, "So shall the people of Israel eat their bread [or food],
unclean (*yokhlu . . . et lachmam tame*), among the nations to which I
will banish them."

Second Isaiah, no less than the eighth-century prophets and his immediate predecessor in captivity, the priestly-minded Ezekiel, exhorts his fellow
Judeans in exile in lyrical language (52:11):

Away, away!
Depart from there!
Unclean, touch it not!
Depart from her midst,
Cleanse yourselves, you who bear the vessels of the Lord!

The prophet had already exclaimed in v. 1:

Awake, Awake!
Put on your garb of might, O Zion,
Put on your robe of splendor,
O Jerusalem, holy city!
For the uncircumcised and the unclean
Shall never enter you again.

Withal, it is noteworthy that the term "Holy Land"[28] (or "Promised
Land") did not become the standard Jewish appellation for the sovereign

territory of biblical Israel; it early became a Christian term that has become popular among Jews only in recent times, as they succeeded in breaking out of the ghettos and entering open society. The standard Jewish term has been "The Land of Israel" (*erets yisra'el*).[29] A parallel to this may be found in the Jewish term, "The Western Wall" (*kotel ma'aravi*), for which the Christian term is "The Wailing Wall."

Another aspect of the Land as Covenant that cannot be discussed here because of the limitation of space is the names of the Land and its boundaries. As everything else, the geographical extent of the Land and the names that it bore depended on the specific circumstances that obtained at any given time. Never was this more manifest and pertinent than since the signing of the Balfour Declaration in 1917 and the rise of the State of Israel in 1948. Thus, for example, all hell broke loose the world over when the Government of the State of Israel began in the later Seventies to use the term "Judea and Samaria" for the territory adjacent to the Jordan River on the west; after all, others had decided that the term "Occupied West Bank" should be employed. A pity indeed — and revealing too — is the simple fact that anyone who knew something about the New Testament was aware that this term had hoary and significant tradition behind it, that it had been used already almost two thousand years ago, when Judea had come under the control of the Romans. Yet who drew public attention to it?

The Book of Acts opens with the account of the meeting of Jesus and his chosen apostles in Jerusalem, following on the Resurrection (1: 1ff.; RSV):

> (6) So when they had come together, they asked him, "Lord, will you at this time restore the kingdom in Israel?" (7) He said to them, "It is not for you to know times or seasons which the Father has fixed by his own authority. (8) But you shall receive power when the Holy Spirit has come upon you; and you shall be my witnesses in Jerusalem and in all Judea and Samaria and to the end of the earth."

With Judea, Samaria, and Galilee constituting at the time the land of Israel under Roman rule (cf. Matt. 19: 1; Luke 17: 11; and John 4: 1ff. for other references to these Districts), it is clear that the expression "in Jerusalem and in all Judea and Samaria (and to the end of the earth)" was used by Jesus — in keeping with Jewish usage at the time — in the sense of "Jerusalem and the rest of the country," namely, the Land of Israel.[30]

Notes

*This study, begun under a Guggenheim Foundation Fellowship in 1968 (as part of "A Critical Study of Certain Biblical Concepts in their Historical Setting"), was reanimated a decade later by the gracious invitation from Spertus College of Judaica to participate in the Colloquium on "America and the Holy Land" that it (along with the Chicago Chapter of the American Friends of the Hebrew University, the Institute of Contemporary Jewry of the Hebrew University, and the American Jewish History Society) sponsored on September 10, 1978. My paper was titled "The Holy Land in the Bible"; and in this connection I wish to thank the then President David Weinstein and Dean Nathaniel Stamfer. Planned as a larger work, the present essay was originally worked up in major part for the Nahman Avigad Volume of *Eretz-Israel* (XVIII, 5745–1985) and was to appear in Hebrew.

1. See the more detailed discussion in H. M. Orlinsky, *The Bible as Law: God and Israel under Contract* (N.Y., 1978; 29 pp.), the Horace M. Kallen Lecture of 1976, sponsored by the Herzliah Hebrew Teachers Institute-Jewish Teachers Seminary, Graduate Division (now a part of Touro College); acknowledgment is herewith made to the then Dean Meir Ben-Horin for his gracious cooperation.

2. In general, the true meaning and intent of the Hebrew text is best gotten from the New Jewish Version (NJV) of the Bible (1962–82) sponsored by the Jewish Publication Society of America; cf., e.g., K. R. Crim, "The New Jewish Version," in the special issue of *The Duke Divinity School Revue* 44, 2 (Spring 1979), ed. L. R. Bailey, pp. 180–191 (the issue reprinted with additions in 1983 as *The Word of God*); H. M. Orlinsky, "The New Jewish Version: Genesis of the Fourth Great Age of Bible Translation," in the Samuel Iwry Volume (*Biblical and Related Studies Presented to Samuel Iwry* [1985]). A one-volume edition of NJV, with a new Preface by the writer, is planned for 1985 [appeared as *TANAKH*].

3. It is very important to note that regardless of the source and date of composition of the passages quoted or referred to in this study—be it J or E or D or P, or some redactor (on which S. R. Driver, *An Introduction to the Literature of the Old Testament*⁹ [1913, frequently reprinted], is still at least as good as any; indeed it has continued to serve many as a source, even if not always acknowledged)—all of them are in agreement insofar as our argument is concerned.

4. Cf. my statement already in *Ancient Israel* (1954), chap. III, p. 43 (= p. 68 in *Understanding the Bible through History and Archeology* [1972]), ". . . In the view of the Biblical writers there could have been no Israel without God and the Holy Land."

Whether the biblical concept of the covenant between God and Israel derived from the Mesopotamian concept of the suzerain treaty—and in which period and milieu—or not, is not relevant to this study. I have never been persuaded by the arguments for the Mesopotamian suzerain origin or nature of the biblical concept, and they appear to have become less convincing to scholars in the last few years. I may but observe here in passing that in his article on "Covenant" in *IDB* (I, 1962, 714a–723b), G. E. Mendenhall, one of the earliest and most vigorous proponents of "suzerainty," while noting the dominance of the word *brit* to express "covenant" in the Bible (286 times), has failed to note (similarly P. A. Riemann, "Covenant, Mosaic" in *IDB Supp.*, 1976, 192a–197a) that the eighth-century prophets hardly constitute a good source for the use of this word as a technical term for God's contract with Israel; thus *brit achim* in Amos 1:9 involves neither the Israelite nor the Judean kingdom. It is rather, on the one hand, God's liberation of Israel from Egypt, their safe trek through the wilderness, and their occupation of Canaan; and on the other, the charge that Israel failed to carry out its part of the contract, that expresses the covenant. Furthermore in this connection, the eighth-century prophets hardly recognized a Sinaitic-Mosaic origin of the covenant. It has been noted, e.g., in the survey by F. F. Bruce of "The Theology and Interpretation of the Old Testament" (chap. XIII, pp. 385–416, in *Tradition and Interpretation: Essays by Members of the Society for Old Testament Study*, ed. G. W. Anderson, 1979), p. 391 (in II, "Covenant and Salvation History"), that "The Abrahamic covenant, related to the land, and the Sinai covenant, related to the Law, differ from each other and from the Davidic covenant . . ."; and note the implications in C. Westermann's stimulating article on "Promises to the Patriarchs" in *IDB Supp.* (690a–693b). Clearly there is ample room, and need, for a fresh approach to the subject.

While the discovery of parallels elsewhere in the Near East to various aspects of the biblical covenant, including that of terminology, is a useful scholarly pursuit, more care should first be taken to determine the precise nature of the biblical covenant; moreover, sight should not be lost of the important fact that parallels in societies that are much the same, in this case agricultural-commercial, do not automatically indicate borrowing and dependence. See my comments on the—alas, still—"current vogue to equate 'parallelism' with 'proof' . . ." on pp. 211ff. of "Whither Biblical Research?," *JBL* 90 (1970), pp. 1–14 (= pp. 211ff. in chap. 11 of Orlinsky, *Essays in Biblical Culture and Bible Translation* [1974], 200–17).

5. It is scarcely necessary to point to or dilate on such generally recognized legal terms as *achuzah* (see, e.g., n. 8 below), *nachalah*, and *yerushah* (see, e.g., the data cited below from Joshua, Hosea, Amos, and Jeremiah).

In connection with *sane* "reject" (vis-à-vis *ahav* "favor"), it may be that the word *garash*, traditionally rendered "cast/drive out, banish, evict," is used in 21:10 above and sometimes elsewhere forensically for "disinherit." Thus in Judg. 11:2–7, his half-brothers disinherit Jephthah, son of a prostitute:

> (2) . . . *vayegareshu*, Jephthah. They said to him, "You shall have no share [*lo-tinchal*] in our father's property [lit., house; *bevet avinu*], for you are the son of an outsider [*ki ben-ishah acheret atah*]"—though he did share with them the same father, Gilead! Later, when his erstwhile compatriots in their time of trouble came to him for help, Jephthah retorted:

(7) You are the very ones who rejected (so NJV, for *senetem;* traditional "hated"] me and disinherited me [*vategareshuni;* traditional "drove me out"] of my father's property [lit., house; *mibet avi*]."

But this matter merits separate study. In the meantime, note similarly the forensic use of (pi'el) *shalach* for "divorce" as against simply "dismiss, send away, allow to leave," and the hiphil of *yarash* "drive out, oust; dispossess."

In his contribution, "Two Biblical Passages in the Light of their Near Eastern Background—Ezekiel 16:30 and Malachi 3:17" (Hebrew) to *Eretz-Israel* 16 (1982), pp. 56–61 (English summary on p. 253*), J. C. Greenfield has noted the possible use of *shlt, chml,* and *chd* as technical terms; thus *shaletet* would denote "to be in control of her property, to have the right to dispose of property acquired." It may well be that *shlt* also has this value in Gen. 42:6 (*veyosef hu hashalit kol ha'arets*), viz., Joseph "was in control of/had the right (or authority) to dispose of the produce (or wealth) of the land"—note the explicatory phrase, also beginning with *hu*, that follows immediately, *hu hamashbir lekol am ha'arets*, "it was he who dispensed rations to all the people of the land" (NJV), and in that case the term *mashal* in the parallel phrase in 45:26 (*od yosef chai vekhi-hu moshel bekhol-erets mitsrayim*) may have the same force: "(Joseph is still alive; yes,) he is in charge [or control] of the produce [or wealth] of the whole land of Egypt"—and note that this phrase follows immediately upon the account in which we are told (v. 23) that "to his father he sent as follows: ten he-asses laden with the best things of Egypt, and ten she-asses laden with grain, bread, and provisions. . . ." (On E and EJ as the sources of these passages, see S. R. Driver, *Introduction*, pp. 17–21.) Eccles. 2:19 may offer another such usage of *shlt*; cf. NJV "and he will control all the wealth . . ." for *veyishlat bekhol-amali*. And since the generally later term *shalat* corresponds to *mashal*, the term used widely earlier, it may be that *mashal* sometimes has the technical real estate value ("to control one's property") also in such passages as Ex. 21:8, Deut. 15:16 (note the context), and Gen. 3:16 (4:7 is too obscure textually and contextually to be considered). [I note now the reference to Ex. 21:8 in Muffs, p. 206, as an Addendum to p. 178.]

6. Among other passages that could be cited, cf., e.g., 13:14ff.,

(14) The Lord said to Abram, after Lot had parted from him, "Raise your eyes and look out from where you are, to the north and south, to the east and west, (15) for all the land that you see I will assign to you and to your heirs forever. . . . (17) Up, walk about the land, through its length and its breadth, for I will assign it to you."

7. It is hypercritical to construe initial *mem* in *mishemanei* and *mital* as privative (traditional "away from"); it is clear from the passages cited here that Esau was blessed with hardly less progeny and bounty than Isaac was, and ought not be deprived of it. Similarly with Ishmael; thus whatever be the original text of Gen. 25:18 and its meaning, received *al penei chol echav nafal* can hardly have been

intended negatively, as is evident from the parallel phrase in 16:12, *al penei chol echav yishkon*, especially when 25:18 begins with *vayishkenv* – and note, too, the use of the same word *shkhn* for Ishmael in 16:12 as for Isaac in 26:2. This is, of course, the thrust of God's assurance to Abraham as recorded in Gen. 21:12–13: "whatever Sarah tells you, do as she says, for it is through Isaac that your heirs shall be continued for you. As for the son of the slave-woman [viz., Ishmael], I will make a nation of him, too, for he is your seed," and is not negated by the Lord's assurance directly to Rebekah (25:23):

> Two nations are in your womb,
> Two peoples shall issue from your body;
> One people shall be mightier than the other,
> And the older shall serve the younger.

It may also be noted here that Abraham adjured the senior servant of his household never to allow his son Isaac to return to Paddan-aram in Ur of the Chaldeans, because of "The Lord, the God of heaven, who took me from my father's house and from the land of my birth, who promised me under oath, saying, 'I will assign this land to your heirs' . . . do not take my son back there . . ." (Gen. 24:1–7).

8. The phrase *vayeshev ya'akov be'erets megurei aviv be'erets kena'an* employed here recalls at once the text of God's earlier promise to Abraham (17:8), "I assign the land you sojourn in to you and your heirs to come, all the land of Canaan, as an everlasting holding. I will be their God" [*venatati lekha ulezarakha acharekha et erets megurekha et kol erets kena'an la'achuzat olam*]. Attention may be drawn here to the legal-real estate term *achuzah* ("holding," traditional "possession"), used both for Abraham and his descendants and for Esau and his descendants (36:43, "Those are the clans of Edom – that is, of Esau father of the Edomites – in their settlements in the land which they hold" [*eleh alufei edom lemoshrotam be'erets achuzatam hu esav avi edom*].

9. Cf. Muffs, op. cit., p. 20 n. 4 and p. 42 n. 1. The matter of acquiring legally, or of refusing to acquire without payment, someone else's property may be worthy of further study; thus the statement is made no less than three times within half a dozen verses in Esther 9 (vv. 10, 15, 16), "But they (the Jews) did not lay hands on the spoil" (of the non-Jews in Shushan and in the provinces) – even though King Ahasuerus had issued an edict (8:14) "to this effect: The King has permitted the Jews of every city . . . to plunder their [enemies'] possessions." In this connection, it is of interest to note Rashi's comment at Gen. 1:1 that the Bible begins with God's creation of the universe – rather than, as one would expect, in a lawbook, with a law or series of laws – to make it clear that as creator and rightful owner of the world He had the right to assign any part of it to anyone He wished; in this case, it was the land of Canaan that He assigned to Israel – a legal transaction to which no one in the world could object. Or as God is said to have

put it to Moses in connection with the Sinai-Law covenant (Ex. 19:5), "Indeed [or For] all the earth is Mine [*ki li kol ha'arets*]"; or, as the Psalmist, e.g., put it (24:1), "The earth is the Lord's, and all that is in it" (cf. Orlinsky, "Who is the Ideal Jew: the Biblical View," Chap. 10 in *Essays*, 197ff.).

10. Moses is the "servant of the Lord" [*eved YHWH*] par excellence in the Bible (see Orlinsky, *The So-called "Servant of the Lord" and "Suffering Servant" in Second Isaiah* [*V.T. Supp.* XIV, 1967; repr. 1977], chap. I, pp. 7ff.)—to which should be added the numerous instances of "My [viz. God's] servant"; and even though God is said to have offered the sort of covenant that He had made with each of the patriarchs, Moses refused the offer (Ex. 32:10ff., Deut. 9:13ff.). What may have motivated the author of this story, while of significance, is not our concern here.

11. The covenant with David was national, i.e., with the continuation of the line of David as the government of God's covenanted partner, Israel. This is clear even from Psalm 89, devoted as it is to the Dynasty of David and the glorification of it:

> (4) I have made a covenant with My chosen one,
> I have sworn to My servant David:
> (5) I will establish your offspring forever,
> I will confirm your throne for all generations. . . .
> (30) I will establish his line forever,
> His throne as long as the heavens last. . . .
> (37) His line shall continue forever,
> His throne (as long) as the sun is before Me. . . .

(cf. N. M. Sarna, "Psalm 89: A Study in Inner Biblical Exegesis," in *Biblical and Other Studies*, ed. A. Altmann, vol. 1 [1963]).

This is likewise true of the statement in II Chron. 34:3, that "In the eighth year of his reign, while still a young man, [Josiah] began to seek the God of his ancestor David [*hechel lidrosh lelohei david aviv*]. . . ." Or cf. the supplementary statement in Amos 9:11ff., "In that day, I will set up again the fallen booth of David . . . (12) declares the Lord. . . . (14) I will restore My people Israel . . . (15) I will plant them upon their soil, / Nevermore to be uprooted / From the soil that I assigned to them. . . ." I am unable to accept several of the central points made, e.g., in M. Weinfeld's article, "Covenant, Davidic" (*IDB Supp.*, 188b–192a) and in Bruce's survey (see n. 4)—both useful discussions, to which may be added the clear and forthright study of *Covenant: The History of a Biblical Idea* by D. R. Hillers (1969).

12. In Gen. 9:26, when Noah blesses Shem, ancestor of Israel, the expression employed is "Blessed be the Lord, / The God of Shem [*elohei shem*]; / Let Canaan be a slave to them"—where Shem vis-à-vis Canaan, rather than expected Ham, clearly stands for Israel. And in Gen. 31:48ff., in the final stage of the dispute between Laban and Jacob—in the course of which God had appeared to Laban the

Aramean and warned him not to do anything to Jacob (v. 24) – Laban declares *elohei avraham velohei nachor yishpetu veineinu elohei avihem vayishava ya'akov befachad aviv yitzchak* (v. 53); but while "(the God of Abraham and) the God of Nahor"– as distinct from the "god(s) of Nahor"– is hardly intended here, both the preserved text (the position in the text and the meaning of *elohei avihem*) and the immediate context are too suspect to provide a positive conclusion in the matter.

13. Briefly put, as the Creator of the universe and the only Deity in existence, God is a universal God; as the God of Israel alone, He is a national God; He is not, however, an international God, since in the biblical view He never became the God of any nation other than Israel. Failure to comprehend this has resulted not only in utter misunderstanding of the biblical concept of God but also in distorting the natural definitions of the terms universal vis-à-vis international. See the detailed argument in "Nationalism-Universalism and Internationalism in Ancient Israel" and "Nationalism-Universalism in the Book of Jeremiah," respectively pp. 78–116 and 117–143 in Orlinsky, *Essays.*

14. Here too, as in the case of the change of the names of Abram, Sarai, and Jacob (see above), the assignment of the land to Israel is the central element in the renewal and fulfillment of the covenant.

15. It should be noted that just as, say, "The Lord" alone is for the Deuteronomist a variant of "the Lord your God," so are such phrases as "that you may live" [*lema'an tichyu*, e.g., 4:1] and "that you may long endure" [lit. prolong your days, *ha'arikh yamim*, e.g., 6:3 – referring back to 5:30] meant to include "in the land that I/God swore [to your ancestors] to assign to you." It is the land of Israel that the authors and redactors of Deuteronomy are talking about, so much so that it is taken for granted by them.

16. Biblical scholarship has tended to overlook or play down the eternality of the Land as Israel's; this aspect merits a full, independent study. One may note in passing specific use of such terms as "forever," "for all time" [*lemin olam ve'ad olam*], "everlasting holding" [*achuzat olam*], "as long as the heavens last / the sun is before Me," and "nevermore to be uprooted"– apart from the clear implication of innumerable other passages; in neglecting this concept, scholars have also failed to do justice to the biblical comprehension of God – as omnipotent and faithful a contractual partner as one could wish.

17. Even Isa. 19:18–25 – hardly original with Isaiah and the bulk of it probably deriving from the Seleucid-Ptolemaic period (cf. Orlinsky, "Nationalism-Universalism and Internationalism in Ancient Israel," in *Essays* [see n. 13 above], pp. 99ff.) – does not have Judeans living in Egypt and worshiping there, let alone in Assyria. The passage is full of difficulties, e.g., the Egyptians will worship Israel's God in Egypt – after God has punished them and they have repented and acknowledged Him – and, presumably, the Assyrians will worship Israel's God in Assyria; but Egypt ends up (v. 23) – in the very midst of its blessings – as subservient to Assyria! Actually, there is no reason for the mention of Assyria in this context in the first

place, except that, apparently, it served as a tie-in with chap. 20 immediately following, devoted as it is to Assyria's invasion and humbling of Ashdod, Egypt, and Ethiopia; but then even Egypt was brought in at this point (vv. 18ff.) by a redactor only because the first seventeen verses of the chapter dealt with Egypt. For other tallywords or themes used in "The Compilation of the Book of Isaiah," see L. J. Liebreich, *JQR* 46 (1955–56), pp. 259–77 (on p. 263, chap. 20 is described as "Transition" between Division IIA [Chaps. 13–19] and IIB [Chaps. 21–27]); 47 (1956–57), pp. 114–38 (especially pp. 119f., 131).

18. In my brief review of this work, *In Jewish Bookland,* Oct. 1974, I noted the anti-Zionist bias that pervades it.

19. Two studies that deal with the postbiblical period are of interest here: Betsy H. Amaru's fine article on "Land Theology in Josephus' *Jewish Antiquities,*" *JQR* 71 (1981), 201–20 (though I find the use of the term "gift" in the biblical context unacceptable; and add to the useful bibliography S. Zeitlin, *The Rise and Fall of the Judean State,* 3 vols. [1962–78]; see, e.g., Samaria, as region of Judean State, vol. 3, Cumulative Index, p. 519a) and W. D. Davies's informative book on *The Territorial Dimension of Judaism* (1982).

20. And note the use of the legal term *riv* in 4: 1 (*ki riv le-YHWH im-yoshvei ha'arets*).

21. Cf. my statement in the "Introduction" to *Ancient Israel* (1954; frequently reprinted), "The Bible as Sacred History and its Interpretation," pp. 8–9 (= pp. 8–9 in *Understanding the Bible through History and Archaeology* [1972]):

> Those who were responsible for the composition of the Hebrew Bible believed that what they uttered and wrote derived from the God who had entered into a mutual Covenant with Israel. . . . The modern historian, however . . . must seek—behind the religious terminology—the same kind of documented human story, with an examination of its underlying dynamics, that would be his proper objective in any other field. Otherwise he would achieve no more than a compilation of myths, chronicles, annals, oracles, autobiographies, court histories, personal apologia.

Consequently,

> . . . in the handling of the biblical material there is the major problem of discovering the fundamental economic, social, and political forces from documents couched almost exclusively in religious terminology and given to interpret all historical experiences as manifestations of divine intervention.

22. Unfortunately, such histories as J. Bright's *A History of Israel* (1959) reflect this biblical view when they attempt to reconstruct the career of Biblical Israel as modern historians: "decay," moral and internal, is a favorite term that is used to account for Assyrian or Babylonian conquests of Israel and Judah, or the cause of the downfall is the rejection of their God and of their covenant with Him. No

wonder that the modern professional historians do not take their contemporary biblical historians seriously. However, in all fairness Bright admitted in his Foreword (p. 10) that he wrote his *History* "with the particular needs of the undergraduate theological student in mind"; see §8, "Biblical History" (pp. 80ff.) in Orlinsky, "Old Testament Studies" (pp. 51–109) in the volume titled *Religion*, ed. P. Ramsey (1965) in the series *Humanistic Scholarship in America: The Princeton Studies,* and the strictures by G. W. Ahlström in his review-article, "Some Comments on [the 3rd edition of] John Bright's 'History of Israel'," *JAOS* 95, 2 (April–June 1975), pp. 236–41.

23. It is of interest to note here that this chapter in Ezekiel is declaimed over the national radio of Israel (*Kol Yisra'el*) during the annual observance of the Day of Independence (*Yom Ha'atsma'ut,* 5th of Iyar, usually toward the end of April or in early May).

24. And where, incidentally, the Masoretes noted that in all three instances the word was spelled *plene.*

25. See Orlinsky, *The So-Called "Servant of the Lord" and "Suffering Servant" in Second Isaiah* (*Studies on the Second Part of the Book of Isaiah,* vol. XIV in *Supplements to Vetus Testamentum,* 1967; repr. 1977), pp. 28ff.

26. It is a pity that A. T. E. Olmstead, one of the very few competent historians of the world of the Bible and author of the fine *History of the Persian Empire* (1948; also a Phoenix paperback), has marred this major work by visiting his uninhibited hostility to twentieth-century (C.E.!) Zionism upon the persons of Ezra and Nehemiah and the policy of the Achaemenid government; concerning his chapters II (23f., 31ff.), XXII, XXV, and XXXII, I wrote on p. 326 of my critical survey of "Jewish Biblical Scholarship in America" (*Essays,* chap. 16, 287–332 – based on my survey in the Tercentenary Issue of *JQR* 45 [1956–57]):

> . . . very few scholars in modern times betrayed publicly their hostility to what such books as Esther, Ezra, and Nehemiah stood for in the manner that Albert T. Olmstead did, in his detailed *History of the Persian Empire* (Chicago, 1948). His loathing for Zionism, ancient and modern, revealed itself in such an expression as "Ezra . . . did not succeed in stopping permanently the activities of the prophets, whose dreams of a coming national kingdom returned again and again, but he did point the way to the only safe policy for the salvation of Judaism – abandonment of nationalistic hopes, reconciliation to the political rule of foreigners, loyalty to the powers that be, and full acceptance of the unique position of the Jew as the guardian of God's moral law. Fortunately for the world, succeeding generations have generally followed his guiding principle: the reactionary minority which has time and again raised the standard of separate nationality has only increased the woe of their fellow-Jews" (p. 307). One wonders which is greater, Olmstead's ignorance of the simple facts of Jewish history or his malice.

See also p. 161 of *Essays*, "Selected Bibliography," and pp. 62f. in my "Old Testament Studies" (n. 22 above), "Extrabiblical Research."

27. The prefatory statement, "The Centrality of Jerusalem," that I wrote for the catalogue of the exhibit of *Maps and Views from the Moldovan Family Collection —Jerusalem: Center of the World* at the New York School of Hebrew Union College-Jewish Institution of Religion (9/18/84–3/1/85), began with the assertion:

> While other major religions have made Jerusalem share their loyalty, affection, and awe with Bethlehem, Nazareth, and Rome, or with Mecca and Medina, only in Jewish life and thought has Jerusalem enjoyed undivided loyalty. Undivided in theology, in prayer, in halacha, in aspiration.

And closed with the explanation:

> And so, if some maps on display at this exhibit show Jerusalem as the center of the world, the geography may not be accurate, but for the Jewish people the fact of Jerusalem's centrality in the world is very real.

28. The term "holy land" found in translations of the Bible represents *admat (kodesh)*, not *eretz*.

29. The term *eretz yisra'el* is found infrequently in the Bible—some half dozen times (I Sam. 13:19; Ezek. 27:17; 40:2; 47:18; II Chron. 34:7); it may be that the writers and redactors of *erets yehudah* avoided it because of the possible confusion with the Kingdom of Israel to the north. See further, e.g., the (barely adequate) article on "Palestine, Holiness of" by J. D. Eisenstein in *Jewish Encyclopedia* (IX, 1905; pp. 502a–503a), where some interesting data are offered (e.g., the term *ar'a kaddisha* in the Zohar); and, of course, the volumes edited by Strecker and by Eckert, Levinson, and Stöhr, and the books by Brueggemann and Davies ([see n. 19], e.g., pp. 28ff., 142f.).

30. I was moved to accept the invitation from Spertus College because the two most widely read national weeklies in the United States had asked me to comment on the term "Judea and Samaria" that the Government of Israel insisted on employing in place of (divinely ordained?) "Occupied West Bank"; but I had refused all comment because I could not be assured that my comment would be reproduced accurately and might well have required correction in a subsequent issue of these magazines.

Land Theology in Philo and Josephus

BETSY HALPERN AMARU

[Editor's note: Both Philo and Josephus stand as counterpoints to the rabbinic conceptions of Judaism being developed in the first two Christian centuries. Their understanding of the role of the Land of Israel forms the subject of Dr. Betsy Amaru's contribution to this book. Amaru, who is Visiting Associate Professor in the Department of Religion at Vassar College, begins by isolating four loci of Land discussion in the Bible: 1) the role of the Land in the Patriarchal covenant; 2) the unique properties ascribed to the Land; 3) the place of the Land in Torah legislation; and 4) messianism linked to the Land in the early and later prophets. She describes how each of these are treated in the work of Philo and Josephus. For Philo, the Land is subjected in all four cases to his thoroughgoing allegorization of biblical content, so that "the Promised Land becomes knowledge of God, wisdom and virtue," for example. "A sense of the real people and the real Land is lost." Josephus, on the other hand, eschewed allegory in favor of the best of Greek historiography. For him, Land is still Land. But for all that, Amaru argues, the Land suffers from Josephus' determined attempt to chip away at its centrality in Israel's covenant with God. Josephus has no trouble with covenant per se, but cannot abide the notion of "a covenanted people limited to a covenanted Land." God makes alliances in history, to be sure, and appears as helper and rewarder, in which the Land may even be the reward, but there can be no sense of covenantal inheritance, in which Land is given as a promise in perpetuity to a specific people, since, for Josephus, it is "conditional on morality and obedience, or even on the fortuitous swing of God's rod." In both cases (Philo and Josephus), we see diaspora thinkers applying the norms of a chosen discipline (Alexandrian philosophy, and Roman historiography) to the Bible and its tale of Jewish destiny. In neither case, argues Amaru, is there "a comfortable place for classical Land theology."]

Separated by less than a century, the two intellectual giants of Hellenistic Judaism, Philo Judaeus and Flavius Josephus, both lived in the Diaspora. The first spent his entire life, the second, the active literary part of his life, outside of the land of Judea. Although differing somewhat in their

attitudes toward the Roman rule under which they lived, both men so ad-
mired Hellenistic intellect that they tried to integrate it into their understanding of biblical Judaism. In Philo's case, the integration took the form
of a philosophic exposition of the Pentateuch. For Josephus, it involved a
treatment of Hebrew Scriptures along the literary, historical style of Greek
classical writers.

While Josephus' *Antiquities* was most certainly written with a gentile,
Roman audience in mind, the extant philosophic writings of Philo are generally thought to have been directed toward Jewish readers.[1] The two writers differed not only in style and purpose of exposition, but also in the source
texts each used for his explication of the Pentateuch.[2] In spite of these differences,[3] exposition of Hebrew Scriptures based on either Semitic or Greek
text would have required the expositor to deal in some way with what we
may term the "Land-centeredness" of classical Jewish history and theology.[4]
The purpose of this study is to examine how Philo and Josephus each han-
dled that "Land-centeredness," and thereby to begin to ascertain the significance of Land theology in Hellenistic Jewish thought.[5]

Land theology appears in Hebrew Scriptures in four general areas,
three of which are concentrated in the Torah books: (a) As a major theme
in the patriarchal introduction to the biblical history of Israel where it is
presented in terms of a covenantal triad of God-People-Land; (b) in the form
of unique qualities ascribed to the "Promised Land"; (c) as a significant concept in Torah legislation which frequently is Land-linked;[6] and (d) in the
context of biblical messianism which in Early Prophets is expressed in terms
of promises to the House of David, and in Later Prophets, in terms of the
loss of the Land and the hope of repentance and return.

Patriarchal History

The patriarchal history opens with God's unexplained direct command
to Abraham to leave Chaldea and move on to "the Land which I will show
thee" (Gen. 12:1). Upon arrival in Shechem, Abraham is promised that his
descendants will inherit the land of Canaan (Gen. 12:7). At every opportunity this promise is renewed: upon Abraham's return from a sojourn in
Egypt and his separation from Lot (Gen. 13:14–17); upon his rescue of Lot
from the Sodomites (Gen. 15:5–7); and upon the prediction of Isaac's birth
(Gen. 17:2–9). The promise is progressively specified: from "this Land"
(Gen. 12:7) to, "all the land thou seest—to the north, south, east, and west"

(Gen. 13:4), to, "from the river of Egypt unto the great river, the river Euphrates" (Gen. 15:18–21). When the promises are formalized, and the term covenant is applied (Gen. 15:18–21; 17:12–14), circumcision of males is commanded specifically as a sign of acceptance of the promise of divine gifts of land and peoplehood to both of which God has a special relationship.

The God-People-Land relationship is renewed with each of the succeeding patriarchs, albeit in less detail than in the case of Abraham. Isaac, confirmed in the covenant before his birth and again at Mount Moriah, is directly confronted at Gerar with a divine promise of land, great numbers, and prosperity (Gen. 26:2–5). Jacob first hears of the promises through the blessings he receives from his father before his flight to Laban in Mesopotamia (Gen. 28:3–4). En route, and again at Bethel years later when he has resettled in Canaan, he receives the promises directly from God (Gen. 28:13–14; 35:10–12). In every instance with Isaac and Jacob, the source of the covenant is referred back to God's relationship with the preceding patriarchs. And in every instance of covenant making, not only is land mentioned, but the specific territory of land promised is denoted as God's gift.[7]

Even with Joseph, a nonpatriarchal figure, the text establishes the covenantal link. Joseph is not confronted by God; rather he is told by Jacob of the promises made at Bethel. Upon his deathbed Joseph then conveys the covenantal promise to his brothers. This attempt to bridge the gap between the patriarchal and exodus periods is set forth entirely in terms of the Land aspect of the covenant (Gen. 50:24).

Thus throughout the biblical narrative of the patriarchs the Land is a central focus for the covenant and for describing God's relationship to the forefathers and their descendants. Within the covenant context, Land may appear without direct reference to the growth and development of the covenanted people. *Never, however, is the covenant presented without some reference to the Land promise.* It is with this biblical emphasis in mind that we turn to Philo and Josephus commenting upon or retelling the patriarchal narratives.

Before examining Philo's treatment of the Land concept, it should be noted that the philosopher's use of allegorical method extended far beyond those works classified as "allegories." Even in treatises such as *On Abraham,* which is considered a literal approach to the biblical text, Philo reaches for the allegorical or "underlying meaning."[8] Much as Philo may defend the literal sense of the law as the body without which the soul cannot function,[9] in his treatment of the Genesis stories, Philo's method involves more and less allegory, never the total absence of it.[10] Given this approach, we can expect that Philo will allegorize the covenanted Land promise. The question then becomes one of the nature and significance of that allegorization.

Philo's treatises on the forefathers are limited to those which deal with Abraham: *On Abraham* and *On the Migration of Abraham*. His full treatments of Isaac and Jacob have not been preserved. Hence, in dealing with the latter, we are limited to *Questions and Answers on Genesis* and to comments on all three forefathers which are scattered throughout Philo's writings.

Philo's treatment of the migration to Canaan involves significant alterations of the Genesis story even at the level which he terms "literal." First, the command to migrate is expressed not directly as "the Lord said," but rather as "under the force of an oracle" (*On Abraham* 61). Secondly, Philo shifts the command from Haran back to Chaldea, thus breaking the migration into two steps: from Chaldea to Haran, and then from Haran to Canaan (Ibid., 69–72). Most significantly, the migrations within Canaan (Gen. 12:6–9) are reduced to a move "into a desert country," and the two specific references to the Land promise (Gen. 12:1 and 7) are totally ignored.

The first of these changes has been attributed to Philo's antipathy to anthropomorphism.[11] Nonetheless, the shift from active to passive voice detracts from the power of the command, and minimizes the expression of intimacy between God, patriarch, and Land felt in the biblical text.

The change of locale for the original command reflects Philo's desire to understand the entire scenario as stages in the spiritual and intellectual development of Abraham, whom he portrays as the prototype of the seeker after truth and knowledge. At both the literal and the allegorical levels he is describing a "virtue-loving soul in its search for the true God" (*On Abraham* 68). The migrations are seen as progressions in this search—from life in a world that ascribes everything to the "movements of the stars" (Chaldea) to a world which turns inwardly to self, perceiving the source of knowledge as coming from the senses (Haran);[12] to a second migration, from sense knowledge to the mystical, nonphysical realm wherein the true God can begin to be known. This last stage, from senses to knowledge of God, involves leave-taking of the familiar, the secure, and a willingness to go off "into the desert country." The concept of "wandering in the wilderness," of the necessity of seclusion and solitude for the mystic, is made much of by Philo.[13] In point of fact, it becomes a substitute for the "land I will show you," the land of Canaan that in Genesis 12:7 is promised at Shechem.[14] When Philo develops these verses allegorically, the Promised Land becomes knowledge of God, Wisdom, and Virtue (*On Abraham* 84; *On the Migration* 28–29). It is the domain of pure contemplation that requires taking leave of the body ("thy land"), senses ("thy kindred"), and of speech ("thy father's land"). At this point Philo is no longer dealing with a physical migration to the desert, but with the migration of the soul. Samuel Sandmel points out that the allegorical interpretation involves a major shift in tone for the departure of the soul is not from the familiar to the foreign, but quite the opposite.[15] In leaving the land of senses, the soul is in the process of self "recovery," ceasing to be the "property of others" (*On the Migration* 10–11). What is vividly described in *On Abraham* as the risk-filled journey into the wilderness, becomes in *On the Migration of Abraham* "a happy life, enjoying in perpetuity the benefit and pleasure derived from good things not foreign to thee, but thine own (*On the Migration*, 11).[16] At the allegorical level it might seem that Philo regains some of what he forfeited in his literal interpretation in terms of a positive sense of Land. But in spite of the positive imagery, the soul's acquisition of its true nature no more evokes the biblical concept of Promised Land than did Abraham's move into "the desert country" at the literal level.

As for the renewals of the Land promise that appear in the biblical text, Philo's treatment of Abraham totally omits any reference to Land save for a comment in *Who is the Heir* where the gift of Land is again equated with the "inheritance" of wisdom (98).[17] In *On Dreams* he does deal with the specific description of the borders of the Promised Land (Gen. 15:18) by telling us that the promise does *not* really mean "a section of country, but rather the better part of ourselves" (255)! The borders enumerated are understood as the limits of what is excluded and included within that better self; Eygpt (i.e. the passions) is excluded, and all territory to the Euphrates (i.e. the virtues) is included (257–58).[18]

Similarly, there is no mention of the Land promise in Philo's exposition of the prediction of the birth of either of Abraham's sons. Instead, the full expression of the covenant idea in Genesis 17 is used by Philo for extensive comment on the change of Abram's name as indicative of the development of the patriarch's character—the student of the supraterrestrial (astrology) has become the student of mind.[19] Furthermore, no mention is made in the patriarchal context of the command to circumcise, the sign of acceptance of the covenant.[20]

The single exception to this neglect of Land as promised real estate may be read into Philo's answer to the meaning of Genesis 17:8.[21] Here Philo states: "the literal meaning is clear, so that the passage does not require any interpretation." But the allegorical interpretation of the verse which follows describes the "eternal possession" of the Land, as eternal control of the body (Canaan) by the Mind (Abraham and his descendants). Moreover the control involves a "sojourn," not a permanent settlement!

In the writings on Isaac that have been preserved there is little if anything to offset the Land treatment in relation to Abraham. To Philo, Isaac represents "the Naturally Wise" one who possesses wisdom from birth, one who knows without instruction "to seclude himself alone with only the invisible God."[22] As such, he never has to leave his country (now Wisdom),[23] and is the single patriarch who is never required intellectually to enter Egypt (body and sense knowledge). The story of the *Akedah* is rendered without reference to the promise that Abraham's seed would inherit the "gates of their enemies," and the extensive direct covenantal Land promise to Isaac at Gerar is reduced at the literal level to "all things belong to the wise man," and to rulership of "corporeal substances" by the Mind at the allegorical level.[24]

Whereas Abraham represents one taught by God, and Isaac, the self-instructed, Jacob becomes the prototype of the "Practicer." In the extant writings (at least) nothing is said of the Land promises made to this third patriarch either by Isaac upon his son's departure to Haran,[25] or directly by God at Bethel years later. However, in *On Dreams* (1.173–82) much is made of the promises made to the sleeping Jacob at Beersheva. In the biblical text he is promised the Land, a posterity that will spread "to sea, south, north, and east," blessings through him and his seed of "all the tribes of the earth," and reassurance that he will be brought back to the Land of Canaan.[26] Philo allegorizes each element of the promise. The promise of Land becomes the promise of wisdom and virtue; posterity becomes the by-product of wisdom which restrains passion, just as the sand holds back the sea; and the blessing of "the tribes" through Jacob and his seed becomes the positive effect of reason (Jacob as Israel) upon the senses (the tribes). The dispersion of Jacob's descendants is not understood as implied in the text, i.e. within the borders of the Promised Land, but rather as worldwide.[27] Allegorically, this dispersion represents the impact of the purified mind on the "earthly" in the individual, and the impact of the man of wisdom on his environment at a social level. As for the assurance of Jacob's return from Haran, Philo makes explicit what was implied in the allegory of Abraham's migration: the body is only the temporary dwelling place of the "reasoning faculty" of the soul. The assurance of return may, in fact, be understood as a "hint" to the doctrine of the immortality of the soul (*On Dreams* 1.181).

Not surprisingly, Philo also does nothing with the transmission of the patriarchal Land promise by Joseph to his brothers (Gen. 50:24). He does comment on the subsequent verse regarding the burial of Joseph's bones in that Promised Land, using it as evidence of Joseph's understanding that the "incorruptible portions of the soul" should not stay with "unrestrained passion," but should go to "the cities of virtue" (*On the Migration* 18).

In his dealings with Land theology, Philo seems consciously to avoid making any connection between divine promise, divine gift, and the Land as real estate. His reluctance to do so is evident even at the literal level. When he does not omit the Land promise entirely, he interprets it in a manner far afield from the biblical sense of covenanted Land.

Philo's problem with the Land idea is not connected to a problem with the concept of a covenant (*diatheke*) between God and Israel. He makes repeated references to "covenant,"[28] and alludes to two treatises, no longer extant, specifically dealing with the subject.[29] In the material available to us, Philo describes the covenant as a "symbol of the grace which God has set between Himself Who proffers it and man who receives."[30] It is this "grace" which each of the patriarchs, in fact, receives. This grace is understood as the development of the rational faculty, release from sense knowledge, as "all the incorporeal principles, forms and measures for the whole of all the things of which this world was made,"[31] not as the gifts of land and peoplehood. Literally and allegorically, Philo views the patriarchs from a universal perspective, i.e. as prototypes of ideal men. At the literal level, Philo's Genesis rehearses the description of the historically rooted human search for true knowledge; and at the allegorical level, of a comparable search by the different types of soul each patriarch represents. Somewhere in that universalistic perspective a sense of a real people and a real land is lost.

When we turn to Josephus' rendition of these narratives in *Antiquities*, we find closer contact with the biblical text, but another problem with the biblical Land concept. Josephus does not set the Land promise within a covenantal context. He deletes those covenantal scenes which he cannot set within the context of clear reward, or he reinterprets the narrative so as to limit the reward to future greatness in numbers. Where he does maintain some idea of Land acquisition, he puts it into the setting of a prediction of providential assistance rather than of promise of Land as divine gift.

Abraham's departure from Chaldea is attributed neither to the direct divine command of Genesis nor to Philo's "oracle," but to Abraham's own initiative (*Ant.* 1.157). The choice of Canaan as a place to settle is presented as God-directed, but only as a parenthetical aside, not as a significant preface to covenant.[32] The initial promise of Land at Shechem is deleted, as is its renewal upon Abraham's return from Egypt, and the narrative moves directly to the war between the Sodomites and the Assyrians. Within that context, Josephus presents for the first time a version of God's promises to Abraham. The promise is made, not as a gift, but as a reward for Abraham's refusal to accept spoils from the Sodomite king. Moreover, the reward is not the full biblical covenant, but the promise of a son "whose posterity would be so great as to be comparable in number to the stars" (*Ant.* 1.183).

The Land idea is first introduced in the context of a "divine voice" predicting that Abraham's posterity will be enslaved in Egypt, but ultimately will emerge from that slavery, "vanquish the Canaanites . . . and take possession of their land and cities" (*Ant.*, 1.185). There is no covenant here, no *berit*, no *diatheke*.[33] Instead, the setting (for what is the third affirmation of a covenantal relationship in Genesis) is constructed by Josephus as a matter of divine prediction of divine assistance, at best.

The same pattern is evident in Josephus' treatment of Isaac's birth and of the *Akedah*. In the former, God reveals that "great nations and kings would spring" from this son, nations which "would win possession, by war, of all Canaan from Sidon to Egypt" (*Ant.* 1.191). In the latter, Josephus elaborates on the predictions of prosperity, power, and great numbers which will accrue to the future descendants. The conquest of Canaan is again mentioned (*Ant.* 1.235), but as with the earlier scene, the language is predictive rather than promissorial. There is no sense of covenanted inheritance here.[34] Moreover, like Philo, Josephus reinterprets the rite of circumcision, it becoming in his case a means of keeping Abraham's posterity from "mixing with others" (*Ant.* 1.192).

As for the covenantal scenes with the adult Isaac (Gen. 28: 3–4, 13–14; 35: 10–12), all are ignored. In their place comes the scripturally ungrounded prayer in which Isaac notes that God has promised his descendants not a Land, but "gracious aid . . . and even greater blessings" (*Ant.* 1.272).

The same theme and language are used in Josephus' version of dialogues between God and Jacob. God's relationship both to the patriarchs and to their descendants is alternately described as a source of "succor," as that of an "escort," "protector and helper," "guide," and even as a matter of destiny.[35] Unlike Philo, Josephus retains and develops the initial covenant scene at Bethel. But the Land promise here and in two additional scenes created by the historian is not the "eternal possession" of Genesis.[36] It is a "grant of power" (*Ant.* 1.282), a "long era of dominion" (*Ant.* 2.175), and a people "destined to find a habitation in Canaan" (*Ant.* 2.194).

The closest Josephus comes to covenantal language in such passages is in the reassurance given to Jacob before he goes to join Joseph in Egypt:

> And now am I come to be thy guide upon this journey, and to fore-shew to thee that thou will end thy days in Joseph's arms, to announce a long era of dominion and glory for thy posterity, and that I will establish them in the land which I have promised.[37]

The limitation of "a long era of dominion" aside, we do seem to have here a "Promised Land." But without a previous covenantal base to refer to, the promise must be understood in terms of the pledge of assistance in conquest made to Jacob at Bethel. The significant fact is that Josephus chose to insert this promissorial language in a nonbiblical passage, while deleting it from his paraphrases of passages where the covenanted Land theology is explicit in the text of Genesis.[38]

Josephus' problem with Land theology in the patriarchal stories is not with covenant *per se*, but with a covenanted people limited to a covenanted Land. To some extent that problem, like Philo's own, is rooted in a desire to "universalize" the special relationship between God and Israel.[39] For Josephus, the tie between God and Israel is one of special concern, but it is only one example of God's providential care for the world. Thus, instead of covenanted Land acquisition, Josephus builds a case for divine "alliance," where acquisition of the Land is conditional on morality and obedience, or even on the fortuitous swing of God's rod.[40]

The other possible impetus to Josephus' significant alterations to Genesis Land theology may be that as a diaspora Jew writing in the year 93 C.E., he was in fact committed to the idea of a diaspora coexisting with a homeland and did not wish to "overstate" the case for the latter. Throughout his renditions of the stories, he gives precedence to the theme of the development of peoplehood over the theme of Land. The first promise made to Abraham is limited to a posterity great in number (*Ant.* 1.183). The prediction that Isaac's posterity would win Canaan by war is directly linked to the promise that he would father great nations. And, most telling, his version of the promise to Jacob at Bethel presents the idea of a wide diaspora as part of a covenantal promise: "To them do I grant dominion over this Land, to them and to their children who shall fill all that the sun beholds of earth and sea" (*Ant.* 1.282)! The similarity between this and Philo's interpretation of the promises made to Jacob at Beersheva is striking.[41]

The Quality of the Land

When we turn to the second major expression of biblical Land theology—the notion that the Land has a peculiar nature and is unique in its relationship to God—we again find that neither Philo nor Josephus sustains the mystical and poetic language of the Pentateuch. In the Torah, Canaan, unlike any other piece of real estate, has a soil that in and of itself cannot tolerate moral pollution; it is a Land that even in the time previous to Israelite habitation would vomit forth those who would pollute it (Lev. 18: 24–30; 20:22–25; Num. 35:34). This peculiar Land never belongs to its conquerors. It is always God's Land upon which even the covenanted people dwell as "strangers and sojourners with God" (Lev. 25:23). Variously described as "flowing with milk and honey," as a "very, very good land" (Num. 14:7), having multiple springs and brooks, and producing delicious fruit and abundant wheat and barley, a land without scarcity even of mineral deposits (Deut. 8:7–9), it is yet a land which, unlike Egypt, is dependent upon God for the most basic source of such prosperity, its water supply (Deut. 11:12).

None of this poetic description of the Land is retained in *Antiquities*. At most, Josephus describes the Land as "favorable" or "fortunate" (*Ant.* 2.269).[42] Philo does occasionally attribute special qualities to the Land, but allegorizes or universalizes them to fit his portrait of the journey to wisdom. The God-given water that enriches the Land becomes the "shower of . . . virtues gushing forth to give drink," the "divine watering of the soul" (*Special Laws* 1.303). The abundance of vineyards and olive trees "represent progress and growth . . . the fruit of knowledge . . . winning for us unmixed gladness as from wine, and intellectual light as from a flame which oil feeds" (*On Flight and Finding* 175).[43] As for the notion that the Land becomes defiled by immorality, Philo interprets the text of Deuteronomy 24:4 so that it is the woman, not the Land, which is defiled.[44]

At the literal level Philo generally avoids romanticized allusions to the Land. He deals with it as a country "occupied by Phoenicians" (*On Moses* 1.214), as "Palestine, then called the land of the Canaanites" (Ibid., 1.163), as a land "afterwards called Palestinian Syria" (*On Abraham* 133). In the context of the journey to the land, Canaan becomes the "land in which the nation proposed to settle" (*On Moses* 1.220); and the sending of the spies is merely a sensible way to check out the fertility or infertility of the land "for if it is poor it would be folly to court danger to win it" (Ibid., 1.225).

Allegorically the land of Canaan represents a stage in the development of the soul, but it is not a particularly positive stage, and certainly no final haven. In several treatises Philo recounts the story of how Canaan was cursed because of his father's exposure of the drunken Noah. In the biblical text (Gen. 9:18–27) it is Ham who is cursed through the fate of servitude placed upon his son. In working his way around this punishment of the son for the sin of the father, Philo explains that while Ham did not "spread abroad" that Noah was "deprived of virtue" (Philo's allegorization of the drunkenness and nakedness of Noah), Canaan actively did so. Thus Ham comes to represent vice in a quiescent state, and Canaan, "which means tossing," is vice "when it passes into active movement."[45]

Philo develops the notion of this "tossing" also in relation to the land of Canaan. It is a stage of adolescence (*Preliminary Studies* 82, 85), a place where "reason is tossed to and fro" (*On the Sacrifices of Abel and Cain* 90),[46] one step up in the progression of the soul from vice (Egypt).[47] One does not get here the biblical sense that the Exodus and the years of wandering culminate in the arrival into Canaan. Instead Philo develops a passage in Numbers (21:16–18) where the Israelites rejoice over discovery of water. In its biblical context the scene takes place on the borders of Moab and precedes entry into the Land. But for Philo the celebration of the well becomes an occasion for expressing joy and gratitude "to the Deity Who gave them the Land as their portion and had, in truth, led them in their migration" (*On Moses* 1.255). The insertion of a divine gift of Land here not only is out of biblical context, but also is presented almost as an aside. Ultimately, as his development of an allegory on the passage indicates, Philo has the Israelites celebrate not the land of Canaan, but the source of water (*On Drunkenness*, 112 and *On Dreams* ii, 270ff.). Having come to the specific piece of land—Canaan—he confronts the contradiction built into his allegorization of patriarchs leaving home to go to the wilderness or returning home by going to the "land of the fathers." And here he makes the well of water at the edge of the desert, not the Land of the fathers, the source of wisdom and virtue.

Erwin Goodenough suggests that this emphasis on the hymn as opposed to entry into the Land occurs because Philo cannot put the culmination of the journey at a place and time where Moses is no longer present.[48] Indeed, for Philo, Moses is the model of perfection. He is the embodiment of the spirit of the Law, of true religiosity, and, as shepherd of the people, their guide from civilization to wilderness, from sociability to contemplation, from enslavement to body and passion to pure thought — but in the Sinai desert, not in the land of Canaan.

Philo maintains a link between Moses and the patriarchs, but it does not include the concept of the Land. When God, speaking to Moses at the Burning Bush, refers to the patriarchs, it is a reference to the virtues they each represent, a means by which mortals can be brought into relationship with God (*On the Change of Names* 13).[49]

When Philo deals with the "Land" in relationship to Moses' leadership (as opposed to "Canaan"), Land is idealized again into a condition of being, a state of virtue, the perfect gift of grace (*Sacrifices of Abel and Cain* 57).[50] The children of Israel must be taken by "way of the desert barren of passions and of wrong doing" and led to the high land from whence spies are sent to view the "whole land of virtue" to see if it is "well fitted both to give increase to the lessons there sown and to raise the stalk of tree-like verities there planted." Unable at this stage to "carry the whole main stalk of wisdom," they cut a single branch and cluster of grapes to show those of "keen mental vision the sprouting and fruit-bearing alike of noble living" (*On Dreams* 2.170–71).

The Land in Torah Legislation

The same approach is used in Philo's explanation of specifically Land-linked commandments: allegorization of the Land and its produce as the gradual acquisition of wisdom and virtue. The requirement to restrain from eating the fruit of the trees until the fifth year (Lev. 19:28) represents the fact that as the mind "has not entered the way of wisdom" (the first year), it "remains barren" and yields "no edible fruit." By the second and third years the mind is "on the way to good sense" but still "only beginning its course," and not prepared to partake of the "fruits of instruction." Only in the fourth year is the soul ready to "trust the produce" (*On Noah's Work as a Planter* 94–138) which then out of thankfulness is offered to God (*On Virtues* 155–60).[51] Similarly, the commands to offer the first fruits of the grain (Lev. 23:10) and the setting aside of the first mixture of the threshing floor (Numbers 15:18) become gifts "not of the land but of ourselves that we may sow and reap ourselves" (*On Dreams* 2.75–77; *Sacrifices of Abel and Cain* 107–09). We are no longer dealing with either a physical land and legislation regarding its cultivation or with a Land particularly dear to God, but with training in virtue, in moral sensitivity. The separation of firstlings "is an avenue to piety," to an "indelible recollection" of God (*Special Laws* 1.132); the observance of the sabbatical laws is to establish a habit of self restraint, to "shackle the mad covetous desires" in dealing with land so that we then may learn "to soften harsh temperaments" in dealing with people (Ibid., 4.215); and the prohibition against selling the Land in perpetuity is to remind us that this world is only a foreign city in which God is the sole true citizen (*On Cherubim* 119–23).

In these allegories Philo not only destroys the sense of real, physical land, but also reduces the Land aspect of the biblical covenantal relationship to a school-house where the adolescent Israel acquires basic sensitivity. This theme leads Philo to the highest level of distortion of the biblical narrative: his treatment of Moses' personal relationship to the Land. Totally reconstructing the events at the waters of Meribah (Numbers 20:7, 13) so that Moses "under inspiration" hits the rock with his "sacred staff" (*On Moses* 1.210), Philo informs us that it is an outrageous calumny against the "all-wise leader" to claim that he was not deserving of entry into the Land. For Philo there was no disobedience on the part of Moses, and hence, no punishment. Moses did not enter the Land because as a perfected soul he did not need to enter it: "children have one place and full grown men another, the one named training, the other called wisdom" (*Migration of Abraham* 46). Indeed, Moses' glimpse of the Land from afar is a far greater gift than actual entry, for while one cannot really possess the things nearest the Divine, it is possible for the "purest and most keen-eyed" to see them (Ibid.)

Just as Philo's treatment of Land in the context of the Exodus and the desert wandering reflects hs desire to emphasize the journey to wisdom under the leadership of Moses, so Josephus interprets the biblical text so as to develop further his picture of a 'normative' "divine providence" operating in the history of the Jews. Ignoring the biblical connections which are set in Land contexts, he connects Moses with the patriarchs through a totally unscriptural reconstruction of a dream in which God recalls how with His assistance "Abraham had journeyed from Mesopotamia to Canaan, and had begotten children to whom he had bequeathed various lands: Arabia to Ishmael, Troglodytis to his children by Katura, and Canaan to Isaac (*Ant.* 2.212–13). There is no Land covenant here; the stress is on the fertility of Abraham; Canaan is presented as a land in no way different from Arabia or Troglodytis; and Abraham, not God, is the bequeather of the various territories. In an earlier passage dealing with Katura's children, Josephus had noted that "all these sons and grandsons Abraham contrived to send out to found colonies (*Ant.* 1.239).[52] Colonies, the spread of the Jews into diaspora, not the Promised Land, lie behind Josephus' stress on the reward of great fertility to Abraham.[53]

The God as "ally" theme recurs throughout Josephus' descriptions of the Exodus, the desert wandering, and the entry into the Land. In treating the scene of the Burning Bush where the God of the patriarchs will now keep His covenanted promise to bring the Israelites out of Egypt into the Land flowing with milk and honey (Ex. 3:6), Josephus shifts the emphasis from Land promise to Moses, the sagacious leader who, with God as companion and ally, will direct the Jews (*Ant.* 2.269). The ally theme and language occurs often in contexts of promise.[54] In each instance the promise is made in the language of alliance—"to tender actual aid," "seconding ardor and championing their cause," "delivering to them the land," "to vouchsafe to us to win this land." Nowhere in these passages is there a promise to grant the Land as covenanted gift. Yet in the biblical parallels there is specific reference to God giving the Land.[55]

In dealing with specific laws, Josephus again avoids the Land promise by deleting the biblical connection between "when you come into the Land" and specific legislation. This deletion is particularly evident in the account of the altar built by the two and a half tribes who had settled on the eastern bank of the Jordan. In the book of Joshua (22:23) the fear is expressed that, in violation of divine direction, they might offer sacrifices in a place outside of the covenanted Land.[56] Josephus completely ignores the connection between altar and Land; and has Phinehas charge the tribes with introducing "strange gods," and going over "to the vice of the Canaanites" (*Ant.* 5.107). Moreover, he puts in Phinehas' mouth a totally ahistorical and unscriptural bit of universalistic theology: "Think not that by crossing the river ye have also passed beyond God's power: nay, everywhere ye are within His domain, and escape from His authority and His vengeance is impossible" (*Ant.* 5.109).

Similarly, when Josephus has Moses exhort the people at Sinai to keep the commandments, the resulting reward—a "fruitful earth,"[57] calm sea, many children, and victory over enemies (*Ant.* 3.88)—includes no mention of covenanted Land. Yet, strangely, in his variations on Moses' final discourses in Deuteronomy 4 and 28, Josephus directly connects observance of the law with retention of the Land, a theme totally consistent with covenantal Land theology. But Josephus is not suddenly inserting a Land covenant into his version of Deuteronomy. Instead, by adjusting and revising the biblical text as necessary, he uses the opportunity to have Moses predict the history of Israel from Josephus' political and personal perspective:

> It is just in this thing that the path of safety lies, and to prevent you from breaking out into any violence against those set over you, by reason of that wealth which will come to you in abundance when ye have crossed the Jordan and conquered Canaan. For should ye be carried away by it into a contempt and disdain for virtue, ye will lose even that favor which ye have found of God; and having made Him your enemy, ye will forfeit that land, which ye are to win, beaten in arms and deprived of it by future generations with the greatest ignominy, and dispersed throughout the habitable world, ye will fill every land and sea with your servitude. And when ye undergo these trials, all unavailing will be repentance and recollection of these laws which ye have failed to keep. (*Ant.* 4.189-91)

The passage runs contrary both to Josephus' earlier versions of the divine promises in *Antiquities* as well as to the biblical source upon which it is based (Deut. 4). Josephus had earlier defined the covenant in terms of great numbers promised to the posterity of Abraham, Isaac, and Jacob,[58] and had (unbiblically) stressed the development of a diaspora as one of the blessings and rewards to that posterity.[59] Moreover, he had had the prophet Balaam predict as a great blessing the future dispersion of the people of Israel.[60] Now he tells us that dispersion is not the product of overflowing numbers and divine blessings, but the result of sin and disobedience. In this particular passage the sin which brings forfeiture of the Land and dispersion is "violence against those set over you." The overall theme of Deut. 4 is the same as the rendition in Josephus, i.e., disobedience and sin bring in their wake dispersion among the nations. But there the similarity ends. In Deuteronomy the specific sin is not violence "against those set over you," but disobedience to God's commandment to make no graven image. The punishment is not just dispersion, but also a great reduction in numbers.[61] Moreover, while repentance ultimately is "unavailing" in Josephus' version, in Deuteronomy it is the very factor which will return the people to the covenanted Land (4:3).

We can understand what Josephus is doing here when we compare his version of Deut. 4 with Josephus' own speech (as well as that of Agrippa) in the *Jewish War*,[62] warning against rebellion. He is interweaving prophecy and history—making history out of the theology of Deuteronomy by the

not so simple technique of retrojecting the history he has experienced back
into biblical prophecy.[63] The "sin" of rebellion "against those set over you"
is how Josephus viewed the revolt of 66–70 against Rome; and the consequence, dispersion without a promise of return, reflects his attitude toward
any effort to undo the Roman conquest of Judea.

Josephus' version of the blessings and curses of Deuteronomy 28 is
another example of reading a historical event back into Moses' prophetic
mouth. This time he does not speak of rebellion or of dispersion, but of
transgressing "His rites," with the consequence of enemy invasion, razing
of cities, destruction of the Temple, and enslavement. But on this occasion
repentance will be effective, and ultimately the cities would be restored and
the Temple rebuilt. The passage parallels its source text exclusive of the last
sentence—"God who created you will restore those cities to your citizens
and the Temple too; yet will they be lost not once but often" (*Ant.* 4.314)
—clearly inserted as a prediction of the Babylonian exile.[64] No secular historian, Josephus cannot explain 586, let alone the Roman destruction, without reference to divine punishment. So he reconstructs the biblical passages
to make them prophesy not only a punishment, but a specific punishment
within an actual historical time. Much as he makes theology out of history
in the *War*, he makes history out of theology in the *Antiquities*.[65]

The Land and Eschatology

Although Josephus develops a relationship between Land tenure and
obedience to law, his account of the threat of dispersion and exile is one-
sided. He deletes the blessings, the parallel promises of redemption and return, all of which scriptural passages significantly are Land-oriented and
covenantal.[66] He maintains this pattern when he deals with the prophetic
portions of the Bible. Josephus' interest in prophecy is almost limited to
prophecy as history already played out. Nowhere does he present the strong
prophetic picture of redemption and restoration to a glorious Land.[67] In
fact he pays little, if any, attention to the major classical prophets who are
associated with messianic eschatology. In their place he uses the Midianite
prophet Balaam and the prophet Daniel as the spokesmen for his own eschatology.

The stature of these prophets in Josephus' eyes is related to the universalistic approach he tries to assume as an historian; i.e., they prophesied
about other nations in addition to Israel (*Ant.* 4.125; 10.266–68, 276). For

reasons of stated political prudence he limits his exposition of Daniel to predictions of events already past. He notes that the Roman power "will have dominion forever through its iron nature," but when he comes to the stone in Nebuchadnezzar's dream, he openly shies away from its dangerous political implications.

> I have not thought it proper to relate this since I am expected to write of what is past and done, and not of what is to be. . . . If . . . any one wishes to learn about the hidden things to come, let him . . . read the book of Daniel. (*Ant.* 10.210)[68]

As for the future of the Jews, Josephus is most explicit. Totally out of scriptural context he has the Midianite priest, Balaam, assure the Jewish people eternal divine providence, indestructibility. As for the Land "to which He Himself hath sent you, you shall surely occupy [it]; it shall be subject forever to your children, and with their fame shall all earth and sea be filled" (*Ant.* 4.115). Suddenly, we find in the mouth of the Midianite priest whom Josephus clearly regards as the instigator of the sin of Baal Peor the promise that Josephus had deleted from its patriarchal context and from its textual setting in the Sinai legislation. In addition, the Balaam passage repeats and further elaborates on the promise to Jacob at Bethel of a diaspora based on overflowing numbers:

> . . . ye shall suffice for the world to furnish every land with inhabitants sprung from your race. Marvel ye, the blessed army, that from a single sire ye have grown so great? Nay, those numbers now are small and shall be contained by the land of Canaan; but the habitable world, be sure, lies before you as an eternal habitation,and your multitudes shall find abode on islands and continents, more numerous even than the stars in heaven.[69]

In order to understand Josephus' treatment of Land we must look back at the threads interweaving the various aspects of classical biblical Land theology. The patriarchal Land covenant is directly tied to the giving of the law.[70] And while the actual occupation of the Land is dependent upon obedience to the law, the Land promise remains eternally covenanted and eternally viable in that repentance and return to God affect restoration to the Land. This return or restoration is then tied to the messianic prophecies regarding the House of David. In each case Josephus weakens, if not breaks, the thread: the Land promise to the patriarchs is *not* covenanted; disobedience of law leads to expulsion or dispersion *without* a covenant-rooted

ingathering of exiles, and there is no mention whatsoever of a Messiah out
of the house of David. Indeed Josephus makes a point of eliminating any
attribution of an eternal or messianic character to David's line. The uncon-
ditional divine promise to David that his "throne shall be established forever" (II Sam. 7:16) is deleted (*Ant.* 7.93); he has Samuel assure David only
that "the kingship would *long continue* to be his" (*Ant.* 8.24); and the promise of an eternal line (of I Kings 8:25) becomes in Josephus a promise of
"numberless successors" (*Ant.* 8.113). As for the promise to maintain Solomon's line forever if the people act righteously (I Kings 9:5), Josephus adds
the unscriptural threat to "cut him off root and branch," not suffering "any
of their line to survive" should they not act righteously (*Ant.* 8.126).

Through Balaam, Josephus replaces the classical messianic eschatology with his own vision of future blessings: a glorious people whose eternal
existence is assured by divine blessing and promise; a people who have a
motherland but whose population is so great that they overflow into every
island and continent. It is not a portrait true to the scriptural source, and
it is perhaps for that reason Josephus puts it into the mouth of Balaam
rather than of a classical prophet. Josephus' eschatology reflects his Hellenistic world—a motherland as a point of reference with an extensive eternal
diaspora which might be characterized as colonial.[71] [Ed. note: See comments on Motherland and colonies by Rosenberg, below, pp. 141–46.]

Philo's eschatology, like that of Josephus, ignores the messianic link
with the line of David. Indeed Philo does not even mention the kingship
of David or of Solomon.[72] When he describes victory over human enemies in a future era, he does predict (on the basis of the Septuagint version
of Numbers 24:7) the emergence of a leader, superior in mind and body
(95), who "shall rule over many nations." Interestingly, this leader, the closest Philo comes to a Messiah figure, is textually elicited not from the words
of a classical prophet, but, like the ultimate eschatological hopes of Josephus, from the prophetic blessing of Balaam![73]

The core of Philo's eschatology is built into his interpretation of the
scriptural blessings and curses (*On Rewards and Punishments*) which he, unlike Josephus, projects into a future messianic age. Although he remains
more than usually within the framework of Deuteronomy in this treatise,
the allegory on the acquisition of wisdom and virtue is by no means omit-
ted. At the literal level obedience to the commandments will be rewarded
in a future era by victory over enemies, man as well as beast; by an end
to war; great prosperity in terms of food, shelter, and fertility; and physical

and mental health. Comparably, disobedience will lead to defeat, destruction of cities and countryside, lack of food and shelter, and physical and mental anguish. A concept of Land is brought into the picture at several levels. In discussing the end to war (93), Philo builds on Leviticus 26:6 to tell us that war will "not pass through the land of the godly at all." Another reference to Land appears (by implication) in the description of the promise of great prosperity. Although he paraphrases Leviticus 26:3, 4 and Deuteronomy 16:13, 14 almost literally, he connects that literal sense directly to his earlier allegorization of the Land as a storehouse of virtue: "For those who possess stored up in Heaven the true wealth whose adornment is wisdom and godliness have also wealth of earthly riches in abundance" (104).

The most significant aspect of Land theology in *Rewards and Punishments*, however, is the notion of the "ingathering of exiles." The idea first appears in a discussion of the importance of role models for virtuous behavior, on the part of an individual, a city, or a nation.

> . . . those who would imitate these examples of good living . . . are bidden not to despair of changing for the better, or of a restoration to the land of wisdom and virtue from spiritual dispersion which vice has wrought. (115) . . . just as God with a single call may easily gather together from the ends of the earth to any place that He wills the exiles dwelling in the utmost parts of the earth, so too the mind which has strayed everywhere in prolonged vagrancy, maltreated by pleasure and lust, the mistresses it honored so unduly, may well be brought back. . . . (117)

The context is clearly allegorical and a far cry from the explicit, literal, physical Land notion of Deuteronomy 30:4.[74] Moreover, Philo chooses to ignore, even at the allegorical level, the next verse which connects the restoration to a Land promise made to the forefathers.[75]

At the end of *Rewards and Punishments* Philo returns to the theme of restoration to the Land, interweaving the physical and spiritual senses of the concept of Land so much so that it is impossible to decipher to what extent he is in fact committed to a physical restoration to a physical Land. He develops a close relationship between repentance, redemption, and return. But here again he departs from the traditional theology by inserting the notion that the Land would produce new settlers who would keep the sabbatical laws the violation of which lies at the heart of the great punishments.[76] "Exhausted by repeated labors," and "unstrung by the numberless mishandlings which it has undergone" (156–57), the land becomes barren until it takes a needed rest, whereupon it again becomes fruitful and produces a new virtuous population (158). Even as he develops this, Philo tells us that it is in fact an allegory for the soul which, full of passions and vices with her children, "pleasures, desires, folly, incontinence, [and] injustice," becomes sick almost to death (159). But once it has cast off these children, the land is "transformed into a pure virgin" and through the implanting of a "divine seed" brings forth new life in the form of the highest of virtues (160).

Just as we are understanding 'land' as soul, Philo returns to the literal level and assures us that with full "acknowledgement of all their sins" (63), the Jews "scattered in Greece and the outside world over islands and continents will arise . . . and pass from exile to home" (165).[77] The work closes with a return to the soul which, like a plant stripped of its stalks, will develop new shoots (i.e. virtues) to supercede the old, if the roots (a seed of virtuous qualities) remain (171–72).

Philo has used the "Land idea" here to interweave in a rather complex way a number of notions which in and of themselves are unrelated to Land theology. The new population generated by the Land reflects Philo's commitment to a Judaism based on common religious ties rather than on common ethnic descent.[78] It is not by accident that into his description of the devastated Land he suddenly and without warrant places the proselyte "exalted aloft by his happy lot . . . that he came over to the camp of God . . . while the nobly born who has falsified the sterling of his high lineage will be dragged right down. . . ."[79] Throughout the treatise and scattered through his other writings are references to the availability of true wisdom to all. God "is the God of all" (*On Rewards and Punishments* 123), who "welcomes the virtue which springs from ignoble birth," and takes "no account of the roots" (Ibid., 152); newcomers are to be given "equal rank" with all the privileges granted "to the native born" (*Special Laws* 1.52); the promise to Abraham that he would be a father of a multitude refers not simply to the nations which would descend from his sons, but also to his concern "not only for his countrymen but also for all others . . . especially for those who are able to receive the discipline of attention. . . ." (*Questions and Answers on Genesis* 3.42). Similarly, Jacob is "registered" under both the name of Isaac his father and of Abraham, his grandfather, one virtuous by birth, the other by instruction. Philo explains that this is done in order to teach Jacob that God is the "inheritance" of both those born to "wisdom" and those who must acquire it (*On Dreams* 1.159).[80]

Broad as he would make the appeal of the covenant, Philo never lets go of the notion that it is rooted in the Jewish people. He uses the "in-gathering of exiles" theme in order to express the ever-available opportunity for a return to wisdom and knowledge of God. The 'land' language seems to serve far more as a metaphor for that return than for a physical recovery of real estate. We must recall that throughout his writings Philo used the Land concept in contradictory ways. Abraham's spiritual migration into the Land is not a 'return' home for the soul, but a journey into the fearful and unknown. On the other hand, Isaac's uninterrupted residence in the Land bespeaks the perfected nature of his soul, and Jacob's temporary departure from the Land is seen as a move away, albeit necessary in his case, from perfection and wisdom. Similar contradictions appear in Philo's description of the history of the Israelites. The Land of Canaan is depicted as an ado-lescent stage wherein the soul tosses about in its pursuit of wisdom; but in association with Philo's Moses, this same Land becomes again a meta-phor for the source of perfect wisdom and its associated virtues. In his es-chatology Philo seems to be using the Land metaphor in such a way as to reconcile these contradictions. The proselyte, like Abraham, must first enter the 'land' as a newcomer, as a stranger. The Jews, like Jacob who becomes Israel, enter as adolescents who must leave temporarily in order to reenter properly.

Admittedly such an interpretation of Philo's eschatology seriously questions the extent of his commitment to a literal restoration. But outside of this treatise there is little, if any, evidence of Philo so understanding the "ingathering of exiles."[81] The appearance of the concept in *On Rewards and Punishments* as more than a contrivance can be credited both to the strength of the idea of Land as a working metaphor in Philo's thought, and to the significance generally of Land theology in the traditional Judaism which Philo espoused in spite of his great interest in Greek thought and culture.

Neither Philo nor Josephus presents Land theology in a manner which can be described as "true to" their biblical source. Through allegory Philo turns biblical history into religious philosophy; and by application of his version of the historian's craft, Josephus turns biblical theology into history. Intellectually they share a love of certain aspects of the Hellenistic world view which taints their interpretations of Hebrew Scriptures. Both read into the text an element of universalism which does not fit well with the explicit particularism of biblical Land theology. Both have a sense of a world far wider than that of Judea, and both speak to some extent out of their personal contacts with that world. Although he mentions having made a pilgrimage to Jerusalem,[82] in neither his political or his philosophical writings, does Philo show much interest in the concrete political affairs of contemporary Judea.[83] His major concern is the diaspora community which he describes in his political treatises as colonies of the "mother city" of Jerusalem (*Embassy to Gaius* 281; *Flaccus* 46). In his treatment of the Land covenant, Josephus is affected as much by the stance he had taken during the revolt of 67 and his fear of the messianism of the Zealots as by the fact that he is writing the *Antiquities* for the Roman reader. Consequently, he too, for reasons of personal commitment, envisions at best a Jewish motherland with a large diaspora as a colonial extension.

Lastly, both Philo and Josephus can be seen as cultivating in their writings a new concept of Judaism reflective of their contacts with the Hellenistic world. In Philo this Judaism is described as a religious or cultural 'nationality' minimally tied to a single ethnic base or territory.[84] Similarly, for Josephus, Judaism is a religion of law, of obedience, which is rewarded not by the classical messianic kingdom, but by "a renewed existence and in the revolution (of the ages) the gift of a better life"[85] (*Against Apion* 2.218). In neither expression is there a comfortable place for the classical Land theology.

Notes

1. There is some difference of opinion among scholars. Erwin R. Goodenough argues that the Exposition of the Laws was written for a gentile audience (*An Introduction to Philo Judaeus* [New Haven, 1940], 40ff.). Samuel Sandmel, citing Tcherikover, questions sufficient evidence that non-Jews read Jewish writings, and suggests that these treatises may have been directed toward Jews "on the threshold of apostasy" (*Philo of Alexandria* [New York, 1979], 47).

2. Philo used the Greek Septuagint (Harry A. Wolfson, *Philo* [Cambridge, Mass., 1947], I, 88). For the section of *Antiquities* dealing with the Pentateuch, Josephus used a Semitic text. See H. St. John Thackeray, *Josephus, The Man and The Historian* (New York, 1929), 81.

3. Josephus' Roman audience aside, he promises at the beginning of the *Antiquities* to set forth "the precise details of our Scripture records . . . neither adding nor omitting anything" (*Ant.* 1.17). All citations from *Antiquities* are from the Loeb Classical Library edition (Cambridge, Mass., 1934).

4. See Abraham S. Halkin, "Zion in Biblical Literature," in *Zion in Jewish Literature*, ed. Halkin (New York, 1961) and William D. Davies, *The Gospel and the Land* (Berkeley, 1974), 15.

5. A significant portion of the material on Josephus herein appears in extended form in my article, "Land Theology in Josephus' *Jewish Antiquities*," *Jewish Quarterly Review* 61:201–29. Permission has kindly been granted by the editor to cite and abstract from that article.

6. This connection involves not only "Land-based" commandments, but also a right of retention conditional upon observance of the commandments. In the Torah books the stress is on faithfulness and rejection of idolatry. In the Latter Prophets, a broader stress is felt.

7. God says to Isaac, "Unto thee and unto thy seed I will give these lands" (Gen. 26:3). In Jacob's dream God says, "The land whereon thou liest, to thee will I give it and to thy seed" (Gen. 28:13); and later again at Bethel, God says, "The land which I gave unto Abraham and Isaac, to thee I will give it, and to thy seed after thee will I give the land" (Gen. 35:12).

8. Samuel Sandmel, *Philo's Place in Judaism* (New York, 1971), 104ff.

9. *On the Migration of Abraham*, 16, 89–93. All citations of Philo both in text and notes are from the Loeb Classical Library edition, trans. F. H. Colson and G. H. Whitaker (Cambridge, Mass., 1958), 10 vols.

10. In his study of Philo, Harry Wolfson attempts to abstract the "rules" for Philo's application of allegory (*Philo*, I, 124ff.). He argues that such treatment of "persons or events in Scripture does not mean his denial of their historicity." Despite Wolfson's argument, the allegorical treatment of text in Philo utterly overwhelms the literal.

11. Sandmel, *Philo's Place*, 111.

12. Philo explains that Haran means "holes," "a symbol for the seats of our senses" (*On Abraham* 72).

13. *On Abraham* 85. See *Who is the Heir of Divine Things* 288 for a similar interpretation of "leaving the fatherland." Goodenough (*Introduction to Philo*, 85) points out that the same stress on "desert living," isolation from society, is made in connection with the giving of the Law.

14. He uses as his textual base the Septuagint version of Genesis 12:9: "And Abraham removed and proceeding forward, encamped in the wilderness." For the significance of this "desert" idea, see Sandmel, *Philo's Place*, 116.

15. Sandmel, *Philo's Place*, 111ff.

16. In the context of discussing Abraham's migration, Philo digresses and makes comparable observations on Jacob's departure from Laban (sense) to return to his father's house (wisdom), and on Moses being "shown" rather than actually entering the Land (*On the Migration* 27–30, 45). Sandmel points out that the metaphysical departure of the soul from the body to its "real" home is clearly spelled out in several other places in Philo. See *Who is the Heir* 69, 289; *On the Virtues* 219; *On Dreams* 1.181; and *Questions and Answers on Genesis* 3.10, 45.

17. See *On Abraham* 90ff., 216ff. Here as elsewhere, Philo does not deal with the narrative in biblical sequence.

18. See also *Questions and Answers on Genesis* 3.16. As for the first part of the verse, "To thy seed I give this land . . ." in *Who is the Heir* 314, Philo again indicates that the land is the wisdom of God.

19. *On Abraham* 81–82; *On the Change of Names* 66ff.; *On the Cherubim* 7; *On the Giants* 62–64; *Questions and Answers on Genesis* 3.43.

20. In *On the Special Laws* 1.7 and in *Questions and Answers on Genesis* 3.48, he presents a variety of explanations for the rite of circumcision: sanitation, facilitation of impregnation; a symbolic reshaping of the organ into the form of a heart; symbolic renunciation of passion, of contempt for man's creative powers. None refer in any way to the rite as a "sign of the covenant."

21. *Questions and Answers on Genesis* 3.45. The verse is: "I will give to thee and to thy seed after thee the land in which thou sojournest, all the land of Canaan as an eternal possession."

22. This is Philo's interpretation of Isaac being "in the field" when he first meets Rebekah (*Questions and Answers on Genesis* 4.140).

23. He identifies land and Isaac with Wisdom. See *On the Migration* 28.

24. *Questions and Answers on Genesis* 4.182. Philo also deals with the Gerar scene in *Who is the Heir* 8, and *On the Confusion of Tongues* 81. In the last, he oddly and awkwardly combines verses 2 and 3 of Genesis 26, understanding the word *katoikei* as a reference to wisdom, and the word *paroikei* as a reference to body. Thus he interprets the full passage as telling Isaac not to go to the land of passions (Egypt), but to stay in the "land" of wisdom and sojourn in the "land" of body only as a stranger. The interpretation involves a "play" on the term 'sojourn' similar to the one done on Genesis 17:8 in *Questions and Answers* 3.45. See page 70 above.

25. Jacob going to Haran, "land of the senses," represents the fact that it is "only right and natural" that the imperfect soul should sometimes "leave the well of boundless knowledge" to dwell in the territory of the body, the senses (*On Dreams* 1.286). But the stay for the wise is short term, and always as a foreigner. Soon enough he is "called back to the land of the father," to virtue and wisdom (*On Abraham* 27).

26. "And the Lord leaned over it and said, 'I am the God of Abraham thy father and the God of Isaac. Fear not. To thee and to thy seed I will give the land in which thou art sleeping. And thy seed shall be as the dust of the earth and shall spread abroad to sea, and south, north and east. And by thee all the tribes of the earth shall be blessed, namely the seed of thee. And lo! I am with thee watching over thee in all the way thou goest and I will bring thee back to this land: for I will not leave thee until I have done all that I have spoken to thee'" (Gen. 28: 13–15 – Septuagint).

27. The notion of dispersion is rooted in Philo's understanding the verb *platuno* to imply outside the Land. The reference to "sea" as the "western" border would belie such an intent in the text. In his comments on Genesis 28:13, Philo

states the universal role of the man of wisdom (i.e. Jacob becoming Israel) quite succinctly. Jacob is "registered under both titles held by his father and grandfather, to the end that the world at large and the lover of virtue may have the same inheritance . . ." (*On Dreams* 1.159).

28. Philo refers to covenant as *diatheke* in *Questions and Answers on Exodus* 2.34; *The Special Laws* 2.16; *That the Worse is Want to Attack the Better* 68; *On the Sacrifices of Abel and Cain* 57; *Questions and Answers on Genesis* 3.10, 40, 60. See also Sandmel, *Philo's Place*, 163, note 287.

29. *Questions and Answers on Exodus* 2.34 and *On the Change of Names* 53.

30. *On the Change of Names* 53.

31. *Questions and Answers on Genesis* 3.40.

32. Compare the direct "Go to the Land which I will show thee" (Gen. 12:1–2) with Josephus' "At the age of seventy-five, he left Chaldaea, God having bidden him to remove to Canaan, and there he settled, and left the country to his descendants" (1.154).

33. The term *diatiki* in Targumic and Talmudic literature was used to indicate "a disposition of property, especially by will and testament" (Jastrow, *Dictionary of the Targumim, the Talmud Babli and Yerushalmi, and the Midrashic Literature* [New York, 1971], p. 294). Josephus might have chosen not to use this term because of this connotation, but this does not account for the absence of the concept of Land covenant. In his presentation of the divine voice predicting to Abraham the ultimate victory of his posterity over the Canaanites, he keeps the appearance of birds of prey (as in Genesis 15:11), but it indicates acceptance of Abraham's sacrifice, not a sign of covenant making. See Livy, *History of Rome* 1.7.

34. Moreover, the grant of great dominion (1.234) is described as coming from Jacob, not from God.

35. *Antiquities* 1.280–83; 2.172–75, 194.

36. The phrase *achuzat olam* in Genesis serves almost as a natural preface and conclusion to the transference of the Land promise from the first patriarch to the blessing of Joseph's children. See Genesis 17:8 and 48:4.

37. *Ant.* 2.175.

38. Moreover, the total passage in *Antiquities* is predictive of God's assistance in Jacob's posterity going to Egypt, gaining power there, and ultimately, leaving and conquering the land of Canaan.

39. In *Covenant: The History of a Biblical Idea* (Baltimore, 1969) Harold Attridge discusses at some length Josephus' replacement of the terminology and theology of covenant with the concept of God as ally.

40. The same idea of God as guide or ally appears in the *Jewish War*. There it is Agrippa who discourages revolt against Rome with whom God is allied (2.390) and Josephus himself who urges surrender because fortune and God have passed the "rod of empire" to Rome (5.366–69). Titus also urges the troops onward to the siege with the assurance of having a divine ally (6.38–41).

41. See above p. 70 and note 27.

42. Josephus uses the most general word, *ge*, for land whether he is referring specifically to Canaan or to land or earth in general. Admittedly a mystical, romantic view of the land is not material for the historian. But certain aspects of the biblical description, such as the contrast with Egypt in terms of sources of water, would have been appropriate in a historical treatment.

43. This allegory is repeated in *On the Unchangeableness of God* 94–96.

44. *Special Laws* 3.30, 31. The text of Deuteronomy deals with a man remarrying his former wife who has meanwhile married another man who also divorces her. The other biblical references to moral pollution of the Land (Lev. 18: 24–30; 20:22–25; Num. 35:29–34) are not commented upon by Philo. In *On Rewards and Punishments* he does, however, develop the notion that nonobservance of the sabbatical laws does violate the Land, causing it to eject the Jews.

45. *Allegorical Interpretation* 2.62; *On Sobriety* 30–34, 44–48; *On the Preliminary Studies* 84.

46. In *On the Posterity and Exile of Cain* (122) he has the word "Canaanites" stand for "opposing doctrines."

47. Philo describes the progress from Egypt to Canaan as from a movement from a state of total submission to passions to the stage of being able to choose between good and evil. Nonetheless, Canaan remains "vice" because of the human proclivity to choose evil; and the customs of Canaan, like those of Egypt, are to be considered hateful to the wise soul (*On the Preliminary Studies* 85–87).

48. "If Moses was the hierophant, it would be extremely embarrassing to have the initiate go beyond the hierophant in attainment" (Goodenough, *An Introduction to Philo*, 200). See also *By Light, Light*, 220–21 by the same author.

49. Philo ignores the references to land in other verses linking the patriarchs, the Exodus, and the land promise (Exod. 6:2–8; Num. 32:7ff.; Deut. 1:8; 4:36–38; 8:16–17).

50. Philo tells us clearly that "the covenant of God is an allegory of His gifts of grace," an unearned perfect gift which can only be "virtue and virtuous action."

51. In *On Virtues* he gives a more literal explanation. The purpose of the law is to produce strength which training gives not only in animals, but also in plants. Implied in *On Virtues* and explicitly stated in *On Noah's Work as a Planter* (94–138) is the notion that the same type of "training for robustness" applies to man's spiritual and intellectual life.

52. Gen. 25:6 simply states that Abraham sent the sons of his concubines "eastward . . . into the east country."

53. As noted above (p. 73), the promise to Jacob includes dispersion of his descendants to "all that the sun beholds of earth and sea" (*Ant.* 1.282). A similar stress comes in Josephus' eschatology. See p. 81.

54. *Ant.* 3.306–14; 4.168; 5.39–40, 94, 115. At the end of his description

of the laws, Josephus creates a passage in the form of a prayer for peace by Moses. Land occupation is mentioned, but again outside the covenantal context – and the major theme again is God as ally. See *Ant.* 4.294–5.

55. Deut. 14:8ff.; Num. 32:7ff.; Josh. 24.

56. In the biblical text, the two and a half tribes defend themselves against the claims "that we have built us an altar to turn away from following the Lord; or if to offer thereon burnt offering or meal offering or if to offer sacrifices of peace-offering thereon" (Josh. 22:23). The charge arises out of the admonition in Deut. 12 to set the altar "in the place that I will show you."

57. *Ant.* 3.88. The context justifies Thackeray's translation of *ges* as "earth" rather than "land." Had he been referring specifically to Canaan, Josephus, to avoid confusion, would have indicated the country by name, as he does earlier in 3.87.

58. See above, p. 72.

59. See above, p. 73.

60. See above, p. 81.

61. "Ye shall be left few in number among the nations" (Deut. 4:27).

62. *War* 3.356–57.

63. The technique is not limited to the Pentateuch. In his accounts of the monarchy, Josephus expands on several passages regarding exile and dispersion in order to point to and explain the cause of the Babylonian exile or of the destruction of the Second Temple. See *Ant.* 8.127, constructed so as to predict 586; 10.59–60 has the prophetess Hulda predicting the Babylonian exile; and 8.296–97, where Josephus turns a positive passage into a warning of the destruction of the Second Commonwealth.

64. *Ant.* 4.312–14. In "The Views of Josephus on the Future of Israel and its Land" (Hebrew), *Yerushalayim,* ed. Michael Ish Shalom and others (Jerusalem, 1953), 43–50, Azriel Shochat argues that this passage refers to the destruction of 70 C.E. He makes a distinction between the language of dispersion and that of exile or total uprootedness. Josephus, he claims, uses the first in talking about his own day, the second, in reference to 586 (pp. 46–47).

65. The tendency to interweave prophecy and history arises out of Josephus' philosophy of God's role in history, a philosophy he sets forth explicitly in the *War* 6.310: "God has a care for men, and by all kinds of premonitory signs shows His people the way of salvation, while they owe their destruction to folly and calamities of their own choosing." To buttress this philosophy, Josephus has rewritten or edited scriptural passages so that they clearly show "premonitory signs." See also *Ant.* 10.277–80.

66. Lev. 26:41–45; Deut. 4:29–38; 30:1–10. "Then will I remember My covenant with Jacob, and also My covenant with Isaac, and also My covenant with Abraham will I remember; and I will remember the land" (Lev. 26:42). "He will not fail thee, neither destroy thee, nor forget the covenant of their fathers which He swore unto them" (Deut. 4:31). "Then the Lord thy God will turn thy captiv-

ity, and have compassion upon thee, and will return and gather thee from all the peoples, whither the Lord thy God hath scattered thee. If any of thine that are dispersed in the uttermost parts of heaven, from thence will the Lord thy God gather thee, and from thence will He fetch thee. And the Lord thy God will bring thee into the Land which thy fathers possessed, and thou shalt possess it" (Deut. 30: 3–5).

67. The return to the Land is a dominant theme in the prophets. See Amos 7: 17; 9: 11–15; Hosea 1: 10–11; 2: 14–24; Joel 4: 18; Isa. 9: 17–23; Jer. 24: 6, 32: 6–25; Ezek. 17: 22–23; 35; 36: 16–38; 39: 25; 47: 15–48; Deutero-Isa. 45: 4–15; 49: 5ff.; 61: 6; Zech. 14: 9. See Halkin (pp. 27ff.) and Davies (pp. 40ff.) for additional passages and descriptions of the restoration theme in prophets.

68. In several other contexts he indicates that the power of Rome is temporary. In the *War* (5.367), he states that the rod of empire now rests over Italy, implying that it can and will move on; in *Against Apion* (2.127), he quietly notes that great imperial powers have been reduced to servitude through the "vicissitudes of fortune," implying a similar fate for Rome; and in his account of Balaam's prophecies (*Ant.* 4.125), he hints at a future calamity. See Shochat on Josephus' attitude towards the future of Rome.

69. *Ant.* 4.115–16. He also comments favorably on the dispersion of the Jews in his own day in the *War* (2.399) and in *Against Apion* (2.282).

70. Exod. 3; 6: 2–8; 13: 11; 33: 1–2; Deut. 1: 8; 4: 36–8.

71. In his account of the Tower of Babel, he has God commanding the people "to send out colonies," "to cultivate much of the earth and enjoy an abundance of its fruit." According to Josephus it is specifically their failure to do so that precipitates the building of the ill-fated tower (*Ant.* 1.110–11).

72. David "the psalmist" is mentioned once by name (*On Confusion of Tongues* 149), and on several other occasions he is merely referred to as "a prophet" (*On Husbandry* 50), as "divinely inspired" and as a "sacred poet" (*On Noah's Work as Planter* 29). Similarly, Solomon is mentioned only once by name and described as "a man of peace," "one of Moses' disciples" (*On the Preliminary Studies* 177). Wolfson (II, 332) sees in Philo's interpretation of Deut. 17: 20 — "the law-abiding ruler, [who] even when deceased, lives an age-long life through the actions which he leaves behind him, never to die" (*Special Laws* 4.169) — an allegorical reference to the divine promise to maintain David's house forever (II Sam. 7: 16). But the connection appears to be more that of Wolfson than of Philo.

73. In the Masoretic text, Numbers 24: 7 reads: "Water shall flow from his branches, And his seed shall be in many waters; And his king shall be higher than Agag, And his kingdom shall be exalted." In the Septuagint, however, there is a completely different verse: "There shall come forth a man from his seed, And he shall rule over many nations: And a kingdom greater than Gog's shall be raised up; And his kingdom shall be enlarged."

74. "Though thy dispersion may have been from one end of the earth to the other, thence the Lord thy God will gather thee" (Deut. 30: 4).

75. "And thence the Lord thy God will take thee, and thence thy God will bring thee, into the Land which thy fathers possessed, and thou shalt possess it . . ." (Deut. 30:5).

76. See above p. 77.

77. Philo uses *anasoizomai* for the "return from exile to home." It has the double meaning of being physically restored and of preserving in mind. See Liddell and Scott.

78. See *Special Laws* 1.51 and Wolfson, II, 355–64, 369–74.

79. *On Rewards and Punishments* 152. See editorial note *b* on the textual distortions involved in this interpretation of Deut. 28:43.

80. See note 27.

81. Scholars have differed in their interpretations of Philo's messianism and the place of Land theology in it. Goodenough argues that Philo's relative silence on the issue was due to political sagacity, and "what he does say shows that there was much more thought of it than he dares write" (*The Politics of Philo Judaeus, Practice and Theory* (New Haven, 1938), 115. Goodenough's reconstruction of Philo's messianism involves a greater stress on his portrait of divine kingship than on the ingathering of exiles. Wolfson argues more subtly that as a "student of Greek literature and histories," Philo looked upon the dispersion of the Jews "as natural growth," "analogous to that of the Roman Empire." But as a student of Scripture he saw this dispersion as "captivity, as divine punishment" (II, 402–03). He also argues that Philo saw the "old prophetic promises" of ingathering as a solution for gentile hostility toward Jews and their peculiar laws (Ibid., 407). My own view, however, is closer to that expressed by E. P. Sanders: "Philo's heart did not lie in awaiting the day of national revival, but in teaching men to follow the 'royal road'" ("The Covenant as a Soteriological Category and the Nature of Salvation in Palestinian and Hellenistic Judaism," in *Jews, Greeks, and Christians: Religious Cultures in Late Antiquity*, ed. Robert Hammerton-Kelley [Leiden, 1976], 35).

82. *On Providence* 2.64.

83. Sandmel, *Philo's Place*, 102–03; Wolfson, II, 402.

84. See Wolfson, II, 401ff.

85. In Josephus, the martyr dies not for the Land but for the law. The most highly meritorious are those who "care more for the observance of their laws and for their religion than for their own lives and their country's fate" (*Against Apion* 1.212).

PART II

The Land of Israel
in the Tannaitic Period

The Borders of Judaism: The Land of Israel in Early Rabbinic Judaism

Charles Primus

[Editor's note: Dr. Charles Primus wrote this essay while serving in the theology department of the University of Notre Dame. Originally delivered as part of a Lecture Series devoted to the Land of Israel in Jewish thought, it—along with a contribution by Joseph Gutmann (see below)—became the basis for what would eventuate in this book. Primus's concern, like that of Sarason (which follows), is the world of the Mishnah, the formative body of rabbinic literature developed during the first two Christian centuries. Illustrative of his interest are three pericopae dealing with the Land of Israel in rabbinic thought from that period, each of which Primus subjects to scrutiny here, hoping to get beneath the surface terms of debate to arrive at models of world conception that generate the comments in question. The first pericope promises "inheritance of the Land" as reward for proper behavior; the second pictures Moses as wanting to enter the Land, not as an end in itself, much less as a reward for performing God's will, but as a means to being able to do God's will in the first place, insofar as much of Torah legislation is operative only within the Land's boundaries. Finally, he turns to a debate between Rabbis Eliezer and Akiba on whether grain harvested within the Land but subsequently turned into dough outside of it requires a dough offering. In the first example, Primus argues that the Land was "relatively neutral," its inclusion in the pericope occasioned by the fact that the rabbinic authors emulated biblical models of language, and in the Bible, the Land is indeed promised as reward. The second example too demonstrates the relative unimportance of Land Theology, compared to envisioning Judaism as a system of commandments, for which occupying the Land is a prior necessity, not a promised consequence at all. These two examples raise the possibility that the Rabbis of the first two centuries were in the process of defining Judaism in terms of a religious system independent of the actual Land boundaries, so Primus turns finally to his third pericope, which he analyzes in terms of an underlying debate over the transferability of the Land's sacrality beyond its borders. According to Eliezer, the Land's sanctity is nontransferable to other places, but in Akiba's view, "the entire world potentially is sacred space." Primus's essay thus raises a question first posed by the Hellenistic Philo and Josephus, and later to be en-

countered again and again in these pages: to what extent is the physical reality of
the Land's geography determinative in Judaism's structure of meaning? And to what
extent can the simple geography be transmuted into conceptualizations where the
location of the actual Land itself ceases to exercise determinative power over Jewish
life?]

I

Religion deals with power. Conflicting views on the nature of physical, psychological, moral, and spiritual powers frequently shape the perception of religious issues. I want to discuss three passages from rabbinic documents which date back to the first three centuries of the present era. Each
passage tells us something about the Land of Israel. I am going to argue
that the three passages reflect different perceptions of the significance of
the Land; and I am also going to suggest that these discussions about the
Land provide an idiomatic vehicle for Jews to discuss essentially religious
issues concerning the nature of God's relation to man, of the historical fate
of Israel, God's chosen people, and of the individual's search for meaning
in his or her own life. In other words, I am going to try to relate these
three passages on the Land of Israel to notions about different sorts of powers,
most notably powers to endure, and to overcome, in situations which threaten
the meaningfulness of human existence.

Two of the passages to which we shall turn in just a moment derive
from Mishnah, a compilation of traditions in the Hebrew language redacted
in Palestine around 200 C.E.[1] Recent study of mishnaic documents suggests
several important points. First, we know little about the men who edited
Mishnah; we cannot be sure we know their names or where they worked,
or the immediate purposes for their project. Second, we cannot be sure that
the masters, or "rabbis," who produced Mishnah in the second century played
roles in the Jewish community in Palestine comparable to the roles of rabbis
in Europe during the middle ages or in the United States today; on balance
the available evidences suggest that we should remain agnostic on the question of the roles, and influence, of rabbis and their disciples during the first
centuries of the present era.[2] And third, mishnaic traditions seem to serve
particularly well for the study of the history—that is, the development and
transmission—of ideas, as opposed to, for instance, the history of political
relationships, or of communal institutions, or of economic development;
this is because we have, in mishnaic documents, a statistically significant

amount of material (in Danby's English translation, 789 pages)[3] on a manageable number of topics and deriving from what seems to have been a relatively small circle of individuals.[4] We can identify major ideas, describe nuances in different approaches to these ideas, and puzzle out developmental relationships in the expression of specific notions.

I hope the foregoing helps to explain two of my presuppositions. First, although mishnaic traditions commonly deal with everyday sorts of actions, as, for instance, rules for dinner table etiquette, or for courtroom procedures, or for holiday practices, or for sexual relations, I pay little attention to these contexts. I assume that it is precisely through rules ostensibly for everyday affairs that mishnaic traditions express ideas which, in fact, present metaphysical notions concerning the lines of structure of reality, of the connection between the realm of the divine and the realm of human beings. And secondly, I assume that mishnaic traditions manipulate for their own purposes Judaic images which had become "traditional" long before the second century C.E. These literary images include Zion, Jerusalem, and the Land.

I spell out these presuppositions in part as response to my friend and colleague, John Howard Yoder,[5] who notes that historians of religious movements which have survived into the twentieth century have a tendency to read back into previous centuries both the issues and also the potential positions of our own time. The former tendency has, I believe, been remarked on frequently; the latter deserves careful consideration, however, for it represents a much more subtle obstacle to historical studies. It is far easier to be self-conscious about the issues which we bring with us to our investigations than it is to put ourselves, through an act of the imagination, into the places of men and women of different times and different cultures and then try to reconstruct both the limits and also the potentialities of their understanding.

Let me translate the problem into Judaic imagery. Assertions of attachment to the Land of Israel, to Zion, to Jerusalem, can be located in sources of Judaism in all ages. Those images will be used, however, in different circumstances to different purposes. In reading the following three passages from early rabbinic documents, we need to be conscious of the preconceptions we bring with us. Many of these, I suspect, have been shaped by association with modern political Zionism and the State of Israel. At the same time, however, I want to see if, in the use of the images in these documents, we may not also glimpse possibilities which might not otherwise be apparent to citizens of the twentieth century.

II

Our first passage occurs at M. Kid. 1:10. That pericope reads as follows:

A. 1. Anyone who performs a single commandment
   2. a. Does well for himself,
      b. And prolongs his days,
      c. And inherits the Land.

B. 1. Anyone who does not perform a single commandment
   2. a. Does not do well for himself,
      b. And does not prolong his days,
      c. And does not inherit the Land.

C. 1. Anyone who has in his possession [knowledge]
      a. Of Scripture,
      b. And of Mishnah,
      c. And of right conduct—
   2. a. Not quickly will such a person sin,
      b. As it is said, "A three-fold cord is not easily broken" (Eccl. 4:12).

D. 1. And anyone who does not have in his possession [knowledge]
      a. Of Scripture,
      b. And of Mishnah,
      c. And of right conduct—
   2. [Such a person] is not of the *yeshuv*. (Danby, p. 323, ". . . has no part in the habitable world.")

References to the Land of Israel occur in A.2.c. and B.2.c. First, I want to discuss the use of the image of the Land in A and in B; and then I want to ask what that usage suggests about the underlying purpose of the entire unit, A–D.

A and B quite obviously balance one another. Each of the phrases in B gives the opposite of the comparable phrase in A. This is accomplished simply by adding the word 'not' to each phrase.

What we have is the announcement of a subject, a person who either performs or does not perform a single commandment, and a list of rewards which ensue from performance or nonperformance. Inheritance of the Land is one of the rewards, we learn, for the performance of even a single commandment; conversely, failure to perform a single commandment results in nonpossession of the Land.

What can we say about the relationship between performance of a commandment and possession of the Land of Israel? Quite clearly the pericope asserts that the former leads to the latter. Can we infer, therefore, that the Land takes priority, in the sense that it is the goal, the end, toward which performance of commandments functions as the means? This argument has been made by the distinguished scholar, W. D. Davies.[6] I am not so sure that the means-end relationship in this tradition necessarily implies the greater importance of the end, possession of the Land. To be consistent one would also have to argue that "doing well for oneself" and "prolonging one's days" also are more important than fulfilling God's commandments.

A more productive question regarding the relation between the Land and performance of commandments might be: What model is suggested by the literary structure in A and B? A biblical model obviously comes to mind. Deut. 5:33 states, "You shall walk in all the way which the Lord your God has commanded you, that you may live, *and that it may go well with you, and that you may live long in the land which you shall possess* [italics added]." A and B in our pericope alter only slightly the biblical injunction: walking in "the way which the Lord your God has commanded" becomes, "Anyone who performs a single commandment"; then, in Mishnah as in Deuteronomy, 'going well', long life, and possession of the Land follow as rewards.

I suspect that, with regard to this pericope, we should see the image of the Land simply as a traditional element: in context, deriving from a biblical model, one of three items specified as rewards for performance of commandments. The central question about this pericope therefore probably is not, 'What notion of the Land is assumed?' Rather we should ask, What is the purpose for using the biblical model?

Let us look briefly at C–D. C1 balances D1 by introducing the word 'not'. These phrases specify the subject and are comparable to, "Anyone who performs/does not perform a single commandment," in A–B. That is, knowledge of three things, Scripture, Mishnah, and right conduct, is juxtaposed with performance of commandments.

Let us look closer at two of the items in C/D1. "Scripture" obviously refers to *Tanakh*, the Hebrew bible. "Mishnah" probably does not refer to the document we call Mishnah, which contains this pericope and nowhere contains specific reference to itself as "Mishnah." Instead we should take "Mishnah" as "teaching," from the Hebrew root, *šnh*. Loosely I would want us to understand it to refer to "traditional teachings," quite obviously not scriptural. By the third century rabbinic masters probably would be refer-

ring to a. and b., Scripture and Mishnah, as the two aspects of Torah—i.e.,
the Written Torah and the Oral Torah. Both derive authority from Moses
at Sinai.

The pericope weaves together different motifs: the biblical harangue
on rewards for the performance of commandments, and knowledge of special traditions as protection from sin and as constitutive of community. The
image of the Land of Israel plays a minor role. Indeed, it is manipulated
as but one aspect of the biblical allusion and is, in context, subordinate to
the polemic in the second half of the pericope.

I think this passage is important, for it illustrates the relatively neutral
quality of the image of the Land. This neutrality, not to say passivity, is
characteristic of most sources on the Land in Mishnah. Approximately one-
third of Mishnah deals with rules relating the the Land, e.g., regulations
regarding agriculture, land tenure, ritual cleanness. [Ed. note: See discussion
of these items by Sarason above, pp. 110–36.] Cursory examination of most
traditions reveals, however, that the nature of the Land, of the soil, or of
the relationship between the people and the Land, is seldom at issue. Instead emphasis is on issues related to the Temple and, as we have just seen,
on study of traditions and on performance of commandments.

Our second passage should make this clearer. b. Sot. 14a reads,

A. R. Simlai expounded:
   1. Why did Moses, our Rabbi, yearn to enter the Land of
      Israel?
   2. Did he want to eat of its fruit or satisfy himself from its
      bounty?
   3. But thus spoke Moses, "Many precepts were commanded
      to Israel which can be fulfilled only in the Land of Israel.
      I wish to enter the Land so that they may all be fulfilled
      by me."[7]

R. Simlai lived in Palestine during the middle of the third century. This
pericope, like M. Kid. 1:10 above, juxtaposes residence in the Land of Israel
with performance of commandments. This time, however, there is no question as to which of the two elements is considered more important. Moses
yearns to enter the Land specifically in order to fulfill commandments which
can be performed only there. Emphasis is on performance of commandments, not on residence in the Land. Curiously, the latter is considered preliminary to the former.

Let me elaborate. M. Kid. 1:10 includes a means-ends relationship.

The Land serves as a reward for fulfillment of commandments. By contrast, at b. Sot. 14a the immediate reward seems to be the opportunity to fulfill commandments. Residence in the Land functions as the means to that other end. Insofar as a further reward is considered, that reward derives from fulfilling the commandments. Desire to enjoy the "fruits" of the Land is, against biblical precedents, explicitly eschewed.

In this second passage the image of the Land of Israel has been set in a completely unbiblical context. Many of the words may be familiar — e.g., the Land, and fulfillment of commandments. The framework is, however, considerably altered. Deuteronomy, for instance, also stresses fulfillment of commandments, but not to the exclusion of enjoyment of the bounty of the Land.

The reference to "Moses, our Rabbi," also is unbiblical. In *Tanakh* Moses figures as prophet, judge, priest, possibly even king.[8] Moses as a rabbinic master, that is, as an individual who learns, studies, and transmits to his disciples the traditions of the Oral and Written Torahs, is a creation of the imagination of the rabbinic movement.[9] Simlai's story vividly demonstrates rabbinic emphasis on one aspect of the biblical heritage — to the detriment of another aspect of that inheritance. Possession of the Land is deemphasized; performance of acts commanded by God and articulated in Torah is made predominant.

The image of the Land in Simlai's story may not be quite so neutral as that same image is in the first passage we discussed. In both pericopae the Land is manipulated for editorial purposes. In Simlai's story, however, the Land carries with it explicit description of traditional rewards, namely, enjoyment of the fruits of the Land, which are being rejected — or at least subordinated to higher sorts of rewards.[10] Nonetheless, neither pericope focuses on the nature of the Land, its qualities, or its relation to the people, Israel.

The foregoing, I hope, will make our third, and final, pericope all the more interesting. M. Hallah 2:1 reads:

A. Produce from abroad which entered the Land [of Israel] is liable for dough-offering.
B. [Concerning produce which] went out from here to there:
   1. R. Eliezer declares it liable [for dough-offering].
   2. But R. Akiba declares it exempt.

Scripture mandates that priests receive a share of all dough prepared for baking (Num. 15:17–21). The gift is called "dough-offering." This pericope assumes that the obligation for dough-offering is incurred at the moment at which the produce is made into dough.

According to A, dough made from imported produce is liable for dough-offering. B gives us a dispute regarding the status of dough made outside the Land, but with raw produce exported from within the Land. Eliezer, a first century sage who reputedly survived the siege of Jerusalem in 70, holds that dough made from exported produce is liable for dough-offering. Akiba, Eliezer's younger contemporary and one of the giant figures in the early rabbinic movement, holds that dough made from produce grown inside the Land but subsequently exported outside the Land is not liable for dough-offering.

The pericope, we note, presents a legal problem: what is the status of dough made outside the Land, from produce exported from the Land? Must a dough-offering be separated for a priest or not?

I suggest that though ostensibly dealing with a legal problem, the dispute in this pericope actually reflects different views on the sanctity that attaches to the Land of Israel. In a sense, these views differ regarding the modes in which holiness enfuses the soil of the Land.

Now, what are these different views? Let us begin with Eliezer's position. He holds that dough made from produce exported from the Land is liable for dough-offering. At this point it is appropriate to refer to Num. 15:17–18, the biblical warrant for the offering:

> The Lord said to Moses, "Say to the people of Israel, 'When you come into the land to which I shall bring you and when you eat of the food of the land, you shall present an offering to the Lord. Of the first of your coarse meal you shall present a cake as an offering. . . .'"

Israelites are commanded to make a cake from coarse meal which they grow in the Land. Eliezer's view seems to be that this requirement holds regardless of the place in which the cake, or dough, is physically prepared; what counts is that the meal, or whatever produce, has grown in the Land of Israel.

How are we to account for the difference between produce which grows in the Land and produce which grows outside the Land? Quite clearly the former is considered to be special in some way in which the latter is not. It would be difficult to maintain that the difference relates to size, taste, color, or some other criterion that affects one or more of the five senses. I do not think it is sufficient to suggest that meal that grows in the Land is special simply because of that fact—or because Scripture says so.

If we are to understand the qualities attributed to the Land I think we must go further and assert that there is assumed here some sort of special element: it is substantive, although obviously invisible; it is attached to the soil and is transmitted to crops that grow in the soil, thereby making those crops special, even if exported outside the Land. Following biblical phrasing, we may call this quality an element of holiness, or of sanctity.[11] It is affective, that is, its effect can be seen in terms of resulting human actions; and therefore I argue that it must be regarded as real, although probably not tangible. I have no objection if someone wants to call this element a magical quality. And please note: I make no claims regarding how many individuals in the history of Judaism have explicitly held this view; I do suspect it is as old as the religion and continues, not without a certain amount of opposition, in our own times.

To return to Eliezer: his position reflects, I believe, the view that an element of holiness associated with dough-offering is inherent in the produce. He therefore requires that a dough-offering be made from exported produce.

Akiba's view reflects a different understanding of the nature of the holiness that attaches to crop which grows in the Land. Akiba seems to assume that the holiness of the Land does not function as an independent entity, inherent in the produce. It has no life of its own, so to speak. Instead, it functions as one element in a complex system, a grid of holiness, if you will. Inside the borders of the Land, an element of holiness attaches to the crop and requires that an action, the gift of dough-offering, be performed. Outside the Land, the gift is not required; the borders of the Land mark off the boundaries of the grid, of the field of operation.

We need to take Akiba's view one step further. Borders of the Land are invisible lines in space, marking off what historians of religion would call "sacred space." Akiba's view gives us a picture of one of the consequences of living in a sacred space. Holiness functions in this area according to a set of abstract rules, which in turn also regulate human conduct.

I suggest that Akiba's position assumes a notion of holiness significantly different from that assumed in Eliezer's opinion. The latter suggests that holiness enfuses objects. It can be transmitted from one object to another and, when in the proper medium, move across territorial borders. By contrast, Akiba's opinion assumes that holiness can be contained by invisible lines in space, that it will be affective within a context described by abstract rules which define sacred space, and not by the qualities of specific objects.

Let us translate this difference into a slightly different context. Eliezer's and Akiba's opinions assume different theories on the nature of holiness — and those theories may not be mutually exclusive. On Eliezer's view holiness enfuses objects and exudes, so to speak, through different media from one object to another. Holiness can be transmitted from soil to a tree or a stalk of wheat; and, I would want to add, from one human being to another human being. If you will excuse an egregious oversimplification, holiness, or sanctity, is contagious.

Akiba's view assumes that sanctity, or holiness, operates within a circumscribed realm, what I have been calling a grid. Sacred space thus is sacred, not because it is enfused with a particular quality, but rather because it is the area in which that quality operates. Within the space, rules, standards, regulations, and laws prescribe the operation of holiness. Sacred space thus is orderly. And on this view holiness, which we must understand as charged with power and apt to be quite frightening (awe-inspiring, or "awful," as phenomenologists of religions might want to tell us), works out its place in creation. Holiness can be plotted, and consequently understood, at least in a minimal sense, relative to the lines of structure of reality reflected in the rules that define orderly operations in a sacred space. The Land of Israel is one sort of sacred space. There are others—notably the city of Jerusalem and, within the city, the Temple-compound. Other possibilities also occur, although within traditional Judaic idiom they may not be obvious.

And here, I believe, we return to the ideas with which I began. References to the Land of Israel reflect efforts to identify God's relation to human beings, and particularly to Israel, God's chosen people, for God is responsible for the rules which order the world. God generates the invisible lines of structure in sacred space. It is God's will that men and women live in sacred space, that individuals perform their roles in the orderly scheme of creation. In doing so, individuals will recognize the cosmic significance of actions in their daily lives—the threat of meaninglessness is beaten back; purposefulness enfuses the individual's life. In Judaic idiom, these thoughts can be expressed in terms of living in the Land of Israel, the promised home of the people, Israel.

And we must state clearly that Israel living in its Land has consequences for the entire world. When Israel lives in its Land, the entire earth can become sacred space. The Land is frequently alleged to be the center of the world, just as Jerusalem, with total disregard of geography, is alleged to be at the center of the Land. How will other nations be affected? We can choose either Eliezer's or Akiba's theory. According to the former, the quality of life characteristic of Israel living in its own Land will be infectious. The nations of the world will perceive, perhaps by witnessing the example, perhaps by other sorts of contact, and they will be affected. Physical barriers, real walls, lack of communications, isolation of the Land, on Eliezer's view, will hinder this process. On Akiba's view the entire world potentially is sacred space. Different areas are subject to different standards, different rules. People in the Land and outside the Land alike have their own special roles to play.

Quite clearly later rabbinic traditions follow Akiba's lead, enlarging the scope of the investigation of what individuals' roles should be, in different places, but especially outside the Land, and at different times. The goal is perception of everyday life as participation in a sacred realm of ultimate significance.[12]

III

The three passages discussed above suggest an effort to assimilate and to reformulate the biblical inheritance. The image of the Land has functioned as an element in the age-old story that Jews have told about themselves. The Land had been promised to Abraham's descendants; those descendants, in each generation, in good times and in bad, in turn have had to explain their identity by reference to the Land. Early rabbinic Judaism, as reflected in the passages discussed above, emphasized a different aspect of the biblical inheritance, namely, Torah, which is to be understood as illuminating the cosmic meaningfulness of actions in the everyday lives of ordinary men and women. Yet rabbinic Judaism also had to come to terms with the Land; the third passage which we read vividly suggested two ways in which the Land might be worked into the system of Torah.

I think we learn from this that the idea of the Land does have its own power. In part rabbinic notions may reflect conscious efforts to tame, or domesticate, the power inherent in the idea. But, because it derives from the fundamental story that the people tell about themselves, the power of the idea of the Land will always lie close at hand, to be tapped for whatever ends individuals may choose to pursue.

108 CHARLES PRIMUS

Notes

1. Jacob Neusner, ed., *The Modern Study of the Mishnah* (Leiden, 1973), surveys the state of mishnaic scholarship through recent times. See also Neusner, "The History of Earlier Rabbinic Judaism: Some New Approaches," *History of Religions* 16 (Feb. 1977), 216–36.

2. Contrast the eclectic use of source materials in supporting conventional assertions regarding the central role of rabbinic authority in Palestine back through early Hellenistic times in, e.g., E. E. Urbach, "The Talmudic Sage—Character and Authority," in H. H. Ben-Sasson and S. Ettinger, *Jewish Society through the Ages* New York, 1971), 116–47.

3. Herbert Danby, *The Mishnah*, (Oxford, 1933).

4. See Neusner, A History of the Mishnaic Law of Purities. Part 12. Tohorot (Leiden, 1976), "Introduction," 1–14.

5. John H. Yoder, "'Anabaptists and the Sword' Revisited: Systematic Historiography and Undogmatic Nonresistants," *Senderdruck aus "Zeitschrift für Kirchengeschichte"* 2 (Stuttgart, 1974), 270ff.

6. W. D. Davies, *The Gospel and the Land: Early Christianity and Jewish Territorial Doctrine* (Berkeley, 1974), 58.

7. Trans. A. Cohen, *Sotah* (London, n.d.), 73.

8. See discussion in Wayne A. Meeks, *The Prophet King: Moses Traditions and the Johannine Christology* (Leiden, 1967).

9. See Neusner, A History of the Jews in Babylonia, Vol. 4 (Leiden, 1969), 279–86.

10. For a felicitous statement of this puzzle, see G. F. Moore's introductory remarks on "Piety," *Judaism in the First Centuries of the Christian Era*, Vol. 2 (New York, 1971), 201f.

11. E.g., Lev. 19:8, 24; 22:10, 14; 27:30, 32.

12. A pericope in Sifre Numbers 110 suggests an alternate explanation for the difference between Eliezer's and Akiba's opinions. The authority behind the pericope in Sifre asserts that the two masters differ on the exegesis of Num. 15:18–19. Without venturing into the complex question of why one would want to connect a difference of opinion among Tannaim to a dispute regarding the interpretation of specific biblical verses, I would simply remark that Akiba's view, as elaborated in the foregoing, recurs with stunning regularity in opinions ascribed to Akiba in disparate legal contexts in *M. T. Zera'im*. See my *'Aqiva's Contribution to the Mishnaic Law of Zera'im* (Leiden, 1977).

The Significance of the Land of Israel in the Mishnah

RICHARD S. SARASON

[Dr. Richard Sarason, of the Hebrew Union College—Jewish Institute of Religion in Cincinnati, continues the theme laid down in this book's introduction. There, our focus was on rules connected with food and tableship; here, he examines the complex of agricultural legislation governing the production of food in the Land. The issue, for Sarason, is one of boundaries, by which he means the social mapping of space. He cites a passage from M. Kelim, which orders the zones of the earth's surface in what amount to concentric circles from the Holy of Holies and the Temple outward, in ever widening arcs, thus producing "an Israelite cultic map of the world. At the very center it places the Jerusalem Temple's central structure, the 'most holy place,' which was construed as the umbilical cord between heaven and earth. . . . At the periphery lie 'all other lands.'" The Mishnah's essential problematic, says Sarason, is the confusion of boundaries, both spatial and social, in that there are actually two taxonomies at work here, one implicating the People Israel, and the other, its Land. When these are not in harmony with each other, conflicts necessarily develop, and the bulk of Sarason's article analyzes four such conflicts: 1) laws of the Land of Israel, when Gentiles inhabit the Land; 2) laws of the Land of Israel for Jews who live, however, outside the Land; 3) the proper setting of the borders of the Land of Israel, given the fact that at least three alternative boundaries are derivable from biblical descriptions; and 4) the unique case of Syria which is contiguous with the Land, but which contains many Jewish inhabitants. Sarason explains all these conflicts as arising out of the fact of a growing diaspora community, present already in the first two Christian centuries, so that a perfect congruence between Holy People and Holy Land—that is, the spatial and social categories "Israel"—no longer held, and Rabbis had necessarily to ask, under such circumstances, who observes the laws, and where? "The tension between the ideal congruence of the social and spatial Israels—between Holy Land and Holy People—and their actual incomplete coincidence," Sarason concludes, "generates the problem of confused boundaries that so preoccupies Mishnah's authors. In one form or another, that problem, for Jews, is at least as old as the time of Sennacherib." As other essays in this book demonstrate, it has not ceased to remain problematic up to our own day.]

Any attempt to grasp the significance of the Land of Israel in early rabbinic Judaism must begin with an analysis of the Mishnah, rabbinism's first text in both priority and sanctity. Redacted in the Land of Israel around the turn of the third century C.E., the Mishnah became the Second Torah (beside Scripture) for subsequent generations of rabbis in both the Land of Israel and Babylonia, and was subjected by them to the same kind of minute analysis as was Scripture.[1] Since all rabbinic texts from late antiquity presuppose the existence of the Mishnah and bear some derivative ideational or formal relationship to it—whether commenting on Mishnah (Tosefta, the two Talmuds), attempting formally to ground Mishnah's rulings in Scripture (the so-called "halakhic" midrashim, to a greater or lesser extent,[2] and portions of the Talmuds), or simply citing Mishnah in passing (the aggadic midrashim)—it is on the Mishnah as foundation-document that this inquiry will focus.[3]

To insure a proper contextual understanding of the Mishnah's valorization and treatment of the Land of Israel, we must first note a few things about the document's literary character, its audience, and the particular *Weltanschauung* that it reflects. While the Mishnah, both thematically and formally, is surely the most systematic and coherent document in the early rabbinic corpus and therefore the one most amenable to systematic analysis, it nonetheless is neither totally systematic nor fully coherent. Mishnah's editors frequently juxtapose conflicting theories of an issue, and sometimes contradictory statements of a problem, without attempting to resolve the conflicts. Most often these conflicts are signalled by the attribution of differing positions to different rabbinic authorities in standard Mishnaic rhetorical patterns (variants of the dispute-form),[4] but sometimes they are not formally signalled at all: unattributed rulings within a single tractate and across tractates occasionally reflect different theories of an issue.[5] Additionally, many individual rulings or sets of rulings have been editorially juxtaposed with no explicit hypotactic connectives. The original status of each ruling and the logic of their juxtaposition was (presumably) clear to the redactors, but in some cases can only tentatively be inferred by subsequent interpreters. The problem of logical connectives becomes even more acute when, as in this study, we juxtapose rulings gleaned from all over the Mishnah.[6] All of these literary particularities bear important consequences for a thematic study like the present one: only at a fairly general level can we validly characterize "*the* Mishnaic conception(s) of X." Beyond that, we must discuss specific issues which are mooted and the range of positions taken.

We also must be clear as to precisely *whose* ideas about the Land of Israel are expressed in the Mishnah. On internal literary evidence alone, it is manifest that the document was formulated solely by and for rabbis in the Land of Israel at the turn of the third century C.E. and speaks, in its present form, only for them. (Views of earlier first- and second-century rabbis are, of course, represented, but have been filtered through the final editing process.) The discourse is technical, specialized, and elliptical, presupposing much prior information and leaving unarticulated many basic axioms that underlie the entire enterprise. The "culture" reflected in the document is quintessentially that of the rabbis and that imagined by the rabbis. It is not the actual culture of other Jews in the Land of Israel at the time of the Mishnah or earlier, although *realia* from that culture are certainly utilized and alluded to.[7]

Of crucial significance to our inquiry is an understanding of the particular worldview expressed in the Mishnah. The document represents a sustained act of imagination on the part of its rabbinic authors; it describes and legislates for an ideal Israelite world of Temple cult, priesthood, Sanhedrin, and king that nowhere existed at the time of its compilation. In particular, the Mishnah embodies the Rabbis' attempts to control and order reality under what they deem to be the unchanging, immutable paradigms revealed by God to Israel in the laws of the Torah and extended logically by themselves. Thematically, the document adumbrates rabbinic conceptions of Scripture's rules and requirements.[8] The most prominent of these conceptions relate to the Temple cult: sacrifices (*Kodoshim*), agricultural offerings (*Zera'im*), purity laws (*Tohorot;* extended beyond the boundaries of the cult), and the cultic calendar (*Mo'ed;* as this applies both inside and outside the Temple)—i.e., those modes of relating to God and the sacred (=that which pertains to God) which the Rabbis viewed as having been divinely ordained for all time and thus of continuing relevance, at least as an ideal program, even after the destruction of the Temple and the cessation of the actual cult. Along the same lines, the preoccupation with order and hierarchy, both social and ontological, characteristic of Scripture's priestly literature is carried forward by Mishnah's Rabbis.[9] The contents of the Mishnah may be described as a series of exercises in definition and classification that construe a variety of (frequently hypothetical) cases in terms of paradigmatic logical-normative categories or principles. Most of these exercises involve gray areas—median cases ("mixtures") in which several principles or categories intersect; the cognitive (and normative) challenge is then to resolve the confusion.[10]

Turning now to the Mishnah's treatment of the Land of Israel, we shall see that this is thoroughly congruent with, and indeed a consequence of, the document's basic orientation as characterized above. Carrying forward the locative, hierarchical ideology of Scripture's priestly codes, Mishnah's Rabbis valorize the Land primarily in terms of its cultic significance as the center of the divine economy and locus of God's Temple.[11] It is preeminently as the "Holy Land" in the cultic sense that the Land of Israel is dealt with in the Mishnah. So, too, in line with the Mishnah's processual concern for categorization, delimiting boundaries, and adjudicating median cases, we shall note that virtually every Mishnaic case involving the Land of Israel deals with issues of boundaries and confusion of boundaries, both spatial and social. The remainder of this article elaborates these two observations.

The locative, cultic significance of the Land of Israel is presupposed throughout the Mishnah and strikingly articulated at the outset of Seder Tohorot, in the opening chapter of Tractate Kelim. Since the most basic assumptions which underlie the document are so rarely stated outright, as we have noted, this passage is particularly noteworthy. It also happens to be the lengthiest sustained set of materials in the Mishnah to deal with the Land of Israel. For both of these reasons, I cite the passage in full (the translation is my own):

> A. There are ten [ascending] degrees of holiness:
>
> B. (1) The Land of Israel is holier than all [other] lands.
>
> C. And in what does its [distinctive] holiness consist?
>
> D. In that people bring [to the Temple] from it[s produce] (a) the *omer*, (b) the first-fruits, and (c) the two [loaves] of bread [on the Feast of Weeks, cf. Lev. 23:9–17], [offerings] which are not brought [to the Temple] from any [other] land.
>
> E. (2) Walled cities [in the Land of Israel] are holier than it [i.e., than the rest of the Land],
>
> F. for (a) lepers are banished from their midst, and (b) people may carry around a corpse in their midst as long as they like, [but] once it has left [the city], they may not bring it back inside.
>
> G. (3) [The area] inside the wall [of the city of Jerusalem] is holier than they [the other walled cities in the Land],

H. for people eat there Lesser Holy Things and Second Tithe.

I. (4) The Temple Mount is holier than it [the city of Jerusalem],

J. for men and women with fluxes, menstruant women, and women who have just given birth may not enter therein.

K. (5) The rampart [surrounding the Temple courtyards] is holier than it [the Temple Mount],

L. for gentiles and those rendered unclean by contact with a corpse may not enter therein.

M. (6) The courtyard of [Israelite] women is holier than it [the rampart],

N. for those awaiting sunset for purification [*tevul yom*] may not enter therein, but are not thereby liable for a sin-offering [if they inadvertently enter the courtyard].

O. (7) The courtyard of [Israelite] men is holier than it [the courtyard of women],

P. for those who lack atonement [-offerings to complete their purification] may not enter therein, and are thereby liable for a sin-offering [if they inadvertently enter the courtyard].

Q. (8) The courtyard of priests is holier than it [the courtyard of Israelite men],

R. for [ordinary] Israelites may not enter therein, except when they must do so for [purposes of] laying hands on [the sacrificial animals; Lev. 3:2], slaughtering [the animals], and waving [the cereal-offerings; Lev. 7:30].

S. (9) [The area] between the porch and the altar is holier than it [the courtyard of the priests],

T. for those [priests] who are blemished and whose hair is disheveled may not enter therein.

U. (10) The sanctuary is holier than it [the area between the porch and the altar],

V. for only those who have washed their hands and feet may enter therein.

W. (11) The Holy of Holies [i.e., most holy enclosure] is holier than it [the sanctuary],

X. for only the High Priest on the Day of Atonement at the time of the [atonement-]rite may enter therein.[12]

(M. Kelim 1:6–9)

This passage comprises an Israelite cultic map of the world. At the very center it places the Jerusalem Temple's central structure, the "most holy place," which was construed as the umbilical cord between heaven and earth, that place where God's in-dwelling presence (*Shekhinah*) was located.[13] At the periphery lie "all [other] lands," elsewhere referred to as "the land of the gentiles" (*erets ha'amim*) or "outside the Land [of Israel]" (*chutsah la'arets*).[14] The degrees of holiness begin with the Land of Israel and increase as one enters walled cities, Jerusalem, and the Temple compound. Those places to which pertain ascending levels of holiness as one approaches the Deity require greater degrees of cultic purification on the part of people who would enter them (so, progressively, F, J, L, N, P, R, T, V, and X). Israelite social taxa here are construed with reference to these degrees of purity: the High Priest stands at the apex of the cultic system, closest in physical proximity to God and the Holy. Progressively excluded from such proximity are ordinary priests, Israelite men, Israelite women, and gentiles (deemed unclean to enter the Temple precincts beyond a certain point). The third axis of differentiation in the list, beside degrees of cultic purity and social groups, is that of cultic offerings. The greater degree of holiness that pertains to the Land of Israel vis-à-vis all other lands is accounted for here by the fact that certain cultic agricultural offerings—the first sheaf of the barley harvest (*omer*), first fruits of the produce, and two loaves of bread made from the new grain —may be brought to the Temple only from produce grown (by Israelites) in the Land of Israel.[15] These gifts elsewhere are contrasted with all other cereal offerings and animal offerings, which may be brought to the Temple also from outside the Land (M. Men. 8:1, M. Par. 2:1).[16] Similarly, Jerusalem is distinguished from the rest of the Land of Israel in that certain cultic offerings, both animal (Lesser Holy Things) and agricultural (Second Tithe), can be eaten only in its midst, in consequence of the centralization of the cult (cf. M. Zeb. 14:8).

That which is deemed important about the Land of Israel in this passage is paradigmatic of Mishnah's treatment of the Land throughout. The four primary points of interest remain cultic purity, those cultic offerings which are viewed as intrinsically connected with the Land (agricultural offerings), social differentiation (boundaries: Israelites vs. gentiles), and spatial differentiation (boundaries: the Land of Israel vs. the land of the gentiles, outside the Land). The first two points are related functionally to the second two, while spatial and social differentiation, as principles that will intersect in problematic ways for the Rabbis, generate a variety of median cases to be resolved. These general observations must now be spelled out.

(1) An enormous number of rulings in the Mishnah deal with matters of cultic purity. Originally this concern was highly localized to the Temple

precincts, Jerusalem, priests who served in the Temple, and Israelites who entered the Temple. In the Mishnah, this locative system is extended symbolically to ordinary Israelites outside Jerusalem who eat unconsecrated food in their homes as if they were priests eating consecrated food in the Temple, a kind of surrogate cultic system.[17] To this extent, actual location no longer matters; the extended system could apply anywhere and everywhere.[18] But, in fact, location *does* matter: Mishnah's rulings make clear that this purity system applies fully only within the Land of Israel. The Land of Israel is deemed to be clean (and its modes of purification, immersion-pools, are always presumed to be clean).[19] The land of the gentiles, on the other hand, is deemed to be unclean and defiling, as are clods of earth from the land of the gentiles[20] and gentile dwellings within the Land of Israel.[21] Gentile immersion-pools, both within and outside the Land of Israel, are deemed valid only for regularly occurring forms of sexually-generated impurity (seminal discharge and, with some qualifications, menstruation), but not for other, more severe forms of impurity.[22] The boundaries between "us" and "them," between "our" land and "their" land, are thus critically preserved even when purity rules are extended beyond the actual cultic situation: Mishnah distinguishes sharply between the "uncleanness" of the land of the gentiles and the "cleanness" and susceptibility to purification of the Land of Israel where Israelites reside. Ideal conditions obtain only where both the spatial and social taxa "Israel" coincide.[23]

(2) Mishnah's first Order, Zera'im, elaborates on those scripturally ordained agricultural offerings which are to be given from produce grown in the Land of Israel: *terumah* (generally translated as "heave-offering") and dough-offering, given to the priests; the Levitical tithe (Num. 18; Mishnah's "first tithe"), given to the Levites; the Deuteronomic tithe (Deut. 14:22ff., Mishnah's "second tithe"), brought to Jerusalem and eaten there by the farmer; first-fruits, brought to the Temple and eaten by the priests; the fruit of vineyards and fruit-bearing trees in the fourth year of their growth (= first-fruits of the trees), brought to Jerusalem and eaten there by the farmer; the "tithe from the tithe" (Num. 18:28, Mishnah's "*terumah* from the tithe"), given by the Levite from his tithe to the priest.[24] The early Israelite theory behind most of these offerings (excluding the Levitical tithe, which was originally for the sustenance of the Levites) is that God is the owner of the Land of Israel and the source of its fertility, while the Israelites working the Land are God's tenant-farmers. The tenants are obliged to return the first portion of the land's yield to the owner, not only as a matter of proprietary right, but in order to insure the land's continuing fertility and the

farmer's sustenance and prosperity.[25] The same theory underlies Scripture's prohibition of agricultural work during every seventh, or Sabbatical, year, as well as the prohibition against eating or using the fruit of a newly-planted tree or vineyard during the first three years of its growth (*orlah*), to each of which a Mishnah-tractate in this Order is devoted.[26] Every seven years the Land must lie fallow; in desisting from working the land, the Israelite acknowledges God's ownership of the Land of Israel (just as he acknowledges God's sovereignty and dominion over the world and over time by refraining from work every seven days).[27] Similarly, the fruit of a newly-planted ("uncircumcised") tree during its first three years of growth is deemed to be the property of God, the guarantor of the tree's subsequent fertility. (In the fourth year, the tree's first-fruits must be brought to Jerusalem, as above.) Mishnah further devotes a tractate to the scriptural prohibitions against sowing together diverse kinds of seeds in the same field or vineyard (*kilayim*), weaving together different kinds of fibers in a single garment (*sha'atnez*), and mating or yoking together diverse species of animals.[28] Such acts of commingling are held to violate or destroy the distinct categories of nature, ordained by God at creation.[29] Finally, Mishnah deals with the scripturally mandated agricultural gifts to the poor from the Land's harvest: the corner of the field (*pe'ah*), the gleanings of the stalks (*leket*), the forgotten sheaf (*shikhehah*), the separated grapes (*peret*) and defective clusters (*olelot*) of the vineyard, and the welfare tithe (Deut. 26:12, Mishnah's "tithe for the poor").[30] These gifts, like the Levitical tithe, are mandated to insure support from the Land's yield for those persons in Israelite society who do not themselves own land, through either dispossession (the poor) or prohibition (the Levites, who are God's servants in the Temple).[31]

(3) The preceding catalogue enumerates all of the elements pertaining to agricultural work and produce that are found in Scripture's various theories of the divine economy obtaining among the God of Israel, Land of Israel, and People Israel, as those theories are homogenized and carried forward in the Mishnah. Mishnah's particular treatment of these materials focuses especially on matters of definition, classification, specification (or extension), and adjudication of conflicting claims, with singular attention devoted to the role of human action and intentionality in this divinely-ordained economy.[32] In this context, both the Land of Israel and the People Israel are interacting and intersecting categories which, for Mishnah's Rabbis, must be clearly delineated. The reason is as follows: Scripture's agricultural laws, and the theory of the divine-Israelite economy which they express, presuppose a total congruence between the spatial and the social

categories "Israel": the rules are directed exclusively to "native" Israelite society at home in the Land of Israel. They express a dynamic unity among
the God who owns the Land and rules over the People, the People who
live on God's Land and render God service through their work on the
Land, and the Land which is under God's special providence and nourishes
the People only if they obey God's laws. But for the Rabbis of the Mishnah, living in the first two centuries of the common era and imagining (for
the most part) the Temple cult and society of the preceding century and
a half, the spatial and social categories are no longer fully congruent: Jews
live both in the Land of Israel and abroad (most in fact living abroad); the
Land of Israel is inhabited by both Jews and gentiles (who do not live under
Jewish jurisdiction). This normatively anomalous, though historically long-
standing, situation poses problems for Mishnah's Rabbis, not least because
it does not conform to their view of the divine order of things laid down
in Scripture. The specific problems raised in the Mishnah deal with defining *who* must observe these agricultural laws (social taxonomy) and *where*
they must be observed (spatial taxonomy) now that the boundaries have
been violated and the categories confused.

The issues of social and spatial taxonomy are thus linked: if we should
find the Rabbis ruling that a gentile living in the Land of Israel must observe Scripture's agricultural prohibitions and separate the requisite offerings, then the spatial category would take precedence in theory; the Land's
special sanctity (i.e., its special relation to God) would appear to be deemed
absolute and inherent, without reference to current inhabitants. If, on the
other hand, we should find that only the Land's Israelite inhabitants were
subject to these rules, then the sanctity of the Land would appear to be
relative to that of the People Israel; the Israelites, by inhabiting and working
the Land, would actively "complete" the Land's "consecration." Finally, if
we should discover that these agricultural rules were extended by the Rabbis
to apply additionally to Israelites living outside the Land, we would have
to consider the implications of symbolic displacement; the Land of Israel
would have gained a nonliteral, nonlocative meaning, just as cultic purity
in the Mishnah has gained such a meaning. Spatial categories thereby would
be fully relativized to social categories.

In fact, elements of all three positions are found in the Mishnah (and
in corresponding materials in the Tosefta), with the second position most
prominent. Frequently the different positions are juxtaposed in the dispute-
form; sometimes they are not. The following paragraphs deal sequentially
with (1) the problem of gentiles living in the Land of Israel; (2) Jews living

outside the Land; (3) the problem of defining the boundaries of the Land of Israel with reference to Jewish observance inside the Land; and (4) the problem of the median case, Jews living in Syria, on the borders of the Land.

(1) Mishnah's Rabbis deem gentiles living in the Land to be exempt from the prohibitions of the seventh year, as are Jews living outside the Land (M. Sheb. 5:7). Toseftan materials deem such gentiles exempt additionally from the requirement to separate dough-offering, and any dough-offering in fact separated by them to be invalid (T. Hal. 2:6, T. Ter. 4:13). Social taxa take precedence in these rulings. Gentiles living in the Land are exempt as well from the obligation to separate *terumah* and tithes. The Mishnaic and Toseftan materials focus instead on the question of whether these offerings, once they have been separated by gentiles, are deemed valid: Mishnah's editors judge them to be so; Tosefta qualifies this judgement (M. Ter. 3:9; T. Ter. 4:12–14).[33] The reasoning behind the Mishnaic ruling is not indicated in the text and can only be guessed at. It might be due to an idealizing wish that these offerings be given from *all* of the Land's produce in conformity with Scripture's norms—required of Jews, but acceptable (minimally) even from gentiles.[34] M. Ter. 3:9 additionally records a dispute over whether a gentile's vineyard in the Land is subject to the offering of the fourth-year fruits. (T. Ter. 2:13, glossing this dispute, refers it rather to a vineyard in Syria!) This item is surely related to the question, discussed below, of whether the *orlah*-prohibition holds universally, both inside and outside the Land.[35] M. A. Z. 1:8 rules that anything attached to the soil in the Land (trees, etc.) may not be sold to gentiles, nor may fields and houses in the Land be rented to them (the latter item subject to dispute), lest they thereby come to acquire proprietary rights in the Land of Israel. The theory here is that the Land properly should belong to Israelites. The ruling may presuppose additionally that gentiles will not (and need not) observe Scripture's agricultural laws, while Israelites, of course, will and must do so. To summarize: the prevailing tendency in Mishnah's rulings is to exempt gentiles living in the Land from the observance of these laws; the divinely ordained economy of the Land is not absolute but relative to the presence and agricultural activity of its Jewish inhabitants. Still, Mishnah records the position that gentile offerings of raw produce are deemed valid after the fact, perhaps indicating a wish that *all* of the Land's produce be subject to Scripture's requirements.

(2) On the other hand, Israelites living outside the Land are exempt from Scripture's Land-bound agricultural laws, with some exceptions to be noted below. M. Kid. 1:9 rules that "any [scriptural] commandment (*mitsvah*)

that is not dependent on the Land [of Israel] is to be observed both in the Land and outside the Land; any [scriptural] commandment that is dependent on the Land is to be observed only in the Land." All of Scripture's agricultural offerings fall into the latter category; here the spatial taxa take precedence.[36] Two exceptions to this ruling (and an appended third) are listed in the same pericope: the prohibitions (1) of sowing together diverse kinds of seeds in a field or vineyard (*kilayim*),[37] (2) of making use of the fruit of a tree or vineyard during the first three years of growth (*orlah*), and (3) (Eliezer adds:) of eating produce of the new spring harvest before the first sheaf (*omer*) has been offered—these apply also to Israelites living outside the Land. (cf. M. Orl. 3:9; T. Ter. 2:13, T. Orl. 1:8, T. Kid. 1:12). The reasons for these exceptions are nowhere stated. It may be that the prohibition against mixing diverse kinds of seeds is viewed by the Rabbis as part of the order of creation and thus applicable everywhere. Some similar reasoning from the universal order of creation might pertain also to the *orlah*-prohibition, though the applicability of this prohibition outside the Land of Israel in fact is disputed at T. Orl. 1:8. M. Orl. 3:9 holds that the applicability outside the Land of the prohibition of eating new grain before the offering of the *omer* is Toraitic (the verse Lev. 23:14—"it is a statute forever throughout your generations *in all your dwellings*"—is used to ground this ruling at Sifra Emor Parashah 10:11, but it is not clear whether the formal-exegetical derivation is the sole or primary reason behind the ruling).[38] Lying outside this framework is the discussion attributed to early Yavneans at M. Yad. 4:3 (and T. Yad. 2:15) of the agricultural tithes which must be given during the seventh year by Israelites living in Ammon and Moab, two lands which border the Land of Israel (see below, paragraph 4). This discussion imagines that Israelites living in both Egypt and Babylonia separate tithes regularly, including during the seventh year (in place of observing the seventh-year prohibitions), and that the custom or requirement in Babylonia is more ancient than in Egypt ("an enactment of the prophets" [*ma'aseh nevi'im*], as opposed to "an enactment of the elders" [*ma'aseh zekenim*]), presumably since the Babylonian Jewish community as a major ongoing settlement of Jews outside the Land was older than the Egyptian community. It is not clear whether this scenario also supposes a symbolic transfer of attributes of the Land of Israel to large Jewish settlements outside the Land ("new Jerusalems"); it certainly supposes a precedence, with respect to tithing laws, of the social over the spatial Israel which is nowhere else assumed in the Mishnah.[39]

(3) We have seen that, with some exceptions, Mishnah's Rabbis deem

the scriptural agricultural rules (particularly those regarding offerings) applicable only to Israelites living in the Land of Israel. A further problem for them is to define precisely the borders of the Land within which these rules apply. Here, too, the underlying issue is the discrepancy betwen spatial and social categories; specifically, that the areas of actual Israelite settlement in the Land, both present and past, do not correspond to the biblically ordained borders. Gen. 15:18 promises to Abraham's descendants all the land "from the river of Egypt to the great river, the river Euphrates." Num. 34:1-10 lists the ideal borders of the Land at the time of the conquest from the perspective of the later Davidic monarchy; additional ideal borders are put forth in Josh. 13-19 and Ezek. 47:13-20. Not all of these areas were in fact settled by the Israelites at the time of the conquest, while even fewer were reoccupied during the Second Commonwealth period. Since all scriptural pronouncements are viewed by Mishnah's Rabbis as divine revelation, they formally acknowledge all of this territory to be "Erets Yisra'el," but distinguish practically among three regions (*aratsot*): (1) that area resettled by the returnees from Babylonia, (2) that area originally conquered by the Israelite tribes at the time of Joshua, and (3) that area never settled at all by the Israelites but included within the broadest scriptural borders (M. Sheb. 6:1, M. Hal. 4:8; cf. T. Sheb. 4:6-11, T. Hal. 2:11, T. Ter. 2:12; also T. M.S. 2:15 = T. B.Q. 8:19, M. Dem. 1:3 and T. Dem. 1:4).[40]

Seventh-year prohibitions and the obligation to separate dough-offering are fully applicable only in the first area, where Israelite settlement had been longest and continued in part to be of some actual as well as ideological significance. These rules are deemed partially applicable in the second area: produce of the land there may be eaten during the seventh year, but the land itself must not be worked; regular dough-offering is separated, but burned on account of the land's uncleanness, while a token offering is given to the priest. (The second and third areas in the biblical Land of Israel are deemed by the Rabbis to be unclean on account of their majority of gentile inhabitants; for practical purposes they are held to be *erets ha'amim*.) Seventh-year prohibitions are not applicable at all in the third area; a token amount of dough-offering is burned there on account of uncleanness and a larger amount given to the priests, who need not eat it in conditions of cultic purity since both dough-offerings are held to be merely symbolic.[41] Within the biblical borders, then, social taxa predominate: Scripture's rules fully apply only in that portion of the Land of Israel which is inhabited by the People Israel, and where the Jews most recently have exercised social and political authority during the period of the Second Commonwealth from the time of Ezra.

The underlying theory of the Land's sanctity is therefore seen again to be *interactive*. The Mishnaic materials comport well with Jonathan Z. Smith's observations in a broader comparative context:

> In order for land to be *my* land, one must live together with it. It is man living in relationship with his land that transforms uninhabited wasteland into a homeland, that transforms the land into the land of Israel. It is that one has cultivated the land, died on the land, that one's ancestors are buried in the land, that rituals have been performed in the land, that one's deity has been encountered here and there in the land that renders the land a homeland, a land-for-man, a holy land. It is, briefly, history that makes a land mine . . . [I]t is the shared history of generations that converts the land into the land of the Fathers.[42]

(4) The willingness of Mishnah's Rabbis to relativize to some degree Scripture's spatial taxa to social taxa[43] generates for them a thorny middle case: the applicability of Scripture's agricultural rules to Syria. Syria is *not* part of the biblical Land of Israel, yet it is spatially contiguous with it on the Land's northeastern border. Syria, moreover, contained a large Jewish population during the late Second Commonwealth period and at the time the Mishnah was being created. Following strict spatial criteria, Syria should be accounted as "outside the Land" pure and simple, yet Mishnah's Rabbis treat Syria as a classic instance of *tertium quid* in which two theoretically opposing principles intersect;[44] thus, in some ways Syria is deemed to be like the Land of Israel and in some ways not.[45]

For example, it is taken for granted throughout the Mishnah (and Tosefta) that produce grown on land owned by Israelite farmers in Syria is liable to the separation of *terumah* and tithes and to the prohibitions of the seventh year.[46] M. Hal. 4:11 records a precedent in which even first-fruits were accepted when brought from Apamea in Syria, and justifies this with the dictum that "one who purchases [land] in Syria is like one who purchases [land] on the outskirts of Jerusalem" (a dictum repeated at T. Ter. 2:10, T. Kel. B.K. 1:15).[47] At the same time, produce grown by gentiles in Syria on their own land is not liable to be treated this way by Jews who purchase the produce—unlike gentile produce grown in the Land of Israel which *is* liable for tithing when purchased by Jews (cf. T. Dem. 1:4, 12). This distinction generates a typical Mishnaic middle case (M. Hal. 4:7, T. Hal. 2:5–6): What if a Jew in Syria merely works the land as tenant-farmer for a gentile? According to one opinion (Gamaliel), the produce is exempt from tithing and seventh-year restrictions, because the land is owned by the gentile and is outside the Land of Israel. The disputing opinion (Eliezer) maintains that the produce is liable, because it is cultivated by a Jew and because Syria is deemed in this regard to be just like the Land of Israel. By juxtaposing this Gamaliel-Eliezer dispute with a second one on the question of the kind of dough-offering to be separated in Syria, Mishnah's editors apparently indicate their view that the main issue in both disputes is the status of Syria vis-à-vis the Land of Israel and "outside the Land." Eliezer holds that only one dough-offering need be separated in Syria, just as in the "core" part of the biblical Land of Israel. Gamaliel, on the other hand, requires the separation of two dough-offerings, just as he does in that portion of the Land which was never conquered by the Israelites (M. Hal. 4:8).[48] Gamaliel thus assigns to Syria a middle status—not quite like the "core" Land of Israel, not quite like the land of the gentiles.[49] A similar status obtains with respect to seventh-year restrictions, which are deemed to apply only to unharvested crops. Harvested produce, however, may continue to be processed in the usual manner, unlike the situation in the "core" Land of Israel (M. Sheb. 6:2; cf. M. Sheb. 8:6). The editorial juxtaposition of this ruling with M. Sheb. 6:1's distinction among the three areas of the biblical Land of Israel (above, p. 120) makes clear that the status of Syria in fact corresponds fully to none of these areas, nor to the situation obtaining outside the Land.[50]

Syria's "middle" status is also articulated with respect to the *orlah*- and *kilayim*-prohibitions and with respect to transferring Israelite-owned property to gentiles. Doubts as to whether a particular item of produce for sale may in fact be *orlah*-produce or a vegetable that was grown in a vineyard (prohibited as mixed seeds in a vineyard) are resolved stringently in the Land of Israel, but leniently in Syria and abroad (M. Orl. 3:9; T. Orl. 1:8; cf. T. Ter. 2:13). Outside the Land, but *not* in Syria, one may even purchase such produce out of the suspected garden.[51] M. A.Z. 1:8 sets forth a dispute as to whether a Jew may sell or rent his house or field to a gentile. Both disputants (Meir and Jose) treat the situation in Syria as a middle case between that in the Land of Israel (where such transactions are forbidden lest gentiles come thereby to own part of the Land and decrease the area cultivated under God's laws of tithing and seventh-year restrictions) and outside the Land (where these considerations do not apply and the transactions are therefore permitted). Since fields owned by Jews in Syria are subject to tithing and seventh-year restrictions, they may not be sold (or, on Meir's theory, even rented) to gentiles, for the same reasons that apply in the Land. The transfer of houses to gentiles in Syria is dealt with by both disputants more leniently than in the Land, but more stringently than "outside the Land." (Significantly, Jose's consistently more lenient theory applies *to the Land of Israel* the ruling that Meir applies to Syria, and to Syria the ruling that Meir applies to "outside the Land"; cf. T. A.Z. 2:8–9.)

In all these cases the status of Syria is deemed to lie somewhere between that of the Land and that obtaining abroad. With respect to the movement of seventh-year produce and heave-offering across borders, however, Syria is deemed to be just like the Land of Israel (M. Sheb. 6:5–6). Thus, unclean oil of heave-offering (which must be burnt) and seventh-year produce (which is deemed ownerless) cannot be transported abroad for gain, but they may be transported to Syria. Similarly, heave-offering, which, as we have seen, is not to be separated outside the Land, cannot be brought into the Land from abroad, but may be brought in from Syria, since it can validly be separated there.[52] (T. Ter. 2:9, on the other hand, wishes to maintain the distinction between heave-offering from the Land of Israel and from Syria: heave-offering from produce of the Land may not be separated on behalf of produce from Syria, and vice versa.[53] Along the same lines, T. Shek. 2:3–4 wishes to maintain the distinction between the annual Temple-taxes [*shekalim*] contributed by Jews residing in the Land and those residing in Syria; cf. M. Shek. 3:4.)

Syria's peculiar status is evident also in the area of purity regulations. Since most of the land is owned and inhabited by gentiles, it is treated as the "land of the gentiles" and deemed to be unclean (just like those portions of the biblical Land of Israel not inhabited by Jews). But those portions of Syria owned by Jews which are *immediately* contiguous with the Land of Israel and into which one can enter from the Land without passing through (unclean) gentile property or a grave-area are held to be clean, just like the Land of Israel (M. Oh. 18:7, T. Kel. B.K. 1:5, T. Oh. 18:2).[54] Significantly, there is no explicit claim that these areas thereby come to form a *part* of the Land of Israel, only that, for the specified purposes, they are to be treated *like* the Land.[55]

To summarize: the intermediate and sometimes vacillating status of the Mishnah's rulings on Syria results from the application of two theoretically opposing principles: the one spatial, which maintains the formal distinctiveness of the Land of Israel against *all* other territories outside the Land, including Syria; the other social, which values a large settlement of the *People* Israel formally outside the Land, but in fact on its very borders. Mishnah's Rabbis clearly wish to do justice to both principles—both Holy Land and Holy People—without *fully* embracing the one over the other. Thus the formal, locative distinctiveness of the Land of Israel is preserved vis-à-vis Syria even while its large Jewish population is acknowledged.

The ideal ("messianic") situation, of course, would be a return to the total congruence of the spatial and social Israels that Scripture's laws originally envisaged. Thus the Rabbis of the Mishnah (who, it must always be remembered, live in the Land) encourage Jewish settlement in the Land of Israel and discourage Jewish emigration from it. They rule, e.g., that while a man may not force his wife to move with him from one of the three administrative units of the Land of Israel (Judea, Transjordan, Galilee) to another, he may compel her and his entire household to move with him to the Land of Israel from abroad or to the city of Jerusalem from outside that city. [Ed. note: see comments below by Saperstein, pp. 190–95; and Bar Asher, pp. 300–02.] Conversely, he may not compel his household to depart from the Land of Israel or from Jerusalem (M. Ket. 13:10–11, T. Ket. 12:5; recall in this context the hierarchical list at M. Kel. 1:6–9). A significant homiletical expression of this attitude toward settlement in the Land of Israel, found not in Mishnah, but in Tosefta, A.Z. 4[5]:3–6, is worth citing here in full:

(4[5]:3)   A. One should rather dwell in the Land of Israel—even in a town in which the majority of the inhabitants are gentiles—

B. than outside the Land—even in a town in which all the inhabitants are Jews.

C. This [ruling] implies that dwelling in the Land of Israel is deemed as important as fulfilling all the commandments in the Torah,

D. and all who are buried in the Land of Israel—it is as if they were buried beneath the altar [of the Temple in Jerusalem].

(4[5]:4)   E. One should not emigrate from the Land of Israel unless the going price of wheat [in the Land] is [as high as] two se'ahs for a sela.

F. Said R. Simeon, "Under what circumstances [does this ruling apply]?

G. "[Only] when one cannot find any [food] to buy [at that price].

H. "But when one can find [food] to buy, even if [the going price of wheat is as high as] a [single] se'ah for a sela, he should not emigrate."

I. And similarly R. Simeon would say, "Elimelech was one of the great men of his generation and one who sustained the community, but because he left the Land, he and his sons died of famine while all the [rest of the] Israelites were able to survive in their own land,

J. "as Scripture states, *And all the city was astir concerning them, and the women said, 'Is this Naomi?'* (Ruth 1:19),

K. "which implies that *all* the city's inhabitants were able to survive, while he and his sons died of famine."

(4[5]:5)   L. Now Scripture states, *[Then Jacob made a vow, saying, "If God will be with me, and will keep me in this way that I go . . .] so that I come again to my father's house in peace . . .* (Gen. 28:20–21), and does it not continue, then *the Lord shall be my God* (Gen. 28:21) [viz., *only* when I return to the Land]?

M. And [Scripture also] states, *[I am the Lord your God who brought you forth out of the land of Egypt] to give you the land of Canaan, and to be your God* (Lev. 25:38),

N. [which implies] that as long as you are in the Land of Canaan, I will be your God,

O. but when you are not dwelling in the Land of Canaan, it is as if I am not your God.

P. Similarly, Scripture states [concerning the conquest of the Land under Joshua], *about forty thousand men ready armed for war passed over before the Lord [for battle, to the plains of Jericho]* (Josh. 4:13).

Q. Now is it conceivable that Israel would conquer the Land *before* the Omnipresent? [the problem is the delimited spatial anthropomorphism if the text is read literally].

R. Rather [we must interpret the verse as follows]: as long as they reside upon the Land, it is as if it is conquered [by them];

S. so when they do not reside upon it, it is as if it is not conquered [by them].

T. Similarly, Scripture states [concerning David when he fled abroad from Saul], *[And David said,] ". . . for they have driven me out this day that I should have no share in the heritage of the Lord, saying, 'Go, serve other gods.'"* (I Sam. 26:19).

U. Now is it conceivable that David would worship idols?

V. Rather, David reasoned from Scripture as follows: Anyone who leaves the Land during peacetime and goes [to live] abroad is as if he were worshipping idols,

W. as Scripture states, *[I will rejoice in doing them good,] and I will plant them in this land in faithfulness, with all my heart and all my soul* (Jer. 32:41):

X. As long as they reside upon it, it is as if they are planted before me [God] in faithfulness, with all my heart and all my soul;

Y. now when they do not reside upon it, it is as if they are not planted before me in faithfulness, with all my heart and all my soul.

(4[5]:6)   Z. R. Simeon b. Eleazar says, "Israelites who reside outside the Land are idolaters.

AA. "How so?

BB. "If a gentile threw a party for his son and went and invited all the Jews dwelling in his town, even if they should eat and drink [only] their own [food and drink], and their own attendant should stand ready to serve them, they still worship idols,

CC. as Scripture states, [. . . *lest you make a covenant with the inhabitants of the Land, and when they play the harlot after their gods and sacrifice to their gods] and one invites you, you eat of his sacrifices* (Ex. 34: 15)."

Recognizing the rhetorical force and intent of passages of this type in rabbinic literature does not diminish their piquancy. The extreme locative stance articulated in the above text is noteworthy: it is "as if" the God of Israel can be served only in the Land of Israel. The various Mishnaic rulings we have been examining indicate both the sense and limits of this "as if," since they maintain that through study of God's Torah and observance of God's commandments, the God of Israel can in fact be served by Jews anywhere and everywhere, but *fully and perfectly* only in the Land of Israel where additional, Land-bound commandments obtain, as Scripture ordains. It is, then, in the interstices between the actual and the ideal that Mishnah's Rabbis map out their world. The tension between the ideal congruence of the spatial and social Israels—between Holy Land and Holy People—and their actual incomplete coincidence, generates the problem of confused boundaries that so preoccupies Mishnah's authors. In one form or another, that problem, for Jews, is at least as old as the time of Sennacharib; from the age of Alexander's conquests it became the problem of the entire Mediterranean world.[56]

Notes

1. This kind of atomizing exegesis, of course, frequently *subverted* the original syntactic logic of both Mishnah and Scripture for the later exegetes' own purposes, a classic instance of overcoming the limitations of a closed canon (Scripture plus Mishnah) through exegetical ingenuity. See Jonathan Z. Smith, *Imagining*

Religion: From Babylon to Jonestown (Chicago, 1982), pp. 36–52. For the application of this insight to rabbinic literature, see Jacob Neusner, *Midrash in Context: Exegesis in Formative Judaism* (Philadelphia, 1983), particularly pp. 53–110; Martin S. Jaffee, "The Mishnah in Talmudic Exegesis: Observations on Tractate Ma'aserot of the Talmud Yerushalmi," in William Scott Green, ed., *Approaches to Ancient Judaism IV* (Chico, 1983), pp. 137–57; idem, "Oral Torah in Theory and Practice: Aspects of Mishnah-Exegesis in the Palestinian Talmud," *Religion* 15 (1985), pp. 387–410; Alan J. Avery-Peck, "Yerushalmi's Commentary to Mishnah Terumot: From Theology to Legal Code," in Green, pp. 113–36; William Scott Green, "On Reading the Writing of Rabbinism," in *Journal of the American Academy of Religion* 51, no. 2 (June 1983), pp. 190–206; and Isaak Heinemann, *Darkhei ha'aggadah*, 2nd ed. (Jerusalem, 1954), pp. 96–195.

2. On Sifra in particular as involving an attempt formally to ground Mishnah's rulings in Scripture, see Neusner, *Midrash in Context*, pp. 35–41, and *A History of the Mishnaic Law of Purities VII. Nega'im, Sifra* (Leiden, 1975); Jack N. Lightstone, "Form as Meaning in Halakhic Midrash: A Programmatic Statement," in *Semeia* 27 (1983), pp. 23–35. Cf. also Neusner, *Formative Judaism: Religious, Historical, and Literary Studies* (Chico, 1982), pp. 153–68.

3. Since I have chosen to limit this article to the Mishnah, for the reasons stated, it is worth remarking here that Mishnah's basic conceptions of the Land of Israel in fact are taken for granted and carried forward in the subsequent rabbinic literature from late antiquity. The Babylonian literature, in a typical process of symbolic transformation and "utopianization" (the term is Jonathan Z. Smith's, *Map is not Territory: Studies in the History of Religions* [Leiden, 1978], pp. 100–103 *et passim*), will transfer aspects of the privileged locative status of the Land of Israel to Babylonia (and the privileges of the Palestinian Rabbis to their Babylonian counterparts!). See below, note 39.

4. For an analysis of Mishnaic rhetorical patterns, see Neusner, *A History of the Mishnaic Law of Purities XXI* (Leiden, 1977), and *Method and Meaning in Ancient Judaism* (Missoula, 1979), pp. 155–81.

5. The matter is further complicated when complementary Toseftan materials reflect still other theories or definitions of that issue.

6. Nonetheless, the problem of paratactic juxtaposition in the Mishnah does not render impossible the present kind of inquiry, or Mishnaic interpretation in general. Frequently the connectives to be inferred are fairly clear. But when they are not, the tentativeness of the proffered explanation must be stated explicitly. On the issue of parataxis and hypotaxis in Mishnah and the larger cultural implications of the issue, see William Scott Green, "On Reading the Writing of Rabbinism," *JAAR* 51, and "Storytelling and Holy Man: The Case of Ancient Judaism," in Jacob Neusner, ed., *Take Judaism, For Example: Studies Toward the Comparison of Religions* (Chicago, 1983), pp. 29–43, especially pp. 29–34.

7. On these points, see the literature referred to in notes 4 and 6.

8. On the precise nature of the relationship between Mishnah and Scripture, see Jacob Neusner, *Judaism: The Evidence of the Mishnah* (Chicago, 1982), pp. 167–229; *Method and Meaning in Ancient Judaism. Second Series* (Chico, 1981), pp. 99–213; and my article "Mishnah and Scripture: Preliminary Observations on the Law of Tithing in *Seder Zera'im*," in William Scott Green, ed., *Approaches to Ancient Judaism II* (Missoula, 1980), pp. 81–96. On the whole, Mishnah's dependence on scriptural laws is not one of formal exegetical derivation but of logical extension. Some Mishnaic topics, however, are totally unknown in Scripture (e.g., the *erub* and *dema'i*, though these topics of course presuppose scriptural rules about the Sabbath and tithing). But, as Neusner so cogently demonstrates, even when Mishnah takes up Scripture's topics, that which its authors wish to address *about* those topics often bears no relationship to scriptural concerns (cf. *Method. Second Series*, pp. 203–04).

9. For a more detailed interpretation and analysis of the worldview expressed in the Mishnah, see Neusner, *Judaism*, especially pp. 230–83.

10. On the ubiquity and significance of "median cases" in the Mishnah, see Neusner, *Judaism*, pp. 256–70.

11. My usage of the term "locative," denoting the importance in cultural imagination of place and spatial orientation, particularly with reference to a "center," is borrowed from Jonathan Z. Smith, *Map is not Territory*, pp. 100–03 *et passim*.

12. In the continuation, a different theory of S-V is attributed to Jose, effectively conflating items 9 and 10 on the list, and probably accounting for the presence of *eleven* items (one subject to dispute) while the superscription at A promises ten. Cf. also T. Kel. B.K. 1: 5–14. See Neusner's commentary, in *A History of the Mishnaic Law of Purities I* (Leiden, 1974), pp. 37–44.

13. On the locative significance of this passage, see Smith, *Map is not Territory*, pp. 104–28, particularly pp. 112–15.

14. *Erets ha'amim* is always used in the context of cultic purity and impurity: M. Naz. 7: 3; M. Oh. 2: 3, 18: 6; M. Toh. 4: 5, 5: 1. On *Chutsah la'arets*: of thirty-eight occurrences listed in Chaim Joshua Kasovsky, *Otsar Leshon Hamishnah I* (Tel Aviv, 1956), p. 272, all but four (M. A.Z. 1: 8 [twice], M. Makk. 1: 10, M. Git. 4: 6) occur in the context of cultic purity and impurity, sacrificial offerings, or agricultural offerings. The four "exceptions" in fact are not exceptional: they deal with intersections between the spatial (Land of Israel/outside the Land) and social (Israelite/gentile) grids discussed below. A.Z. 1: 8 rules that an Israelite may not sell land or landed property to a gentile in the Land of Israel, but may do so outside the Land; Git. 4: 6 states that an Israelite's slave sold to a gentile in the Land of Israel or to anyone outside the Land thereby gains his freedom (viz., the sale is invalid); Makk. 1: 10 rules that the Sanhedrin's authority extends to Israelites living outside the Land.

15. These three agricultural offerings are specifically linked by Scripture with the Land of Israel: cf. Lev. 23: 9–17 (*omer*, two loaves); Ex. 23: 19, 34: 26, Num.

18:13, Deut. 26:1–11 (first-fruits). Mishnah's Rabbis here emphasize that fact in their own reading of Scripture.

16. Cf. the full set of rulings in Seder Kodoshim which follow the fixed formal pattern: "X is observed/may be brought both in/from the Land of Israel and outside the Land." In addition to M. Men. 8:1 and its parallel at M. Par. 2:1, there is M. Hul. 5:1 (the law prohibiting the slaughter of "an animal and its young" on the same day; Lev. 22:28), 6:1 (the law of "covering the blood" of slaughtered animals; Lev. 17:13), 7:1 (the prohibition against eating "the sinew of the hip"; Gen. 32:32), 10:1 (the gift to the priest of "the shoulder and the two cheeks and the maw" from the slaughtered animal; Deut. 18:3), 11:1 (the offering of "the first of the fleece"; Deut. 18:4), 12:1 (the rule to "let the dam go from the nest" before taking its young; Deut. 22:6–7); M. Bekh. 9:1 (the tithe of cattle). Only three of these rulings, M. Hul. 10:1, 11:1, and M. Bekh. 9:1, refer to cultic offerings. These three priestly gifts are not specifically linked by Scripture with the Land of Israel, nor are they inherently (i.e., logically) Land-bound; thus they can be observed outside the Land as well. M. Tem. 3:5 rules that the firstborn of the cattle and the tithe of cattle should not be brought from abroad to the Land of Israel because their status can be dealt with abroad (cf. T. Tem. 2:17: one need not scruple to bring them from abroad). Cf. also T. Sanh. 3:5.

17. Neusner deals with the ramifications of this observation; see *Method and Meaning*, pp. 101–31; *Method. Second Series*, pp. 55–81.

18. See J. Z. Smith on "locative" vs. "utopian" visions of the world, *Map is not Territory*. Note particularly his "afterword" on p. 128.

19. M. Mik. 8:1. The point may be mooted. See Neusner's commentary, *Purities XIII* (Leiden, 1976), pp. 173–77.

20. M. Oh. 2:3, 17:5, 18:6–7; M. Toh. 4:5, 5:1; M. Naz. 3:6, 7:3; cf. T. Mik. 6:1, T. Oh. 17:7–18:11. See Shmuel Safrai's discussion of the rationale for this impurity, "The Land of Israel in Tannaitic Halakhah," in Georg Strecker, ed., *Das Land Israel in biblischer Zeit* (Göttingen, 1983), pp. 206–07, and notes *ad loc.*

21. M. Oh. 18:7, because gentiles are suspected of throwing abortions down the drain.

22. M. Mik. 8:1. Cf. T. Mik. 6:1, which deems Samaritan territory and its immersion-pools to be clean. Samaritans comprise a median social category for the Mishnah's Rabbis, falling between Jews and gentiles (not unlike Syria on the spatial axis).

23. Cf. M. Naz. 3:6, where a Nazirite vow taken outside the Land of Israel and fully observed there becomes effective only after the man has entered the Land of Israel, and must be observed again.

24. For exegesis and analysis of the relevant Mishnah- (and Tosefta-) tractates, see the following: on Terumot, Alan J. [Avery-]Peck, *The Priestly Gift in Mishnah: A Study of Tractate Terumot* (Chico, 1981); on Ma'aserot, Martin S. Jaffee, *Mishnah's Theology of Tithing: A Study of Tractate Ma'aserot* (Chico, 1981); on Ma'aser

Sheni, Peter J. Haas, *A History of the Mishnaic Law of Agriculture: Tractate Ma'aser Sheni* (Chico, 1980); on Dema'i, Richard S. Sarason, *A History of the Mishnaic Law of Agriculture III. A Study of Tractate Dema'i* (Leiden, 1979); on Bikkurim, Margaret Wenig Rubenstein, "A Commentary on Mishnah-Tosefta Tractate Bikkurim, Chapters One and Two," and David Weiner, "A Study of Mishnah Tractate Bikkurim, Chapter Three," both in William Scott Green, ed., *Approaches to Ancient Judaism III* (Chico, 1981), pp. 47–88 and 89–104; on the first chapter of Hallah, Abraham Havivi, "Mishnah Hallah Chapter One: Translation and Commentary," in Green, *ibid.*, pp. 149–84. On Seder Zera'im as a whole, see now Alan J. Avery-Peck, *Mishnah's Division of Agriculture: A History and Theology of Seder Zera'im* (Chicago, 1985).

25. The same theory applies to the offering of the firstborn of the cattle and the firstborn human sons (redeemed by the Levites, who serve God in their place). See further my article cited at note 8 above, particularly pp. 84–86 and the literature cited there, as well as W. D. Davies, *The Territorial Dimension of Judaism* (Berkeley, 1982), pp. 15–21.

26. For analysis of M.-T. Shevi'it, see Louis E. Newman, *The Sanctity of the Seventh Year: A Study of Mishnah Tractate Shebiit* (Chico, 1983). On M.-T. Orlah, see Howard Scott Essner, "The Mishnah-Tractate Orlah: Translation and Commentary," in Green, *Approaches III*, pp. 105–48.

27. See, for example, Matitiahu Tsevat, "The Basic Meaning of the Biblical Sabbath," in *Zeitschrift für die Alttestamentliche Wissenschaft* 84 (1972), pp. 447–59. On the seventh year, see further Newman, pp. 15–22.

28. For analysis of M.-T. Kilayim, see Irving J. Mandelbaum, *A History of the Mishnaic Law of Agriculture: Kilayim* (Chico, 1982).

29. Cf. Mary Douglas, *Purity and Danger: An Analysis of the Concepts of Pollution and Taboo* (London, 1966), p. 53: ". . . holiness is exemplified by completeness. Holiness requires that individuals shall conform to the class to which they belong. And holiness requires that different classes of things shall not be confused. . . . Holiness means keeping distinct the categories of creation. It therefore involves correct definition, discrimination, and order."

30. For analysis of M.-T. Peah, see Roger Brooks, *Support for the Poor in the Mishnaic Law of Agriculture: Tractate Peah* (Chico, 1983).

31. Cf. Brooks, pp. 17–19: "God supports both the priests [viz., Deuteronomy's Levites] and the poor because they neither own land nor attain the economic prosperity promised to all Israelites who live in the Land (see Deut. 8:7–10)" (p. 18).

32. Cf. my article cited at note 8 above, pp. 86–89; Peck, *Priestly Gift*, pp. 2–7; Jaffee, pp. 4–8; Mandelbaum, pp. 3–4; Newman, pp. 17–20; and Neusner, *Judaism*, pp. 174–81. On the role of human action and intentionality in Mishnah generally, see Neusner, *Judaism*, pp. 270–83, and Howard Eilberg-Schwartz, *The Human Will in Judaism: The Mishnah's Philosophy of Intention* (Atlanta, 1986).

33. The formulaic linguistic usage at M. Ter. 3:9, "*terumah* separated by gen-

tiles . . . is [deemed valid] terumah [*terumatan terumah*]," throughout the tractate's first chapter refers to categories of persons who are not obligated (or are forbidden) to separate *terumah* but whose offering, once separated, is nonetheless deemed to be valid. Cf. Peck, p. 31, and pp. 122–29. (*Pace* Peck, T. Ter. 2:12 does not maintain that produce grown by a gentile in the Land of Israel is liable to the separation of *terumah* and tithes.) The status of *terumah* separated by gentiles is disputed at M. Ter. 3:9; Simeon does not deem it fully valid, but rather to have the status of *terumah* separated from produce on account of doubt as to whether it had to be separated (*dema'i*). The Toseftan materials question the validity of *terumah* and tithes which the gentile brings out of his house; his reliability is suspect. The status of *terumah* separated by Samaritans is also the subject of these rulings. Samaritans, as we have observed in note 22, comprise a median case on the Rabbis' social grid; they are neither true Israelites nor true gentiles. Their status is subject to dispute: sometimes like Israelites, sometimes like gentiles. For the purposes of this article, we need not deal with the issues raised in connection with Samaritans. It is not clear whether T. Hal. 2:6's ruling that "[with respect to] dough-offering separated by a gentile in the Land and *terumah* separated by a gentile outside the Land, one informs him that he is not obligated [to give these offerings]" implies that a gentile in the Land *is* obligated to separate *terumah*, and thus contradicts M. Ter. 3:9.

34. If this ruling on the *post facto* validity of gentile *terumah* in the Land and the ruling in the same Toseftan pericope (T. Ter. 4:12–13) on the *post facto* invalidity of gentile dough-offering in the Land follow the same theory, the diverging conclusions might be due to the fact that dough-offering is not an offering of raw produce from the Land but a product of human labor, made from grain and water, while *terumah* is an offering of the Land's raw produce. *Terumah* separated even by a gentile could thus be deemed to come from the Land, while dough-offering does not (see further below, n. 44).

35. T. Ter. 2:13 also regards the *orlah*-prohibition and the prohibition against mixing diverse kinds of seeds in a vineyard as applicable to gentiles both in and outside the Land. This would accord with the view that these two prohibitions are universally operative, not Land-bound (M. Kid. 1:9, below).

36. Cf. M. Maas. 3:10: the produce of a tree the roots of which are in the Land of Israel and which extends over the border outside the Land is liable to be tithed; the produce of a tree the roots of which lie outside the Land, even if its branches extend into the Land, is exempt from tithing (cf. T. Maas. 2:22).

37. M. Kid. 1:9 and M. Orl. 3:9 use the general term *kilayim*, which applies to both the field and the vineyard. T. Ter. 2:13 refers only to *kilay hakerem*, mixed seeds in a vineyard.

38. In the same pericope, M. Orl. 3:9, the applicability outside the Land of the *orlah*- and *kilayim*-prohibitions are acknowledged not to be scriptural in origin. The former is deemed to be *halakhah*, while the latter is a "ruling of the scribes" (*midivrei soferim*). At M. Orl. 3:9 and T. Orl. 2:8, doubts concerning possible vio-

lations of the two prohibitions are dealt with more stringently within the Land than outside it.

39. Mishnah's rulings on *terumah* separated from produce grown outside the Land (M. Ter. 1:5, 7:3, 9:4, M. Sheb. 6:6; cf. T. Ter. 2:9, T. Sheb. 5:2) do not deem it to be true *terumah* (cf. Peck, pp. 50–52, 216–17, 256–58, and pp. 338–39, notes 74 and 76). M. Sheb. 6:6 specifically prohibits bringing *terumah* from produce grown outside the Land of Israel into the Land; presumably this also means that it is forbidden to separate *terumah* outside the Land (M. Hal. 4:10–11, a series of precedents, similarly notes that dough-offering was not accepted from abroad). Traditions in the Babylonian and Palestinian Talmuds, on the other hand, indicate that *terumah* and tithes were separated by third-century Babylonian Rabbis who deemed this obligation to be incumbent upon Jews living outside the Land of Israel. See P.T. Hal. 4:4, B. Bekh. 27a. This may indeed have been an instance of symbolically applying the attributes and stringencies of the Land of Israel to the major Jewish settlement in Babylonia for ideological reasons. See Neusner's discussion, *A History of the Jews in Babylonia II* (Leiden, 1966), pp. 260–62; 51, n. 3.

40. M. Sheb. 9:2–3 (cf. T. Sheb. 7:10–15), M. Ket. 13:10, and M. B.B. 3:2 (and T. Sanh. 2:3) additionally distinguish among three regions (*aratsot*) within that portion of the Land resettled by the returnees from Babylonia: Judea, Transjordan, and Galilee. These distinctions are not relevant to our discussion here. They acknowledge climatic-topographical differences within the Land of Israel for agricultural, calendrical, and administrative purposes (i.e., proper observance of the laws of removal during the Sabbatical year—see Newman, p. 179ff.—and intercalation of the calendar; adjudication of marital and property rights—e.g., that a man may not move his wife to another region without her consent, that valid usucaption requires both the owner and the squatter to be located within the same region). The issue of M. Sheb. 9:2–3, as explained by Newman, *Sanctity of the Seventh Year*, *is* broadly related to our inquiry. In ruling that the time for removal from the household, during the seventh year, of each species of produce grown in the Land varies from region to region, Mishnah's Rabbis again relativize the blanket applicability of Scripture's Land-bound laws to nonarbitrary conditions (in this case, to regional differences in the growing season).

41. From the equivalence of T. Ter. 2:12–13 with T. Hal. 2:11–12 it would appear that, at least to Tosefta's editors, the geographical applicability of the obligation to separate *terumah* is the same as that of dough-offering, but it is not clear whether the strictures of M. Hal. 4:8 would apply to *terumah* as well.

42. Smith, *Map*, p. 110, with references to biblical theories of the Land of Israel. See also Newman, pp. 121–24.

43. On this point I have benefitted from a conversation with Prof. Roger Brooks, University of Notre Dame.

44. W. D. Davies, *The Territorial Dimension of Judaism*, pp. 34–35 [= *The Gospel and the Land* (Berkeley, 1974), pp. 54–56] wants to explain the Rabbis' exten-

sion of scriptural tithing and seventh-year laws to Syria in political-economic terms: "conservative sages, such as Rabbi Eliezer . . . in order to protect Palestinian agriculture wanted to subject Syrian agriculture to all the requirements of tithing and the sabbatical year so as to check the emigration of farmers to Syria [after the war of 66–70 C.E.]," with reference to M. Hal. 4:7–8. Whatever the (now inaccessible) reasoning of the historical Eliezer may have been, the redactional context of this opinion in the Mishnah as finally edited suggests to the contrary that the "Mishnaic" issue regarding the status of Syria is less "practical" in this sense than "theoretical": lying just outside the borders of the Land of Israel but filled with Jewish inhabitants, Syria is yet another "middle case" for ratiocination. Cf. Neusner, *Judaism*, pp. 259–60, and Newman, p. 239, n. 50. Other significant "middle cases" relevant to our topic deal with the movement of produce across the borders of the Land of Israel. Thus, e.g., grain grown outside the Land of Israel which is imported into the Land is deemed liable for dough-offering, since the dough in fact is made inside the Land, but it is mooted whether grain grown inside the Land which is exported is liable to dough-offering (M. Hal. 2:1; cf. Sifre Numbers, Shelach 110 [ed. Horowitz, p. 113], where the prior case also is mooted). On the one hand, the dough will be made outside the Land; on the other, the grain originates in the Land. Similarly, produce grown in clods of earth from abroad which is brought into the Land by ship is deemed liable to tithes and seventh-year restrictions as soon as the ship makes physical contact with the shoreline of the Land of Israel (M. Hal. 2:2; cf. the refinements at T. Ter. 2:13, and cf. M. Dem. 5:10); from that point the clods are adjudged to form part of the earth of the Land. A classic "middle case" involves the liability to tithing of mixtures of foreign-grown and domestic produce sold in markets in the Land of Israel (or in Syria); see T. Dem. 1:4, 1:9–14, 4:11–18. The alternative positions set forth here mandate either following the status of the majority of the produce or following the presumption that produce sold in the Land has been grown in the Land until we have firm knowledge to the contrary (T. Dem. 1:9, 4). See my *Demai*, pp. 39–50, 132–37.

45. The word "like" should be underscored here. Mishnah's editors never claim that Syria has actually become part of a "greater Land of Israel"; merely that, for the reasons indicated, it is to be treated as *analogous* to the Land. The same kind of analogous, "as if" reasoning undergirds the Mishnaic extension of the cultic purity system beyond the immediate domain of the cult. Cf. Neusner, *Purities XI* (Leiden, 1976).

46. Explicitly at M. Maas. 5:5 and M. Oh. 18:7, presupposed at M. Dem. 6:11, M. Hal. 4:7, M. A.Z. 1:8, M. Sheb. 6:2, 5–6; cf. also T. Maas. 3:14, T. Ter. 2:11 (the produce remains liable to tithing and seventh-year restrictions even if the field is subsequently sold to a gentile), T. Kel. B.K. 1:5, T. Oh. 18:4, T. Dem. 1:4, T. Hal. 1:8, 2:5–6, T. A.Z. 2:8–9, T. Sheb. 4:12. It is, in fact, the very taken-for-grantedness of this proposition that generates the moot, secondary issues on which Mishnah's creators focus their attention, e.g., whether a Jew must

tithe the produce if he purchases the field *after* the point in its growth at which the produce is deemed edible and becomes liable for tithing (M. Maas. 5:5, T. Maas. 3:14—Akiba: no, since at that point the field still belonged to the gentile; sages: yes, but only in proportion to the amount of growth after the field's ownership has changed hands); whether a Jew who simply *leases* a field from a gentile in Syria must tithe the produce, since he does not own the land (M. Hal. 4:7, T. Hal. 2:5–6—Eliezer: yes, Syria is like the Land of Israel; Gamaliel: no, Syria is not like the Land of Israel [see the discussion below]); whether a Jew can rent a field to a gentile in Syria, thus adversely affecting the liability of the produce to tithing (M. A.Z. 1:8, T. A.Z. 2:8–9—Meir: yes, Jose: no [see the discussion below]).

47. Contrast with this the dispute at M. Bikk. 1:10 over the acceptability of first-fruits brought from Transjordan. Jose the Galilean (vs. the anonymous opinion) does not permit this, since Transjordan is not deemed by him to be part of "the Land flowing with milk and honey," though it is obviously part of the biblical area of settlement. That the dispute in part has an exegetical basis, harmonizing Deut. 26:9 with Exod. 13:5, is clarified at Sifre Deuteronomy 301 (ed. Finkelstein, p. 319; cf. *Mekhilta derav Shimon bar Yohai*, Bo 13:5, ed. Epstein-Melamed, p. 39). See Jack N. Lightstone, *Yosé the Galilean I: Traditions in Mishnah-Tosefta* (Leiden, 1979), pp. 18–19. (Cf. further M. Bikk. 3:11's ruling that additions to the first-fruits are treated like the first-fruits themselves only when they come from the Land of Israel, not from abroad.)

48. The separation of dough-offering in both Syria and that part of the biblical Land of Israel never conquered by the Israelites is understood to be symbolic. One portion of dough-offering is burnt as unclean, since both geographical areas are deemed unclean as "land of the gentiles" (here social reality is taken into account: a majority of the population in both areas is gentile). The second, larger offering is eaten by the priest and, in conformity with its status, need not be eaten in strict conditions of purity (see M. Hal. 4:8). With respect to both disputes at M. Hal. 4:7, Mishnah's editors report that "at first they [sages] seized upon the leniencies of both Gamaliel and Eliezer, but then they decided to follow the opinion of Gamaliel in both cases." The position finally endorsed, then, holds that Syria is *not* to be treated in these respects like the "core" Land of Israel (but cf. T. Hal. 2:5–6, where the tradition ascribed to Eleazar b. Tsadok modifies Gamaliel's position in the direction of Eliezer's!).

49. Cf. the dispute at T. Hal. 2:6 over whether Jews who purchase bread in Syria must separate dough-offering on account of doubt as to whether the offering must be separated (as must be done under these circumstances in the Land of Israel; so T. Hal. 1:8). Here the opinion that Syria is to be treated like the Land of Israel is assigned to Gamaliel (!)—perhaps in conformity with the immediately preceding Eleazar b. Tsadok materials?

50. It is not clear how Mishnah's editors mean us to understand Akiba's opin-

ion at M. Sheb. 6:2, nor indeed what the opinion meant on its own—"R. Akiba articulated a general rule: All [forms of work] that are permitted [during the seventh year] in the Land of Israel are to be performed in Syria"—viz., whether this is to be understood as an objection to items in the immediately preceding list of labors which are not to be performed in Syria (so, e.g., Albeck, *ad loc.*), or whether Akiba's ruling in fact diverges radically from the entire conception of M. 6:2 and maintains that the status of Syria is fully identical with that of the Land of Israel respecting seventh-year restrictions (so Newman, pp. 124–25). T. Sheb. 4:12 would support the first reading, but this still leaves open the question of what Akiba's opinion originally meant. On a different matter of seventh-year law, T. Sheb. 7:10 notes that, unlike the situation obtaining in the Land of Israel, no distinctions are made in Syria among climatic regions with regard to the removal of different species of produce from households.

51. The equivalence in these cases of Syria and the Land of Israel is the opinion attributed at M. Sheb. 6:5–6 to Simeon. Since the anonymous rulings there which distinguish between the Land of Israel and "outside the Land" do not mention Syria at all, it is not clear whether Mishnah's compilers understand Simeon's position to contradict them (as Newman, p. 134, maintains) or merely to refine them.

52. See Peck, p. 55, and p. 339, n. 76. Peck rightly points to the ambiguity in this ruling: whether it refers to produce grown in Syria by gentiles or by Israelites. If the former is the case, then the ruling is self-evident; if the latter, then Syria is not, in this view, deemed equivalent to the Land of Israel.

53. T. 1:8 does not distinguish in this regard between Syria and "outside the Land." Judah's opinion there disputes the Mishnaic ruling, maintaining that the status of Syria in this case follows that of the Land of Israel (i.e., for stringency). A more complex case is then given where, according to Judah, the status of Syria follows that of "outside the Land." Thus, on Judah's view, too, Syria remains a middle case.

54. Cf. in this regard T. Oh. 18:4—gentile cities such as Ashkelon which do not form part of the Land of Israel but are surrounded by the Land are not deemed liable to tithing and seventh-year restrictions (unlike Syria), but are not deemed unclean (like those parts of Syria contiguous with the Land which are owned by Jews). Cf. also T. Oh. 18:14.

55. Toseftan materials indicate that in administrative matters Syria is treated like any other foreign country, distinct from the Land of Israel. Thus, a writ of divorce brought from Syria to the Land of Israel requires validation like one brought from abroad (T. Kel. B.K. 1:5; cf. M. Git. 1:1–3); a slave sold in Syria is like one sold abroad—the sale is valid and the slave need not return to the Land of Israel (T. Kel. B.K. 1:5, T. A.Z. 3:18; cf. M. Git. 4:6); staple foodstuffs cannot be exported from the Land to Syria (or even from one hyparchy to another), as insurance against famine (T. A.Z. 4:2); in case of famine, drought, or plague, the *shofar* is

to be sounded to alert the people only in the affected areas, not in the Land of Israel for Syria or vice versa (T. Taan. 2:11).

56. Shmuel Safrai, "The Land of Israel in Tannaitic Halakhah," Georg Strecker, ed., *Das Land Israel in biblischer Zeit: Jerusalem-Symposium 1981* (Göttingen, 1983), came to my attention after the present article had been submitted for publication. Safrai deals with many of the same sources, but focuses partly on other issues than I do here (he is concerned, e.g., with ascertaining the antiquity of some of the anonymous Mishnaic rulings.

PART III

The Land of Israel in the Medieval Period

The Link to the Land of Israel in Jewish Thought: A Clash of Perspectives

Shalom Rosenberg

[Editor's note: Shalom Rosenberg, who serves on the faculty of the Hebrew University in Jerusalem, first published the following examination of the role of the Land of Israel in Jewish thought in a contribution to the Hebrew language journal *Cathedra*; its scope quickly established it as a classic, and the fact that it was beyond the reach of English language readers virtually demanded the inclusion of an English version here. Accepting as a given the fact of the Jewish people's historic link to the Land, Rosenberg provides a typology of that linkage: a paradigmatic model of the conceptual subheadings that comprise it and of the forms in which it may be found. The author surveys biblical and Hellenistic thought; then medieval philosophy (primarily Maimonides—1135–1204—and Halevi—1075–1141); and finally, modern thinkers such as Abraham Isaac Kook (1868–1935) or the lesser known R. Tzadok HaKohen of Lublin (1823–1900); and contemporaries as well —like Nathan Rotenstreich and Eliezer Schweid; thus giving us an essay of incredible magnitude. At the outset, he examines the concept of mother/fatherland, and the symbol of Land as Mother, against the background of Hellenistic institutions and ideas, and the biblical heritage. But he moves rapidly to a comparison of Maimonides and Halevi who represent two polar opposites in their conception of the Land's role. For the former, the Land is "instrumentality, in that the Land exists as a requisite instrument for Jewish self-governance," necessary for the complete observance of the commandments; for the latter, the Land "holds its own intrinsic value." No means to an end, for Halevi, it is an end in itself; not simply, "a mere territory in which a Jewish state happens to exist." Halevi's doctrine is tied to medieval geography, a combination, really, of climatological and astrological notions that go back to the fifth century B.C.E., but are filtered through the prism of Arabic translations and treatises until they emerge in medieval philosophy, particularly (for our purposes) in mystical writings that emphasize the unique consonance of Land, People, and heavenly destiny—an idea that Rosenberg traces as late as the work of Martin Buber. But the concept of the Land of Israel as geographical center is ultimately extended to include also a cosmological vision of the Land as Foundation Stone for Creation; the natural locus also for revelation; and a critical location for the process of redemption as well. These considerations too are surveyed by the author who concludes with a discussion of Jewish philosophy's treatment of *aliyah*, immigration to the Land, that is so central to Judaism's metaphysical concerns.]

   Few subjects in the study of Judaism have merited as much scholarly attention as that of the affinity of the Jewish people for the Land of Israel. Articles on the subject have explored a variety of methods and perspectives: thus, the need to justify the nature of this contribution, written from the viewpoint of the history of Jewish thought. This work seeks primarily to ask: Among the variety of forms of attachment to the Land, can we distinguish a typology that transcends the specificity of concrete systems shaped by the course of history? From the historical perspective, the discussion will focus on Jewish thought of the Middle Ages. The very nature of the subject, however, demands breaching the chronological boundaries of that period, and using texts that are themselves not philosophical according to the accepted definition of the term.

   Preoccupation with the typology of categories of affinity presupposes from the start the existence of such affinity. We shall not enter into this question, nor into problems of legitimatizing it. As necessary and as real as these questions may be, they are almost completely ignored in the pages that follow.

   These, then, are the formal limitations of this work. Its intent, however, will be even better understood, if we add one final note of clarification. We are concerned here not with redemption, but with the Land of Israel. The distinction between the two, which has so often been blurred, is nonetheless at the core of what follows. Distinguishing the anticipation of redemption from the attachment to the Land of Israel is excruciatingly difficult, but it is imperative, if we wish to arrive at an understanding of a flesh-and-blood people's affinity for a land of stone and dust, in days that are not messianic.

   Any typological work of this nature carries with it, from its inception, the danger of oversimplification, with the result that the typology appears remote from the empirical data themselves: a condition brought about by the author's construction of those data and his speculation on them. This author accepts the responsibility of such a risk, in the hope that the critique that is practically assured on that account will enrich the subject and deepen our understanding of one of the most remarkable chapters in the history of Jewish thought.

Motherland and Mother

If asked about their connection to their land, contemporary men and women would doubtlessly respond with some word drawn from their own language that is semantically equivalent to the notion of Fatherland or Motherland. [Ed. note: The author uses the Hebrew term *moledet*, and later, refers explicitly to the imagery of *em*, "mother." Thus, the following translation utilizes "Motherland," despite, for example, the Greek equivalent *patria*, on which he also draws, in his various citations.] Such too would be the response of an Israeli of our time, born in the Land, a child of his or her Motherland. Did such a concept exist in the ancient Jewish sources? The accepted answer is, "No." The search for such a concept in classical Jewish thought is seen as a pursuit after anachronism: so that contemporary usage of a term such as Motherland with respect to the Land of Israel is assumed to be erroneous, uncomprehending, or simply neologistic.

This position is amply summarized by Judah Elitzur in his article on "The Land of Israel in Biblical Thought":

> In the Bible, the word *moledet* cannot be interpreted as "Fatherland" (homeland, *patria*). That is a modern idea, created by 19th-century Europe. We do find *moledet* in the Bible, as in "But progeny [*moladetekha*] born to you after them shall be yours; they shall be recorded instead of their brothers in their inheritance" (Gen. 48:6). Here *moledet* means "offspring, clan, family, patriarchy" not what is signified by the modern Hebrew of our day. That is to say, the simplistic modern definition, the Land of Israel as the Motherland of the Jewish people, does not hold in biblical thought.[1]

The search in classical Jewish thought, then, for the motif of the Motherland would appear to be an illegitimate reading back into the past.

Yet appearances are deceiving here, at least in one respect. Isaac Heinemann has shown that in the Jewish literature of the second-Temple period, under the influence of Hellenistic literature, the concept of citizenship — that is, the link between an individual and his Land — holds a central position.[2] According to II Maccabees, the Hellenizers trespassed against their Motherland. Judah Maccabee, in opposition, roused his soldiers to prepare to die for the Torah, and for the "Fatherland" (*Patris:* 8:21), or "for the Torah, the Temple, the Holy City, the Motherland, and the State" (13:14), in a war against the intruders, for the sake of "their Torah, their Motherland, and their Temple" (13:11). According to Heinemann, this concept is absent from I Maccabees; nonetheless, in this book too, parallel motifs regarding the Land as parental inheritance may undoubtedly be found.[3] The Mother-land motif is also found in Philo. Philo sees a human being as a citizen of the world ("cosmopolitan"), yet also obligated to his Motherland, since only criminals who do not honor God may be characterized as evading their obligations thereto.[4] [Ed note: On Philo see discussion above, by Betsy Halpern Amaru, pp. 65–86.]

One could multiply examples, but from the perspective of "Jewish" thought, the problem of "Jewish legitimization" would remain: is the term "Motherland" not borrowed from the culture of the Greek world, a foreign transplant in the world of Jewish thought?

A student of the history of Jewish thought would have difficulty answering this question, because an answer is possible only by presupposing an a priori definition of the nature of Jewish thought from the outset. However, I think that here, at least, an investigation of the development of Jewish thought would lead us to answer in the negative. Jewish borrowing of the term "Motherland" from Greek culture may constitute a semantic question, but it presents us with no revolutionary conceptual change. This claim may be demonstrated by indicating the parallel concept in various instances of Jewish thought. However, we will have to consider the parallels in terms of the distinction between an abstract concept and a legendary image. By the latter, I mean the perception of the Land of Israel as an actual Mother.[5]

The image of the Land as Mother has a long history. It originates in scripture, mainly with the book of Isaiah, where Zion is identified with the people Israel: ". . . say to Zion, you are my people" (Is. 51:16). Yet elsewhere, the people Israel is identified with the "*daughter* of Zion" (as opposed to the daughter of Edom, Lam. 4:22), so that Zion becomes a mother. At the Destruction, she becomes bereft; at the Redemption, her children will return to her: "You will say in your heart, Who gave birth to these? For I have been bereaved and alone, an exile wandering to and fro—and as for these, who raised them? . . ." (Is. 49:21). "For the children of the desolate one are more than the children of the married woman . . ." (Is. 54:1); "to bring in your children from afar . . ." (Is. 60:9).

The symbol of Mother is found in both Apocrypha[6] and rabbinic writings.[7] Interpolating, the Septuagint translates the verse in Psalms (87:5), "And of Zion, it shall be said, this one and that one were born in her . . ." as, "Zion" has become "Mother Zion." In IV Ezra, Zion is "the Mother of us all." The parallel in Baruch is particularly striking (4:17–29).

There are abundant examples in rabbinic literature too. One of the loveliest is expressed by the Midrash to Deuteronomy 22:7: "'You will surely send away the Mother'—that is, Jerusalem; 'but the children you will take to yourself'—these are Israel" (*Yalkut Makhiri*: Ps. 147). Perhaps the most dramatic expression of the vision of the Land of Israel as Mother is the story of Ulla who went to Babylonia. As he was about to die, he wept, saying, "One who expires at his mother's breast cannot be compared to one who expires at the bosom of a stranger" (P.T. Kel. 9:4). So the legendary image of the Land of Israel as Mother is a symbol of outstanding vitality in midrash (and *piyyut*).

But its ideological significance did not disappear in succeeding generations. At the beginning of the eighteenth century, R. Moshe Chagiz [1672–1751?] championed the Land's standing in a libertarian world where "Everyone says in his own city, 'I am well, for this is my Jerusalem.'"[8] Chagiz spoke of two important loyalties: worship of God and love of the Land of Israel, which are like honoring Father and Mother.[9] Here, another stratum makes its appearance, Kabbalistic thought, where the Land is "supernal Mother, that is, the Land of our birth."[10] [Ed. note: for the Land in Kabbalistic thought, see comments by Moshe Idel, pp. 170–80.]

The parallelism between the mythic image of "Mother" and the concept of "Motherland" did not escape the thinkers who witnessed the rise of new nations and modern patriotism. Isacco Samuel Reggio [1784–1855; director of the Collegio Rabbinico Italiano in Gorizia] expressed this connection cryptically by commenting on Isaiah's words, "Where is your mother's bill of divorce, with which I sent her away?" (Is. 50:1): "Nations are not called 'Mother,'" he explains, "because the nation is always the children. Rather, the mother is the land they are on, or the city where they were born. For just as the foreign speaker says *patria*, so the Hebrew one says, 'Mother' . . ."[11]

Motherland: *Moledet Ha'am*

For Jews dwelling in their Land, seeing that Land as Mother requires no explanation. But how can diaspora Jews do so? They might mean that they are strangers in their actual land of residence, "a people living the lives of sojourners in a land of their sojourning," "outside of their home," in the words of III Maccabees. Such a person is a *xenos*, that is, a stranger under divine providence, to whom is owed decent treatment without affliction or oppression, but not equal rights.

Isaac Heinemann proposes the hypothesis that we consider here also the coming into being of yet another motif, it too being found in Hellenistic literature: the Metropolis.[12] According to him, this concept in Jewish-Hellenistic thought is the missing link in harmonizing the perception by diaspora Jewry of the Land of Israel as its Homeland, and its claim to have rights in the various lands where it has settled. We see an important conceptual alteration here. The concept of the Motherland depicts an established connection between territory and individual, or between territory and a people, with the people viewed, however, as a collection of individuals; in both cases the "one born" in the Motherland is seen as an individual. With the concept of Metropolis, however, the "one born" is not the individual qua individual, but the individual as member of a people, a community.

The idea of a Metropolis is found in Jewish Hellenistic literature and in Philo.[13] Philo claims that the dispersion is a result of the increased numbers of Jews dwelling in the many lands of Europe, Asia, Africa, and the Mediterranean isles. Having dwelled in most of these lands from their founding, Jews see them as "Motherland." But besides their loyalty to the Motherland, they feel loyally bound—through the people of which they are a part—to the Holy City which is their Metropolis.

The concept of the Metropolis has different implications still in the teachings of the Rabbis. In the words of R. Johanan, for example, it designates the relationship between the Land and all the peoples of the world: "In the future, God shall make Jerusalem a metropolis to all the world."[14] Normative Judaism of that period did not absolutely repudiate such a doctrine;[15] but there remains an enormous difference between the Metropolis in the case of Jewish communities, and the Metropolis in the case of other peoples. In common, however, is the notion of a "Mother" who is both "city and Mother," a Mother whose daughters are cities and settlements.

This vision of a link to the Land of Israel mediated by the individual's membership in the community, and that community's link to the Land recurs in modern Jewish thought with various forms and nuances. Doubtless, this demonstrates how fundamental are the distinctions among the different meanings of the concept "Motherland." However, it functions here not so as to provide a rationale of the rights of Jews wherever they may be, but to reinforce their attachment and right to the renewed state in its historical territory.

An acute expression of this distinction has been given by Nathan Rotenstreich, in his definition of the essence of Zionist emancipation:

> It is possible to understand this return to the Land demographically, as a population's return to, or its taking possession of a Land in which

it has not dwelled; and it is possible to understand this from a Zionist vantage point, as a renaissance. . . . We have understood our renaissance as a return to a historical Motherland. That has created the conflict. On this point, it seems to me that Zionist policy took the only stand possible, a compromise, to the effect that the return does not in and of itself negate the right of the population existing there, despite the conceptual difference between the Motherland of a people and the Motherland of settlers . . . [16]

The Motherland of a people implies that the people is "represented by the Land of Israel, even when not actually present in it." And this Motherland need not necessarily conflict with "the existence of people actually living there." The opposing elements are essentially different in character.

This concept has clear legal roots, tied to the distinction between the rights of aliens living on the Land, and their rights as a people. The distinction acquires its full political gravity in Rotenstreich's words. However, it has important implications also for our understanding of the processes taking place among ourselves. Eliezer Schweid[17] has considered the change with respect to the relationship of belles-lettres to the Land, wherein we may distinguish between the writers of the second and third *aliyah*s (waves of immigration) on one hand, and writers born in the Land of Israel on the other. The former retain always a certain sense of distance, of estrangement, of alienation; the latter succeed in neatly expressing those direct impressions of the Landscape, which arouse in them a genuine religiosity of spirit. Belles-lettres literature thus attests to the linkage of successive generations to the Motherland. We ourselves are equal witnesses to the striking phenomenon that precisely that relationship which appeared at the outset as alienated and indirect, ended up in producing a link stronger than the direct and unmediated one. Schweid explains this paradox in terms that parallel the distinction that we made above.[18]

> Linkage to the Motherland is an act of consciousness, proceeding from a prior act of consciousness, an act of national identification. That is, it expresses not a personal connection to the environment in which one has been raised, but a national tie to the Land that constitutes the foundation for the national creation of the people. That connection is founded in historical culture—not the landscape or nature, the flora and fauna, or the archeology. To the degree to which one identifies with one's people, one recognizes in the Land that bears its culture and that is reflected in its creativity—a Motherland . . .

And in a single sentence—"Only as one is a child of the entire Jewish people, is the Land of Israel one's Motherland."

We close this survey of the concept of Motherland with its exemplification in another realm: Halakhah; as expressed in Rabbi Joseph Dov Soloveichik's sermons on repentance:

> The right to possess the Land of Israel is derived from our fathers (B.B. 119a/b). Does that mean that each Jew has an equal share in its ownership? No. The Land does not belong to each and every individual, but to a collective Israel as a singular independent entity. . . . My personal right derives from the fact of my being part and parcel of the Congregation of Israel [*Kenesset Yisra'el*]; since the Land belongs to the Congregation of Israel, it belongs also to me. The Jew's title to the Land is not the possession of the individual, but of the collectivity; it is the holding of the Congregation of Israel, seen as a metaphysical individual. To be sure, each one of us has a right to the Land, but this right comes with, and only with, an unequivocal cleaving to the Congregation of Israel, and a full identification with it.[19]

Thus, halakhic thought retains the legal implications of the Land viewed as a "Motherland of the people," by preserving the link between the Land and the individual as a member of the people; and this situation holds even after a loss of personal connection regarding the governance of property and rights.

Between Two Kinds of Linkage

We come now to the central problem: the linkage to the Land of Israel, in medieval Jewish thought. From those who have studied Jewish thought regarding its portrayal of the link to the Land of Israel, it is evident that the Land is more than a Motherland there. One's tie to a Motherland is an empirical fact, albeit a contingent not a necessary one, that does not derive from the essence of human nature itself; whereas Jewish thought attempts to derive an a priori link to the Land, arising out of the very nature of the system. More than a "Mother-legacy," the Land becomes "the Betrothed," the Promised Land, so that the tie between people and Land is transformed from a chance occurrence into a marriage made in heaven;

in the same sense that in marriage, a given woman X is declared to be betrothed to a given man Y, so with regard to the Land, its field X is said to be allotted to a given owner Y—all this, even before the coming into being of the people. This a priori enactment is presented amidst the contradictory tensions of the various medieval philosophical systems, as we can see from a comparison of Moses Maimonides (1135–1204) and Judah Halevi (before 1075–1141).

The place of the Land of Israel in Maimonides' system is connected to the doctrine of the End of Days; at its core is the renewal of the messianic kingdom of the Davidic dynasty. For Maimonides, messianic liberation will make possible the renewal of prophecy, the apex of personal fulfilment, as he tells us in the *Guide* (2:36):

> [Melancholy] is without doubt the direct cause of the cessation of prophecy in the time of the Exile. For there can be nothing worse than to be a purchased slave, indentured to wanton fools, and powerless to oppose them, as they combine in themselves the absence of true wisdom and the reinforcement of bestial appetites. This evil state was foreseen for us, in the words, "They will wander to and fro to seek the word of God, but will not find it" (Amos 8:12); and, "Her king and princes are among the nations and have no instruction; nor have her prophets found the Lord's vision" (Lam. 2:9). This is a real truth, occasioned by the fact that prophecy's prerequisites have been lost. But in the messianic period—may it soon begin—prophecy will again be in our midst, as God has promised.

Thus, the renewal of prophecy is conditional upon the establishment of a free Jewish state, living in accordance with God's law; and the Land of Israel is only the territory of that state. The cessation of prophecy is not a function of the departure from a particular territory, but of life without the appropriate political structure.

Even before Maimonides, the Rabbis had themselves already considered the necessary connection between the Land and prophecy; for example: "It would have been proper for the Divine Presence to rest upon our Master, but his being in Babylonia [that is, outside the Land] prevented it."[20] Our citation from the *Guide* certainly constitutes a sort of exegetical twist to this rabbinic judgment, in that it places emphasis not on the negative geographical properties of the diaspora but on the existential state of diaspora life itself. Clearly perceiving this exegetical deviation, Isaac Abravanel

(1437–1508) juxtaposed against it the words of Halevi, an obvious criticism of Maimonides' doctrine of prophecy:

> We have also seen that after the Exile, prophecy did not dwell among the nation, which is not to say that this was because of the Exile and its woes, for at certain times, under the righteous kings, there was gladness and rejoicing, when every person could enter his home in peace. Rather, the matter was like what the Chaver wrote to the Kuzari king (2:12) that the prophets all prophesied in the Land of Israel, or for her sake, in accordance with scripture's statement, "Her king and princes are among the nations and have no instruction; nor have her prophets found the Lord's vision" (Lam. 2:9). That is to say, even those prophets who were in a state of preparedness received no vision, because such was God's will. . . .[21]

Halevi's formulation in the Kuzari, "All who prophesied did so only in the Land of Israel or for her sake," (2:12) explicitly links prophecy to the Land. Thus, it becomes possible to juxtapose two perspectives: the first (Maimonides) sees the territory as having instrumental value, in that the Land exists as the requisite instrument for Jewish self-governance; the second (Halevi) views it as having its own intrinsic merit. The distinction is necessary, I believe, if we are to take into consideration (within the framework of an Aristotelian world view) the difficulties implicit in explaining the uniqueness of a specific territory, a subject to which we shall shortly return. One might hypothesize that Maimonides' position here approaches his treatment of the problem of the reasons behind the commandments, with regard to which he holds that one may fully search out the rationale for commandments in general, but not for their details.

We can clarify the conceptual distinction by observing the difference in illustrative motifs employed by Maimonides and Halevi, in their respective interpretations of a specific biblical verse that has always denoted the Jewish people's link to the Land, I Samuel 26:19. It is cited frequently to prove the Land's unique quality. "For they have driven me out this day, that I shall have no share in the heritage of the Lord, saying, 'Go, worship other gods.'" In this verse, Halevi finds support for his view of the Land of Israel as elite among all lands. By contrast, in his *Epistle on Apostasy*, Maimonides writes:

> God has already explained by way of the prophets that all who dwell among non-believers [i.e., outside the Land] become like them, for

so said King David, may he rest in peace, "For they have driven me out this day that I should have no share in the heritage of the Lord, saying, 'Go, worship other gods.'" He considered his sojourn among the nations as if he were worshipping other gods.[22]

This verse is adduced in Maimonides' *Epistle* as additional evidence for the ruling that one must try to save oneself from an evil place in which one cannot properly maintain one's religion, by traveling until one reaches a better place, even if, by so doing, one would endanger one's existence. "The heritage of the Lord" is understood here not in terms of relationship to a territory, but to any society anywhere that is supportive of the fulfillment of religious commandments. To substantiate his interpretation, Maimonides was able to depend on the words of the Targum, to the effect that it is preferable "to dwell among the inheritance of the people of the Lord, than to say that David went among peoples worshipping idols."

As we said, this conclusion is necessitated by Maimonides' Aristotelianism, though, to be sure, one should not conclude that it constitutes his entire stand on the subject. The tensions in his system can be seen from the fact that in his code (*Hilkhot Melakhim* 4:12) he adduces the verse, "For they have driven me out this day . . . ," just as it is found in the Talmud (Ket. 10b) in order to support the ruling that "One should always live in the Land of Israel, even in a city whose majority is not Jewish, rather than outside the Land in a city where the majority is Jewish."[23] There can be no doubt that it is Maimonides' faithfulness to his Talmudic sources that preserved in his own teachings even those motifs that are not directly derivative from his philosophical doctrine. The Talmudic source constitutes a sort of outer limit to all possible reinterpretation.

Philosophically, on the other hand, this faithfulness is expressed by the acceptance of an additional domain for the application of Aristotelian rationalism. Thus, it is possible to take Maimonides' philosophical explanation of a central problem: the nature of God's selection of the people Israel; and to relate it to the Land. "If we believe in creation," he says, "then every other question falls by the wayside . . . as, for example, why God set His Torah within one specific people, and not with another" (*Guide* 2:25).

By way of contrast, in order to understand in full Halevi's position, I want to cite from Chasdai ibn Shaprut's letter to Joseph, King of the Kuzars.

The One who examines the heart and comprehends the inner self knows that it was not for my own aggrandizement that I did all of this, but in order to find out the truth: whether there is still a sovereign lamp lighting the way for Israel's exile to a place where they are not subjected to tyrannical subjugation. If I knew that it were so, I would contemn my glory, abandon my station, leave my family behind, and trek over hill and dale, land and sea, until I reached the place where my lord the King was stationed, that I might behold his greatness, the glory of his excellence, the dwelling of his subjects and the standing of his servants, and the tranquility of the remnant of Israel. My eyes would light up, and my inner organs delight; my lips would formulate praise to God, whose favor has not left his humble ones.

Whatever the historical facts concerning Chasdai's letter, we have here evidence of the fundamental values embodied within a Jewish state: "the tranquility of the remnant of Israel," "a sovereign lamp," and, above all, honor and freedom where "they are not subjected to tyrannical subjugation."

In the light of this dream, the significance of the *Kuzari*'s conclusion stands out seventy fold. With the conversion of the Kuzar king, Chasdai's dream becomes real for the Chaver. As Halevi organizes the story, the dialogue between the king and the philosopher appears at the book's beginning. The deprecatory treatment of the Exile, which permeates Christian and Islamic theology, loses its sting in this literary framework. Thus, Halevi creates a surprise in having the Chaver decide that "He has agreed to abandon the Kuzar's land for Jerusalem" (5:22). Despite the risk of drawing conclusions from a literary context, we certainly have here an explicit expression of one kind of affinity for the Land of Israel, which differs from the affinity for a mere territory, like the land of the Kuzars, in which a Jewish state just happens to exist.

Mystical Geography

In Halevi's thought, the connection between the people and the Land is a synthesis of naturalistic concepts and historical categories. As we have already remarked, this connection must be analyzed from the particular vantage point of medieval philosophy and science, which are formulated in general rules, and do not, therefore, recognize a personal or individual side to reality. Hence, it is possible to explain the phenomenon of humanity in general, but difficult to understand its differentiation into particular peoples, languages, and creeds. Movement from the general laws of nature to the facts of historical particularity was facilitated by the development of the laws of climatology, whose source lay in the Hippocratic tradition.

We first hear of the relationship between climate and the characteristics of a people dwelling in it in a 5th-century B.C.E. composition belonging to the Hippocratic school of medicine.[24] This composition, with its beginning of climatology, influenced the development of philosophy in the classical and medieval periods.[25] Later, climatological and astrological interpretations were conflated, and from these, other, more "rationalistic" theories followed, in attempts to posit an astronomical context for the phenomenon of differentiated peoples and languages, and thus to derive historical laws from natural ones.

An interesting illustration of such a derivation is the explanation of language. In the dispute between those who saw language as a natural property and those who saw it as a human convention, many philosophers strove to establish a mediate position, according to which various astronomical conditions were responsible for the differences among peoples and tongues. Thus, Abu Nasr Al-Farabi (c. 870–950) explained, "The first natural cause for the existence of different nations is this: there are differences in the celestial elements above their heads. . . ."[26]

It now became possible to postulate a congruence between peoples and lands, and hence, within the framework of medieval philosophy, to explain the special standing of the Land of Israel, as well as the Jewish people's affinity for it. It is within this ideational framework that Halevi's geographical-climatological doctrine should be seen.

> The Kuzar said, "I haven't heard that the inhabitants of the Land of Israel have an advantage over people in the world at large." The Chaver replied, "But the same is true of the rugged mountain ridge that you say makes the vineyard flourish . . . (2:12). However, if they did not plant the vines within it and perform the appropriate labor for them, they would not produce grapes."[27]

This approach influenced the Aristotelian school, so that Maimonides too explicitly taught that certain geographic areas are better than others. However, this is so for the area known in medieval geography as the Fourth Climate, a general area that included the Land of Israel, but other lands as well.[28] Gersonides' (1288–1344) system, by contrast, accepted the geographical hermeneutic in such a way as to explain "why God selected this particular Land of Israel, and that is because of its exceptional readiness to receive divine emanation" (*Commentary to Gen.* 12:1). Apparently through the influence of Gersonides, Chasdai Crescas (?–1412?) too accepted this conceptualization, speaking of "the advantage of providence in one place over another," as a function of "natural differences among places regarding the necessary readiness for the worship of God."[29]

A new chapter in mystical geography opens up in the thought of Maharal of Prague [Judah Loew ben Bezalel, 1525–1609]. The transition from the world of nature to the world of history was accomplished simply by expanding the Aristotelian law of natural sites: not just the elements of nature, but people too have natural locales, and the natural place of the Jewish people is the Land of Israel. Thus, the law of natural sites generates a model applicable to historical reality too, from which Maharal derives the political moral that it is unnatural for one nation to be subjugated to another. Correlatively, all such subjugation—Jewish Exile included, since it is not natural—must some day be annulled, so that those who are exiled will one day return to their proper locale.

An important additional innovation in geographical theory developed from its contact with Kabbalah. The classic illustration, in my opinion, is found in *Chesed Le'avraham* by Rabbi Abraham Azulai [c. 1570–1643].[30] According to Azulai, the status of the Land was determined in the wake of cosmic events. Following Adam's sin and the triumph of the "external impurities" (the *chitsonim*), the Divine Presence (the *Shechinah*), departed the blemished world, but:

> There arose the merit of former generations (*harishonim*), and the mercies of the Holy One, and the merit of the sainted Fathers, and an opening was created so that all the shells [of evil] (*kelippot*) were smashed, and a breach was opened so that the holiness might bypass the impurities (*chitsonim*) and illuminate Israel, and come to rest upon them without any of the garb of the *chitsonim* or a separating veil made by these *chitsonim*.[31]

The entire earth is here seen as enveloped by *kelippot*, shells of evil, or impurity, chaos and void (*tohu vavohu*). In one place only is there a breach, a portal of holiness connecting heaven and earth, and this gateway is the Land of Israel, which is positioned beneath the heavenly window. Should this window which opens up onto the portal of holiness close, the world itself would be lost. It actually did close once, during the Destruction of the Temple in 70, but only momentarily, and "immediately after the Temple was destroyed, the Holy One opened the window . . . and diminished the realm of the Ophanim within the window so that it might not close again. This portal is never closed . . ." because when the window reopened, it stayed that way forever, even now, during the post-70 epoch following the Temple's destruction. Thus, the path to unity and reparation (*tikkun*) of the universe leads through the Land of Israel.

The mystical significance of the Land of Israel in *Chesed Le'avraham* is not restricted to its difference from other lands. It is possible to sketch a mystical map of the Land and other regions. "Each portion of the earth's lands was given to a nation with which it is connected," so that there is a three-way tie binding a land, a people, and an "angel responsible for that people's powers of soul and of cognition." This is true, for example, of Ar, which God gave to the descendants of Lot; and of Seir, given to Edom, "because he [Edom] is ruddy [in Hebrew, *edom*], so his land is called Edom [= ruddy]. Each people thus has its own guardian angel, except the People Israel which is bound directly to God alone and to God's law, and thus there follows its attachment to the Land of Israel. Even its internal division into tribes is conditioned essentially "by the secret of each tribe's soul, in that the harmonious composition of their souls corresponds to the coherent interrelationship of the Land's divisions."

The conclusion that Azulai derives from this analysis is particularly interesting: "Just as the Divine Presence is not whole as long as the Temple is not intact on its foundation, so too it will not be whole as long as the Land of Israel does not extend to the fullness of its borders."[32]

In Jewish thought, therefore, a type of mystical geography was continuously being elaborated with the principle goal of explaining the uniqueness of the Land of Israel. At the root of this mystical geography was the search for the meaning behind the Land's sacrality, the particular trait "allotted to this people and this Land, in that God has chosen them both," as Martin Buber puts it.[33] At its heart is the recognition that the purposes of history can be actualized only in the conjunction between people and land: land—not a dead and inert object, but a living and active mate. Mystical geography is nothing other than a natural attempt to throw light on this primal intuition.

Creation and Revelation

Certainly the simplest expression by far of this mystical geography is the claim that the Land of Israel is the center of the world.[34] However, the doctrine of the Center was linked to a parallel doctrine of Creation. Hence the Center of the World went from being a geographical concept to a cosmological one: the Foundation Stone (*Even Shetiyah*) of the universe.[35]

This centrality of the Land took a further turn in the writing of Nachmanides [1194–1270].

> When God created heaven and earth, He subjected the lower world to the higher, and put each people, according to their lands and their nations, under a planet and a star, as we know from the science of astrology. That is what is meant by the verse, "The Lord your God apportioned them to all the peoples" (Deut. 4:19): to everyone, He apportioned planets in the heavens, and put supreme angels above them to rule over them. . . . But the honored God is the God of gods and Lord of lords for all the world. The Land of Israel is the center of the inhabited earth and God's own inheritance, so over it he put no angels, nor officers, rulers or sovereigns.[36]

The connection between peoples and lands is expressed here as a sort of relativity of providence. The essence of various peoples is said to follow from the influence of their respective angel and planet, whence there can emerge but a partial perspective on reality. But as the center of habitation,[37] the Land of Israel transcends planetary rule. So the essence of its designated people is not incomplete. Its law is not merely an emanation of a specific planet, but the revelation of God Himself. To resort to anachronism, we have before us a type of medieval anticipation of Nachman Krochmal's [1785–1840] law of the absolute connected here not with Israel the people, but with Israel the Land.

The Land of Israel, then, receives divine providence with no mediating "officer, ruler, or sovereign"; however, it is also the Land of revelation. Here, Halevi's doctrine in the *Kuzari*, regarding the revelation of the Divine Presence (the *Shekhinah*) or of the Divine Influence (the *Inyan Elohi*) finds expression.

The Divine Presence is to be found among the people when it is on its own Land (*Kuzari* 1:109); outside the Land, the Presence may still be found, along with angels, but solely among the pious and only *in potentia;* whereas in the Land of Israel, they combine their forces *in actu* (3:11). Thus, Abraham, for example, "was uprooted from his [native] land, and only then was he fit to be joined with the Divine Influence" (2:14). "The Divine Influence is connected to him and to all his everlasting posterity to govern their thought and conduct, not simply in terms of physical contact" (4:3). It is this spiritual connection to which we give the name "revelation."

Thus far, we have seen familiar themes expressed in a system's normative concepts and terminology. However, an important innovation now deserves attention: the distinction between the visible Presence (*Shekhinah*) and the hidden one (5:23).[38]

Rabbinic literature presents three different motifs on this topic:[39]

1. *The Divine Presence accompanying Israel into Exile.* Regarding the verse, "Who is like Thy people Israel, a singular nation in the earth whom God went to redeem unto Himself for a people, and to make Him a name, and to do for Thy land great and wondrous things, even for you, in [driving out] from before Thy people, whom Thou didst redeem to Thee out of Egypt, the nations and their gods?" (2 Sam. 7:23), Rabbi Akiba says, "Were it not written in Scripture, this would be impossible to say! Israel remarked (as it were) to God, 'You redeemed Yourself.' And so, you find that wherever Israel wandered, the Divine Presence wandered with them . . . and in the future, when they return, the Divine Presence (as it were) will return with them."

2. *The withdrawal of the Divine Presence.* Other statements speak of the departure of the Divine Presence, the classic example being the description of its withdrawal during the destruction of the Temple.

3. *The Divine Presence remaining in the Temple's ruins alone.* This third direction is found in rabbinic legend as expressed in the words of R. Elazar b. Pedat: "Destruction or no Destruction, the Divine Presence has not budged from its place."

In Halevi's teaching these three motifs appear together as one. Preparation for revelation is to be found among select individuals who form "a dwelling place for the Presence wherever they happen to be (#1). In the Land of Israel, however, it is as if the Divine Presence and the Divine Influence watch for a person who merits their attachment, to be as God to such a person, as in the case of the prophets and the pious; it is like the faculty of reason that "watches for a person whose natural endowment has been perfected, whose soul and character are in harmony, such that in all its perfection, it falls upon such a one, as is the case with philosophers" (2:14). So even though the Divine Presence is not presently visible in the Land of Israel (#2), it remains concealed there (#3), awaiting the opportunity to be revealed to the appropriate person. The Presence has thus departed (#2) but has not moved from its place (#3). This doctrine concerning the hidden Presence that has not left its place but awaits those who merit its attachment, implies that the attachment to the Land of Israel was not broken even when the Land was destroyed. With the return of Israel to its Land, "The Divine Presence too (as it were) will gather there," as Martin Buber puts it. Immigration to the Land means a return to the designated site of revelation.[40]

Nachmanides' attachment to the Land is closely allied to Halevi's here, but is given a halakhic turn. The Land's settlement constitutes a "positive commandment to the generations" obligating each and every Jew, "even in the time of the dispersion." Relevant here is another discussion drawn from the *Sifre* to *Parashat Ekev* (#43): "[God says], 'Even though I banish you outside the Land, you should retain your distinctiveness by keeping the commandments, so that when you return, they will not be new to you.' This implies that the fulfillment of the commandments outside of the Land merely foreshadows their true fulfillment when redemption dawns."[41]

Nachmanides' ideas on the commandment to inhabit the Land created a tradition in thought and in Halakhah, represented prominently, for example, by R. Solomon ben Simeon Duran [1400–1467]. His father, R. Simeon ben Zemach Duran [1361–1444] maintained that inhabiting the Land made possible the fulfillment of the commandments dependent on the Land; by contrast, his son understood the settlement of the Land as an independent commandment in its own right. However, we have here more than a passive assimilation of the ideas of Nachmanides. Duran developed Nachmanides' views, systematizing their existing motifs in such a way that the influence of philosophic discipline is patently perceptible. In the complex of concepts found in the sources, Duran distinguishes three: habitation [*yeshivah*], immigration [*aliyah*], and settlement [*yishuv*]. In order to explain the structure of this triad, he uses philosophical distinctions derived from the analysis of causality. Philosophers distinguish two causes, the efficient (or prior) cause and the formal (or immediate) cause. The efficient cause activates something, while the formal cause sustains it once it already exists. It is possible to apply these categories to inhabiting the Land of Israel, so that the commandment itself is "habitation"; the prior, or efficient, cause is "immigration"; and the sustaining, or formal, cause is "settlement":

> The commandment itself is "habitation," that is, residence, and the efficient cause is "immigration," for without immigration, no one would even enter the Land. "Settlement" implies such matters as planting gardens and orchards, and acquiring homes, for wherever there is food and shelter, there you find habitation. It is possible, however, to have

gardens and orchards, the cause of settlement, without actually dwelling there. Thus settlement is not the same as habitation. It thus appears, from the application of philosophical introspection,[42] that inhabiting and settling are not the same thing. Thus I say that settling and immigration are both causes of the commandment, one bringing it about, and the other sustaining it, but that the commandment itself is habitation alone.[43]

Redemption

Above, we considered two possible schematic affinities: one instrumental, and the other seeing in the Land intrinsic value in and of itself. Both of these affinities lead to a post-redemption Jerusalem, a Jerusalem of the future. There is no denying the holy status of Jerusalem as it was when it was built up. But the question arises as to what one's relationship shall be to Jerusalem of the post-Destruction era, to Jerusalem destroyed and contemned, swallowed by legions. A purely instrumental attachment leads inevitably to a territorialist conclusion, that, in fact, is absent from classical Jewish thought, because of the authority of Halakhah. However it is certainly evident in Karaite thought; as H. H. ben Sassoon demonstrated in his study of early Karaites, Anan ben David believed that the Land is not the Land of God unless it is held by Israel the people. If it is not so held, its sanctity escapes and is gone.[44] The Land remains, however, the site of the ideal society of the future.

But it is conceivable that in any specific historical situation, the society most closely approximating the ideal may exist precisely outside its borders.[45] If the Land of Israel has instrumental value only, the attraction of a flourishing and creative center elsewhere would be detrimental to the actual Land's appeal. In the writings of Pirkoi ben Baboi [8th century, Babylonia], for example, we find — alongside an unabated trust in redemption — a legitimization of the diaspora, for surely settlements in diaspora communities are also Zion, in that, speaking instrumentally, they too are "gates distinguished by Halakhah."[46] Babylonia, where the Halakhah resides, thus looms as an alternative, through the merits of whose settlements, "the messiah and redemption will come to Babylonia first." Similarly, in later ages, the people, the community, is transformed into a "Jerusalem of Lithuania," a "Jerusalem of the north," and all those other "Jerusalems of . . ." which have accompanied us throughout the generations, and which arose in opposition to their mother, the unredeemed Jerusalem "of dust and stone."

Parallel to this communal approach to redemption, however, there is another system that emphasizes the individual, for by Maimonides' time, we witness the appearance of a different tradition, which believed that the possibility of perfecting society lay only in the ability of the solitary individual to guide his own soul to true *eudaemonia*. Does this path to personal redemption also pass through the Land of Israel? Solomon Duran's response to R. Haggai ben Alzuk preserves the record of this dispute:

> I have seen all that you wrote with regard to immigration to the Land of Israel, and you have written much. Implicit in your words is the notion that perfection of the soul comes about through apprehension of ideas alone, to which immigration to the Land neither adds nor detracts.[47]

By way of refutation, Duran objects that R. Haggai's position is overly intellectualized; it is built on the delusion that it is possible to attain perfection and *eudaemonia* through the intellect alone, whereas, in truth, only the commandments bring us to perfection. Hence—the importance of the Land, which is itself commanded, and which is the locus for the performance of other commandments too.[48]

The confrontation of perspectives could be elucidated through a host of illustrations. We considered above the verse, "For they have driven me out this day that I shall have no share in the heritage of the Lord, saying, 'Go worship other Gods'" (I Sam. 26:19). A survey of commentaries to this verse reveals that their authors differed sharply on the question of whether the principle it expresses is relevant to the situation after 70 (the era of Destruction) or not. (For example, a comparison of Rashi [1040–1105] and of Isaiah ben Abraham Halevi Horowitz [1565?–1630] regarding the Land's sanctity during its Destruction epoch would emphasize this difference in approach.) [Ed. note: On Rashi, and the Land in the thought of medieval commentators, see remarks by Michael Signer above, pp. 000–000.]

Different attitudes underlie different halakhic positions also. The author of *Megillat Esther* [Isaac ben Eliezer de Leon, who wrote this commentary to Maimonides' *Sefer Hamitsvot* in 1592] defends Maimonides' system, explaining, "The commandment [to settle the Land] applies precisely when we are not subjugated to other nations [i.e., either before the era of Destruction that commenced in 70, or in the future era of messianic

Redemption]." Numerous halakhic discussions elaborate this motif,[49] saying, for example, that the demise of Jewish sovereignty imposes limitations on the degree of applicability of those commandments that are dependent on the Land. Thus, *Pri Megadim* to *Orach Chayim* (#575) explains that we no longer blow the trumpets on public fast days, even in the Land of Israel, "because it [the Land] is not in our hands." R. Zadok Hakohen of Lublin [1823– 1900] applied this principle even to the commandment to settle the Land:

> The commandment to settle the Land seems to me to be fundamentally applicable along the lines laid down by *Megillat Esther* to *Sefer Hamitsvot*: that is, it comes from the time when the Temple still stood. . . . It cannot even be called "settlement" [*yishuv*] unless they dwell in tranquility, that is, they [the Jews] are masters of the Land . . . just as dwelling in the Land in tranquility under one's own government is called "settlement" in the time when the Temple stood, but when the Temple was destroyed, and not everyone was exiled, even those who still lived within the Land were not called its inhabitants, and did not constitute "settlement" in it, because they were subject to the gentile kings who ruled there, just as I am, outside the Land. We do not refer to those outside the Land as constituting "settlement," but only as sojourning in general; this does not fulfil the commandment of "You shall settle. . . ." (*Divrei Sofrim*, 14)

There is, therefore, only "sojourning," not "settlement," in post-70 Jerusalem. A sense of the commandment to resettle, despite the necessary limitation of "sojourning" is expressed in Judah Halevi's famous poem, "Your words traverse the distances." He goes to a destroyed Land, feeling that:

> If wild beasts and owls are her present dwellers,
> Was she not given to the patriarchs?
> Now it is an inheritance of thorns and brambles,
> And they traverse its length and breadth
> As if they wandered among the plants of a garden,
> But they are strangers and sojourners—seeking
> A place to be buried, and the lodging of guests.[50]

Under consideration here is the Jew's attachment to an actual destroyed Land, not just a utopia of the future. Contrary to the previous view, which emphasizes the obligatory nature of this attachment, is Rav Abraham Isaac Kook's [1868–1935] introduction to *Shabbat Ha'arets*, where he relies on the verse from Psalms which treats of the Israel "of dust and stones" prior to the final redemption, a time, that is, when the Land is still ruled by non-Jews:

> [The psalmist] informs us that even prior to the completed conquest . . . it is still accounted the Land of the gentiles, so that not all the commandments could have been fully performed in it. But even then, the Torah commands its settlement, and the sacred obligation to settle the Land is in no way diminished.

Among the different possibilities of relationship to the concrete unredeemed Jerusalem, the distinction alluded to by Martin Buber deserves mention. In one section, Buber describes the character of R. Zeira who realized in his own life the commandment to immigrate to the Land [*aliyah*].

> This was the fruition of his fundamental desire to dwell in the Land and among the people, to do God's will from the vantage point of a people, and that alone. Not to quibble over the Redemption, not to meditate on it, or to hasten the end, but solely to live in the Land *as the people* of God. The Messiah will come when we have stopped thinking about it. [Italics added; see below.][51]

Buber describes here the attachment of a Jew to the Land of Israel even when it is not predicated on the basis of a messianic expectation or promise. This is a bond to a real Land of Israel, characterized solely by the anticipation to live in it.

However, Buber's description contains a gloss on the sources, which testifies to the great distance between two polar opposites implied by his phrase, 'as the people': that is to say as a national community and not merely as individuals.[52]

Here we return to the important distinction that we saw when analyzing the concept of "Motherland"—this time, in the treatment of more traditional categories of immigration to the Land that we looked at above: "inhabiting" [*yeshivah*] and "settling" [*yishuv*]. Are we confronted with a group attachment, or an individual one?[53] Time and again, for example, the significance of Nachmanides' formulation of the commandment has been understood as obligating the individual and not the group.

If this description is accurate, we are confronted with a dialectical process which brings each of these types of affinity—the individual and the group—to its own particular ideological pitfall which redefines its limits. We again illustrate the facts from the responsa of Simeon Duran. We saw

above that for him, the habitation [*yeshivah*] of the Land is a commandment; but, he adds, "This commandment does not include all [the People]
Israel; it is denied to the general collectivity, as the sages maintained: It is
subsumed under the category of those oaths with which God charged Israel, 'that they may not hasten the end of days nor go up to the Land of
Israel [all together] like a wall'" [Ket. 112a].[54] The collectivity's bond with
the Land of Israel endures in theory, but it is withheld in practice on account of the oaths administered by them that they "neither hasten the end
of days nor go up to the Land [all together] like a wall."

With the development of the idea that immigration to and habitation
of the Land are necessary prerequisites of redemption, a new motif was added
to the Jewish affinity for the Land. Pervasive throughout Jewish tradition
is the theme that redemption is linked not merely to the fulfillment of the
commandments, but first and foremost, to the command to inhabit the Land,
a commandment realized through immigration, which thus takes on unique
redemptive significance. This new emphasis too is linked to the thought
of Halevi. At the close of *Sefer Hakuzari*, Halevi deals with the custom
of the sages to kiss the Land's very dust and stones. Their support for this
custom came from a verse in Psalms that had doubtlessly been cited hundreds, if not thousands, of times in another context. But Halevi reads it
anew, by including the preceding verse along with it, and thereby suggesting
a new message.

> You shall arise and have pity on Zion; it is the time to favor her; the
> appointed time has come. For Thy servants hold her stones dear, and
> love her dust. (Ps. 102:14–15)

The words of the Chaver are clear: "That is to say, Jerusalem will surely
be rebuilt, but only when the children of Israel yearn for her so much that
they love her stones and her dust . . ." (5:27).

Halevi's basic intuition of immigration as the means of bringing redemption later permeates the thinking of the Safed period, as well as that
of the nineteenth-century heralds of Zionism,[55] where, however, the influence of Maimonides, as well as that of Halevi can be detected. Maimonides'
influence is expressed first, by the emphasis on the affinity to the Land as,
above all, a collective enterprise; and second, by his predilection for giving a naturalistic interpretation to the processes of redemption. (A striking
expression of this predilection was his stand on the possibility of the renewal of rabbinic ordination.) Both of these directions attain their full import among the nineteenth-century Zionist visionaries.

Jerusalem and her Daughters

Jerusalem has been both city and mother. But her daughters, of whom I now treat, are not found on any conventional map, and certainly not on the maps of Judah and Benjamin's inheritance. Some of those daughters have been mentioned above: the important Jewish communities which became centers, the "Jerusalems of . . . ," that is, Jerusalem's rivals. Occasionally, one of these daughters is transformed into a rival, in the name of Jewish life; occasionally, it is for the sake of freedom in a new world: "For in his own city, everyone will say, 'I shall be well, for this is Jerusalem for me. I am tranquil and at ease, unrestrained by the law and propriety. Why should I care now about Jerusalem's troubles?'"[56]

But there is another daughter, even though Rashi labels her a "companion," rather than a daughter. It is the heavenly Jerusalem.[57] Contrary to accepted opinion, the notion of a heavenly Jerusalem is not to be found ubiquitously in rabbinic literature. Statements concerning the "heavenly temple" are pervasive and early, but a heavenly "Jerusalem" is mentioned only once in the entire Talmud.[58] Rabbi Johanan said, "The Holy One Blessed be He has said, 'I shall not arrive at the heavenly Jerusalem until I come to the earthly one'" (Ta'an. 5a). The heavenly and earthly Jerusalems are rivals here, with the earthly Jerusalem taking precedence. Victor Aptowitzer (1871–1942) theorized that this was an anti-Christian diatribe, but Professor Urbach has demonstrated that the polemic is directed against the post-Destruction apocalypts who stressed the *opposition* between the heavenly and the earthly Jerusalems. By this statement, R. Johanan intended to deny such a conceivable opposition, and thus, to prevent our seeking refuge in a celestial Jerusalem.

In a later age, this rivalry returns in a different garb, this time, Christian. Despite its "Zionist" phase during the Crusades, Christianity generally showed little concern for the Jerusalem of flesh and blood, and the Zion of dust and stone. But this was true of various developing trends in Jewish thought also. Jerusalem became a cosmic, spiritual reality, and this spiritualization made Jerusalem distant and sterile.[59] [Ed. note: see below, pp. 180, 201–03 on the Land of Israel in Hasidic thought, for example, by Moshe Idel and Marc Saperstein.]

R. Johanan mentions yet another of Jerusalem's daughters: "Jerusalem of the world to come is not like the Jerusalem of this world . . ." (B.B. 75b). Rivalry with the heavenly Jerusalem is not just a cosmological construct; it implies also a historical, eschatological rivalry.[60] This is the Jerusalem

of the future, the Jerusalem of "next year," Jerusalem rebuilt, of the dreams
and visions and legendary descriptions. Yet between us and the Jerusalem of the future yawns an immeasurable historical chasm, which may be
breached, perhaps, only by a path that contravenes the oath not to "go up
[together] like a wall." This vision of the future Jerusalem may well be sufficient to create within us a sense of exile; but it will not suffice in the creation of an attachment to the Jerusalem of today, the Jerusalem of dust and
stone. The classic illustration of this impotence, it seems to me, is found
in the thought of Maharal [Judah Loew ben Bezalel of Prague, 1525–1609].

We hear here the words of the rich Italian who says to David Reubeni
[d. 1538?]: "I have no interest in Jerusalem, neither concern nor desire anywhere but in Sienna."[61] He negates Jerusalem without even recognizing the
fact of his own exile. But even those who recognize Jerusalem face the danger of reinterpretation, in which Jerusalem's daughters become her rivals.

The investigation of the attachment to the Land of Israel in Jewish
thought encounters two difficulties: on one hand, it must distinguish among
the various modes of attachment and their objects—hence the specific importance of an attachment to a Jerusalem which is neither celestial nor eschatological, the Jerusalem of dust and stone. On the other hand, it must
take cognizance of the thematic dialectic intrinsic to this affinity. Thus, for
instance, it has always been stressed that inhabiting the Land of Israel is
tantamount to being a guest at the table of the Almighty. But Nachmanides
demonstrated the astounding responsibility that such a role entails:

> Those who merit sitting before the Holy One Blessed be He in His
> own Land, those who are to behold the King's face, do well to be
> zealous of His honor, for should they rebel against Him, their woe
> would be greater than any creature that wages war and angers the
> King in His palace.[62]

Summing up this dialectic in one concise statement, Nachmanides remarks, "The fact of Israel's intimacy to the Holy One Blessed be He is itself
a cause of estrangement."

We have attempted here to consider yet an additional dialectic that
complicates the affinity for the Land of Israel: the Land as means, and the
Land as end. It is the divergent paths typical of these two modes of attachment that Rav Kook addresses in his classic essay on the Land of Israel:

> Love for our holy Land is the foundation of the Torah . . . but love
> of the Land differs according to different people's levels of conscious-

ness—for there are those who love our holy Land for her precious qualities . . . while others love it because they recognize in it the essence of physical respite for the community of Israel. But the Land is not a superficial thing . . . not merely the means to an end, to her collective unification, or the strengthening of either her material or spiritual existence. . . .[63]

Thus, beyond all rational interpretations, the mysticism of the Land of Israel too is found in Jewish thought, but it is a mysticism in which the Land is not merely a symbol of something else, but an end unto itself.[64]

Notes

My thanks are extended to the late Prof. Ch. H. Ben-Sasson, Prof. A. Schweid, and to Prof. Y. Elitsur for their important comments. I also wish to thank Rabbi Ze'ev Gothold and Dr. Moses Chalamish for drawing my attention to various sources and for the assistance provided by their insightful comments.

1. Y. Elitsur, "Erets-Yisrael Bemachshevet Hamikra," *Erets Nachalah.* Judah Shabiv, ed. (Jerusalem, 1975), pp. 21–28.

2. Y. Heinemann, "The Relationship between a People and Its Land in Jewish Hellenistic Literature (Hebrew)" *Zion* 13–14 (1948–49), pp. 1–9.

3. I Maccabees 15:33.

4. Philo, *The Life of Moses* II, 98. See additional sources in Heinemann, *A People and Its Land,* p. 4, n. 20.

5. Regarding this symbol, see the article of B. Ts. Dinur, "The Image of Zion and Jerusalem in the Historical Consciousness of Israel" (Hebrew), *Zion* 15 (1951), pp. 1–17.

6. For a putative connection between the image of Zion as mother and the story of Hannah, see G. W. E. Nickelsburg, *Resurrection, Immortality and Eternal Life in Intertestamental Judaism* (Harvard, 1972), pp. 106–109.

7. Compare Nachmanides' remarks in his Rosh Hashanah sermon, *Kitvei Haramban,* C. B. Chavel, ed. (Jerusalem, 1963), I, p. 251.

8. Compare the words of Jacob Frank: "This is the land promised to our ancestors. If they were to offer all of the lands filled with precious stones, I would not leave Poland, for it is the inheritance of God and the inheritance of our mothers." See note 44 below.

9. Rabbi Moshe Chagiz, *Sefat Emet* (Vilna, 1876: Jerusalem, 1968), p. 16a. See note 56, below.

10. Ibid., p. 12a. The use of "Supernal Mother" for the Land of Israel is found before Rabbi M. Chagiz in the writing of Rabbi Aaron Berekhiah of Mo-

dena. See Y. Tishby, "The Confrontation between the Kabbalah of Rabbi Isaac Luria and the Kabbalah of Rabbi Moses Cordovero in the Writings and Life of Rabbi Aaron Berekhiah of Modena" (Hebrew) *Zion* 39 (1974), p. 42, n. 114: ". . . So long as I know that my thoughts will ascend satisfactorily first to those dwelling in the bosom of the Supernal Mother."

11. *Letters of Y. Sh. Reggio* (Vienna, 1836), Notebook II, p. 89. The symbol of the mother is not the only parallel to the concept of "homeland." The phrase "alien land" (Psalms 137:4) is nothing but the antithesis of the people's relation to their homeland. This is a topic deserving of further study.

12. See Heinemann, *A People and Its Land*, pp. 6–9; R. Z. Werblowski, "Metropolis for all Lands," *Jerusalem through the Ages—The 25th National Congress for the Knowledge of the Land of Israel* (Jerusalem, 1969), pp. 172–178.

13. On the Special Commandments, see I, 68; for additional sources, see Heinemann, *A People and Its Lands*.

14. *Tanchuma Devarim* (ed. Buber), Sec. 3, p. 4. See Y. A. Zeligman, "Jerusalem in Jewish Hellenistic Thought," *Judah and Jerusalem* (Jerusalem, 1957), p. 198.

15. Compare M. Men. 13:10: "If one said: 'I pledge myself to offer a whole offering . . . which I will offer in the House of Onias' he should offer it in the Temple, but if he offered it in the House of Onias he has fulfilled his obligation . . ." (H. Danby, *The Mishnah* [Oxford, 1933] pp. 512–513). (Onias was the head of a sacrificial cult in Egypt which competed with the Jerusalem Temple. On this passage, see E. E. Urbach, *Muda'ut shel Mercaz Utefutsot Betoldot Yisra'el Umashma'utam Beyameinu* (Shazar Library, The Institute for Contemporary Judaism, Hebrew University, Jerusalem, 1975). On the attachment to the Land of Israel through the generations, also see: Y. Ben Shlomo "The Jewish People's Attachment to the Land of Israel" (Hebrew), *Sekirah Chodshit* (April 1973), pp. 3–12, Y. M. Grintz, "Between a People and Its Land" (Hebrew), *Ha'umah* Tevet 5728 (1968).

16. N. Rotenstreich. "To Be a Zionist in the Year 1976—An Interview with Yeshiahu Ben Porat" (Hebrew), *Sefer Hashanah shel Ha'itona'im 1976*, p. 29ff.

17. "The Relationship of Israeli Youth to the Land of Israel," *Hayisra'eli Kiyehudi*, (Givatayim, 1976), pp. 13–21.

18. Ibid., p. 20.

19. See J. B. Soloveichik, *On Repentance*, P. Peli, ed. (Jerusalem, 1975), pp. 75–76. Regarding the sanctity of the Land, see Ibid., pp. 300ff.

20. M. K. 25a. Cf. *Sifrei Shoftim* 175.

21. Abravenel's commentary on Maimonides' *Guide to the Perplexed* II, 32 (Jerusalem ed. photocopy of Warsaw ed., II, 68b).

22. *Iggeret Hashmad*, (ed. Rabinowitz, Mosad Harav Kook) p. 65.

23. Compare Maimonides' remarks in his Commentary to the Mishnah (A.Z. 4:11): "It is forbidden to dwell in a city which allows idolatry, except when we are compelled, since we dwell in their lands because of our sins, and we fulfill the verse "And you shall worship there . . . the work of human hands. . . ." Amongst

the famous comments on the phrase "All who dwell outside the Land . . ." is Maimonides' in his laws: "All who leave the Land of Israel and settle outside the Land are as if they were idolators."

24. See A. Altman, "Rabbi Judah Halevi's Theory of Climatology" (Hebrew), *Melilah* 1 (1944), pp. 1–17; also see E. Barker, *National Character and the Factors in its Formation* (London, 1928), p. 69.

25. Compare, for example, Plato's *Laws* 705a, and 747d ff.

26. See Al-Farabi's Hebrew translation edited by Philipowski, *Sefer He'asiph* (Leipzig, 1849), p. 33. Compare *Kovets Teshuvot Harambam*, II, 22a–23a.

27. H. Wolfson suggested that Judah Halevi's theory of climatology is a reaction to the theory of Ihwan al-Safa, who considered Iraq to be the chosen land: *JQR* 33 (1942), pp. 65ff. and n. 193.

28. For sources, see A. Altman, *Judah Halevi's Theory of Climatology*, p. 17.

29. *Or Hashem*, Art. 2, Sec. 2, chap. 6. Vienna ed.; 39b).

30. *Chesed Le'avraham* (Amsterdam, 1805) Ma'ayan 3.

31. Ibid., *Nahar* 2 (25:1).

32. Ibid., *Ma'ayan* 2, *Nahar* 7 (26:1).

33. M. Buber, *Bein Am Le'artso [Between a People and its Land]* (Jerusalem-Tel-Aviv, 1945), p. 2.

34. Regarding the "navel of the earth" in the Bible, cf. J. A. Zeligman, *Jerusalem in Jewish Hellenistic Thought*; S. Talmon's review of W. Davis' *The Gospel and the Land* in *Christian News from Israel* 25 (1975), p. 135; and Heinemann, *A People and Its Land*, p. 2. Another prevalent motif is the elevation of the Land of Israel; see Kid. 69a; Heinemann, *A People and Its Land*, p. 2.

35. See *Kuzari* I, 95; II, 20 and compare Rabbi David Kimchi in his commentary to Psalms 87:3 and Bachya Ben Asher in his *Kad Hakemach* (Lemberg ed. 56a). In my opinion, the theory of the center in the thought of Rabbi Judah Halevi is related to the problem of the climatological balance which creates the necessary conditions for the possibility of prophecy.

36. From his Rosh Hashanah sermon, Chavel, *Kitvei Haramban*, I, 240; Nachmanides makes similar observations in many places in his Torah commentary. Also, compare *Zohar* II, 108b.

37. Under the influence of medieval geographical theory, "The center of the world" became "the middle of civilization."

38. According to Rabbi Judah Moscato, this distinction is parallel to that between potentiality and actuality.

39. For a list of sources, see E. E. Urbach, *Chazal — Pirkei Emunot Vede'ot* (Jerusalem, 1969; English trans., *The Sages*), p. 42, n. 59.

40. See Buber, *People and Its Land*, p. 70.

41. See Nachmanides, *Torah commentary to Genesis* 26:5, Lev. 18:25, 25:2, Num. 35:33–34. Dt. 11:18. On this issue see: Rabbi Joel Teitelbaum (the Rabbi of Satmar), *Vayoel Moshe Ma'amar Yishuv Eretz Yisra'el* VII; and G. Scholem, "Mitz-

vah Haba'ah Be'averah" in *Mechkarim Umekorot Letoldot Hashasta'ut Vegiguleha* (Jerusalem, 1975) p. 66.

42. The text requires emendation; read *iyyun* in place of Hebrew *inyan*.

43. *Responsa of Rabbi Shlomo Ben Shimon Duran*, par. 1. (Hebrew). Similarly, Rabbi Shneuer Zalman Horowitz compares *aliyah* to acquiring tzitzit (ritual fringes), (*dehaynu lehakhsharat hamitzvah*) *Shnei Luchot Haberit*, *Sha'ar Ha'otiyot*, Ot Kuf, "Kedushah."

44. S. S. Ben Sassoon, "The First Karaites—Aspects of their Social Theory" (Hebrew), *Zion* 36 (1970), p. 47. Anan's commentary on "Every place where I shall cause to be remembered . . ." is identical to the words of the rich man in *Sefat Emet* of Rabbi M. Chagiz (see below n. 56). On territorialism amongst the Sabbatians and the Frankists, see Scholem, "Mitzvah Haba'ah Be'averah," p. 48 and n. 50: "For the messiah shall not give any sign or portent of ingathering the exiled or the return of Israel to their Land, except amongst the nations; rather, they will actually find mercy amongst the peoples. Gratitude to the community of Israel . . . shall be in all the places of their dwelling amongst the peoples. . . ." Scholem holds that Jacob Frank broke the Sabbatian movement's attachment to the Land of Israel: "We believe that Jerusalem will not be built even after the demise of history (in halachic terms, *Ad ve'ad bikhlal*)," ibid., p. 121. A purely territorial concentration replaced the vision of the return to Zion: "You used to turn to the land where the heads of the citizenry are turbaned, but all the good, the beauty and the niceness is hidden in Poland," ibid., p. 122. See above, n. 8.

45. E. E. Urbach (*Muda'ut shel Mercaz*) has addressed the unusual position of Y. Kaufman on the problem of territorialism. The fact that the affinity for the Land of Israel kept the Jews from establishing a state in the diaspora, while it did not prevent them from settling in it, is paradoxical and inexplicable in Kaufman's eyes.

46. See ibid.

47. *Responsa of Rabbi Shlomo Ben Shimon Duran*, Sec. 3. On this question, see Rabbi Israel Shtepianski, *Erets Yisra'el Besifrut Hateshuvot (The Land of Israel in Responsa Literature)*, (Jerusalem, 1967–68), I–II.

48. Notes to *Sefer Hamitsvot*. Apparently, this was the reason for his *aliyah*. "This is what brought me out of my land and led me from my home. . . ." Rosh Hashanah sermon. Chavel, *Kitvei Haramban*. See also Ch. H. Ben-Sasson. "Rabbi Moses Ben Nachman—A Man of the Conflicts of His Age" (Hebrew), *Molad*, pp. 360–366.

49. Rabbi Moshe Zui Neryah dwelt on these tendencies in his article "The Centrality of Israel in Halakhah" (Hebrew), *Torah Shebe'al Peh*, Isaac Raphael, ed. Vol. II (Jerusalem, 1969). I have been greatly helped in this section by Rabbi Neryah's article. It would be appropriate to point out the dialectical paradox in the fact that Rabbi Neryah builds his concept of "centrality" as a halakhic idea upon the very sources which different legal decisors (*poskim*) have employed to limit the *mitsvot* of settling in the Land of Israel and *aliyah* to it.

It is difficult to summarize the bibliography on the relation to the Land of Israel in the halakhah. One of the best works, in my opinion, paradoxically, is *Vayoel Moshe*, a publication of the Satmar Rebbe (see above n. 41). Amongst the new research worthy of mention are: M. A. Tanenblat. *Perakim Chadashim Letoldot Erets Yisrael Ubavel Bitekufat Hatalmud* (Tel-Aviv, 1967); and Sh. Bialoblotski "Yerushalayim Bahalakhah" *Em Lamasoret* (Ramat Gan, 1971).

50. H. Brody, *Diwan Judah Halevi* (Berlin, 1893–94), II, pp. 164–166. Also see: B. Ts. Dinur, "Rabbi Judah Halevi's Aliyah to the Land of Israel and the Messianic Agitation of his Time" (Hebrew), *Minchah LeDavid Yellin* (David Yellin Jubilee Volume, 1935), pp. 157–192.

51. Buber, *People and its Land*, p. 60.

52. It is possible to identify the personal motives within the complex of beliefs associated with the Land of Israel and the resurrection of the Dead. See B. Ts. Dinur, "Pilgrims' Inscriptions in the Temple Mount from the Beginning of the Arab Conquest" (Hebrew), *Be Maavak Dorot* (Jerusalem, 1975), pp. 117–134. On the settlement of the Land as a communal or personal commandment, see also Y. K. Miklishinski, "The Land of Israel in the Light of the Sources," *Arakhim Vehearachot* (Jerusalem-Tel-Aviv, 1976), pp. 298–308.

53. See Y. Praver, "Medieval Lovers of Zion—Pilgrimages to the Land of Israel in the Crusader Period" (Hebrew), *The 19th National Congress on the Knowledge of the Land* (Jerusalem, 1965), pp. 131ff.

54. *Responsa of Rabbi Shlomo Ben Shimon Duran*, sec. 3.

55. See Y. Katz, "Messianism and Nationalism in the Thought of Rabbi Yehuda Alkalai" (Hebrew), *Shivat Tsiyon* (1955–56), esp. pp. 14–20. The success of Western Jewry in the Damascus Affair was, in his opinion, a most significant influence in the movement toward change in a realistic direction.

56. See above, nn. 9, 10; See Dinur, *op. cit.*, (n. 5).

57. Ta'anit 5a: "The rebuilt Jerusalem . . ."

58. See V. Aptowitzer, "On the Supernal Temple" (Hebrew), *Tarbiz* 2 (1931), pp. 137–154, 254–277.

59. See E. E. Urbach, "Jerusalem of Below and Jerusalem of Above," *Yerushalayim Ledoroteha* (Jerusalem, 1969), p. 163. On the spiritualization of the Land of Israel in Kabbalistic and Hasidic thought, see Rivka Shatz, "The Messianic Foundation in Hasidic Thought," *Molad*, n.s., 1:1 (Iyar-Sivan 5727 = 1967), pp. 105–111 and the bibliography cited there.

60. See Werblowski, "Metropolis For All Lands."

61. *Sippur David Ha-Reuveni* (ed. Neubauer), p. 163.

62. Chavel, *Kitvei Haramban*, p. 249.

63. Abraham Isaac Kook, "The Land of Israel," *Orot* (Jerusalem, 1950), p. 9.

64. In addition to the articles cited in the various notes, it is necessary to add these three important contributions, to which I am indebted: R. J. Z. Werblowski, "Israel et Eretz Yisrael," *Les Temps Modernes* 253 (1967), pp. 371–393; S. Et-

tinger, "Le peuple juif et Eretz Yisrael," ibid., pp. 394–413; S. Talmon, "The Biblical Concept of Jerusalem," in J. M. Oesterreicher and Anne Sinai, eds., *Jerusalem* (prepared under the auspices of the American Academic Association for Peace in the Middle East) (New York, 1974), pp. 180–202.

The Land of Israel in Medieval Kabbalah

MOSHE IDEL

[Editor's note: Perhaps more than any other body of literature, Kabbalah is rich with metaphor and symbol. Here, Dr. Moshe Idel, Associate Professor in Kabbalah at the Hebrew University in Jerusalem, analyzes its symbolic references for the Land of Israel, asking whence these are derived. He turns first to the Land of Israel as the "supernal female" or the "feminine aspect of divinity" and posits a lost rabbinic tradition that was suppressed in Jewish circles, but was carried by Gnostic and Christian sources, until it surfaced again in rabbinic writings in the middle ages, beginning with the twelfth-century *Book of Bahir*. Other sources picture living in the Land of Israel as a special case of *imitatio Dei*, a derivation again from the Kabbalah's preference for vivid sexual allusions, in which "the human righteous dwelling in the Land of Israel imitate the 'possession' of the upper Land by the divine male in the Pleroma." Borrowing Levi-Bruhl's term, "participation mystique," Idel describes this settlement in the Land as acting upon the Godhead, by bringing about the divine union of male and female. His survey turns next to a debate in Geronese circles between R. Ezra ben Solomon (d. 1238) and his better-known contemporary, Moses ben Nachman (Nachmanides) over the merit of actively seeking to settle the Land. Finally, he deals with prophetic — or ecstatic — Kabbalah, in which the Land of Israel loses its locative specificity, and emerges as a metaphor for the human body itself, but properly descriptive, therefore, of Jewish life outside the actual geographic Land of Israel too — a theme later picked up by Hasidic masters in Poland. His analysis concludes with a critique of Eliade's conception of sacred space, and the extent to which it is applicable to Kabbalistic symbolism.]

Kabbalah, more than any other Jewish trend of thought, developed an elaborated geosophy of Eretz Yisra'el. Although it mostly expanded upon already existing motifs connected to the Land found in the Bible and in the Talmudic-Midrashic literature, Kabbalah gave a peculiar turn to some of them — such as its description of the Land of Israel as the "omphalos" or the anatomical center of the universe (*tabur ha-aretz*) — and contributed some new perspectives and perceptions which seem to be either the result of Kabbalistic ways of thinking, or of the assimilation of alien influence. Given the vastness of Kabbalistic literature and the recurrence of the theme of the Land of Israel throughout this body of literature, we shall confine ourselves to what seem to be the most original perceptions of the aforementioned theme, consciously neglecting most of the Kabbalistic treatments of older motifs. [Ed. note: on the Land as Center of the earth, see remarks above by Shalom Rosenberg, pp. 153–54.]

I. The Sexualization of the Land of Israel

With the exception of Tantric mysticism, Kabbalah is the single type of mystical thought which regarded sexual relations as fraught with theurgical and mystical implications. Most of the 613 commandments, and especially licit sexual relations solely for the purpose of reproduction, were intended to restore the primeval harmony and union of the two Divine Powers, *Tiferet* and *Malkhut*, which were commonly symbolized as bridegroom and bride, or King and Queen. Being the most influential couple among the ten divine manifestations (*sefirot*), this pair had to remain in a state of dynamic union—often conceived symbolically in sexual terms (*zivvug*)—in order to maintain the descent of the divine efflux upon our world. One of the most important symbols of *Malkhut*, the female aspect of the couple, is *Eretz Yisra'el*, the Land of Israel.

The personification of earth as a female is widely known in ancient Jewish sources, where it is represented as Mother Earth,[1] but no explicit sexual features attributable to the Land of Israel can be found in the Bible or in the Talmudic-Midrashic corpus. As a symbolic sexual counterpart, the Land of Israel plays no role in this body of literature. However, it seems reasonable to assume that such a conception existed among the Jews of remote antiquity, was excluded from Rabbinic sources, and flowered again in the Kabbalistic literature. Evidence for this assumption can be found in ancient non-Jewish sources. The New Testament (Rev. 21:1–2), for example, states:

> And I saw a new heaven and a new earth; for the first heaven and the first earth were passed away. . . . And I, John, saw the holy city, new Jerusalem, coming down from God out of heaven, prepared as a bride adorned for her husband.

A possible association of the "new earth" with the "new Jerusalem" described with sexual overtones as a bride, seems also to be suggested by a Gnostic text.[2] According to Irenaeus, the Valentinian Gnostics[3] "maintain that their aeons and gods and fathers and lords are also still further termed heavens together with their Mother, whom they also call 'the Land' and 'Jerusalem,' while they also style her many other names." As in Revelation, so too this Gnostic text seems to imply a polarity of heaven and earth, or male and female. It is evident that we face here not only the well known *topos* but also a particular issue where the Land of Israel is apparently synonymous with earth, standing in contradistinction to heaven. This is implicit in the use of the terminologically specific *Ha'aretz* ("The Land") rather than *Eretz* ("Earth") in general; and also in the parallel term "Jerusalem."[4] Another reference to the Land of Israel in a Valentinian source deals with the Enneads, the divine powers forming the Pleroma: "Each one makes myriads upon myriads of Glories, and each Ennead has a Monad in it, and in each Monad there is a Space called *Incorruptible*, that is to say, *Holy Land*."[5] The last phrase seems to be a translation of the Hebrew *Eretz ha-Kodesh*.

Two important features emerge from these texts. The concept of Eretz Yisra'el is apparently applied not only to a geographical place on earth but to a spiritual entity placed above. Such a usage of this concept is unparalleled in Hebrew non-Kabbalistic texts, which know of a supernal Jerusalem but not of a supernal Land of Israel.

The above material strengthens the assumption that Eretz Yisra'el was conceived of as a symbol of a Divine power. The second feature of this concept, its sexual characterization, seems to me also obvious and constitutes a perception which differs from that found in classical Jewish sources. Nevertheless, the possibility that these two characteristics of the concept of Eretz Yisra'el stem from non-Jewish circles—Christian or Gnostic—is highly improbable. It would be odd for non-Jewish, often anti-Jewish, authors to introduce a new positive perception of the Land of Israel, thereby reinforcing the values of the Jewish religion, the only faith which emphasized the importance of the Land.

I should like therefore, to submit the thesis that an ancient Jewish conception of Eretz Yisra'el was preserved in non-Jewish texts, while it was suppressed in Rabbinic sources. Such an ancient Jewish conception could, presumably, have been handed down in Jewish esoteric circles, until it reached the Middle Ages, whence it was committed to writing in the *Book of Bahir* (12th century) which is presumed to be the first Kabbalistic book:[6]

> What is [the meaning of the verse], "The whole earth is full of His Glory"? (Isaiah 6: 3) It is that "whole earth" which was created on high, on the first day. It is parallel to Eretz Yisra'el and filled with the Glory

of God. And what is it (i.e., this Glory)? It is Wisdom of which it is written, "The wise shall inherit Glory." (Proverbs 3:35) It furthermore states, "Blessed be the Glory of God from His place." (Ezekiel 3:12)

The supernal Earth which corresponds to the Land of Israel is related to the Glory of God and to His place. It seems that the last quotation testifies to the existence of a tradition concerning a supernal Earth reminiscent of the Valentinian Gnostic text quoted above, wherein the Holy Land was related to the Glory and Space *topos*.[7] Moreover, as Gershom Scholem notes,[8] the supernal Earth in the *Book of Bahir* symbolizes a female entity—the last *Sefirah, Malkhut.* We may, therefore, assume that already in one of the oldest Kabbalistic documents, the Land of Israel became a symbol of a supernal female entity.

The sexual implications of the feminine imagery of the last divine manifestation, *Malkhut,* seem to be implied already in one of the first Kabbalistic treatises written in Spain. R. Jacob ben Sheshet (13th century) tried to decode the Kabbalistic significance of the order of three items mentioned in the second blessing of the Grace after Meals—"the Blessing over the Land" [of Israel]: the Land, circumcision, and the Torah.[9]

> Concerning "the Blessing over the Land:" after one mentions the good and spacious Land, he must mention circumcision. The commentators explain this as based on the fact that the Land was given (i.e., promised) to Abraham simultaneously with the commandment of circumcision (Genesis 17:8–14). However, this reason is not convincing to me. . . . The real reason seems to be that when the Israelites entered the Land, Joshua was ordered to circumcise them (Joshua 5). . . . In order to achieve a juxtaposition within the blessing of the reference to circumcision and the reference to the Land, we mention circumcision before mentioning the Torah. Thus, this sequence is so formulated for a fitting and laudable purpose, as one hint within another hint (*ofan be-tokh ofan*). Firstly, he mentions the Land (which is the core reference of the blessing), afterwards he mentions circumcision, to juxtapose them, and only afterwards does he mention the Torah.

The sequence of Land, circumcision, and Torah point, according to Ben Sheshet, to a special relationship between these subjects. What the nature of this affinity is, ben Sheshet does not explicitly reveal, although his cryptic reference to "a fitting and laudable purpose, as one hint within another hint" certainly suggests a deeper, more esoteric level of meaning.

It is commonplace in medieval Kabbalistic thought that the Land of

Israel symbolizes *Malkhut,* also called *Shekhinah,* the *Sefirah* that represents
the feminine aspect of divinity. Torah (the Written Law) is symbolic of *Tiferet,*
the masculine principle among the *Sefirot.* The covenant of circumcision
(*brit*) alludes to the *Sefirah Yesod,* which is symbolized by the masculine member and conceived as a connecting channel through which the divine efflux
moves down from *Tiferet* to *Malkhut/Shekhinah.* Another symbol of *Yesod*
is the *Zaddik,* the Saint or Righteous One who resists sexual sin and thus
safeguards the holiness and purity of the supernal procreative function.

In light of this, R. Jacob ben Sheshet seems to be suggesting that the
thematic sequence of the Blessing over the Land symbolizes, *in nuce,* the
proximity of the divine female and male principles conjoined appropriately
by the phallic power of the latter. Moreover, the biblical juxtaposition of
the Promised Land and circumcision (in Genesis 17 and Joshua 5) is interpreted as a veiled allusion to the mystical relationship between the sexual
purity and holiness symbolized by the covenant of circumcision, and the
Holy Land, the former being a prerequisite for attainment of the latter.

What seems to be implicit in R. Jacob ben Sheshet's discussion became explicit in several passages found in the cornerstone work of Jewish
Kabbalah, the *Book of Zohar,* wherein we find:[10]

> "And I have also set up my covenant of circumcision with them, to
> give them the Land of Canaan";[11] because they were circumcised. For
> whoever is circumcised inherits the Land, as none can inherit the Land
> but the righteous[12] and whoever is circumcised is called "righteous,"
> as it is written, "Your people shall all be righteous and shall forever
> possess the Land" (Isaiah 60:21). Whoever is circumcised and keeps
> that sign of the covenant [pure] is called "righteous."

These statements have to be interpreted on two levels: The straightforward
meaning asserts that the Land of Israel can be possessed only by righteous
Jews, with circumcision being a *sine qua non* condition for its inheritance.
But a full understanding of the text eludes us if we fail to have recourse
to a much deeper realm of signification. The Land here symbolizes the female power (*Malkhut*) in the divine realm, which is "possessed" by the male
power (*Tiferet*) by means of the "righteous" (*Zaddik*) who is at the same time
the "sign of the covenant" (*brit*), that is, the phallic principle of *Yesod.*

This theosophical dimension of the Zoharic text is corroborated by
a further parallel passage:[13]

> By [the name] God the Almighty, He reveals Himself to them [the
> Patriarchs]—out of the dark mirror.[14] But He did not reveal Himself

out of the shining mirror.[15] And should you assert that they [the Patriarchs] used[16] only the female [aspect] and not more,[17] come and see that they [the male and female aspects] never separate, as it is written, "And I have also set up My covenant of circumcision with them."[18] Behold, the covenant of circumcision[19] unites with her. From the Holy One, blessed be He, one must learn.[20] It is said that He does not separate them, as it is written, "by God the Almighty"; and it is written, "And I have also set up My covenant of circumcision with them," this being in order to maintain the covenant[21] in [perpetual] union.[22] "And I have also set up My covenant of circumcision with them to give them the Land of Canaan." See that it states: whoever safeguards [the purity of] the covenant of circumcision, inherits the Land.

This text explicitly discloses the theosophical *substratum* of interpretation and its sexual perception of the relation between the righteous and the Land; it reflects the supernal dynamic union of the male and the female divine powers. The human righteous dwelling in the Land of Israel imitate the "possession" of the upper Land by the divine male in the Pleroma. It seems that we can recognize here a special interpretation of living in the Land of Israel as an instance of *imitatio Dei*.

The impact of the sexualization of the relationship between the Land of Israel and its Jewish inhabitants is especially evident in the Kabbalistic discussion of the quandary concerning the fate after death of Jacob, Joseph, and Moses. In several texts, Kabbalists discuss these ancestors' separate fates: Jacob was buried in Hebron—that is, within the borders of the Land of Israel; only the bones of Joseph were brought there, while his body was not; Moses was interred, bones and all, outside the Promised Land.[23] I shall cite here a relatively late version of a Kabbalistic solution. R. Abraham Azulay (17th century) states, in the name of a certain R. Kalonymus:[24]

Joseph's body was not buried in the Land of Israel, but only his bones, because he experienced a seminal pollution in the attempted seduction by [the wife of] Potiphar. But since the [sexual] act was not accomplished, his bones were buried in the Land of Israel. Moses, our teacher, may his memory be blessed, married a Cushite woman . . . and, therefore, even his bones were not buried in the Land of Israel—for it [the Land] is called a "God-fearing woman." But Jacob our ancestor refused to marry Timna, Esau's mistress, who came to him and requested him to marry her, and, therefore, he merited [that even his body] be buried in the Land of Israel.

Extreme sexual purity is presented as an indispensable condition for entry into the Land, which is explicitly portrayed here as a woman.

But this peculiar symbolism of the Land as Woman implies more than a mere human imitation of the divine union of male and female powers. The Kabbalists were interested not only in *imitatio Dei*; beyond their own imitative role, they strove for a certain participation ("participation mystique") in the supernal processes which they understood to be intrinsically linked to their own behavior as a sort of *imitatio* in reverse. This is the reason why they conceive of the habitation of the Land of Israel as meaning more than a mere reflection of the divine in the realm of the material. According to them, actual historical "possession" of the Land of Israel by righteous Jews has theurgical overtones: the supernal processes can be influenced by means of sympathetic corresponding actions performed below. In other words, the divine dynamic union between *Tiferet* and *Malkhut* can, and must, be reinforced by religious acts performed in the Land of Israel. There are several texts which assert this impact of commandments performed in the Land upon the promotion of supernal union. According to the *Book of Zohar*:[25]

> When [the people of] Israel dwelled in the Holy Land, everything was harmonious, as it should be . . . and they performed [their] worship, and the firmaments of the world [conceived as curtains] were penetrated,[26] so that worship (i.e., prayer) ascended to its place above. For the Land is exclusively suited to worship by the people of Israel.

Supernal harmony as achieved by the union of *Tiferet* and *Malkhut* is, therefore, to be induced by the performance of Jewish ritual in the Land of Israel. Later on, the Safed Kabbalists (16th century)[27] repeat the lesson: "Supernal union is achieved by Israel's prayers only in the Land of Israel, but not abroad," and holy harmony can be restored only by the complete return of all the tribes of Israel to their peculiar areas in the Land.[28] Without the return of the entire people, the Divine Pleroma fails to reach its supreme and perfect status.

II. Two Attitudes Toward the Land in Geronese Kabbalah (13th century)

The conception of the Land of Israel as the center of the world was widespread in Talmudic and Midrashic literature; nevertheless, a new turn can be detected in Kabbalistic comments upon this theme. In a letter writ-

ten by R. Ezra b. Solomon (d. c. 1238), one of the Kabbalists belonging
to the school of Gerona, we read:[29]

> The inner line[30] of the populated world is the Land of Israel, which
> is called the omphallus (i.e., the navel) of the world[31] and around it
> there are seventy nations; so also regarding the Glorious Name (*shem
> ha-nikhbad*);[32] the inner line and the heart (i.e., the center) are [the
> source of the] power of Israel . . . and around it there are seventy
> names and all of them depend upon and are sustained by [the efflux]
> from the center. . . . This is the reason why the inhabitant of the Land
> of Israel [receives directly] from its [i.e., the Land's] power and is under
> its [sphere of] influence and is similar to someone who has a God;[33]
> whereas whoever dwells abroad actually must resort to [the efflux]
> he receives from the name[34] which is appointed [i.e., has dominion]
> over him. . . . But at the time of the resurrection, the souls, even of
> those who died in the Land of Israel, will return through its area,[35]
> using the inner path[36] which ascends to the inner line of the Glorious
> Name which is called "the bundle[37] of life."

It is obvious that we face here a Kabbalistic version of the well-known al-
chemical statement that asserts, "That which is above is like that which is
below and that which is below is like that which is above."[38] Thus the Land
of Israel corresponds to the center of the creative divine powers. This correspondence is no mere structural paradigm. According to the last statement
in the passage, "an inner path" links the two centers by which the souls of
the dead return to their bodies. This "path" seems to constitute an ontological *nexus* and may reflect the influence of the Islamic concept of the
straight line that connects two centers and is used by souls in their ascent
to their source.[39]

The perception of the Land of Israel qua center remains a mere theory
in the words of R. Ezra. He maintains:[40]

> Nowadays the Jews are already released from the obligation[41] [to dwell
> in] the Land of Israel. Their suffering—out of the love of God—the
> [vicissitudes of] the dispersion, and their afflictions and subjugation
> are like an atoning altar for them, as it is written (Psalms 44:23) "Yea,
> for Thy sake are we killed all the day long."

This rather non-activist attitude is reflected also in R. Ezra's *Commentary
to the Song of Songs* where he asserts that in the Messianic time the people
of Israel "will go to the Land of Israel with the permission and help of the

gentile Kings."[42] As R. Ezra explains, "Not by [the power of] their bows and their swords will you inherit the Land, and not by horses or chariots, but by the will of God, who will cause the fall of the nations and will humiliate them before you."[43]

This passive orientation towards the return of the Jews to their Land contrasts sharply with the extremely activist, even militant, position of R. Ezra's younger contemporary—the renowned R. Moses ben Nahman (Nachmanides).[44] A distinguished Kabbalist, he subscribes to the perception of the Land of Israel as corresponding to a supernal divine power[45] and being directly influenced by it.[46] But regarding the practical consequences of this theory, his attitude is diametrically opposed to R. Ezra's.

Dwelling in the Land of Israel becomes for him not only a religious obligation but the single way to attain perfect Jewish life. The performance of the commandments in the Diaspora is, in Nachmanides' view, a mere preparation intended to enable their true performance in the Land of Israel.[47] Moreover, the Promised Land being the only proper forum for a full religious life, the Jews must live in their own Land even if this aim can be achieved only by fierce wars with its gentile conquerors.[48] Nachmanides considers this fight as one of the daily religious obligations incumbent upon every Jew and not a matter to be postponed until the Messianic era.[49] Since R. Ezra and Nachmanides were contemporaries, and possibly also colleagues, the basic differences between their attitudes toward the Land of Israel may be the result of an inner controversy in Kabbalistic circles in Catalonia. Since R. Ezra's views were formulated before the bulk of Nachmanides' works, the latter's views are, at least partially, a reaction to R. Ezra's position.[50]

III. The Land of Israel in Prophetic Kabbalah

Alongside the theosophical brand of Kabbalah, which is mainly concerned with the inner processes in the Godhead, there exists another type of Kabbalah, the prophetic, or ecstatic, one.[51] This latter Kabbalistic school was interested in techniques of reaching ecstatic experience rather than in influencing the divine powers. The focus of discussion in the works of the representatives of prophetic Kabbalah is the inner processes taking place within human consciousness. According to the theosophic Kabbalah, the Land of Israel becomes symbolic of a supernal manifestation; the prophetic Kabbalah perceives it as a metaphor for human status.

According to R. Abraham Abulafia, the outstanding proponent of this brand of Kabbalah, the true analogue of the Land of Israel is the human body. Commenting upon the Rabbinic dictum[52] which asserts that prophecy will not dwell (i.e., occur) outside the Land unless it dwells beforehand within the Land, Abulafia[53] maintains that a simplistic, i.e., merely geographical, understanding of the meaning of "Land of Israel" is untenable. He emphasizes the fact that the first prophecy reported in the Bible occurred in Ur Chasdim when Abraham was told to leave his homeland for the Promised Land. In Abulafia's opinion, the Land of Israel is the body of the righteous man,[54] whereas the term *"chutsa la-aretz"*—outside the Land—points to the soul,[55] which is different from the body. Therefore, the geographic meaning of the Land of Israel is irrelevant in the context of the gift of prophecy; the Divine Presence (i.e., the *Shekhinah*) dwells everywhere, although only in someone who is worthy to receive prophetic inspiration.[56]

The same Rabbinic dictum was interpreted by R. Isaac of Acre, another outstanding Kabbalist who was influenced by the prophetic Kabbalah. In his mystical diary, entitled *The Treasure of Life*, we read:[57]

> The secret of "outside the Land" and of "the Land of Israel" is that . . . "The Land (*eretz*) does not signify the earth of dust (i.e., the geographic land), but the lump of dust (i.e., the human body) in which souls dwell. "The Land" is the palace of the souls; it is flesh and blood. The soul that dwells in earth (*ha-aretz*) which derives from Jacob's seed certainly dwells in the Land of Israel. Even if the soul dwells outside the Land (i.e., geographically), the *Shekhinah* (the presence of God) will rest upon it since it is definitely in the Land (i.e., earth) of Israel. But the soul which dwells in the Land (i.e., geographically) which does not derive from the seed of Jacob . . . who is Israel, our father, certainly dwells "outside the land," even if it is in the Land of Israel, [even] inside Jerusalem. Neither the *Shekhinah* nor the spirit of prophecy will dwell upon it, since it is certainly "outside the Land."

Like Abulafia before him, R. Isaac of Acre uses a pun on the word *eretz*, which means both land and earth; by changing "land," as mentioned in the *dictum,* into "earth," which is taken to signify the human body, he transfers the focus of the discussion from the geographical-national level to the individual one. The Land of Israel thereby loses its geographical centrality of the theosophical Kabbalah, so that its national and, eventually, its messianic role,[58] is neutralized by its transformation into a metaphor of the human body. According to R. Isaac, the Land of Israel exists wherever a Jew goes;[59] in Abulafia's view, the body of any person who is worthy to receive a prophetic inspiration may be considered as a "Land of Israel."

At least from the phenomenological point of view, the views of these

two Kabbalists may be considered as the precursors of attitudes which flour-
ished much later in the Hasidic literature (18th century). Some Hasidic
masters considered the place where they established their court as the "Land
of Israel,"[60] an assertion closely related to their emphasis on the possibility
of individual salvation,[61] which (for them) is independent of both the Messiah and the actual geographical Land of Israel.[62] [Ed. note: On Hasidic
thought, see also comments by Saperstein, below, pp. 201–03.]

IV. Conclusion

Some final remarks may be helpful in order to elucidate the peculiar
character of the Kabbalistic perception of the Land of Israel. In its early
stages, Judaism developed an elaborated conception of its "sacred space," the
Land. Its center, Jerusalem, or the Temple within it, was conceived of as
an *axis mundi* or the starting point of the ascending ladder leading to heaven.
So far the categories employed by comparative religion à la Eliade are fully
pertinent also to the Jewish texts.[63] Nevertheless, the dramatic changes in
the history of the Jews after the destruction of the Second Temple radically
altered the Jewish perception of their "sacred space." In the civilizations whose
concepts of "sacred space" were analyzed by Eliade, the contact between the
people and their "space" was direct and concrete, and their perception of
the center was almost tangible; their concepts were living realities whose
material expressions were the single way to experience them. For medieval
Jews, on the other hand, these features of one's relationship to sacred space
were no longer actual. They learned about the importance, centrality, or
holiness of the Promised Land from their sacred texts: the Bible and the
Midrashic-Talmudic literature, which were the main source of their images
of the nature of the Land of Israel. Most of the descriptions a medieval
Jew found in these texts were, roughly speaking, accurate, since their authors were inhabitants of the Land they described. But the most important
contribution to the image of the Holy Land, made by the medieval Jewish
literature, was afforded by the *Book of Zohar*, which combined and embel-
lished fragmentary descriptions of the Land found in the antecedent texts,
and even invented details which sometimes are in flagrant contradiction to
the real geography.[64] The Zoharic literature created an imaginary "sacred
space" with an illusory sacred shrine or fabulous assemblies. These had an
impressive impact on the Kabbalists, especially on those who established
the Kabbalistic center of Safed in the second half of the sixteenth century.

Even when living in the real Land of Israel, the phantoms of the imaginary accounts were much more influential than such ancient and concrete *loci sacri* as the Western Wall. (To give only one example: Zoharic literature turned R. Shimeon bar Yohai into the chief hero of ancient mysticism; the Safed Kabbalists "discovered" his grave at Meron, near Safed, and it became for them a place of pilgrimage, second only to the remnants of the Temple.)

But let us return to medieval Kabbalah; the interest of the Kabbalists in the "center" imagery manifestly confirms the importance Eliade attributed to this motif. But his affirmation that[65] "man can live only in a sacred space, in the 'center,'" must be corrected when applied to the medieval Kabbalists. Though preoccupied, it is true, by the problem of the Land as their Sacred Center, they yet found a way to live outside that "sacred space" in a dialectical relationship to it. They could thus build their existence around "sacred space" as a living reality, without having to uproot themselves in order to live in it. The substitutes for the real effort to reach the concrete Land were exegesis of and meditation upon texts dealing with the Land, or contemplation of various aspects implied within the concept of the Land. In other words, most Jewish mystics have preferred to concentrate upon literary symbols of the supernal center, in lieu of direct contact with the geographical center;[66] and their mystical interpretation of the mythical center either partially attenuated the ritual aspect related to the center (as in the Zoharic literature), or even totally obliterated it (as in the prophetic Kabbalah). The growing interest in the mystical meaning of the Land of Israel, or of Jerusalem, for that matter, was a symptom of a weakening of the tendency to live there. In the eyes of many of the Kabbalists intent on glimpsing something of the nature of the divine, contemplation of literary symbols of the supernal Land was more effective than the more natural but remote contact with the concrete extension of the divine—the terrestrial Land itself. In modern times, the waning of Kabbalistic symbolism may have contributed to the emergence of a more productive perception of the Land as a national home, not just sacred space.

Notes

1. See Menahem Stein, "Mother Earth in Old Hebrew Literature," *Tarbiz* 9 (1936): 257–77 (Hebrew); Raphael Patai, *Man and Earth in Hebrew Custom, Belief, and Legend* (Jerusalem, 1942), vol. I, pp. 70ff. (Hebrew).

2. On Jerusalem as a female in Gnostic and Kabbalistic texts, see my paper, "Jerusalem in Medieval Thought" in Joshua Praver, ed., *History of Jerusalem in the Middle Ages* (Jerusalem, forthcoming) (Hebrew).

3. Irenaeus, *Against Heresies*, IV, 1f. *The Ante-Nicene Fathers*, I (Grand Rapids, Michigan, 1977), p. 463. Compare also to Hippolytus, *The Refutation of All Heresies*, VI, 29, *Ante-Nicene Fathers*, V (Grand Rapids, Michigan, 1977), p. 88, where the term "Good Land"—apparently a translation of the Hebrew phrase *haaretz hatovah* (Deut. 1:35, etc.)—refers to *Sofia*, the female power in Gnostic theosophy.

4. On Jerusalem as a female entity see my paper referred to in note 2, above.

5. Charlotte A. Baynes, *A Coptic Gnostic Treatise Contained in the Codex Brucianus* (Cambridge, 1933), p. 112. Compare also pp. 104–05, where "The god begetting Land" is referred to. On the affinity between this work and medieval Kabbalistic views, see my "The Image of Man Above the Sefirot," *Da'at* 4 (1980), pp. 46–47 (Hebrew).

6. Paragraph 130 in Reuven Margalioth's edition (Jerusalem, 1978), p. 57. German translation in Gershom Scholem, *Das Buch Bahir* (Leipzig, 1923), par. 90, pp. 97–98.

7. Scholem had already pointed out the affinity between this passage in the *Book of Bahir* and other Gnostic texts. See his *Les Origines de la Kabbale* (Paris, 1966), pp. 105–07. But the texts referred by him (p. 106, n. 71) deal with "earth" as *Sofia* without the connotation of Eretz Yisra'el. Therefore, Scholem concludes, Gnostic material may be the source of the *Bahir* text. Traditions on Eretz Yisra'el (as Holy Land, Good Land) preserved in Gnostic texts apparently suggest a different explanation. The *Book of Bahir* may have inherited a genuine Jewish tradition which could have been also the source of the Gnostic views.

8. See Scholem, *Les Origines*, pp. 106–07.

9. See his *Book of the Faith and the Trust*, c. VIII, in *The Works of R. Moses ben Nachman*, ed. H. D. Chavel, vol. II (Jerusalem, 1964), pp. 378–79.

10. Vol. II, fol. 23r; compare also fol. 40v, 59v, etc.

11. The Hebrew wording is identical to the biblical verse Exodus 6:4, but I have rendered it as it was understood by the author of the Zohar. The sexual perception of these words was discussed by Yehudah Liebes "Tsaddiq Yesod Olam — A Sabbatian Myth," *Da'at* 1 (1976), p. 107, n. 171 (Hebrew).

12. For the sexual characteristic of the Righteous as a Kabbalistic symbol, see Gershom Scholem, *Elements of the Kabbalah and its Symbolism* (Jerusalem, 1976), pp. 224–36 (Hebrew).

13. *Zohar*, vol. II, fol. 26r.

14. A typical symbol of the *Sefirah Malkhut*, the supernal female power.

15. Symbol of *Tiferet*, the male *Sefirah*.

16. The Aramaic verb *ishtamshu* means also "having a sexual relation with." In this context, it seems to suggest the intensity of identification of the Patriarchs with the corresponding *Sefirot*.

17. The female—*Nukba*—is the last of the ten *Sefirot*. The text asserts that though the Patriarchs related directly only to the female aspect (*Malkbut*), indirectly they had access to the male aspects (*Yesod* and *Tiferet*) as a result of the continuous union of all three.

18. Exodus 6:4. See above, n. 11.

19. *Brit.*

20. This perpetual supernal union is perceived as the highest harmony which it is the duty of man to imitate. See above, n. 17.

21. *Kiuma*—in Aramaic, "covenant," but clearly it assumed the meaning of covenant of circumcision like its Hebrew counterpart *brit*. See Yehudah Liebes, *The Messianic Idea in Jewish Thought* (Jerusalem, 1982), p. 128 (Hebrew).

22. "*Beyichuda.*" The Aramaic term means, in the Zoharic terminology, "union" in general and "sexual union" of the male and female supernal powers.

23. See R. Moses de Leon's Kabbalistic *Responsa* edited by Isaiah Tishby in *Kobets al Yad, Minora Manuscripta Hebraica*, vol. V (15) (1950), pp. 24–30 and the Zoharic parallels referred by Tishby in his notes.

24. See *Chesed Le'avraham* (Lvov, 1863), fol. 22r.

25. Vol. I, fol. 84v.

26. The imagery of penetrating the airs coincides with the Kabbalistic view on the ascent of the prayer of the inhabitants of Eretz Yisra'el. See, e.g., R. Joseph Gikatilla's *Sha'arei Orah* (Warsaw, 1883), fol. 31v–32r.

27. See Azulai's *Chesed Le'avraham*, fol. 19v–20r. As Bracha Sack has shown, most of the material collected in this work stems from the writings of R. Moses Cordovero. See her article "The Tracing of Sources in R. Abraham Azulai's Work *Chesed Le'avraham*," *Kiryat Sefer* 56 (1981), pp. 164–75 (Hebrew), and her paper "The Influence of Cordovero on Seventeenth Century Jewish Thought" in *Jewish Thought in the Seventeenth Century* in the proceedings of the international colloquium at Harvard University, March, 1982.

28. *Chesed Le'avraham*, fol. 19v.

29. The original Hebrew text was printed by Gershom Scholem, "A New Document on the History of the Beginning of the Kabbalah," *Sefer Bialik* (Tel Aviv, 1934), pp. 161–62 (Hebrew).

30. The "inner line" sometimes signifies the *Sefirah Tiferet* which R. Ezra usually refers to as the central line. See especially his commentary on the *Song of Songs*, ed. H. D. Chavel in *The Works of Moses ben Nachman* (Jerusalem, 1964), II, p. 508, 511–12, 515, and George Vajda, *Le Commentaire d'Ezra de Gerone sur le cantiques des cantiques* (Paris, 1969), p. 347, n. 14, p. 351, n. 47. Sometimes the central line functions as a symbol for the *Sefirah Malkhut*.

31. Cf. *Tanchuma*, Kedoshim 10.

32. The divine name refers to the *Sefirah Tiferet*, whereas the seventy names signify the seventy angels which are appointed—according to several Rabbinic sources—over the seventy nations. The angels above depend, according to R. Ezra,

upon the divine efflux emanating from the sixth *Sefirah*, i.e., *Tiferet*, as the seventy nations depend upon the power of Israel below. The use of the term "center" implies that in the supernal world the angels are arranged in a circle around the *Tiferet* which is its center, like the seventy lands surrounding the Land of Israel which is, according to Rabbinic sources, the center of all the other lands.

33. Cf. B. T. *Ketubot*, fol. 110v.

34. I.e., the angel appointed over the land in the Diaspora where the Jew is living.

35. *Derekh gevulo.*

36. The Hebrew term *hamesilah hapenimit* may also be translated as "the central path" since R. Ezra conceives the adjectives "inner" and "central" as interchangeable. See his *Commentary on the Song of Songs*, pp. 508, 511–12, 515 and his *Commentary on the Talmudic Legends*, printed in *Likkutei Shikhechah Ufei'ah* (Ferrara, 1556), fol. 15r. The term *mesilah* is reminiscent of the biblical reference to the path to Beit El (Judges 21:19).

37. *Zeror Hachayim*, cf. I Samuel 25:29. This expression refers to the *Sefirah Tiferet* compared to the text quoted by R. Ezra in the name of his teacher, R. Isaac the Blind and cited by Scholem, *Les Origines*, p. 315, n. 174.

38. See opening of The Emerald Table. R. Ezra stresses that the process of emanation in the divine world is strictly parallel to the process of creation of the lower world. See Gottlieb, *Studies*, pp. 66–68.

39. See A. Altmann, "The Ladder of Ascension," *Studies in Mysticism and Religion Presented to Gershom G. Scholem* (Jerusalem, 1967), pp. 3ff. Altmann has pointed out (pp. 27–29) the possibility that the Kabbalistic term *kav hamishor* and *kav ha-yashar* were influenced by theories found in Islamic sources, as part of that material's influence on R. Jacob ben Sheshet and other later Kabbalists. The assumption that already R. Ezra might have been influenced by this concept should substantially strengthen Altmann's assertion.

40. In this letter (above, n. 29, pp. 161–162) in the middle of the passage on the Land of Israel which was quoted and discussed above.

41. *Chiyuv.* Compare to the statement of one of the Tosaphists on B. T. *Ketubot*, fol. 110v: "Nowadays there is no religious obligation to dwell in the Land of Israel." See also Israel Ta-Shema, "Eretz Israel Studies," *Shalem*, vol. I, ed. Joseph Hacker (1974), pp. 81–82 (Hebrew). It seems that in the text dealt with by Ta-Shema, we can perceive the "terrible aspects of the sacred center," which were one of the obstacles which withheld Ashkenazi Jews from going to the Land; see Mircea Eliade, *Patterns in Comparative Religion* (New York, 1972), p. 384.

42. Ed. H. D. Chavel, p. 515.

43. Ibid., p. 517.

44. Nachmanides' attitude towards the Land of Israel was discussed by several authors, the latest being Chaim Henoch, *Nachmanides: Philosopher and Mystic* (Jerusalem, 1978), pp. 141–159 (Hebrew); idem, "Inquiries into Nachmanides' con-

ception of Erez Israel," *Or Hamizrach*, vol. 100, Special Jubilee Edition (New York, 1980), pp. 31–41 (Hebrew). Nevertheless it seems that no one has compared in detail Nachmanides' view to R. Ezra's. I shall shortly refer to those statements of Nachmanides which are pertinent to a comparison to R. Ezra's position.

45. See the prayer composed by Nachmanides on the ruins of Jerusalem: Nachmanides' *Works*, ed. Chavel, vol. I, p. 424, as well as his commentary on Genesis 14:18, 28:17.

46. See his *Torat Ha'adam*, *Works*, II, pp. 296, 298.

47. See Nachmanides' *Sermon for Rosh Hashanah*, *Works*, I, p. 251.

48. Interestingly enough, Nachmanides formulated his militant view against the background of the continuing fighting being waged in the Land of Israel between the three superpowers: Mongols, Christians, and Muslims. See Joshua Prawer, *A History of the Latin Kingdom of Jerusalem* (Jerusalem, 1971), vol. II, p. 388.

49. See the sermon cited by Prawer, ibid., p. 388, n. 5.

50. On the differing perceptions of the Kabbalah in Nachmanides and in R. Ezra's works see my article "We have no Kabbalistic Tradition on This" in Isadore Twersky, ed., *Rabbi Moses Nahmanides (Ramban): Explorations in His Religious and Literary Virtuosity* (Cambridge, Mass., 1983), pp. 56–64.

51. For details on this Kabbalistic school, see Gershom Scholem, *Major Trends*, lecture IV.

52. I could not locate the exact source to which Abulafia refers. For the Rabbinic texts which assert that prophecy is a phenomenon unique to the Land of Israel see L. Ginzberg, *The Legends of the Jews* (Philadelphia, 1946), vol. V, p. 301, n. 215.

53. See his *Sefer Hacheshek*, ms. New York, JTS, 1801 (EMC 858), fol. 32r-v. The passage discussed here was treated briefly by Abraham Berger, "The Messianic Self-Consciousness of Abraham Abulafia," *Essays on Jewish Life and Thought Presented in Honor of Salo W. Baron* (New York, 1959), p. 60. His interpretation of the passage is erroneous since it takes into consideration only a short part of the discussion. As a result, Berger views the "land" as a metaphor of the "inner soul" —a term which does not occur in Abulafia's terminology—instead of as a metaphor of the body.

54. Ms. New York, fol. 32v: *Guf Tsaddik*. In other passages, Abulafia identifies "the land" with the "the heart" hinting at its "material" meaning. Some other texts, written by contemporaries of Abulafia and corroborating this view, were discussed in my article "Jerusalem in Medieval Jewish Thought." See above, n. 2.

55. The numerical value of the Hebrew letters that make up the words *chutzah la'aretz* is 430, exactly like that of the letters *nefesh*—soul.

56. As Berger rightly pointed out (n. 53, above), Abulafia's mystical perception of the Land of Israel has to be understood against the background of his polemics with R. Shelomo ben Abraham ibn Adret, who maintained that prophecy can be attained only in the Land of Israel. See RaShBa, *Responsa*, I, no. 548.

57. Ms. Moscow—Ginzburg, 775, fol. 95r. The original Hebrew text was printed in Moshe Idel, "Erez Israel and Prophetic Kabbalah," *Shalem: Studies in the History of the Jews in Erez Israel,* ed. Joseph Hacker, vol. III (1981), p. 126, n. 40 (Hebrew). In this article I have attempted to prove the influence of Abulafia's Kabbalah on Kabbalists in Acre and Safed at the end of the 13th century. See now its English translation in Richard I. Cohen, ed., *Vision and Conflict in the Holy Land* (New York, 1985), pp. 102–110.

58. Although Abulafia considered himself to be the Messiah, he never referred to the Land of Israel as the scene of eschatological events. See also Berger, n. 53, above.

59. As Gottlieb has already remarked, R. Isaac does not agree with the concept of R. Judah Halevi that only people born as Jews are able to become prophets. R. Isaac asserts that even proselytes may receive prophetic inspiration. See Gottlieb, *Studies,* p. 242.

60. See Arthur Green, "The *Zadiq* and *Axis Mundi* in Later Judaism," *JAAR* 65, no. 3 (1977), pp. 339–42, 344, n. 18. However, even R. Nahman of Brazlav viewed his journey to Eretz Yisra'el as the only way to achieve a higher esoteric understanding of the mizvot. See Arthur Green, *Tormented Master: A Life of Rabbi Nahman of Bratslav* (Alabama, 1979), pp. 76–79. It is worth mentioning a surprising parallel perception of one's own journey to the Land of Israel. At the beginning of the 14th century, R. Shem Tov ben Abraham ibn Gaon writes of his immigration in the company of R. Hananel ben Abraham Esquira: "We left our place in order to come to the Holy Land, since we thought that outside [the Land] may not be worthy of the usage of these wondrous subjects (i.e., Kabbalistic items)." (*Baddei Ha'aron,* Ms. Paris, 840, fol. 95v.)

61. However, there were also other trends in Hassidic thought. See Isaiah Tishby, "The Messianic Idea and Messianic Trends in the Growth of Hassidim," *Zion* 32 (1967), pp. 1–45 (Hebrew).

62. See also the Frankists' perception of Poland as Eretz Yisra'el in Gershom Scholem, *Studies and Texts Concerning the History of Shabbetianism and its Metamorphosis* (Jerusalem, 1974), pp. 42–48, 121 (Hebrew).

63. Mircea Eliade, *Images and Symbols: Studies in Religious Symbolism* (New York, 1969), pp. 42–45, indeed uses examples from Rabbinic sources.

64. See Gershom Scholem, "Questions Concerning the Critical Analysis of the Zohar Connected to its Information on Eretz Yisra'el," *Zion* 1 (1925), pp. 40–56 (Hebrew); idem, "The Book Shevilei Yerushalaim, attributed to R. Isaac Helo—a Forgery," *Zion* 6 (1934), pp. 39–53, 220–21 (Hebrew).

65. *Images and Symbols,* p. 55. Compare also to his *The Sacred and the Profane* (New York, 1961), p. 65.

66. The hypothesis that the profanation of the Holy Land and the destruction of the Temple have broken the concrete link between the Land and the Divine Realm cannot be substantiated from the classical Kabbalistic texts. See, e.g., the

material referred to in n. 36, above. For the transformation of the Jewish "sacred space"—the Temple—in "sacred time," see Arthur Green, "Sabbath as Temple: Some Thoughts on Space and Time in Judaism," *Go and Study—Essays and Studies in Honor of Alfred Jospe*, ed. R. Jospe, S. Fishman (Washington, D.C., 1980), pp. 287–305. Compare also to Ch. N. Bialik's essay, "Halakhah and Aggadah," *Kol Kitvei Ch.N. Bialik* (Tel Aviv, 1968), pp. 216–17 (Hebrew).

The Land of Israel
in Pre-Modern Jewish Thought:
A History of Two Rabbinic Statements

MARC SAPERSTEIN

[Editor's note: How important was the Land in the daily life of medieval Jewry? Did people take seriously the many adages regarding its religious centrality? Dr. Marc Saperstein, Professor of Jewish History and Thought at Washington University in St. Louis, tests the binding force of such homiletical statements by examining a specific legal issue. According to the letter of the law, a man planning to migrate to the Land of Israel may divorce his wife without paying her a marriage settlement (a *ketubah*), if she refuses to accompany him. Saperstein surveys the legal literature surrounding this law, to see if it was, in fact, ever followed. In the process, he discovers a variety of facets regarding medieval Jewry's conceptualization of the Land, especially under circumstances when the values implicit in living one's life there conflicted with other religious considerations, such as sustaining one's family where they happened to be, or endangering one's life by travel. His treatment of this legal issue leads him to consider a purely homiletical one, again a traditional "proverbial" remark to the effect that living outside the Land is tantamount to living without God. If people persisted in living outside the Land anyway, how did they uphold the veracity of this statement, but still reinterpret it so as to avoid passing negative judgment on their decision to remain in the diaspora? Saperstein's discussion again reveals the extent to which living in the Land was actually a consideration for medieval Jewry, either because they tried to live there, or, because, having decided not to, they found it necessary to reinterpret traditional wisdom to avoid its extreme devaluation of their decision.]

> The Jewish people . . . forced to leave their ancient country, has never abandoned, never forsaken, the Holy Land; the Jewish people has never ceased to be passionate about Zion. It has always lived in a dialogue with the Holy Land.[1]

These words, written by Abraham Joshua Heschel, express a sentiment reiterated by dozens of Jewish thinkers of the past generation. The passion-

ate attachment of Diaspora Jewry to *Eretz Yisra'el,* from the destruction of
the Temple at least until the Emancipation, is an ideological axiom shared
by the vast majority of contemporary Jews. Why this is so widely assumed
to be true might be worthy of a study in itself; it was certainly not the case
seventy-five years ago, when anti-Zionists sought to temper the passion of
the attachment through quietistic and universalistic teachings, and Zionist
writers berated medieval and contemporary Jews for having made peace with
life in *galut* [lit. "Exile," outside the Land].[2] Our question, however, is different: to what degree does a statement like that of Professor Heschel reflect
a demonstrable historical reality? What kinds of source material would be
relevant for such a test; how might the statement be documented or proven;
how is the role of the Land of Israel in Jewish thought and consciousness
from 70 to 1800 to be evaluated?

The technique most frequently employed for this purpose is not especially fruitful. This is the method of anthology, the collection of sources
from all periods and genres of Hebrew literature which praise the merits
of the Land of Israel, emphasize the importance of living there, articulate
yearnings for its holy places, and so forth. Such collections of passages,[3]
generally removed from their historical and literary context and presented
without indication of opposing viewpoints or analysis of what they might
really mean, are at best a starting point; at worst they may be biased distortions. It is not enough merely to collect rabbinic pronouncements—
"Whoever dwells in the Land of Israel lives without sin"; "Whoever walks
four cubits in the Land of Israel is assured of a place in the world to come";
"Dwelling in the Land of Israel counterbalances all of the divine commandments"[4]—as if they were self-explaining and sufficient as evidence for the
view of "the Jewish tradition." Questions fundamental to any historical
investigation must be raised: whose view does this represent? why was it
said? to what extent does it typify Jewish attitudes and conduct? how does
the sentiment relate to other statements concerned with Jewish values and
obligations?

The present study is therefore concerned both with substantive matters and with methodological issues relating to the use of sources bearing
on the Land of Israel. The following principles might be suggested at the
outset: First, religious leaders usually do not bother denouncing sins that
are not being committed; preachers generally emphasize values that are challenged and problematic. As historical evidence, a rabbinic statement warning against leaving the Land of Israel or underlining the importance of living
there is therefore double-edged: it reveals not only the commitment to the

Land of at least one (and possibly many) religious leaders, but also a weakness of commitment among the Jews such leaders were trying to convince.[5] Second, a statement from either Talmud or Midrash cannot be assumed to be equally valid for all periods of subsequent Jewish history. For legal statements, one must attempt to determine to what extent they were actually enforced in Jewish courts throughout the ages. For aggadic statements, it is instructive to trace the history of their use: whether a particular statement had significant repercussions or was consigned to virtual oblivion, who quoted it and for what purpose, how was it interpreted and applied. Finally, we learn most about the role of the Land of Israel not from hyperbolic praise, but rather from discussions that reveal tension or conflict between loyalty to the Land and other values in Jewish life. I shall attempt to apply these principles to a well-known halakhic and aggadic statement, from the most important locus of rabbinic views on the Land, the Babylonian gemara at the end of tractate Ketubot.

"She Must Be Compelled To Go Up [to *Eretz Yisra'el*], And If She Does Not Consent, She May Be Divorced Without Her *Ketubah*."

The following text, a *baraita,* and, therefore, datable before the year 200 C.E., raised legal dilemmas for generations of rabbinic judges:

> Our Rabbis taught: if the husband desires to go up [to *Eretz Yisra'el*] but his wife refuses she must be compelled to go up, and if she does not consent, she may be divorced without a *ketubah* [a marriage settlement]. If she desires to go up and he refuses, he must be compelled to go up, and if he does not consent, he must divorce her and pay her *ketubah.* (B. Ket. 110a)[6]

This passage concerns a conflict between two important Jewish values: encouraging settlement of the Land of Israel, and protecting the contractual rights of a wife. The law unambiguously states that the settlement of the Land takes priority. While a husband cannot ordinarily compel his wife to move with him to a different country,[7] he may do so if he wants to settle in *Eretz Yisra'el,* even if it means moving from a fine dwelling to an inferior one. If the wife refuses, the husband may divorce her and be freed of the obligation to pay the amount specified in her marriage contract.

Was this law actually enforced? Based on actual cases recorded in the rabbinic responsa literature, the answer would appear to be "Sometimes, but often not." For example, the following problem was presented to Maimonides in Egypt near the end of the twelfth century. A young man married the daughter of a leading Jewish family in Alexandria. When their first son was three months old, the husband quarreled with his in-laws, and tried to pressure his wife to renounce certain contracted rights. The court determined in favor of the wife, leaving the husband bound to all stipulations of the marriage agreement. Then a friend suggested that the husband ask his wife to settle with him in Israel; she would certainly refuse to leave her entire family and move with an infant to a strange country, and then he could divorce her without any financial obligation whatsoever. This time the court, following the clear dictum of the Talmud, ruled that the wife was obligated to accompany her husband or she would lose her rights to the stipulated payment upon divorce. The dumbfounded leaders of the community complained, "From now on, everyone who dislikes his wife and wants to divorce her without paying will fabricate this claim; many women will consequently be divorced by their husbands."

Maimonides, responding, reported the practice of many Jewish courts to pronounce a general ban of excommunication upon anyone who would claim a desire to settle in Palestine for any reason other than the pure motivation of enjoying the blessing of the Holy Land; only after the husband answers "Amen" to such a ban do they enforce the rule in his case, permitting him to go. Maimonides himself would go even farther in restricting its enforcement, despite the absence of Talmudic support: the husband must have a general reputation for honesty, and there must be no known strife between husband and wife, for "It is a light matter for most men to cause grief to their wives and to free themselves from the obligation of paying their *ketubah,* and we must guard against such a sin."[8] In other words, in the case at hand, he would dissent from the court and refuse to enforce the Talmudic law.

The noted German authority, R. Meir of Rothenberg [d. 1293], suggested a different provision, also apparently intended to protect the wife against the machinations of a husband not sincerely committed to living in *Eretz Yisra'el.* The wife may be divorced without her *ketubah* "provided that he goes to the Land of Israel and does not return. But if he should come back to settle outside the Land, even after many years, if she is still alive she may demand [the money stipulated in the *ketubah*], and if, God forbid, she has previously died, her heirs may claim it." R. Meir was also careful to limit enforcement to precisely what is stated by the Talmud so that the woman would not be excessively penalized. The wife may lose her right to the amount stipulated in the *ketubah* as compensation for divorce, but dowry property she has brought to the marriage is certainly to be protected for her.[9] Neither Maimonides nor Meir of Rothenberg was prepared to go so far as to change the principle of the law or to reverse the theoretical hierarchy of values. But the potential for abuse generated an effort to ensure greater protection for wives and a mandate for judges to investigate closely the circumstances and the motivations of the proclaimed desire to settle in the Holy Land.

An even more radical view was recorded in the Tosafot to the Talmudic passage. Quite simply, "This law does not apply at the present time, because of the dangers of the journey."[10] The Talmudic position was understandable on the part of Palestinian tannaim [Rabbis prior to the Mishnah's promulgation, c. 200 C.E.] who wanted to attract immigration from the relatively nearby countries of the second-century Diaspora. But for twelfth and thirteenth-century French rabbis, it was not so simple. Factoring in all the hazards of travel between northern Europe and Palestine during the period of the Crusades, when even armed nobles knew they might not reach their destination safely, the French rabbis decided that the balance of the equation had shifted, and that the value of settlement in wartorn *Eretz Yisra'el* could no longer justify compelling a wife to undertake the venture against her will. The result they recommended was a benign neglect of what the Talmud clearly mandated.

Later rabbis, especially those living in Mediterranean countries, generally agreed in principle that the law should not be enforced under conditions of serious danger, and the question shifted to whether or not such danger actually existed in their time. The matter was never finally resolved; problems relating to this rule continued to appear in the responsa literature of almost every generation. R. Solomon b. Simeon Duran [Rashbash 1400–1467; ed. note: see also below pp. 156, 158, remarks by Shalom Rosenberg] maintained that a full discussion of the law was necessary, despite its unambiguous formulation in the Talmud, "because times change, so that novel circumstances that have not occurred in a thousand years can arise very quickly; in our times we see new misfortunes and new dangers constantly arising for those who travel by sea and on land." His conclusion, cited as halakha in the *Shulchan Arukh*, is that the wife is not compelled to accompany her husband to Israel by land if she lives anywhere west of Alexandria, but that she may be compelled to travel by sea in the summer "provided there are no pirates"—a provision leaving the door ajar for subsequent litigation. As for his own personal experience, "This case has already come before me, and I have adjudicated several times that we do not enforce going up."[11] In the sixteenth century, R. Samuel di Medina (Maharashdam) used the danger principle as the basis for an *a fortiori* argument relating to a different issue. Asked whether a mother's death-bed command to transfer her body for burial in Palestine should be enforced, he replied, "If in the matter of settling in the Land, the hazard of travel is sufficient to nullify the law so that we do not compel either the husband or wife . . . how much more in regard to the present matter of burial is the fact of danger to the living and the dead sufficient to justify refraining from any action."[12]

But this was not all. One of the Tosafists, R. Hayim b. Hananel ha-Kohen [ca. 1150–1200], went considerably beyond the rationale of "dangers of the journey" in arguing for the unenforceability of the Talmudic law. He stated that at present, "living in the Land of Israel is not a religious obligation at all, owing to the difficulty or impossibility of fulfilling many of the precepts attached to the soil."[13] Here is an unmistakable reversal of the tannaitic hierarchy of values; according to R. Hayim, the importance of living in *Eretz Yisra'el* had diminished to the point where it was obviously outweighed by other considerations. The Talmudic rule of compulsion was abrogated not because of conditions that might readily be changed, such as the geographical location of the couple or the peacefulness of the region, but because of the very nature of Jewish life itself.

R. Hayim's statement caused considerable consternation among later authorities, and the majority did not accept it as normative.[14] One went so far as to deny its authenticity. R. Joseph b. Moses of Trani (Maharit, sixteenth-century Safed) noted R. Meir of Rothenberg's repudiation of a distinction between the religious significance of *Eretz Yisra'el* in the time of the Temple and in his own day, that is, after the period of the Temple's destruction. From this, he concluded that R. Meir, the outstanding expert on the Tosafists, did not consider the statement attributed to R. Hayim to be part of the Tosafot, for Meir would surely not have ignored such an important authority as R. Hayim. Maharit concluded that R. Hayim, like the other Tosafists, recognized only the argument based on danger; the statement that it is not a *mitzvah* to live in the Land was "the marginal note of a student, bearing no authority at all."[15] In short, Maharit insisted that it was indeed a *mitzvah* to live in *Eretz Yisra'el*, even at the time in which he lived. But this insistence impelled him to formulate the central question in a manner that could not be more lucid and succinct: "Which *mitzvah* takes precedence, sustaining one's wife and children or going to live in the

Land of Israel and thereby leaving them in hunger and thirst? . . . When you
sit and weigh the obligations of these *mitzvot,* you find that it is more obligatory to remain with one's wife and children and provide for their needs and
guide them in the right way and raise them to the study of Torah than to go
physically to the Land of Israel."[16] Again we see the Talmudic law not being
enforced in a vacuum, but weighed in the balance with other vital needs.

The following responsum provides another fine example of the dynamic issues impinging upon the decision whether to implement the rule
of the *baraita.* In this case, a woman went to the court claiming that she
wanted to settle in the Land of Israel in order to escape from her sick husband, who was mistreating her badly and giving away his property to relatives so that there would be nothing left to pay the *ketubah* obligation at
his death. It might appear that the situation would provide good grounds
for enforcing the Talmudic law. While the woman's motivation for living
in the Land was apparently not the purest, all she was asking was that the
court grant her the money stipulated in her *ketubah,* to which she would
certainly be entitled at the husband's death, before he could succeed in his
devious attempt to deprive her.

R. Tam ibn Yahya [Turkey; 1475–1542] refused to enforce the law.
The husband's sickness meant that he was not unwilling but unable to go,
and the rule of compulsion therefore did not apply.

> All the more so since he can claim that food is extremely scarce in
> the Land of Israel and there is not enough to earn a livelihood, and
> [this is why] he does not want to go there: this is certainly a legitimate
> claim. . . . Especially if he is knowledgeable in Torah, we do not com-
> pel him, because there is a scarcity of food. One who lives in Israel
> may leave it in order to study Torah;[17] therefore one who is able to
> study outside the Land is obviously not to be compelled to go there.
> All the great rabbis of France and Germany relied upon this reason,
> in addition to the danger of the journey, in not going to Israel. I
> have a tradition that this is why the amoraim of Babylonia did not
> go. And perhaps this is why Maimonides did not, even though he
> was close to Israel and safe caravans were readily available to travel
> there from Egypt. . . . He would not have been able to provide for
> himself in accordance with his dignity in the Land of Israel and also
> to study Torah.[18]

This passage articulates a position that goes beyond the immediate
case at hand, justifying not only the refusal to enforce the Talmudic law

but the historical reality of great centers of Jewish learning led by pious scholars who theoretically could have decided to live in the Holy Land but chose
not to. Ibn Yahya then cited one final reason for his unwillingness to act
in the present case. After a detailed discussion of the Tosafot, including the
statement of R. Hayim, he concluded, "Since there is a dispute among the
giants, we will not act to compel the husband to divorce her and pay."[19]

In short, the undisputed Tannaitic ruling intended to promote settlement of *Eretz Yisra'el* cannot be assumed to have governed Jewish life in
all ages. While it was indeed sometimes enforced,[20] other interests relating
to the institution of marriage and its contractual obligations, intellectual
aspirations, economic realities, and a judicial reluctance to intervene in a
highly controversial and problematic matter, often made the Talmudic law
a dead letter. [Ed. note: See also remarks by Shalom bar Asher, pp. 299–303
below, for opinions attributed to rabbis in North Africa during the eighteenth and nineteenth centuries.]

"Whoever Dwells Outside the Land Is As One Who Has No God"

The second statement, also a *baraita* from Ketubot 110b, raises problems totally different from the legal dilemmas of the first. This statement
has no halakhic significance, yet it is quoted in virtually every discussion
of *Eretz Yisra'el* in medieval and early modern Hebrew literature: "Whoever
dwells in the Land of Israel is as one who has a God, and whoever dwells
outside the Land is as one who has no God." Here too, a tension is generated between important values. On the one hand, there is the centrality
of *Eretz Yisra'el* for Jewish religious experience; on the other hand, there
is the universality of God and the danger of implying that access to God
is limited to one geographical location. This is compounded by the problems of undermining the religious status of pious Jews who were born, lived,
and died in the Diaspora. Indeed, the statement is challenged immediately
in the gemara itself: "Does one who lives outside the land really have no
God?" It is as if some amora were arguing that the original formulation is
too extreme, that the Tannaim had been carried away with their own rhetoric.
It is appropriate to assert that God has a special relationship with the Land
of Israel, but it is not appropriate to say that God has no relationship with
other lands.[21] Therefore a more moderate form is suggested: "Whoever dwells
outside the Land is as one who worships idols." This way, at least, the possibility of a relationship with God in the Diaspora is not denied.

Significant modifications were occasionally made in quoting these statements. Commenting on Genesis 17:8, Rashi wrote "and *there* I will be to them as God, but an *Israelite* who dwells outside the land *in the time of the Temple* is as one who has no God." In accordance with the context of God's promise to Abraham, "Whoever" has been changed to "Israelite"; without any obvious justification, the qualification "in the time of the Temple" has been added. In this formulation, it was clear that the statement did not apply either to Rashi and his contemporary Jews, or to his Christian neighbors. If we turn to Rashi's commentary on Leviticus 25:38, the verse that the gemara adduced as its basis for the aggadic statement in question, we see that Rashi actually ignores the Talmudic exegesis, following instead an alternative lesson drawn from Sifra: "To whoever dwells in the land, I am as God, but whoever *departs from it* is as one who worships idols." Not being born and living one's life in the Diaspora, but emigrating there from the Holy Land, is presented as sinful. [Ed. note: See below, pp. 216–17, 225–27 for further discussion of Rashi's attitude toward the Land.]

Maimonides incorporated the same change into his Code: "Whoever *departs from* the Land [of Israel] is as one who worships idols."[22] In the sixteenth century, Maharit Zahalon defended this alteration not on textual but on logical, or, one might say, ideological, grounds:

> Maimonides' intent was to defend the merit of those who dwell outside the Land. He did not want to say that all who lived outside the Land are, as it were, Godless; he therefore wrote that the gemara was not intended to apply to one who lived [in the Diaspora] as his ancestors had since the time they were expelled from holy soil and compelled through divine decree to live outside the Land. What was he to do? Of such a person it is not said, "He must not live outside the Land"; if it were, what should we say about all the Jews, and especially our sainted rabbis, who have lived in the Diaspora?[23]

In other words, Maimonides emended the Talmudic teaching because its implications were distasteful; how could he possibly codify the assertion that all the great Diaspora rabbis were like idolators? But there is more than this in Zahalon's comment; indeed, he seems to be attributing a critical historical sense to Maimonides' halakhic technique. The original Talmudic statement had been made by a Palestinian tanna to a Palestinian audience; the problem it addressed had actually been as Maimonides understood it: *leaving* the Land of Israel. Simply to have reproduced verbatim the original wording in his medieval Diaspora context would have been to falsify its intent, by equating a Jew born in the Diaspora who decided to remain there with a Jew born in the Land of Israel who decided to leave it. What Zahalon appears to be arguing is that Maimonides changed the wording of the Talmudic statement in order to convey its original intent most effectively—and accurately—to the audience he was addressing.

Despite Maimonides however, it was in its original form that the statement was most frequently cited in subsequent literature: "Whoever *dwells* outside the Land is as one who has no God." This was generally associated with the doctrine that God has a special providential relationship with the Land of Israel. This assertion, with strong roots in the classical texts of the tradition—"a land which the Lord thy God careth for; the eyes of the Lord thy God are always upon it" (Deut. 11:12); "the Land of Israel is watered by the Holy One praised be He Himself, the rest of the world through an emissary" (B. Ta'anit 10a)—was not particularly controversial. But the conclusions drawn from this premise could point in markedly different directions, depending on the theory of divine providence being used.

Some Jews writing in the philosophical tradition applied the Maimonidean doctrine that God's providential protection of any individual is directly proportional to that individual's intellectual apprehension of God.[24] This was combined with the assumption—unquestioned by medieval Jews— that the Land of Israel possessed a climate and air quality uniquely conducive to intellectual activity.[25] [Ed. note: See above, pp. 150–53, and below, pp. 214–16, for further discussion of medieval climatography associated with the Land.] Its inhabitants were therefore likely to have reached a higher level of intellectual perfection than the inhabitants of other lands, and consequently there would be greater providential attention directed to the Land of Israel. The difference, however, was not absolute but relative, a question of degree. A clear expression of this view is given by Yedaiah Bedersi [c. 1270–1340], in his discussion of a passage from Sifre on Deuteronomy 11:12. According to Yedaiah, the Bible and the Rabbis speak

> as if to indicate that the part of the world most providentially supervised is the Land of Israel. But the reason for this degree of providence is the high status of its inhabitants, who are watched over by God more than any other nation . . . for the degree of providence is proportional to the degree of knowledge and guidance.

The combination of appropriate conditions for intellectual activity (climate and air quality) and proper guidance for this activity (the Torah) makes Jews

living in the Land of Israel capable of perfecting their souls and attaining
a direct providential relationship with God.[26]

It is against this background that the Talmudic statement is to be understood. In a different context, Yedaiah himself made the connection: "the
superior status of that Land and its air is well known, as the Rabbis said,
'The air of the Land of Israel makes one wise,' and 'Whoever lives outside
the Land is as one who has no God,' and it is therefore called 'the place
which the Lord has chosen.'" This formulation is rather laconic, omitting
the critical doctrine of intellectual apprehension and divine providence, as
if it could be assumed that the reader was already familiar with the argument linking the two rabbinic statements. A fuller statement of the entire
theory is given by Abraham Bibago in the fifteenth century:

> The reason why they said that whoever lives outside the Land is as
> one who has no God is that such a person will not have a balanced
> temperament, and consequently his intellect will not be settled, as it
> would be with a proper corporeal environment. If a person's tempera-
> ment is not appropriate, he will resist philosophical enlightenment.
> . . . This is why one who dwells outside the Land is as one who has
> no God. . . . For the Land of Israel is moderate for its inhabitants,
> situated in the fourth climate, in the center of the inhabited world;
> those who are born there and live there will not be frozen by cold
> nor scorched by heat; their temperament will therefore be perfect for
> rational speculation, and their intellect clean and pure.[28]

This mode of interpreting the rabbinic statement does not imply that it is
impossible for anyone outside the Land of Israel to attain philosophical enlightenment and thereby to merit God's providential attention. Rather, the
conditions outside the Land are more difficult, fewer will reach the aspired
level, and therefore, in general, those living in the Diaspora will be more
likely to be "as one who has no God."

A very different explanation of the uniqueness of *Eretz Yisra'el*, not
dependent on the controversial Maimonidean doctrine of providence, was
widely accepted. In the rabbinic formulation, the other lands were under
the jurisdiction of "princes" (*sarim*) while the Land of Israel was governed
directly by God. A medieval reformulation of this idea taught that the
events occurring outside the Land of Israel were part of the ordinary pattern
of nature, the end result of a long chain of intermediate causes in which
the stars were generally considered to have a dominant role. The Land of
Israel was different; there God acted directly, not through the stars and the

effects they generated. R. Solomon b. Adret (Rashba [Spain, c. 1235–c. 1310]) was asked for a formal responsum in explanation of the statement that "Whoever dwells outside the Land is as one who has no God."[29] Following his teacher Nachmanides, he formulated the fundamental, metaphysical difference between *Eretz Yisra'el* and the other lands in this manner: "[God] did not give the Land [of Israel] and the people [of Israel] to [the jurisdiction of] a star or to one of the heavenly princes whom He apportioned to all the [other] nations; . . . our Land is perpetually chosen, for it is not handed over to an emissary, but to God's own providence."[30] For some writers, therefore, merely living in a foreign land under the dominion of "princes" or stars was enough to explain the rabbinic comparison with Godlessness.[31]

Others carried the implications of this status further. Living under the intermediaries which God ordained to govern the affairs of the world in a natural manner might be viewed as diminishing the efficacy of prayer. This was the conclusion of R. Nissim Gerondi (Spain, c. 1310–c. 1375) in his fourth *derashah:*

> "Whoever dwells outside the Land is as one who has no God." This is because the other lands of the idolators are given over to the government of the heavenly princes, which cannot be changed except through a miracle . . . ; consequently, the prayer of one who dwells outside the Land and is under [the jurisdiction of] a constellation or star *is not heard as much* (*ein tefilato nishma'at kol kakh*) as if he were in the Land of Israel, which is not under the governance of any ruler but God Himself.[32]

An even more extreme formulation, is attributed by a later author to the "Yalkut":

> "Whoever dwells in the Land of Israel is as one who has a God," for he prays to God and God hears his prayer; he is not under [the jurisdiction of] a constellation, but under the power of the Holy One Himself. But "whoever dwells outside the Land is as one who has no God," for even when he prays to God, *God does not hear his prayer,* as he is under [the jurisdiction of] princes and constellations.[33]

It would be hard to find a more radical theological negation of the Diaspora in post-Talmudic literature.

Application of the rabbinic statement could be extended beyond prayer to the entire corpus of the commandments. It was not merely that certain commandments applied exclusively to the Land of Israel, although certain commentators did, in fact, use this fact in their interpretations.[34] The more powerful doctrine held that even those commandments not dependent on the Land, those that *could* be observed by the Diaspora Jew, were somehow incomplete when performed outside of *Eretz Yisra'el*. Based on statements of the rabbinic literature, this doctrine was given classical formulation by Nachmanides in two central passages.

In his commentary on Leviticus 18:25, Nachmanides addressed the notion that the Land of Israel expels its inhabitants because of sexual misconduct. He began by discussing the distinctiveness of the Land of Israel in familiar terms: the other nations are assigned to their own constellations which in turn are overseen by special angels, but the Land of Israel is the estate of the Eternal, subject to no intermediate power but only to God. This is why the Land is unable to tolerate idolatry, the worship of intermediate beings, or the sexual immorality so often associated with it. Even nations which practice idolatry with impunity outside the Land are punished for the very same actions when they dwell upon it (II Kings 17:26). After quoting several additional rabbinic statements to this effect, Ramban continued,

> This is the meaning of the saying of the rabbis, "Whoever dwells outside the Land is as one who has no God. . . ." And in the Tosefta of tractate Avodah Zarah, the Rabbis said . . . "When you are in the land of Canaan, I am your God; when you are not in the land of Canaan, I am so to speak (*kiveyakhol*) not your God." . . . On this basis the Rabbis said in the *Sifre:* "'And you perish quickly from off the good Land.' Although I banish you from the Land to outside the Land, you should make yourselves distinctive (*metzuyanim*) by the commandments, so that when you return they shall not be novelties to you. . . . And so did the prophet Jeremiah say, 'Set thee up waymarks' (*tziyunim*): these are the commandments, by which Israel is made distinctive." . . . For the essence of the commandments (*ikar hamitzvot*) is for those dwelling in the Land of God. Therefore the Rabbis said in the *Sifre* . . . "Dwelling in the Land of Israel is of equal importance to all the commandments of the Torah."

There is much in this passage that Nachmanides has left unexplained.[35] Most important for our purposes is the new conclusion drawn from the premise of God's special providential relationship with the Land. The commandments performed in exile have little intrinsic importance; they have an instrumental value, preserving Jewish distinctiveness, and keeping Jews in practice, for the time when they would return to the Land and perform them as they were truly intended to be observed. In short, the very same actions have a totally different significance when they are performed upon the "Estate of the Eternal." The Jew outside the Land is as one who has no God because the commandments he performs, mediated through the long chain of intermediate causes, have little direct effect upon the Godhead.

Such conclusions, which appeared to make the efficacy of prayer or the value of the *mitzvot* dependent upon geographical location rather than on inner, spiritual factors, were abhorrent to other Jewish thinkers. The problems inherent in the Talmudic assertion are evident in Hasidic literature, where several striking reinterpretations use various rhetorical techniques to nullify the simple meaning and to make the highest spiritual status available to Jews outside the Land [Ed. note: On Hasidism, see remarks above, p. 180 by Moshe Idel.] For example, the following was attributed to the Baal Shem Tov by his disciple, R. Ya'akov Yosef of Polnoye:

> I heard from my teacher that wherever a person is in his thought, there he is indeed. If he dwells outside the Land, but yearns and thinks of *Eretz Yisra'el* constantly, he is *similar (domeh)* to one who has no God, but he actually has one. . . . This is not the case if he is in *Eretz Yisra'el*, but his status and livelihood are outside the Land, for he will always be thinking of such matters. . . . Such a person is *similar* to one who has a God, but in reality, he has none, for his thought is outside the Land.[36]

This interpretation focuses on the use of the word *domeh* in the rabbinic statement; the Rabbis did not say, "Whoever dwells outside the land *has* no God," but "*is as one*" or "*appears like one* who has no God." According to the Besht, the similarity is one only of appearance.

A similar reinterpretation is given by R. Elimelekh of Lizensk, who wrote,

> a person who wants his prayer to be heard must focus his thought as if he were praying in the Land of Israel, with the Temple rebuilt and the altar set in its proper place. . . . This is the meaning of "whoever dwells in the Land of Israel," namely, whoever imagines to himself that he is standing in the Land of Israel; through this exercise, he attains clarity in prayer. "Is as one who has a God" means he is like one who investigates God's exaltedness in order to apprehend the

Creator through His works, namely, the heavenly bodies in their courses. And "whoever dwells outside the Land," who does not conduct himself during his prayer in this manner, "is as one who has no God," meaning, he is like one who does not investigate the world around him in order to know that there is a God.[37]

In both these interpretations, the Land of Israel remains central — as an ideal. But the distinction between physically living in the Land and living outside it has been abandoned for a spiritual distinction; it is the ability to think of *Eretz Yisra'el*, and to imagine oneself praying in the reconstructed Temple, no matter where one happens to be living, that is now critical.

A more radical spiritualization of *Eretz Yisra'el*, not explicitly applied to this statement but clearly in the same tradition, is proposed by R. Menahem Nahum of Tchernobil in his homiletical interpretations of selected *aggadot*:

> Even though the physical *Eretz Yisra'el* exists, its essence is a spiritual matter, namely, the life force coming from God. Although we are outside the Land, we nevertheless have an aspect of *Eretz Yisra'el* . . . for in every house of worship and study, the life force of *Eretz Yisra'el* is emanated from God. Therefore the sages said, "Houses of study and worship are destined to stand in *Eretz Yisra'el*" (B. Meg. 29a), for they themselves are an aspect of the vitality of *Eretz Yisra'el*. Understand this. If so, one who stands in the house of worship or study, and prays in words suffused with thought is indeed in *Eretz Yisra'el*, that is, in the life force of the creator. But if he thinks vain thoughts . . . then even though his body is in the house of worship, his essential part, which is his thought, is not in '*Eretz Yisra'el*,' namely the house of worship.[38]

Here a further step has been taken. It is not even necessary to imagine oneself being in the Land of Israel or to yearn for it, but merely to be in the synagogue and to pray with devotion and purity of thought. This in itself constitutes "being in the Land of Israel" in the most important sense.

Perhaps the most astounding reinterpretation of the statement is attributed to the Baal Shem Tov by R. Benjamin b. Aaron of Zalosce [late eighteenth century]. According to this view, the rabbis were not referring to the Land of Israel at all, but rather to two spiritual levels to be found in different Jews. First, there is the Jew who is bound up by his terrestrial nature (*artziyut*), by his corporeality; this is the one who "dwells in the Land." He thinks that he worships God fully and completely, that there is nothing lacking in his service. But he thinks this only because he fails to recognize the awesome greatness of the Creator. In this way, "One who lives in the Land—that is, ensconced in his corporeality—imagines himself [still another interpretation of *domeh*] to have a God," but in reality he has no God at all, and has not even begun the appropriate service of the Almighty.

The opposite is true of the Jew who lives "outside his terrestrial nature" (*chutz la-aretz*). He understands the greatness of God and realizes that he has not even begun to serve Him properly. As his thought cleaves to God's exalted nature, he is constantly abashed at the shortcomings of his own service when measured against the standard of perfect love and awe. This man, who lives "outside the Land," imagines that he has no God, but in reality he does have God within him.[39] In this interpretation of the Baal Shem Tov, the physical Land of Israel has totally disappeared from the rabbinic statement, even as an ideal. Dwelling "in the Land" has become a negative characterization, dwelling "outside the Land" a positive one. The statement is transformed into an expression of paradox emphasizing the distance between appearance and reality; the ultimate value has nothing to do with one's geographical location, but lies rather in the humble recognition that the human being can never hope to worship God in accordance with His true greatness.

We have traced some of the vicissitudes of two tannaitic statements affirming the aboslute centrality of *Eretz Yisra'el* and denigrating the value of life in the Diaspora, and we have seen how these statements, reverberating in many different contexts of Jewish life and thought, have been used to draw a panoply of conclusions.[40] While some have reaffirmed the centrality of *Eretz Yisra'el* with all its implications in accordance with the straightforward meaning of the rabbinic pronouncements, others have in effect repudiated the simple meaning, de-emphasizing the significance of *Eretz Yisra'el* (at least in premessianic times) in favor of other important Jewish values. This is not to suggest that the millennial Jewish attachment to the Land of Israel had little basis in reality. It is, rather, to suggest that beginning with the amoraic period, intellectual and spiritual leaders of the Jewish people had to walk a treacherous tightrope, balancing diverse and sometimes conflicting goals, all of which were in some sense critical to Jewish survival. They had to maintain the importance, the centrality of the Land of Israel, Jerusalem, and the Temple Mount, without undermining the possibility of continued and creative Jewish life in the Diaspora. They had to instill the consciousness that Jewish religious life was somehow incomplete without

Land and Temple, yet make certain it would remain full and rich enough to merit the loyalties of adherents tested by powerful rivals. They had to foster yearnings for the Land of the Bible, the Land that God had chosen, without cultivating the idolatrous worship of soil and stones. While occasionally one element or another got out of balance, the full history of interpretation of rabbinic statements about the Land reveals a rather impressive harmonization of these goals.

Notes

1. Abraham Joshua Heschel, *Israel: An Echo of Eternity* (New York, 1969), pp. 58–59.

2. E.g. Y. H. Brenner, "Self-Criticism," in *The Zionist Idea*, ed. A. Hertzberg (New York, 1975), p. 310. Pre-emancipation Jews, when in the mood for self-criticism, would also have dissented from a generalization such as that of Professor Heschel; cf. the retrospective characterization of Spanish Jewry by R. Jacob Emden: "Misfortune befell us when Israel enjoyed honors in countries like Spain and assimilated with the people among whom they lived. *No one at all yearned for Zion; it was abandoned and forgotten*" (Introduction to *Amudei Shamayim*, translated in Philip Birnbaum, *A Treasury of Judaism* [New York, 1962], p. 405).

3. A representative but certainly not exhaustive list would include Yehiel Michael Guttman, *Eretz Yisra'el Bemidrash Vetalmud* (Breslau, 1929); Joseph Zahavi, *Eretz Israel in Rabbinic Lore* (Jerusalem, 1962); Avraham Holtz, *The Holy City: Jews on Jerusalem* (New York, 1971); Itzak Raphael, *Hachasidut Ve'eretz Yisra'el* (Jerusalem, 1940); Simeon Federbush, *Hachasidut Vetsiyon* (Jerusalem, 1963); Moses Tiberg, *Mishivchei Ha'aretz* (Tel Aviv, 1975); Hen-Melekh Merhavyah, *Kolot Korim Letsiyon* (Jerusalem, 1980).

4. The first two quotations are from B. Ket. 111a, the third from Sifre on Deuteronomy 12:29.

5. Consider, for example, R. Simeon b. Yohai's comment, "Elimelech, Mahlon, and Chilion were great men and leaders of their generation. Why then were they punished? Because they left Palestine for a foreign country" (B. BB 91a). As historical evidence, this probably tells us little about the theological underpinnings of the Book of Ruth. It may indeed serve as evidence for the emigration of powerful Jews in the wake of devastating economic conditions following the disastrous Bar Kokhba revolt in the middle of the second century. A late thirteenth-century author, faced with a quite different problem in his environment, concluded that Elimelech and his sons were punished because they married alien women (*Zohar Chadash*, Ruth [Livorno, 1866], p. 99a).

6. According to a different version of this statement, preserved in a manu-

script of the Tosefta and in the Palestinian Talmud, the husband who refuses to accompany his wife to the Land of Israel is *not* compelled to do so; see Saul Lieberman, *Tosefta Kifeshutah, Ketubot* (New York, 1967), p. 386. The Palestinian text would appear to reflect the view that this technique of fostering the settlement of *Eretz Yisra'el* was not worth undermining the husband's supremacy in the marital relationship.

7. B. Ket. 110b; Maimonides, Hil. Ishut, 13.17.

8. *Teshuvot Harambam*, ed. J. Blau (Jerusalem, 1958), II, 639–41.

9. R. Meir of Rothenburg, cited in Yisrael Schepansky, *Eretz Yisra'el Besifrut Hateshuvot* (henceforth, "Schepansky"), I (Jerusalem, 1966), 156. R. Meir's decision about the obligation of the husband to pay his former wife if he subsequently left the Land of Israel was accepted by later codifiers; see Isserles' *Darkhei Moshe* on *Tur*, "Even Ha'ezer," 75 and *Mappah* on *Shulchan Arukh*, ibid.

10. Tosafot Ket. 110b, "Hu." For other examples of Tosafistic determinations that Talmudic rulings were not applicable in their time, see Ephraim Urbach, *Ba'alei Hatosafot* (Jerusalem, 1968), pp. 50, 79, 151–52, 203, 290, 320–21; Jacob Katz, "Ma'ariv be-Zemano ve-she-lo be-Zemano," *Zion* 35 (1970), 35–60; idem, *Exclusiveness and Tolerance* (New York, 1962), p. 30.

11. R. Solomon b. Simeon Duran, in Schepansky, I, 129–32; cf. *Beit Yosef* and *Shulchan Arukh*, "Even Ha'ezer," 75 end.

12. R. Samuel di Medina, in Schepansky, I, 439. In this responsum, di Medina reviews the widely differing positions recorded in the rabbinic literature on the value of burial in *Eretz Yisra'el* for one who lived and died outside the Land. This remained a matter of controversy in post-Talmudic times. While the halakha recognized burial in the Land of Israel as important enough to justify disinterment (*Shulchan Arukh*, "Yoreh De'ah" 363), opposition in principle to the burial in *Eretz Yisra'el* of someone who had never lived there continued through the Middle Ages, and can be seen both in the Zohar (e.g. "Terumah" 141b) and in philosophical sources; see my "Yedaiah Bedersi's Commentary on the Midrashim," *Proceedings of the Eighth World Congress of Jewish Studies*, Division C (Jerusalem, 1982), p. 65, n. 15.

13. Tosafot Ket. 110b, "Hu"; on R. Hayim, see Urbach, *Ba'alei Hatosafot*, pp. 107–110. R. Hayim's point, recorded rather elliptically, appears to be that those who live in the Land of Israel would be liable to punishment for transgression of the commandments that are incumbent in *Eretz Yisra'el*, yet difficult or impossible to observe at present. Under such circumstances it should not be considered a religious obligation to live there. (This is how his words were understood by R. Hayim Jair Bachrach, *Chavot Ya'ir*, responsum 210, p. 110a. Bachrach used the analogy of going to live in the Land of Israel to clarify his position on the value and perils of studying Kabbalah; the analogy *ba lelamed venimtza lamed*. I am grateful to Professor Isadore Twersky for directing me to this source.)

14. See, for example, the discussion by R. Isaiah Horowitz in *Shenei Luchot Haberit*, "Sha'ar ha'otiyot," Letter Koph: R. Hayim's statement is "the view of an

individual, his reason is illogical . . . we need pay no attention to his words" (Warsaw, 1852; I, 234b).

15. R. Joseph b. Moses of Trani, in Schepansky, I, 318.

16. Schepansky, I, 319.

17. See B. AZ 13a (a priest may incur ritual impurity by leaving the Land of Israel in order to study Torah) and Maimonides, *Hil. Melakhim* 5.9. R. Meir of Rothenberg, asked why a group of French rabbis who had emigrated to Palestine later commanded their sons to return to Europe, replied that "they were unable to engage in Torah because they were compelled to work so hard to provide physical sustenance, and as there was no learning, the Jews there were not expert in the details of the commandments" (Schepansky, I, 120).

18. R. Tam ibn Yahya, in Schepansky, I, 363. Compare R. Solomon b. Simeon Duran's listing of all the values that, in his view, outweigh the precept of living in the Holy Land: "One is not obligated to emigrate to Israel if there are serious obstacles, for those who live there are permitted to leave in order to marry or to study Torah. . . . This is all the more true if a husband wants to go and his wife does not, and he would have to divorce her, and perhaps he would not find a wife there, or would find one demanding too much money, as is fashionable these days; or if the man has children and cannot bring them and would leave them orphans. Or if he cannot study Torah there on an appropriate level, while he can outside the Land. Similarly, if he can support himself outside Israel but not there, or if he would have to borrow money to pay the expenses of his voyage. Neither the Torah nor the sages have obligated a man to become a beggar in order to go to the Land of Israel. . . . All of these reasons have prevented many great Jews from moving there" (Schepansky, I, 133; cf. also III, 43).

19. Schepansky, I, 363.

20. For a literary example, see S. Y. Agnon, *In the Heart of the Seas (Belevav Hayamim)* (New York, 1947), p. 16.

21. This is the way R. Samuel Edeles (Maharsha) understood the objection of the gemara; see his *Chiddushei Aggadot*, ad loc. Compare the discussion by the preacher R. Joseph b. Hayim Zarfati of Adrianople: the objection comes from one who understood the statement literally to mean that those who live outside the land have no God, and protested that "this is something that reason cannot tolerate." Zarfati's own interpretation of the statement, influenced by Nachmanides, is that God immediately punishes the sins of those who dwell in *Eretz Yisra'el* because of the holiness of the Land, whereas the sins performed on impure soil are not immediately punished. This is why those who dwell in the Land appear to have a God watching over them, while those outside the Land do not (*Yad Yosef*, [Amsterdam, 1700] Va-Yehi, p. 86d).

22. *Hil. Melakhim*, 5.12; cf. *Shitah Mekubbetzet*, ad loc.: "whoever dwells outside the Land—who leaves the Land of Israel to [live] outside it—is as one who has no God."

23. R. Yom Tov Zahalon, in Schepansky, I, 403.

24. Maimonides, *Guide for the Perplexed*, III, 51. On this rather controversial doctrine, see Zevi Diesendruck, "Samuel and Moses ibn Tibbon on Maimonides' Theory of Providence," *HUCA* 11 (1936), 341–66, and, more recently, Alvin Reines, "Maimonides' Concepts of Providence and Theodicy," *HUCA* 43 (1972), esp. pp. 188–94.

25. This view, supported by the Talmudic statement "The air of the Land of Israel makes wise" (B. BB 158b), was integrated into a general theory of the relationship between climate and national character. See Shalom Rosenberg, above, pp. 150–53.

26. Yedaiah Bedersi, *Perush Hamidrashim, Sifre* on Deut. 11:12, Parma MS 222, folios unnumbered. Cf. R. Joel ibn Shu'eib, *Olat Shabbat* (Venice, 1577), p. 129a: "His eyes roam throughout the entire world, but His providence is revealed and seen in the Land of Israel, because of the degree of preparation the air affords to its inhabitants."

27. Yedaiah Bedersi, *Perush Hamidrashim*, "Bereshit Rabbah" (96.5), Paris MS 738,3, f. 208v; on this entire passage, dealing with the issue of burial in the Land of Israel and esoteric doctrines in the aggadah, see the article noted above, n. 12.

28. Abraham Bibago, *Derekh Emunah*, Constantinople, 1522 (reprinted Jerusalem, 1970), p. 94c–d.

29. *Teshuvot Harashba*, I, 134.

30. *Chiddushei Harashba al Aggadot Hashass*, ed. S. M. Weinberger (Jerusalem, 1966), p. 67; cf. R. Moses b. Nachman (Nachmanides), Torah Commentary on Leviticus 18:25 and *Derashah Lerosh Hashanah*, in *Kitvei Ramban*, ed. C. Chavel (Jerusalem, 1963), I, 250; Zohar, beginning of "Lekh Lekha" (78a).

31. See, for example, R. Isaiah Pinto in *Ein Ya'akov*, ad loc; R. Abraham Bornstein in Schepansky, III, 42. Maharal of Prague wrote in *Gur Aryeh* on Genesis 17:8, "It means that he has no God to aid and to help him through a divine act, for the Land of Israel is especially sought out, while the other lands are the portion of the angels, and whoever dwells outside the Land, it is as if he had departed from the dominion of the Holy One, God forbid!"

32. *Derashot Haran*, ed. Leon Feldman (Jerusalem, 1973), p. 54.

33. R. Samuel Shalem (18th century), in Schepansky, III, 609.

34. R. Isaiah Pinto in *Ein Ya'akov*, ad loc.

35. In particular, the Kabbalistic assumptions with which Nachmanides seems to be working here are not made explicit; cf. R. Jerohman Perelmann, "The Great One of Minsk," in Schepansky, III, 61, mentioning Ramban's doctrine and leaving it without further comment because "we do not deal with esoteric teachings" (*ein lanu esek benistarot*). Indeed, there seems to be a reluctance among certain authors to explore the implications of this doctrine fully; see the treatment of R. Judah Rosannes, *Parashat Derakhim* (Warsaw, 1871), Sermon 22, p. 91b. On the other

hand, note the rhapsodic praise of Ramban's teaching by the sixteenth-century Salonika preacher R. Solomon le-Veit ha-Levi: "Woe to the eyes that see this and the ears that hear this and do not make for themselves wings like a dove to fly and dwell in the Holy Land as he himself [Ramban] did; not only did he preach beautifully, he fulfilled what he preached, leaving his home and his portion [in Spain] and making his way to Jerusalem"; *Divrei Shelomo* (Venice, 1596), p. 73a.

For modern treatments of this important aspect of Nachmanides' thought (which he reiterated in a climactic passage at the end of his "Sermon for Rosh Hashana"), see Dov Rafel,"Haramban al Hagalut ve'al Hage'ullah," *Ma'ayanot* 7 (1960), p. 107, and Aryeh Newman, "The Centrality of Eretz Yisrael in Nachmanides," *Tradition* 10 (1968–69), p. 24 ("His thesis is that none of the laws of Judaism have any intrinsic validity outside *Eretz Yisra'el*"). No discussion that I have seen has noted the conflict between this and another striking Nachmanidean doctrine: that Judaism does not depend upon the future advent of the Messiah or the restoration of the Jewish people to the Land of Israel, that the essence of the Torah would be unaffected if the Jewish people were to remain permanently in its exile, and that indeed the ultimate reward of immortality for the soul may be greater when the commandments are observed in *galut* than would be the case when they are observed in Israel under the messianic kingdom (see his "Vikkuah" in *Kitvei Ramban*, I, 310, and "Sefer Ge'ullah," ibid., I, 279). See also Yitzhak Baer, *A History of the Jews in Christian Spain* (Philadelphia, 1961), I, 248, where both doctrines are presented without any indication of the tension between them.

36. *Ben Porat Yosef* (New York, 1970), p. 87b. Cf. Louis Jacobs, *Hasidic Thought* (New York, 1976), p. 209.

37. *No'am Elimelekh* (Jerusalem, 1977), pp. 32–33.

38. *Yesamach Lev* on Ketubot (Slavuta, 1798), p. 26b–c; I am grateful to Professor Arthur Green for bringing this source to my attention. Joseph Perl referred to this passage in his parody *Megalleh Temirin* (Vienna, 1819), Letter 128, n. 1; for Perl's critique of the Hasidic spiritualization of *Eretz Yisra'el*, see Tovah Cohen, "Ha-Hasidut ve-Eretz Yisra'el—Aspekt Nosaf shel ha-Satirah be-Megalleh Temirin," *Tarbiz* 48 (1979), pp. 332–340. The same passage would also seem to be in the background of Agnon's story "Ha-Meshullach me-Eretz ha-Kodesh," where, to the amazement of everyone, the magnificent *beit midrash* of an arrogant Polish community flies away in literal fulfilment of the aggadah that had been spiritualized by Menahem of Tchernobil. For another example of Hasidic de-emphasis of the geographical land of Israel, see R. Nahman of Bratslav, *Likkutei Moharan* I, 44 ("A Jew may purify the atmosphere of a place by praying there, and he may then breathe holy air just as he does in *Eretz Yisra'el*") and II, 40.

39. *Amtachat Binyamin* (Minkowitz, 1796), p. 3b. According to this report, the Baal Shem Tov cited the *aggadah* as if the word "Israel" did not appear and it read simply "whoever dwells in the Land is as one who has a God." With this interpretation of "eretz," compare the striking allegorization at the beginning of

No'am Elimelekh, "Shalach" (Jerusalem, 1977; p. 215): God's command to send forth men to scout out the land of Canaan (*eretz Kena'an*) means that the proper way to serve the Creator is for man to look carefully at his own corporeality and earthiness (*artziyut*), and thereby to subdue (*lehakhni'a*, from the same root as *Kena'an*) it.

40. At least three other statements in the same gemara have been similarly controversial and repercussive, and a study of the history of their interpretation and use would reveal other dynamics of the Jewish link with *Eretz Yisra'el*: "Israel shall not go up [to the land of Israel all together as if surrounded] by a wall"; "The dead outside the Land will not be resurrected"; and "Whoever walks four cubits in the Land of Israel is assured of a place in the world to come" (all B. Ketubot 111a).

The Land of Israel
in Medieval Jewish Exegetical and
Polemical Literature

MICHAEL A. SIGNER

[Editor's note: Trained first as a rabbi in Hebrew Union College, and later, receiving his doctorate at the University of Toronto's Pontifical Institute of Medieval Studies, Dr. Michael Signer has regularly contributed to our knowledge of how Jews and Christians explicated their traditions for each other, especially from the eleventh to the thirteenth centuries. He does just that here, with regard to what he calls "the ideological crucible of the Land of Israel debate" which formed a prism through which was focused the larger issue of scriptural promise, as Jews and Christians in Christian Europe understood it. The debate is revealed for us in a novel literary genre, designed especially for unlocking Scripture's mysteries: biblical commentary, which Signer designates, "sequential narrative," that is, the literary means by which discrete and disparate pericopes are unified into a single exegetical whole; so that "historical meaning and metahistorical or religious meaning live side by side within a biblical text." Secondarily, there emerged polemical treatises, beginning in twelfth-century Provence, and culminating in public disputations in the thirteenth and fourteenth centuries. Surveying these two literary fields, Signer examines the medieval Jews' dialogue with their Christian neighbors, as well as with themselves, as they adapted their lives to the novel conditions of medieval life. In detail, we see their fascination from afar with (1) the geographical *realia* of the Land, "its flora and fauna, its cities, hills and valleys"; (2) the place of the Land in the religious system where Jews found themselves, of necessity, living outside the Land's boundaries, still hoping, however, to keep that system's commandments; and (3) the Land's role in foreshadowing redemption and restoration.]

Scripture bears the narrative of the Jewish people's encounter with God, their redemption from oppression, and their return to their Land. This redemptive drama in Scripture is thus profoundly linked to the Land of Israel in that the same God who exiled and chastised Israel would ultimately redeem them by the determinative act of restoring their link to the Land of the Covenant.

Emphasizing the aspiration to return, of course, betrays the historical circumstances of the diaspora experience which may not have completely spiritualized the Land in Jewish consciousness, but certainly placed it in a dialectic for the Jews: on the one hand certain legal obligations could be fulfilled only in the Holy Land—and yet, on the other hand, the Land itself was demonstrably unavailable to diaspora Jewry. It would necessarily remain unredeemed until the incursion of the Lord into history, and the redemptive return of God's people into the Land again. In the meantime, successive generations of Jews attempted to reduce the dissonance of Jewish life lived outside the Land by reinterpreting the biblical text so that the classical texts of rabbinic Judaism (ca. 135 C.E.–ca. 600 C.E.) reflected the Land of Israel as both a locative and a utopian reality.[1]

It was this modified scriptural stance which became the cultural inheritance of the communities of Jews who settled along the banks of the Rhine, the Seine, and elsewhere in Northern Europe. With the Islamic conquest in the eighth century from the south it penetrated the Iberian peninsula, and later still, became part of the cultural heritage of those Jews who lived under the monarchs of the Christian *Reconquista*. In this way, a uniquely European civilization developed from the tenth through fifteenth centuries and evoked the latest creative response from Jewish communities intent on reinterpreting the literary heritage of the Bible and the Rabbis so as to explain new dilemmas typical of the new era.[2]

One of the major challenges to Jewish creativity arose from the fact of the parallel transmission of the Patristic heritage to the surrounding Christian culture of Northern Europe. While accepting the ongoing existence of the Jews as "Israel according to the flesh," the writings of the Church Fathers expressly denied the legitimacy of the Jewish interpretation of Scripture. Following the writings of the New Testament, the Patristic authors argue that with the coming of Christ there was no further need for rabbinic legislation at all, since the "law" was no longer to be identified as a means of salvation.[3] The continued existence of Israel was itself dependent wholly upon the mercy of God who maintained them as an outward sign of the victory of Christian faith. The Jews were *caeci*, blind to the truth of Christ, so they were unable to see that the truth of Christ was announced in the words of their own Scripture.[4] Jews were condemned to live by the letter of Scripture, while the Church vaunted itself to see beyond the letter and to partake of the deeper mysteries of Scripture. Even those theologians of the eleventh and twelfth centuries who saw value in the study of the letter of Scripture, such as Hugh of St. Victor (d. 1140) and St. Stephen Harding

(d. 1134), and who were, therefore, willing to consult with Jews for the determination of an authoritative scriptural text, recognized that the letter was only the foundation of the house, whose walls and roof could be erected only through the application of proper interpretation and exposition to the letter, until the latter's moral and mystical senses became apparent. In the *Didascalion,* a work devoted to the relationship between the arts and theology, Hugh of St. Victor claims that it is an error to stop with the literal sense and not to press for the deeper meaning.[5]

Part of the validation for the Church's claim to the only licit interpretation of Scripture, and the concomitant rejection of Jews and Judaism, was the "fact" that the Jews, no longer able to worship at their Temple in Jerusalem, were in evident exile from the Land of Israel. Jewish protagonists in Jewish-Christian disputations are thus constantly asked to compute the excessive duration of time that the Lord had kept them in exile since the coming of Christ, as opposed to the relatively brief exile of four hundred and thirty years in Egypt and four hundred years in Babylonia.[6] Even such a detached individual as Andrew of St. Victor (d. 1175) whose intellectual efforts were completely dedicated to the exposition of the literal sense of Hebrew Scripture, was aghast at the fact that the Jews really seemed to believe that they would again be returned to their Land of Israel:

> The Jews, deluded by vain hope, promise this to themselves – that they will recover the Land which was once theirs by means of their deliverer, and that nothing will ever be lacking for them again. Rather, they and their children will inhabit the Land forever. Animals which are utterly downcast and looking at a deserted land do not dare promise themselves a home which is superior and more noble.[7]

The contrast between Jewish hope and Christian scorn in this passage of a twelfth-century commentary on the prophet Ezekiel demonstrates a tension inherent in Christian exegetes who were intent on consulting Jews to arrive at accurate scriptural readings and understanding, but who could only view as ludicrous the theological conclusions of those same Jewish consultants.[8] We see how the larger issue of scriptural promise on which the two faith communities based their stand was highlighted, and even symbolized, in an ideological crucible of the "Land of Israel" debate, which focused the issue in the greatest of clarity.

It was in the midst of this tension with the larger Christian world that European Jewry developed its own tradition of biblical interpretation which significantly differed from the classical sources in Talmud and Midrash.

Undergirding this development lay the evolution of biblical commentary as a literary genre.[9] In these commentaries, the biblical text and its narrative were inseparably connected by the thread of the exegetical comment, so that the reader was forced to see the biblical text as a continuous narrative suggestive of a given series of meanings that transcended the historical situation within the narrative itself. However, the reader was encouraged to move through a biblical pericope in its entirety, rather than to see a particular series of words in isolation. In this manner, the second psalm, for example, could be seen as referring to both an historical event in the life of King David and at the same time as pointing to an adumbration of the messianic deliverer who would save Israel.[10] The effort to make the historical meaning and the metahistorical or religious meaning live side by side within a biblical text thus constitutes one of the great achievements of the genre of biblical exegesis in medieval Europe.[11]

Out of this same intense study of the language of the Bible considered as a part of what we may call a "Sequential Narrative," with deeper signification, there emerged yet a second genre of biblical exposition: the polemical treatise.[12] Beginning in Provençe of the twelfth century those passages in Scripture which were most frequently employed by Christian expositors to prove the messiahship of Jesus as well as the humble status of Israel after the coming of the Christ were collected, and these Christian arguments were examined for their failures of logic. Treatises were written which examined biblical passages according to the order of the canon of Hebrew Scripture. Other polemical compositions were written in the form of letters to apostates. The public disputations held in France and Spain during the thirteenth and fourteenth centuries also inspired Jewish participants to put their answers to the Christian challenge into written form. Although these polemical treatises focused largely on messianic passages in Scripture, the question of Jewish sovereignty over the Holy Land or the length of Jewish exile was often raised.[13]

Scriptural interpretation, therefore, became a two-edged sword for medieval Jewry. It provided a vehicle of discourse which enabled them to find the scriptural basis of their religious teachings, and a means to refute those who claimed that their understanding of God's word was inadequate. Biblical exegetical and polemical literature were the vehicles of transmission of classical Jewish views, the views of the talmudic Rabbis, into a world which challenged the very foundation of that inherited tradition. The methods of biblical exegesis would reflect the different cultural environments where Jews lived. Philological exegesis among Spanish Jews would be more ad-

vanced than in Christian Europe. Philosophic and Kabbalistic discourse would
be integrated into the exposition of the Bible depending upon the extent
to which those disciplines had developed within the Jewish intellectual milieu.
Most important to remember is that Jewish biblical exegesis did not flourish
in isolation from other areas of Jewish study such as Talmudics, Jewish legal
responsa, and Jewish liturgical poetry.[14] Biblical exegesis is the focus of this
essay because it gives us deeper insight into Scripture—the area which might
have been most conjunctive for Jews and Christians during the Middle Ages,
but because of the exclusivity of truth in revelation claimed by Jews and
Christians was the most disjunctive.

In this essay we will present the exegetical views of (1) Northern France
and Germany, as well as those of (2) Provençe and (3) Spain with regard
to the Land. We will include exegetical statements from the polemical treatises
wherever appropriate. We shall discover that there was exposition of the
biblical narrative on three levels: 1) the concern with elements in the biblical narrative which deal with the geography of the Land itself, its flora and
fauna, its cities, hills, and valleys; 2) the place of the Land within the life
of the Jew insofar as the Land was associated with keeping the divine commandments; 3) the focus on the Land as foreshadowing the ultimate redemption and restoration of the Jewish people. Throughout, we shall observe a constant tension between metareality and social reality, the former
being the Jew's patient faith, to which Andrew of St. Victor attests, that
somehow life in the Land would constitute a genuine part of the facticity
of the Jew's daily life, just as Scripture itself promised; and the latter being
the grim recognition that redemption remained as yet unfulfilled.

From Geography to Theology:
From Biblical Locus to Covenantal Focus

The biblical narrative locates various places within the Land of Israel,
often weaving them into its account of the movements of individuals or
into the narratives describing the conquest of the Land itself. In such instances medieval exegetes carefully explain the position of the cities relative
to one another. Rashi expounds the words "Going on more and more towards the Negev" in Gen. 12:9 as "by stages: he stayed here a month or
more, then travelled on and pitched his tent in another place." He then details the geography of Negev as "to proceed to the South of the Land of
Israel which is the direction where Jerusalem is—which is in the territory

of Judah who had their portion in the South of the Land of Israel — to Mount Moriah which is Judah's possession." The reader is led to combine the general direction in which Abraham travelled with the focus of the Rabbis in *Genesis Rabbah* whose emphasis was on Abraham's proximity to the Temple mount and Jerusalem.[15]

Utilizing the literature of the Talmud and Midrash the medieval exegetes pay special heed to the etymology of place names, especially where it appears that one biblical location has two or more names. The resolution to such problems is often derived from the biblical text itself: for example, by cross-reference to other instances in the biblical narrative which explicate the location or character of the area in question.[16] But beyond the Bible, these exegetes regularly consult rabbinic literature as both map and guide to the flora and fauna of the Land of Israel.[17] Nachmanides went beyond literary resources to personal observation. His commentary on the Torah was completed while he actually lived in the Land of Israel. He, therefore, attempts to give approximate distances between places based upon direct observations by himself and others. This "empiricism" appears to have forced Nachmanides to revise his commentary.[18]

Medieval geography extended beyond this empirical world of nature. Exegesis of place and names and geographical locale also provided the commentators an occasion to resort to metaphysical descriptions of the Land of Israel. Most striking is their repeated insistence on the rabbinic dictum that "the Land of Israel is the center of the earth." From this idea of its "centeredness" they derive the further consequences that the Land of Israel is geographically higher than all other lands.[19] Contiguity to the Land of Israel increases the physical size of an area. For example, the Euphrates is identified with the biblical "great river" because it is the river closest to the Land.[20]

Even the climate of the Land is unique. Fruit ripens more quickly there than in other places. Animals grow larger. Precious stones are more easily found there.[21] All of these are based in the medieval commentators' conviction that the Land is the object of unique divine benevolence:

> Israel is not like Egypt which is irrigated at certain seasons by the Nile and its lakes, like a garden. It is almost exclusively a land of hills and valleys for the absorbing of the dew of heavens and nothing else.[22]

This relationship between divine provision for natural phenomena in the Land is read back into the narrative of the Flood. Even during the deluge the waters did not enter the Land directly from the heavens, but flowed toward her from other lands. Trees were destroyed all over the world, but not in the Land itself.[23]

This focus on the superiority of the Land of Israel and its natural resources even forces the exegete, at times, to interject the "Land of Israel" as a causative factor into a narrative where it is acutely absent, and thus to heighten the effect for the reader of the passage. Rashi understands the *migdanot* (Gen. 24:53) which Eliezer the servant of Abraham presented to the family of Rebecca to be "sweet fruits," which owe their charm to the fact that they are "fruit from the Land of Israel."[24] The narrative of Genesis does not even suggest the context of fruits from the Land of Israel, but Rashi introduces the notion of Israel into the narrative to heighten the majesty of the gift. The image reenforces the extraordinary quality of the Land of Israel for the reader, and reveals that even when outside the Land of Israel, Eliezer could present a marvelous gift which was itself a product of the Holy Land.

The name of a geographic zone of the Land sometimes afforded an opportunity to present an excursus that combines the geography together with the superiority of the Land. When Moses ordered the spies to investigate the Land, he sent them to the *Negev*. Rashi quotes the Midrash Tanchuma: "God showed them the *Negev* or the worst part of the Land, just as merchants show the worst of their wares before they reveal the best."[25] Thus geography served as the gateway to a theology of covenant between God and the Jews.

We have seen the medieval exegetical effort to link names of places and objects in the Land with the biblical narrative. The commentaries draw upon the text of the Bible, the literature of the Rabbis and their own empirical observations to keep the covenantal promise before the eyes of the reader. Isolated philological units are constantly drawn into the overall narrative of the Pentateuch and historical books. From the perspective of medieval exegetes this narrative focused on the entry, departure, and reentry into the Land.

From Narrative to Salvation:
From Covenantal Promise to Lifelong Praxis

Theology is apparent in the exegetes' exposition of narrative portions of the Pentateuch which focus on the Land as a portion of the covenant between God and the people Israel. However, Jews living in Moslem and

Christian lands during the Middle Ages were faced with an essential dissonance between the narrative, rich in the lore of the Land, and the fact of
their own exile from it. This contrast presented the commentators with a
considerable hermeneutic challenge. Further, the book of Deuteronomy and
the historical books of Scripture indicate that possession of or exile from
the Land is dependent upon the collective conduct of the people Israel. Our
commentaries, therefore, regularly return to the theme of inhabiting the
Land as both a significant event in Israel's past and the hope of a future
physical reality.

In this moment between past and future glories, biblical narratives
are viewed as prefiguring redemptive promise. The patriarchal narratives of
Genesis were, for example, seen by the medieval exegetes as adumbrating
both Israel's immediate future entry into the Land (after the Exodus and
desert wandering) and its ultimate eschatological entrance there (with the
advent of the messiah).[26] Even before the Land was promised to him, Abraham's sojourn in Shechem prefigures the conquest of the city by his descendants and their acceptance of the covenant before their entry into the
Land:

> *And Abram passed through the Land unto the place of Shechem, unto the
> oak of Moreh.* In order to pray on behalf of Jacob's sons anticipating
> the time when they would come to fight against Shechem. *The plain
> of Moreh.* He showed him Mt. Gerizim and Mt. Ebal where Israel
> took upon themselves the oath to observe the Torah. *And he builded
> there an altar.* In anticipation of thanksgiving for having descendants,
> and in anticipation for receiving the Land as a sign of the Covenant.[27]

Rashi's comments on these verses are derived from Talmudic texts. They
move the reader from the Land as Abram perceived it, through the Land
as the possession of the people. In addition, Rashi joins the possession of
the Land to the fulfillment of the mandates prescribed in the Torah.[28]

Nachmanides pushes beyond the explications of Rashi with respect
to the patriarchal narratives as expressions of the Covenant of Israel. For
him the patriarchal narratives function as a map of Israel's future.

> I shall tell you a rule you will comprehend in all subsequent passages
> concerning Abraham, Isaac, and Jacob. It is an important matter which
> our Sages mention briefly, saying, "Whatever occured to the fathers
> is a sign to the sons." That is why Scripture prolongs the story of the
> travels of the Patriarchs and of the digging of wells and the like. One

might deem them to be redundant useless matters. However, all of
them come to teach about the future. For when an event occurs to
any of the three patriarchs, one may attempt to divine prophetically
what may occur to his seed. And know that every divine decision,
wherever it turns from the potentiality of a decree into the actuality
of a similitude, such a decree will be fulfilled under all circumstances.
. . . Therefore, God fortified Abraham in the Land and performed similitudes on his behalf with respect to all the things which would happen to his descendants.[29]

This lengthy statement from his commentary on Genesis 12:6 indicates that Nachmanides understood "events" in the lives of the Patriarchs
as having a prophetic force which was binding upon the lives of their descendants. In a recent study of Nachmanides' exegesis, Amos Funkenstein
points to the similarity between Christian typological reading of Scriptural
narratives and the "similitudes" which Nachmanides illuminates.[30]

The patriarchal narratives are, therefore, predictive of the ultimate conquest of the Land:

And it came to pass in the days of Amraphel King of Shinar. This event
happened to Abraham in order to teach us that four kingdoms will
arise to rule the world. In the end, Abraham's children will prevail
over them, and they will fall into their hands. Then they will return
all their captives and their wealth.[31]

For medieval Jews who viewed the mention of the Four Kingdoms
of Daniel as a prophecy of hope, Nachmanides' reading of Genesis 14 provided a message of comfort.

The link between the exile from the Land and the return to the Land
focused on the commandments which God had given to Israel. So medieval
exegetes constantly demonstrate the bond between the Jews' observance of
the commandments and their link to the Land.[32] The Land is the paradigmatic locus for the observance of the commandments, as the injunctions
in Deuteronomy reiterate, "It shall come to pass when you enter the Land."[33]
If the Land is God's gift to the people, then the people demonstrate their
love most completely by carrying out the divine mandates. We noted above
the importance played by the idea of "narrative sequence." As a particularly
noteworthy sequence, we find our commentators drawing conclusions regarding the commandments in the Pentateuch relative to the time at which

entry into the Land occured. Thus, the new commandments mentioned in the book of Deuteronomy are said to have been known to Moses at Sinai (i.e. in the book of Exodus) but were not stated until Deuteronomy because they were to be observed in the Land.[34] With recourse to the theory of similitude, the exegete concludes for his own time that the entire purpose of keeping the commandments during exile is so that they will be remembered when Israel is restored to its Land.[35] The exile from the Land of Israel is thus again linked with the failure to observe the commandments.

Some exegetes, however, identify the cause of the exile, both in biblical and postbiblical times, with the failure to observe the Sabbatical and Jubilee years specifically.[36] Their narrowing of the focus to these commandments as the cause for exile, instead of the numerous alternative causes for exile mentioned in rabbinic literature, those, for example, that have to do with moral vices, demonstrates how deeply the Land covenant was rooted in medieval mentality. Thus the medieval exegete himself became a prism through which the totality of rabbinic literature was refracted to his readers. This "refraction" is illustrated in Nachmanides' explication of Leviticus 25:2.

> *A Sabbath unto the Eternal.* Bend now your ear to understand that which I am permitted to inform you about it in the words that I will cause you to hear, and if you will be worthy, you will contemplate them and understand them. I have already written in my commentary on Genesis that the six days of creation represent all the days of the world, and the seventh day is a Sabbath unto the Eternal thy God, for it will be the Sabbath to the Great Name, just as we have been taught in a Mishnah: "On the seventh day what psalm did the Levites sing in the Sanctuary? They sang A Psalm, A Song. For the Sabbath day, A song for the World to Come, which will be wholly a Sabbath, and rest for life everlasting." Thus the seven days of the week allude to that which He created in the process of creation, and the seven years of the Sabbatical cycle refer to that which will occur during the creation of all the days of the world. It is for this reason that Scripture was more stringent regarding the transgression of the laws of the Sabbatical year than with respect to those guilty of transgressing all other negative commandments, and made it punishable with exile just as He was stringent with respect to forbidden sexual relations for which the punishment of the people as opposed to that of the individual is also exile.[37]

From Teachers of Tradition to Defenders of the Faith:
The Land as Witness to the Redemption of the People Israel

We have seen thus far that medieval Jewish exegetes often proclaim that their purpose was to transmit the tradition. This explicit aim was often complemented by an implicit need to "answer the *Minim*" (Christians) and strengthen the faith of their co-religionists.[38] Though it would be an exaggeration to assert that Jews were preoccupied with Christian interpretation or that Christians were exclusively desirous of refuting Jewish claims to Scripture, nevertheless, the premodern world gave little ground for mutual tolerance, in that Jews and Christians knew with absolute certainty that they each possessed exclusive knowledge of divine truth in Scripture. Thus, both in their exegetical literature and in polemical treatises they pointed out why the other side was mistaken.[39]

Bartholomew, Bishop of Exeter (d. 1184) formulates the Jewish "error" as follows:

> The chief cause of disagreement between ourselves and the Jews seems to me to be this: they take all the Old Testament literally, wherever they can find a literal sense, unless it gives manifest witness to Christ. Then they repudiate it, saying that it is not in the Hebrew Truth, that is, in their books, or they refer it to some fable, as that they are still awaiting its fulfillment, or they escape by some other serpentine wile, when they feel themselves hard pressed. They will never accept allegory, except when they have no other way out. *We* however, interpret not only the words of Scripture, but the things done, and the deeds themselves in a mystical sense, yet in such a way that the freedom of allegory may in no wise nullify either history in the events, or proper understanding of the words of Scripture.[40]

This summary of differences between Christian and Jewish approaches represents a "scholarly" view of the problem. It lacks the rhetoric of *caecitas* or blindness which characterizes much of the Christian literature about Jewish interpretation.[41] Whatever the tenor of the argument, Christians since the period of the Church Fathers had pointed to the conquest of the Temple and Jerusalem by the Romans as the end of the Jewish dispensation. From that point onward one had to interpret all passages about the Land with a spiritual eye.[42]

I believe that I shall see boundaries of the Lord in the land of the living.
David clearly leads us to the spiritual sense. What boundaries did he
seek? What did this king lack?. . . . The "land of the living" is that in
which the bounties of the Lord are prepared for the saints and the
meek. Before the advent in the flesh of the Lord and Savior these were
not accessible to Abraham, Isaac, and Jacob or any prophet. . . . The
blood of Christ is the key to paradise. . . . Does any one believe that
this is a physical land which we can see and which is possessed by
sinners of whom it is said, "Cursed be the land for your sake." (Gen.
3:17)

      Those who believe that this land was possessed by the Jewish
people, let them tell me, how much of it did they possess after they
returned from Egypt? Dan to Beersheba is scarcely one hundred and
sixty miles. Scripture attests that even the very powerful kings David
and Solomon possessed no more than this, if we exclude that which
they received in peace treaties after their victories.

      You object that the Promised Land is that which is defined by
the book of Numbers? Now I will admit that these lands were once
promised to you; although not handed over to you on the condition
that you observe God's commandments and live according to God's
precepts. . . . Because you chose idols over God you have lost all the
land of God promised to you.[43]

St. Jerome's statements in this letter probably were unknown to most
Christian and Jewish exegetes during the Middle Ages, but they reflect the
questions which do appear with respect to the Land.[44] The issue for Christians and Jews was formulated about the nature of the exile of the Jews
from their Land. According to Christians, Jews read the Scripture incor-
rectly, failed to recognize the Christ, and had been exiled from their Land.

    To the Christian accusation that Jews understood the Scripture only
according to the letter, Joseph Kimhi responded:

Tell me, when the Holy One Blessed be He gave the Torah to Moses
who taught it to Israel, did he [Moses] understand it figuratively or
not? If you say that he did not understand it figuratively but literally
and taught it so to Israel, then Israel is not to be held accountable
in this matter. . . . Know that the fact is that the Torah is not to be
taken altogether literally or figuratively.[45]

Much of Jewish polemical literature retains this ironic tone. Christian interpretation was not true in that it purposely perverted or at least twisted each biblical passage to arrive at an explanation with respect to Jesus as the messiah. Jewish interpreters invented countercharges to refute their views:

> In this same manner you reverse Scriptural citations and expound them according to your opinion, so with respect to the Torah and the Prophets you can turn them around and say that they speak of your Messiah. . . . How can they [the Christians] claim that Ps. 48:9 refers to the Magi or that Ps. 48:2–3 refers to the Messiah when it is a known fact that he was born in Bethlehem, and not "the city of the king?"[46]

Many of the polemical treatises examine passages in the New Testament for the inconsistent use of geographic terms with respect to the places visited by Jesus. Their literary aim is to demonstrate that Christian scriptural use of the Land as a background for the life of Jesus is in error.[47] According to the logic of their polemical treatises, if the interpretation of Scripture was in error, and the "realia" of Jesus' life were inaccurately portrayed, then Christianity would pose no challenge to the truth of Judaism.

Although the Land is not presented as a central theme of argumentation within the disputation and polemical literature, the lack of sovereignty appears to be recognized as a potential reason for apostasy. In his letter to Solomon HaLevi, baptized Paul de Santa Maria at Burgos on 21 July 1391, Joshua HaLorki wrote that aside from material considerations or spiritual reasons, Solomon might be turning to Christianity because of the "doom of our homeland and the multitude of the afflictions that have recently befallen us, which ruined and destroyed us." HaLorki continues to admonish the apostate:

> You cannot have overlooked the reports from travellers' accounts, the letters of Maimon, and the merchants who currently travel there, that most of our nation in the East, except those in Persia, are under the power of the Sultan. Those who are not under his power are under the yoke of another king, such as those who live in the furthermost part of the land of Kush. Have no doubt about this: The Jews who live in the lands of the Christians are only those who returned with Ezra and Nehemiah, who were not the nobles, but the most impoverished part of the people. If there were a divine decree to destroy all the peoples, our nation would be preserved in its integrity.[48]

The traveller's account to which HaLorki refers may well have been *The Itinerary* of Benjamin of Tudela, which was written in the latter half of the twelfth century. Benjamin of Tudela's work reflects concern with those geographic areas where Jews were "not under the yoke of the gentile kings."[49] We therefore have a continuity within Spanish Jewry of a concern for Jewish sovereignty.

Jewish exegetical literature reflects these concerns for sovereignty in its emphasis that biblical prophecies concerning the Land of Israel have not yet been fulfilled.[50] In this way the Christian accusation that the Jews lack a land and a king as a sign of punishment is turned back upon itself. It is precisely the length of the exile that is said to prove that the messiah has not yet come. Only when the twelve tribes have been restored to their Land will the biblical promises be fulfilled:

> We can see that Jesus did not establish himself in Jerusalem. Most of its inhabitants did not follow him. Most of the people who travel there today are attacked by evil soldiers.[51]

Far from demonstrating Israel's rejection by God, the continuing desolation of the Holy Land proves that God's word has not yet been fulfilled. Israel is cursed with exile, true, but only because it has failed fully to fulfill the Torah given at Sinai, not because a new Torah was given that Israel refuses to observe. Israel's sufferings in exile may indeed bring about the purification of the world. For they may hasten his arrival.[52]

The exegetes emphasize that in Israel's current exile, all other people have failed fully to establish themselves in the Land. This fact proved to their satisfaction that God had given the Land to the Jews in perpetuity, ultimately destining it to be returned to them. The Land of Israel is "allergic" to foreigners; it spews them out, and this is so despite the fact that the Land is attractive to gentile kings who wish to imagine themselves as possessing a share within its midst.[53] The failure of the gentile kings to conquer the Land is a repeated theme in the polemical and exegetical literature from the eleventh through thirteenth centuries, with many commentaries identifying these monarchs specifically as Christians and Moslems.[54] Understandably, the awareness of the Crusaders' failures seems to have been a source of great comfort to Jewish medieval exegetes and apologists.

> Since the time that Israel has not dwelled on the Land, from the Temple's destruction until now, our enemies have been unable to establish themselves firmly upon it. How many cities have been destroyed, re-

built, and destroyed since then? The gentiles always stir up war over
the Land of Israel. Rome exiled us, and held the Land for a time, but
not for long. After that came the Ishmaelites who hold the upper hand
to this very day. Three times the Christians have made war, and three
times the Ishmaelites have responded with war since the destruction
of the second Temple until now. Now the two nations live on the
Land, but in insecure and uneasy peace. They constantly threaten one
another.[55]

In the end, the Land is personified as patiently awaiting the redemption of its exiled children, an eventuality which will come about in due
time at the will of God. The diaspora is projected as living under the final kingdom of Edom whose fall will presage Israel's restoration. To carry
out this task of restoration, Israel must keep the commandments (as we saw
above), but in addition, it must achieve a state of spiritual cleanliness.

> *And if the Eternal your God enlarge your border.* This section deals with
> a future event. . . . When your merit attains a degree that you ob-
> serve all the commandments, loving God with a perfect everlasting
> love, so that it should be apparent to Him that you will never sin
> again, then He will broaden your boundary and give you all the ten
> nations He promised to Abraham. This is a reference to the days of
> which he said, "The Lord your God will circumcise your heart and
> the hearts of your offspring to love the Lord your God with all your
> heart and soul."[56]

In addition to this broad statement, Nachmanides utilizes passages from
the books of Numbers and Deuteronomy to develop the argument that different borders of the promised Land prefigure successive periods in the Land's
restoration.[57] Nachmanides believed that it was a positive divine commandment for Jews to return to the Land of Israel and to settle there even before
the final restoration, there to await the ultimate redemption.[58] When they
do the will of God the broadest possible borders shall be restored there:

> And from the desert and Lebanon until the farthest sea shall be your
> border . . . for you are obliged to capture it and destroy the people
> there, and to uproot idolatry. The Lord has promised you no opposi-
> tion wherever your foot shall tread.[59]

Medieval exegetes reveal a triumphalist spirit in their description of
Israel's messianic conquest of the Land. When redemption does occur, God
will lead the dispersed people in a bloody conquest. Israel will witness God's

vengeance upon both Christians and Moslems according to the measure of Israel's suffering.[60] When the Jews reconquer their Land, they will purify it from all idolatry. We even find idolatry identified explicitly as Christianity![61] The idolatrous nations of the Bible are identified with Christianity and Islam, but the restored Israel will be the "light unto the nations" as they teach the true revelation of God to others. Specifically, Israel will then take all Christians and Moslems who convert to Judaism and teach them Torah.[62] In this final apocalyptic vision, we see how medieval biblical exegetes balance the Talmudic literature's expectations of a restored Israel, which will fulfill all the commandments of God, against the immediate experience of medieval Jewry still suffering exile at the hand of Christians and Moslems.

Summary

In general, then, medieval Jewish exegesis and polemics attempt to provide a focus for the Land of Israel within the biblical narrative. Much of this exegesis is rooted in the notion that the Land of Israel is the center of the world, and that God has a unique relationship to it. Geographical *topoi* in the Bible which relate to the Land become opportunities to explicate the narrative and to point to future reality marked by restoration. The veracity of future hopes rests upon careful reconstruction of the story of the ancestors of Israel.

The assumption that Scripture itself is the locus where one finds testimony to the unique relationship of God and the Jewish people to the Land of Israel is stated most clearly, perhaps, in the introductory comments of Rabbi Solomon ben Isaac of Troyes (Rashi) to his commentary on the book of Genesis. He raises a question based on the midrash Tanchuma about the reason the Pentateuch begins with the narrative of the world's creation rather than with the first commandment given to Israel, the celebration of the Passover (Ex. 12:1). In response he cites Psalm 111:6, "God tells His people the might of His deeds to give them the inheritance of the nations," and explains:

> For if the nations of the world say to the people of Israel, "You are robbers because you stole the land of the seven Canaanite nations," They [the Jews] should say to them, "The whole earth belongs to the Holy One Blessed Be He. He created it, and He gives it whomever is upright in His eyes. By His will He gave it to them, and by His will He took it from them and gave it to us."[63]

This statement provides a synthesis of the nature of Torah for the Jewish people, and of the connections between the Jewish People and its Land. It emphasizes the necessity of reading Torah as a "story," a sequential narrative. Torah *begins* with the creation narrative, thus implying that it is not a book of laws, but a record of God's beneficence to the people of Israel.[64] In particular that beneficence is the Land of Israel, given them as an "inheritance of the nations" (Ps. 111:6). In this way, Psalm 111:6 is said to answer a question placed in the mouths of the nations of the world.

Should anyone question the possession or capture of the Land by the Jewish people, the answer is that all the earth is ultimately the possession of God who distributes it according to the righteousness of each nation. "The mighty acts of God" are performed to give Israel "an inheritance," their Land. The Jewish reader of this passage would also notice the paranomasia of the Hebrew word *aretz* which means both "earth" and "land," recognizing full well that *ha-aretz*, "*the* land" can refer in context only to the Land of Israel. In this way Rashi would join the possession of land (in general) at the discretion of God with the more specific idea that the possession of the Holy Land must itself be by the grace of God and directly dependent upon the righteousness of God's people.

Rashi's introduction to the Torah reveals a synthesis of the Jewish exegetical and polemical traditions about the Land of Israel during the medieval period. The Pentateuch began with the story of creation because, despite the consequence of exile that befalls Israel when it fails to keep the commandments, the covenant between Israel and its God is not exclusively rooted in Israel's obedience to God through the observance of the law. Certainly the covenant would never be so dependent upon observance of the law that God's ultimate promise to Israel would be nullified. Rather, God acts beneficently to Israel long before commanding any laws at all. The universality of the creation story is refracted into the particular act of the bestowal of a land upon Israel. Israel, behaving righteously, inherits the Land, and the Land rejects all other conquerors, awaiting the return of its true owners, Israel redeemed.

It should be noted that Rashi does not present the negative aspect of Israel's exile from the Land. For him the Torah is not the narrative of Israel's debilitating exile but of its proud possession of the Land. As the covenant is eternal, so Israel's possession of its Land is eternal. God cannot be so capricious as to take back what was graciously bestowed from creation's very inception!

This passage by Rashi became the commentary *par excellence* for the

Jewish people. For Jews reading through Holy Writ, it stood as the very first lesson in a traditional Jewish reading of the Pentateuch. As Rashi's commentary grew in popularity and authority to the point where it was conflated with the meaning of the text itself, his introductory explanation constituted the normative framework for a Jewish interpretation of the Bible.[65]

The exegetical traditions about the Land of Israel during the medieval period follow the contours suggested by Rashi. Wherever possible, the medieval interpreters focused the reader's attention on the restoration of the people to the Land. The biblical message represented more than a glorified past; it was an adumbration of a more glorious future. The Christian world, on the other hand, saw the Jewish diaspora as verification that Israel of the spirit had taken the inheritance of Israel of the flesh. So in their exegetical writings of the Middle Ages, Jews sought out refutations of these claims. The failure of Christians to capture the Land of Israel from the Moslems and the failure of Christianity to convert the Moslems were validations of Jewish claims. Their biblical commentaries promised that even in exile, Jews could be comforted knowing that by holding fast to the religion of their ancestors they would some day return to their Land.

Notes

1. The ambiguity of the term "Israel" as both a geographic locus and a name for a social aggregate appears in Scripture itself. Rabbinic literature continues this tradition. Some of the most significant thinking about the relationship between Rabbinic literature and Scripture is to be found in the writings of Jacob Neusner. See in particular "Map without Territory: Mishnah's System of Sacrifice and Sanctuary," *Method and Meaning in Ancient Judaism* (Missoula, Mont., 1979), 133–54; *Major Trends in Formative Judaism: Society and Symbol in Political Crisis* (Chico, Cal., 1983). An important focus on the narrative elements in relation to the Bible and rabbinic sources has been developed by Geza Vermes, *Scripture and Tradition in Judaism* (Leiden, 1961) and *Post-Biblical Jewish Studies* (Leiden, 1975).

2. There is no comprehensive history of Jewish exegetical literature during the medieval period which compares to Beryl Smalley's *The Study of the Bible in the Middle Ages* (Notre Dame, Ind., 1960; 3rd ed., Oxford, 1985), nor is a full survey of the exegetical methods employed by Jewish exegesis as there is for Latin exegesis in Henri de Lubac's *Exegese medievale: les quatre sens de l'Ecriture* 4 vols. (Lyon, 1959). The best integration of the insights of Jewish exegetical literature with the history of medieval Jews is to be found in H. H. Ben-Sasson, *A History of the Jewish People* (Cambridge, Mass., 1976), pp. 385–726 and in Salo W. Baron,

A Social and Religious History of the Jews: High Middle Ages (New York, 1958), vol. 6, "Laws, Homilies, and the Bible." In Hebrew one should consult B. Z. Dinur, *Yisrael baGolah* (Tel Aviv, 1958–) for exegetical material reflecting the life of medieval Jewry.

3. For Patristic attitudes with respect to Judaism, cf. Marcel Simon, *Verus Israel* (Paris, 1964); James Parkes, *The Conflict of the Church and Synagogue* (Cleveland, 1964); Rosemary Radford Reuther, *Faith and Fratricide* (New York, 1974). An examination of early medieval Latin literature about Jews and Judaism is to be found in Bernhard Blumenkranz, *Les Auteurs Chretiens Latins du moyen age* (Paris: 1963).

4. This accusation was rooted in the text of Romans 11:7: "quid ergo quod quaerebat Israel hoc non est consecutus, electio autem consecuta est, ceteri vero excaecati sunt." Cf. B. Blumenkranz, *Les Auteurs Chretiens*. This theme of Jewish blindness revealed itself in Christian representational art: cf. B. Blumenkranz, *Le Juif Medieval au miroir de l'art chretien* (Paris, 1966), 53–55, 74–77; and W. Seiferth, *Synagogue and Church in the Middle Ages: Two Symbols in Art and Literature* (New York, 1970).

5. Beryl Smalley, *The Study of the Bible*, pp. 34–111. For further investigation of Hugh of St. Victor's relationship to Jewish exegesis, cf. Marianne Awerbuch, *Christlich-Jüdische Begegnung im Zeitalter der Fruscholastik* (Munich, 1980), pp. 197–230; and my own "Between Text and Tradition: Victorines, Jews and the Development of the Sensus Litteralis," forthcoming.

6. See Blumenkranz, *Les Auteurs, passim*.

7. Andrew of St. Victor, *Expositio in Ezechielem* 37:25. The text of the *Expositio in Ezechielem* is forthcoming in *Corpus Christianorum Continuatio Medievalis*, vol 53. That edition will include a discussion of Andrew's relationship to Jewish exegesis. At present, see B. Smalley, *Study of the Bible*, pp. 112–95.

8. We still lack a full investigation into the nature of Christian Hebraism during the eleventh and twelfth centuries. A. Grabois, "The Hebraica Veritas and Jewish-Christian Relations in the Twelfth-Century," *Speculum* 50:4 (October 1975), 613–14, presents a limited view.

9. F. Baer, "Rashi and the Historical Reality of his Time" (Hebrew), *Tarbitz* 20 (1949), pp. 320–33, and J. Rosenthal, "Anti-Christian Polemic in Rashi's Exegesis of the Bible" (Hebrew), *Mechkarim Umekorot* (Jerusalem, 1967), 1:101–16, suggest that the pressure toward *peshat*, "literal," exegesis was the Christian allegorical reading of Scripture. In my own study of Rashi's younger contemporary, R. Joseph b. Simon Kara, I suggest that the narrative emphasis in medieval biblical exegesis with the Franco-German schools may have originated in pedagogics: "Exégèse et enseignment: les commentaires de Joseph ben Simeon Kara," *Archives Juives* 18:4 (1982), 60–63. By far the most brilliant and synthetic study of exegetical form and content is F. E. Talmage, *David Kimhi: The Man and the Commentaries* (Cambridge, Mass., 1975).

10. M. Signer, "King/Messiah: Rashi's Exegesis of Psalm 2" *Prooftexts* 3 (1983): pp. 273–84.

11. This formulation is my own but it is discussed in great detail by E. M. Lifschütz, *Rabbi Solomon Yitshaki* (Hebrew), (Warsaw, 1912); S. Kamin, "Rashi's Exegetical Categorization with Respect to the Distinction between *Peshat* and *Derash*," *Immanuel* II (1980), 16–32; and B. J. Gelles, *Peshat and Derash in the Exegesis of Rashi* (Leiden, 1981).

12. On the history of Jewish polemical literature, cf. B. Blumenkranz, *Juifs et Chretiens*, 220ff.; and D. Berger, *The Jewish-Christian Debate in the High Middle Ages* (Philadelphia, 1979), 3–32.

13. Surveys of interpretation which relate to the question of Jewish sovereignty can be found in A. Posnanski, *Schiloh: Ein Beitrag Zur Geschichte der Messiaslehre* (Leipzig, 1904); and A. Neubauer and S. R. Driver, *The Fifty-Third Chapter of Isaiah according to the Jewish Interpreters* (Oxford, 1876–77).

14. M. Steinschneider, *Jewish Literature from the Eighth Century* (New York, 1965), 60–202. For more specialized studies of the relationships between all of these genres, one should consult S. Baron, *Social and Religious History*, vols. 6–7; E. E. Urbach, *Ba'ale HaTosafoth* (Jerusalem, 1980), 2 vols; A. Grossman, *Reshit Chokhmei Ashkenaz* (Jerusalem, 1981); and I. Twersky, "Aspects of the Social and Cultural History of Provençal Jewry," *Jewish Society through the Ages*, H. H. Ben-Sasson and S. Ettinger, eds., (New York, 1971), pp. 185–206.

15. Rabbi Solomon b. Isaac (hereafter Rashi), *Commentary on Genesis* 12:9. The citation is from Genesis Rabba 39:17.

16. Rashi, *Commentary on Genesis* 14:10, 17; *Commentary on Joshua* 1:4; 8:2. Nachmanides, *Commentary on Numbers* 28:12.

17. Cf. frequent references to the Aramaic Targumim to describe natural phenomena such as flowers, birds, etc. in I. Löw. *Die Flora der Juden* (Vienna, 1934), 4:148–231.

18. Cf. Nachmanides' lengthy comment on Genesis 11:28 with respect to the location of Haran and Genesis; and 35:16, where he claims "This I originally wrote while still in Spain but now that I was worthy and came to Jerusalem . . . I saw with my own eyes that there is not even a mile between Rachel's grave and Bethlehem. . . . And I have also seen that Rachel's grave is not in Ramah or near it." On the reasons for Nachmanides settlement in the Land of Israel see Martin A. Cohen, "Reflections on the Text and Context of the Disputation of Barcelona," *Hebrew Union College Annual* 35 (1964).

19. This phrase is found in *Talmud Babli Zevachim* 54b, in relationship to the central location of the Temple in Jerusalem. Medieval exegetes use only that part of the phrase which refers to the Land being more elevated than all other lands. Rashi, *Commentary on Genesis* 45:9; *Deuteronomy* 1:25; 32:13. David Kimhi, *Commentary on Joshua* 15:8; Jer. 4:3, Ez. 16:40; 17:3. Nachmanides, *Commentary on Leviticus* 18:25.

20. Rashi, *Commentary on Genesis* 15:18. "*The Great River:* Because it is mentioned in connection with the Land of Israel, Scripture calls it 'great' although it is the last mentioned of the four rivers that went out of Eden." Cf. also *Commentary on Genesis* 2:14 and *Deuteronomy* 1:7; and Rabbi David Kimhi, *Commentary on Genesis* 2:14; 15:18.

21. On animals' size, see Nachmanides, *Commentary on Exodus* 3:9, *Leviticus* 26:6. On the fruit of Israel, see Rashi, *Commentary on Deuteronomy* 32:13. On precious stones, see Nachmanides, *Commentary on Deuteronomy* 9:9. For the natural qualities of the land increasing during the day of the Messiah, see Rabbi David Kimhi, *Commentary on Ezekiel* 47:17; 49:12; *Commentary on Joel* 4:18.

22. Nachmanides, *Commentary on Deuteronomy* 11:10.

23. Nachmanides, *Commentary on Genesis* 8:11, quoting *Pirkei d'Rabbi Eliezer* 23.

24. Rashi, *Commentary on Genesis* 24:53. One can contrast Rashi's comment with Rabbi David Kimhi's explanation, "This word includes anything which may be considered the finest whether it be fruit, vessels, or clothing."

25. Rashi, *Commentary on Numbers* 13:17 quoting *Tanchuma, Shelach* 6.

26. See Rashi, *Commentary on Genesis* 12:6. The treatment is more sharply articulated by Nachmanides, *Commentary on Genesis* 14:1 and 15:2. The term *remez* is frequently used by the exegetes to mean "allusion" or "hint." See W. Bacher, *Arkhe Midrash* s.v. *remez*.

27. Rashi, *Commentary on Genesis* 12:6–7.

28. Mount Ebal and Mount Gerizim were the locations prescribed in Deuteronomy 27–28 for the people to hear the consequences of the covenant. The supercommentary on Rashi *Gur Arieh* written by Judah Loew of Prague (*ad loc*) emphasizes that the reason Rashi focused on the location was to demonstrate that these matters in the life of Abraham were concerned with "heavenly matters." Judah Loew, "*Gur Arieh*" in *'Otzar Haperushim al Hatorah* (Jerusalem, 1976), 38a. *Mishnah Sotah* 7:5 described the reading of the "blessings" and "curses."

29. Nachmanides, *Commentary on Genesis* 12:6. I am basing my translation on C. Chavel, *Ramban: Commentary on the Torah: Genesis* and Amos Funkenstein, whose article will be cited in the following note.

30. Amos Funkenstein, "Nachmanides' Symbolical Reading of History," *Studies in Jewish Mysticism*, J. Dan and F. Talmage, eds., (Cambridge, 1982), 129–50. Funkenstein's article is most important because it points out both similarities *and* differences between Christian typological reading of Scripture and Jewish "symbolic" reading.

31. Nachmanides, *Commentary on Genesis* 14:1; 15:12. I have included only the beginning of the comment. Nachmanides continues to elaborate the four kingdoms, utilizing texts from rabbinic literature, T. B. *Avodah Zarah* 11a. For a discussion of the concept of the "Four Kingdoms" in medieval Jewish exegetical and historical writings, cf. Gerson D. Cohen's *The Book of Tradition by Abraham Ibn Daud*

(Philadelphia, 1967), 223–62 and B. Netanyahu, *Don Isaac Abravanel* (Philadelphia, 1968), 130–94.

32. Rashi, *Commentary on Genesis* 17:2, links the commandment of circumcision and the Land. The conquest of the Land becomes the point in time for the observance of commandments: *Commentary on Deuteronomy* 11:28; 12:8; 26:1. Nachmanides comments on similar themes: *Commentary on Genesis* 1:1; 19:5; *Leviticus* 13:47.

33. The Hebrew construction which translates "It shall come to pass" occurs more frequently in Deuteronomy than in the other books of the Pentateuch. Exodus, with its description of laws and the cultus, has the next most frequent use of this construction.

34. Nachmanides, *Introduction to Commentary on Deuteronomy*.

35. Nachmanides, *Commentary on Leviticus* 18:25.

36. Nachmanides, *Commentary on Leviticus* 25:2, links the verse to the cosmological process of creation and redemption. He expands upon the statement in *Mishnah Avot* 5:9 that exile comes about because of false justice and the perversion of justice and the failure to observe the Sabbatical year. It should be noted that Nachmanides cites a different text than is to be found in other editions of *Avot*.

37. Ibid.

38. Cf. F. Talmage's Introduction to Joseph Kimhi's *Book of the Covenant* (Toronto: 1972). See also O. S. Rankin, *Jewish Religious Polemic* (New York, 1970); B. Blumenkranz, *Juifs et Chretiens dans le monde occidental* (Paris, 1960), 213–90. A. Funkenstein, "He Temurot Bevikuach Hadat Shebein Yehudim LeNotzrim Bameah HaYod-Bet," *Zion* 33 (1968), 125–44.

39. J. Rosenthal, "Sifrut Havikuach Haanti-Notzrit," *Areshet* 2 (1960): 130–79; 3 (1961): 48–66, provides a full bibliography of Jewish polemical works. P. Browe, *Die Judenmission im Mittelalter und die Päpste* (Rome, 1942), 99–110 provides a bibliography of the Latin polemical treatises from 700–1600. Jacob Katz, *Exclusiveness and Tolerance* (New York, 1961) puts Jewish-Christian argumentation into a sociological framework.

40. Bartholomew of Exeter, "Dialogue against the Jews," Ms. Bodl. 482. f. 1ᵈ, quoted in B. Smalley, *Study of the Bible*, 170–71.

41. Cf. *supra* note 4. Also, B. Blumenkranz has composed an index to themes in Latin Christian literature relating to Jews: 496–1100 in his edition of *Altercatio Aecclesie contra Synagogam* (Strasbourg, 1954), 130–54; s.v. "L'aveuglement des Juifs."

42. Cf. H. de Lubac, *Exégèse médiévale*, 1:305–63; 489–548; 2:99–198.

43. Excerpt from Jerome, "Letter 129" quoted in F. E. Talmage (ed.), *Disputation and Dialogue: Readings in the Jewish Christian Encounter* (New York, 1970), 174–80. Talmage's reader contains important excerpts from Jewish and Christian authors on the topic.

44. The writings of Jerome were probably better known through his bibli-

cal commentaries than through his letters. The letters might have been quoted in *Florilegia*, collections of excerpts from the Fathers, which circulated in monastic libraries during the Middle Ages. Jerome's statements about Jews and Judaism seem to have been less well known than Augustine's.

45. Joseph Kimhi, *The Book of the Covenant* 46.

46. Jacob b. Reuben, *Milchamot Hashem*, J. Rosenthal, ed., (Jerusalem, 1963), 74.

47. Jacob b. Reuben, *loc. cit.* Joseph ben Nathan Officiel, *Sefer Yosef Hamekaneh* (Jerusalem, 1970), 81, par. 94.

48. Joshua HaLorki's letter is published in J. D. Eisenstein's *Otzar Havikuchim*, (rpt. Israel, 1969), 98–103. For further information on the correspondence, see Y. Baer, *A History of the Jews in Christian Spain* (Philadelphia, 1978), 2:139–50.

49. I explain this concern about freedom from "the yoke of the gentiles" in my introduction to *The Itinerary of Benjamin of Tudela* (Los Angeles, 1983), 13–36.

50. The anticipation of unfulfilled prophecies forms the introductory section of Joseph b. Nathan Officiel's *Sefer Yosef Hamekaneh*, 15–25; Jacob b. Reuben's *Milchamot Hashem*, 157–85. Yair b. Shabbetai da Corregio, *Cherev Pipiyot* (Jerusalem, 1958), is devoted entirely to this theme. The problem of Jewish sovereignty is discussed frequently in the *Commentary on Psalms* by David Kimhi; see Joel Rembaum, "The Development of a Jewish Exegetical Regarding Isaiah 53," *Harvard Theological Review* 75:3 (1982), 289–311.

51. Joseph Kimhi, *The Book of the Covenant*, 74.

52. Joseph b. Nathan Officiel, *Sefer Yosef Hamekaneh*, 67, par. 50.

53. David Kimhi, *Commentary on Isaiah* 52:1, 63:1; *Jeremiah* 49:7; *Joel* 4:19; *Psalms* 127:5. D. Berger, *The Jewish-Christian Debate*, 29; 89; 203; 270.

Nachmanides' *Commentary on Leviticus* 18:25, indicates that Israel will not tolerate idolators or sinners. It literally vomits them out. This comports with his *Commentary on Genesis* 1:1 where he claimed that "It is fitting if a people continues to sin that it loses its place and another nation come to inherit its land." Similarly the inhabitants of Sodom and Gomorrah were punished severely because "the Land of God's inheritance will not suffer abomination" (*Commentary on Genesis* 19:5). David Kimhi, *Commentary on Ezekiel* 11:18, indicates a purification of the Land from idolators; and that the Land is "allergic" to foreigners and spits them out (*Commentary on Ezekiel* 17:5).

54. R. Nissim b. R. Moses of Marseilles, *Hechalutz* 7, 102–03; R. Joseph Ibn Kaspi, *Tam Hakesef* 43–45, quoted in B. Z. Dinur, *Yisrael Bagolah*, 2:1, 446–47.

David Kimhi, *Commentary on Isaiah* 63:1; *Jeremiah* 49:7; *Obadiah* 1; *Micah* 7:20. See also, Nachmanides, *Commentary on Leviticus* 26:16.

55. Nachmanides, *Commentary on Deuteronomy* 19:8.

56. Nachmanides, *Commentary on Numbers* 21:2, 26:54; *Deuteronomy* 8:18; 9:4; 11:24; 18:1; 19:8; 31:18.

57. Nachmanides was the first to include settlement in the Land as a positive commandment. Cf. his comment on Maimonides, *Sefer Hamitzvot* part 2, positive commandment number 4, and his *Commentary on Numbers* 33:53.

58. Nachmanides, *Commentary on Deuteronomy* 11:24.

59. David Kimhi, *Commentary on Isaiah* 26:2; 52:1; *Commentary on Ezekiel* 11:18; *Joel* 4:19. Joseph Kimhi, *Book of the Covenant*, 74; Joseph b. Nathan Officiel, *Sefer Yosef Hamekanneh* 77, par. 80; 81, par. 94; 91, par. 98; 94, par. 100. In the account of the trial of the Talmud in Paris (1240) R. Yehiel of Paris indicates that all who have oppressed Israel will be destroyed except the Pope and the King of France because they protected Israel, *Otzar Havikuchim*, 86. Calling upon God's vengeance against earthly kings is a frequent theme in the Chronicles of the Crusades: see S. Eidelberg, *The Jews and the Crusades* (Madison, Wis., 1977).

60. For the history of the identification of Christians as idolators, see J. Katz, *Exclusiveness and Tolerance*, 3–66.

61. The most complete articulation of Christianity and Islam as a *praeparatio evangelica* for Judaism is by Maimonides, *Mishneh Torah, Hilkhot Melakhim*, end.

62. Rashi, *Commentary on Genesis* 1:1.

63. For Rashi's use of the technique of rhetorical questions in his exegetical works, see my "King/Messiah: Rashi's Exegesis of Psalm 2," *Prooftexts* 3 (1983), 275–76.

64. Traditional Jewish exegetes of Rashi would certainly disagree with my assessment of the importance of sequential narrative here. Cf. Elijah Mizrahi and Judah Loew on Rashi's comment to Genesis 1:1 in *Otzar Haperushim 'al Hatorah*. "All the stories of the Torah are there for a purpose, but the principal subject matter (*ikar*) is for the purpose of the commandments."

65. Rashi's commentaries have the status of a *Glossa Ordinaria* within Jewish biblical exegesis. He was called "Parshandata," "the exegete par excellence." Cf. H. Hailperin, *Rashi and the Christian Scholars* (Pittsburgh, 1963).

Return in Mercy to Zion:
A Messianic Dream in Jewish Art*

Joseph Gutmann

[Editor's note: Not all our knowledge of Jewish ideas comes to us by way of the written word. That abundant literary corpus must often be augmented, and even corrected, by testimony of the arts which bear equally poignant witness to what people have valued most in their lives. Dr. Joseph Gutmann, Professor of Art History at Detroit's Wayne State University, surveys synagogue art from the thirteenth to the eighteenth centuries, to see if and how recollections of the Land are to be found there. Beginning with twenty-three thirteenth- to fifteenth-century Spanish Hebrew Bible manuscripts which portray details of the Tabernacle that do not conform to its biblical description, he argues that medieval artists envisioned no mere historical reproduction, but a messianic Temple modeled after Solomon's achievement and symbolic of the Jews' ardent hope that they be restored to their Land. In Ashkenazic northern and central Europe, the synagogue itself was outfitted as a temporary surrogate temple, "so as to insure its rebuilding in the messianic future." Thus, for example, by the thirteenth century, the Torah ark was renamed after the Temple ark — *aron hakodesh* — and, a century later, it was outfitted with a curtain, called *parokhet*, just as the biblical one had been. Gutmann describes those curtains still extant, as well as similar means of recalling the biblical prototype, such as the sixteenth-century practice of inscribing the ten commandments on ark doors in Italy, the seventeenth-century introduction of an eternal light (*ner tamid*), the eighteenth-century custom of outfitting the ark with a valance called *kapporet*, and, above all, perhaps, the deliberate manufacturing of lampstands for Chanukah, which dominated the interior architecture and resembled the seven-branch lampstand (*menorah*) of the Temple of old. The Jew's yearning for redemption to the Land is borne out also by Passover Haggadah art, which Gutmann surveys as well, along with parallel evidence from illustrated itineraries of pilgrims anxious to return to the Land, and even late eighteenth-century Sabbath cloths with floral borders and inscriptions extolling the Land of Israel.]

I

From the end of the thirteenth century into the fifteenth century we frequently find in Spanish Hebrew Bible manuscripts two or more pages devoted to depictions of what appears to be the splendid vessels of the wilderness Tabernacle described in the books of Exodus, Leviticus, and Numbers. Some twenty-three surviving manuscripts represent objects like the golden lampstand, its tongs and snuffers, the jar of manna flanked by the budding rod of Aaron, the Ark with its rings and poles and Ten Commandments, the golden incense altar, two silver trumpets and the *shofar*. To be noted also are the altar of burnt offering and some shovels and bowls (Figs. 1–2).[1]

Closer examination of these sacred vessels reveals some unexpected and unaccountable details:

1. What, for instance, are the stones with steps and the mortars next to the menorah, and why are the loaves of showbread placed in compartments on a table—none of these details mentioned in or conforming to the biblical descriptions?
2. What, we may ask, is the Mount of Olives doing in the midst of the Sanctuary vessels?
3. Why are these objects confined to the preliminary folios preceding the Hebrew Bibles and not in proximity to the descriptive passages of the cult objects in Exodus, Leviticus or Numbers?

One clue to this enigma lies in the inscription to folio 13 of one of the earliest manuscripts, dated 1299, of this unique Spanish iconographic tradition (Paris: Bibliothèque Nationale, Ms. hébr. 7). It reads:

All [implements existed] while the Temple was [still] upon its site and the holy Sanctuary was upon its foundation. Blessed is he who beheld it in all its glory and splendor and [witnessed] all the acts of its power and might.

And happy is he who waits and will live to see it. May it be Your will that it [the Temple] be speedily rebuilt in our days[2] so that our eyes may behold it and our heart rejoice.[3]

An additional clue can be found in the *Mishneh Torah*, the legal code of the most influential and widely read twelfth-century Spanish Jewish philosopher, Maimonides. In his Book of the Temple Service (*Avodah*, Book 8), Maimonides discusses many of the above-mentioned objects.[4] He explains that all these cult implements existed in the Solomonic Temple, the same structure which a King-Messiah would rebuild in the messianic period.[5] At that time a Jewish kingdom, governed by Jewish law, would be established under the King-Messiah in the Land of Israel. The stone with steps, according to Maimonides, is for the priest to ascend in order to trim the lamps of the *menorah*; the mortars are for grinding and compounding the ingredients used for the Temple incense.[6]

The enigmatic Mount of Olives is explained by such Bible commentators as the twelfth-thirteenth century David Kimchi. He and others tell us that God will make underground caverns through which the dispersed of Israel may roll until they emerge at the Mount of Olives at Jerusalem in messianic times.[7]

One miniature in a manuscript, dated 1404, from Saragossa is entirely devoted to the Mount of Olives. Around the illustration runs a passage from Zechariah 14:4:

> On that day, He shall set His feet on the Mount of Olives near Jerusalem on the east; and the Mount of Olives shall be split in two from east to west [forming] a huge gorge. . . .[8]

A mural in the third-century Dura-Europos synagogue actually depicts this momentous event. A cleft Mount of Olives, topped by two olive trees, discharges on Resurrection day the dead corpses of the righteous buried within (Fig. 3).[9] The meaning of the Mount of Olives is clear. The righteous dead, on that final day, will emerge from the Mount of Olives and be enabled to view from that vantage point some of the beautiful objects of the Third Temple—the rebuilt Messianic Temple.

Maimonides claimed that:

> When Solomon built the Temple, knowing that it was destined to be destroyed, he built underneath, in deep and winding tunnels, a place in which to hide the Ark. It was King Josiah who commanded that the Ark be hidden in the place which Solomon had prepared. The staff of Aaron, the jar of manna, and the oil for anointing were also hidden with the Ark.[10]

Furthermore, in fourteenth-century Spain, and especially in Catalonia, the Hebrew Bible itself came to be called the "Lord's Sanctuary" (*mikdashyah, mikdashiyah, magdessia*). Its threefold division—into Pentateuch, Prophets, and Hagiographa—was likened to the division of the ancient Solomonic Jerusalem Temple.[11] Placement of the hidden Solomonic Temple appurtenances on the opening pages of Spanish Hebrew Bibles—rather than accompanying the descriptive passages of these cult objects in the books of Exodus, Leviticus, and Numbers, as is the usual practice in both Christian and Hebrew manuscripts—visually expressed and affirmed the Spanish Jew's belief in resurrection and kept alive his hope that he would be privileged to view the Third Temple in messianic times.

Where and when did the idea of the Messianic Temple arise? It must be remembered that the year 70 C.E. proved cataclysmic for Judaism. The Temple in Jerusalem lay in ruins. A religious system which was a thousand years in the making and had focused on the centralized Jerusalem Temple, a hereditary priesthood, and sacrifices—all to insure the fertility of the Land of Israel—had come to an abrupt end. A salvational Judaism which featured a new religious edifice—the decentralized synagogue—had arisen. Not priests, but scholars (Pharisees, later called rabbis) were its leaders. For the lapsed cultic sacrifices in the now defunct Temple, prayers, ceremonies, charity, deeds of loving kindness (*mitzvot*), and the study and observance of God's Torah were substituted. Fertility of the Land was no longer the primary goal; life eternal of the soul and bodily resurrection were the central promises given the faithful.

Loss of the sacred Jerusalem Temple could, however, not easily be eradicated from Jewish memory. It had after all been God's house—a visible symbol of God's love and concern for Israel. Why had it been destroyed? Why had God abandoned it? Rabbinic scholars, particularly the Amoraim, tried to demonstrate that God had no alternative. He had, however, not abandoned Israel, but His divine wrath was kindled against Israel's sins and against the untrustworthy, wicked guardians (= priests) of His Temple. These guardians were sinners who had violated God's trust by making His place unworthy for worship. God, therefore, decided to employ the Romans to destroy His Temple. The Rabbis tried to show that God would build a more splendid Solomonic Temple in the future; that the destroyed Second Temple had never measured up to the sanctity of the First, for God's *Shekhinah* did not dwell in it; and that it was therefore not worthy of being rebuilt.[12]

God, however, had hidden or caused to be hidden for his faithful the splendid vessels of Solomon's Temple. Moral reconstitution would bring about restoration of the Solomonic Temple in the messianic future. This hope was nurtured by its insertion into the daily liturgy:

> At time's end He will send our Messiah to save all who wait for His final help. God, in His mercy, will revive the dead. . . . (Maimonides' Creed, *Yigdal*)

> May it be Your will, Lord our God and God of our fathers, that the Temple be speedily rebuilt in our days. . . . Return in mercy to Your city Jerusalem and dwell in it, as You have promised; . . . rebuild it soon, in our days as an everlasting structure, and speedily establish in it the throne of David. (Daily *Tefillah*)

Messiah, the son of David—they fervently prayed—would come in the future, return the exiles to their Land, deliver them from their enemies, and restore the Jerusalem Temple.[13]

This abiding belief in a messianic redemption in the Holy Land, a belief affirmed daily, also served as a denial of the insistent Christian claim that Christ (= Messiah), son of David, had already come for the Israel of the Spirit (*verus Israel*). No wonder that the Spanish Jew valued a visual image of the future Jerusalem Temple, while he recited his prayers and read from his *mikdashyah* (= Bible), sheltering himself, as it were, in a surrogate Sanctuary.

II

Just as the Spanish Jew visually beheld the future *mikdashyah* in the Land of Israel, so much of Ashkenazic Jewry testified to a related rabbinic belief that the synagogue itself constitutes a surrogate, a temporary substitute, for the Temple—a *mikdash me'at*.[14] The worshipper had been instructed to face, in his prayers, towards Jerusalem. Synagogal buildings, therefore, were frequently oriented towards Jerusalem or, at any rate, the East.[15] As the surrogate Temple, the synagogue took over practices which formerly had been exclusive prerogatives of the Jerusalem Temple. Furthermore, charity, deeds of loving kindness, Torah reading or study and the recitation of prayers, regular practices in the synagogue, were equated with offering sacrifices in the Temple.[16]

Ashkenazic rabbis, especially in medieval Central Europe, wanted the synagogal appurtenances to resemble those they associated with the ancient Solomonic Temple, so as to insure its rebuilding in the messianic future.[17] By the thirteenth century in Central Europe, the Torah ark was given the same designation as the biblical Temple ark—*'aron ha-kodesh*.[18] A curtain, called *parokhet*, was hung in front of the ark, since the biblical ark had also been placed "behind the *parokhet*" (Exod. 26:33). Rabbinic sources from the fourteenth century on refer to Torah curtains in Ashkenazic synagogues; some apparently, by the sixteenth century, had birds embroidered on them, as the biblical curtain had had "a design of cherubim worked into it" (Exod. 26:31).[19] No Torah ark curtain of this period has survived; the oldest one extant dates from 1590, comes from Prague, and does not conform to the above description.[20] From seventeenth-century Italy unusual curtains have survived with the walled city of Jerusalem and its Temple embroidered on them. They also carry such verses as "I keep Jerusalem in memory even at my happiest hour" (Ps. 137:6)[21] (Fig. 4) and "If I forget you, O Jerusalem, let my right hand wither" (Ps. 137:5).[22] Not only did the *parokhet* itself recall the ancient Temple, but its embroidered centerpiece emphasized the longing for Jerusalem and its messianic Temple.

By the sixteenth century, we find the practice of placing the words of the Ten Commandments on the wooden interiors of Italian ark doors, "for the tablets were deposited in the [biblical] ark" (Exod. 25:16 and Deut. 10:2).[23] The analogy with the ancient Sanctuary is carried further in the Ashkenazic *mikdash me'at*. In 1530 Antonius Margarita, a convert to Christianity, observed in his book, *The Entire Jewish Faith:* "They open the [ark] doors, which they call *kapporet*, the [biblical] Mercy Seat, and take out the Decalogue [i.e., the Torah or pentateuchal Scroll]."[24] By the eighteenth century, the designation *kapporet* is applied to a valance specially designed to hang above the Torah curtain. Literary sources are silent as to how, why, and when this transformation of *kapporet* from the Torah ark doors to the Torah valance occurred. These valances come predominantly from eighteenth-century workshops in Southern Germany and Bohemia (Fig. 5). They had either seven or five scallops, and were donated with the curtain or made separately. In any case, the dogmatic assertion of Samuel Krauss—"In the house of prayer [synagogue], free of sacrificial offerings, [the *kapporet*] rightly had no place"[25]—is not borne out by the evidence. Usually embroidered on the *kapporet* were three crowns—symbolic of the crowns of learning (Torah), priesthood, and royalty (M. Avot 4:17)—and a Hebrew inscription giving the name of the donor and the occasion. In the center, two cherubim with outspread wings hover over the ark (Exod. 37:1ff.) with its Decalogue. On the scallops, we sometimes find such cultic appurtenances as the ephod (Exod. 28:6f.; 39:2f.), the copper altar (Exod. 38:30; 39:39), the *menorah* (Exod. 25:31f., 31:17f.), the table of showbread (Exod. 25:25–30; Lev. 24:6), the copper laver (Exod. 38:8) and the frontlet of pure gold (Exod. 28:36; 39:30). Just as the ancient *kapporet* rested on top of the ark, with the cherubim spreading their wings above it, so the synagogal *kapporet* (valance) in a sense also rested "on top of the ark." Like its ancient counterpart, its embroidered cherubim "had their wings spread out above, shielding the cover with their wings" (Exod. 25:20; 37:9).[26] By the seventeenth century, the *ner tamid* (eternal light) had been introduced into Central European synagogues in remembrance of the Temple. It was hung in front of and above the Torah ark and curtain. This *ner tamid* alluded to the lights set up "to burn regularly" (*ner tamid*, Exod. 27:20; Lev. 24:2) outside the curtain. Many of these eternal lights, in fact, closely resemble those hung in neighboring churches (Fig. 6).[27]

The final object introduced into the Central European synagogues was the large synagogal lampstand that stood on the south side of the ark. Used for the *Chanukah* holiday, these lampstands began to resemble, by the seventeenth century, the seven-branched Temple lampstand, but usually, of course, had two additional branches for light. Isaac Tyrnau, a fourteenth-century Hungarian rabbi, wrote: "One kindles the Chanukah [lights] in the south of the synagogue, in memory of the Temple *menorah* that stood in the south (Exod. 26:35; 40:24)."[28] According to Israel Isserlein (15th-century Austria):

> We kindle [the lights] in the synagogue towards the southern side as a memorial of the [Temple] *menorah*; it would appear that we ought to arrange the lights as they were arranged on the [Temple] *menorah*.[29]

The 1656 Chanukah *menorah* from the destroyed Worms synagogue testifies that such bronze Chanukah lampstands once stood in European synagogues during the seventeenth century. A similar bronze *menorah*, dedicated in 1706 to the Achaffenburg synagogue in Germany, is now in the Hebrew Union College Skirball Museum.[30] Naming the ark *'aron ha-kodesh*, inscribing the Decalogue on its inside doors, utilizing a *parokhet* (curtain) and *kapporet* (valance) to cover the ark, suspending a *ner tamid* (eternal light) in front of it and placing a Chanukah *menorah* (lampstand) on its south side—all practices that arose in Ashkenazic Central European synagogues between the fourteenth and eighteenth centuries—these all attest to the fact that to the Ashkenazic Jew, the synagogue was a surrogate Temple, a small sanctuary (*mikdash me'at*) in the Exile. Praying in his *mikdash me'at* promised him that he would behold the magnificent appurtenances of the messianic Temple of the future when all the exiles would be gathered to the Holy Land.[31]

III

The unbearable miseries—persecutions, vilifications, charges of well-poisoning, blood-libel accusations—to which Jews were subjected regularly in the declining structures of medieval Central Europe evoked something more concrete than the abstract symbolism of the *mikdashyah* and the *mikdash me'at*. From the fifteenth century on—primarily in Ashkenazic South German Hebrew manuscripts—we find depictions of the arrival of Elijah and the Messiah. The Passover Haggadah, also called *sefer ha-ge'ulah* ("Book of Redemption"),[32] recited at the Passover *seder*, served as the artistic vehicle for the awaited redemption on the "Night of Redemption." *Shefokh*, the initial word of the verse, "Pour out Your wrath upon the nations that do not know You" (Ps. 79:6 and Jer. 10:25), is the designated page for these illustrations. In a German (?) Haggadah, dated 1478, for instance, the head of the household is shown opening the door of his home, holding the prescribed fourth cup of wine, and reciting the *shefokh* as he welcomes the messianic guest (Fig. 7). The Messiah is depicted as a bearded old man riding upon a richly adorned ass. Seated behind the Messiah are a man and a boy, along with a woman holding a cup of wine. A young girl is precariously balanced on the tail of the ass, while still another youngster clings to the tail. The messianic ass and its many riders no doubt symbolize the household of Israel travelling with the Messiah to the promised and hoped for Redemption in Zion, the Land of Israel. Rabbi Joseph Yuspa Hahn of sixteenth-century Frankfurt explains this custom associated with *shefokh*:

> After drinking, as is customary, from the cup of blessing (i.e., the third cup of wine), he [the head of the household] grasps the fourth cup of wine and opens the door. The moment that the door is opened, he begins reciting *shefokh*. And what a lovely custom it is, done in remembrance of the Messiah, that when the recitation of *shefokh* begins, someone stumbles into the threshhold in order to demonstrate, on the night of our first redemption, our strong faith in our final redemption.[33]

Printed Haggadot, such as the Venice Haggadah of 1609, continue this medieval motif, but with some interesting variations. A passage from the "Grace" to be recited after the Seder meal reads,

> Our God . . . may the remembrance . . . of Messiah, son of David Your servant, and of Jerusalem, Your holy city, and all Your people, the house of Israel, ascend and come and be accepted before You for deliverance. . . .

Illustrations of this passage show the prophet Elijah walking in front of the Messiah, who is seated on the ass, and blowing the shofar of Redemption. The figures approach the Gate of Mercy of the city of Jerusalem, whose rebuilt Temple already stands within the walls. In fulfillment of the prophecy heralded by the messianic Redeemer, we witness the ingathering of the exiled Jews who are seen flocking from all corners of the world to the Holy City.[34]

Some Jews, not content with simply waiting for the anticipated arrival of the Messiah at Passover, undertook pious pilgrimages to the sacred sites of the Holy Land. At the graves of the righteous dead prophets, kings, and patriarchs, they appealed for intercession for themselves and all Israel before the divine throne. By the sixteenth century, Jewish itineraries, especially from Italy, had come to be illustrated with the sacred sites of the Holy Land. By the late eighteenth century, printed Sabbath cloths had also appeared. An example from Italy has a deep, lavishly decorated foliage and floral border with a Hebrew inscription praising the Holy Land (Fig. 8). In its center is a roundel revealing the Temple, Solomon's House of Learning, and the Wailing Wall. This centerpiece is in turn framed by another circle depicting other holy places in Jerusalem. Next we note an octagonal shape within a square which has some twenty conventionalized representations of other sacred Holy Land sites, all radially arranged and identified by Hebrew inscriptions. These Sabbath cloths became popular and continued with some variations throughout the nineteenth century. Not only did such a cloth serve as a *vade-mecum* – a tour guide – but it was a pious memento of the fulfillment of a *mitzvah* – a pious pilgrimage to the Land of Israel. Moreover, the visit forged for the Jew a spiritual link with the Land of his ancestors which would one day be redeemed by the Messiah.[35]

It was only at the turn of this century, that the age-old hope of a return through the agency of a supernatural Messiah gradually gave way to a new political demand. The German artist, Ephraim Moses Lilien, who designed the souvenir drawing for the Fifth Zionist Congress meeting at Basel in 1901, best summed up the dawn of a new dream as embodied in political Zionism – the pioneer return to the Land (Fig. 9). A bearded old man, symbolic of the religious ghetto Jew, sits huddled in a corner, his eyes downcast; his hands lean on a cane and he is imprisoned by thorns that surround him. Above him stands a winged male figure (a personification of Zionism) pointing to the future – a Jewish farmer diligently plowing the land at sunrise. The Hebrew inscription reads: "May our eyes behold Your return in mercy to Zion" (*Tefillah*).[36]

The old messianic longing was soon to become a living, political reality. Yet *mikdashyah, mikdash me'at*, the Messiah at the Seder, and the pilgrimage mementi of the Holy Land represent diverse aspects of Israel's messianic dream – the return to Zion.

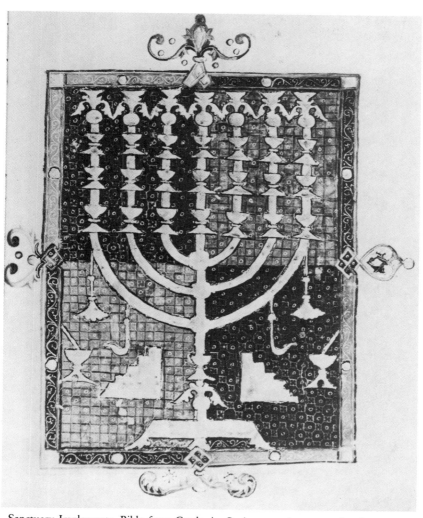

Sanctuary Implements, Bible from Catalonia, Spain, second quarter of 14th century. London, British Library, MS Add. 15250, fols. 3v–4.

Sanctuary Implements, Bible from Catalonia, Spain. See photo 1.

Mount of Olives and Ezekiel's Vision, Painting from North Wall of the Dura-Europos Synagogue, 244/45 CE. Damascus National Museum, Damascus, Syria.

Torah Ark Curtain, Italy, 1680/81. The Jewish Museum, New York, F. 2944.

246

Kapporet, Prague, Bohemia, 1763/64. The State Jewish Museum, Prague, No. 117.216.

247

Interior of Men's Prayer Hall, Worms, Germany, 1174/75. (The Eternal Light is from 1842.) Destroyed by Nazis in 1938.

The Messiah at the Seder, Haggadah, Germany (?), 1478. Washington, D.C., Library of Congress, fol. 19v.

Printed Sabbath Cloth, Italy, 18th century. Jerusalem, Israel Museum, 161/26.

From the Ghetto to Zion, Souvenir Drawing for the Fifth Zionist Congress, Basel, Switzerland, 1901. Artist: Ephraim Moses Lilien.

Notes

*I am deeply grateful to my good friend, Prof. Stanley F. Chyet, for his valuable criticisms of this paper.

1. Cf. J. Gutmann, "The Messianic Temple in Spanish Medieval Hebrew Manuscripts," *The Temple of Solomon: Archaeological Fact and Medieval Tradition in Christian, Islamic and Jewish Art*, ed. J. Gutmann (Religion and the Arts 3, Missoula, 1976), 125–44.

2. Cf. *Mishnah, Taanit* 4:8 and *Avot* 5:20.

3. See discussion in Gutmann, *op. cit.*, 128. This manuscript comes from Perpignan, Kingdom of Majorca, and not from Aragon, as indicated in ibid., 126 and 134, n. 6 (1). Ibid., p. 136f. (11a) should be corrected to read: Gottheil, No. 16, Bible, Spain, second half of 14th century, three folios and Gottheil, No. 17, Pentateuch, Spain, second quarter of 14th century, folios 3v–4. Ibid., 138 (18) should read: Solsona, Catalonia, 1384. Cf. B. Narkiss, *Illuminated Hebrew Manuscripts in the British Isles*, I (Oxford, 1982), 110ff. Cf. also Paris, Companie des Prêtres St. Sulpice, Ms 1933, folios 5v–6 and 7v–8 in M. Garel, "The Foa Bible," *Journal of Jewish Art* 6 (1979), 78–85, a Spanish Bible from the second half of the fourteenth century. The newly discovered folio (Paris, Bibliothèque de l'Ecole Nationale Supérieure des Beaux-Arts, Collection Masson, Ms 4, folio 1) probably should be dated to the second quarter of the fourteenth century as it closely resembles the unpublished miniatures in a Spanish Pentateuch in Istanbul, cf. Gutmann, *op. cit.*, 136 (11). The inscriptions around the Temple instruments come from Exodus 25:39, 30:27, 31:8; see M. Garel, "Le mobilier du Sanctuaire: Un folio détaché," *Journal of Jewish Art* 9 (1982), 105–07.

4. Cf. Ibid., 131–32.

5. Maimonides, Book 8, Treatise 5, 2:14 and Book 14, Treatise 5, 11:1: "King Messiah will build the Third Temple." Cf. also *Leviticus Rabbah* 9:6. Rabbinic sources frequently do not distinguish between the Temple and the Tabernacle, for "we find that the Tabernacle was called *Sanctuary* and that the Sanctuary was called *Tabernacle*," cf. Babylonian Talmud, *Erubin* 2a–b; *Shevu'ot* 16b. Some sources claim that God himself is to rebuild the Temple—*Numbers Rabbah* 15:10, *Leviticus Rabbah* 30:16: "I [God] shall rebuild for you the 'first' Temple." Cf. *Targum* to Zechariah 6:12f.; Isaiah 53:5 and Abravanel, Commentary to Zechariah 4. Cf. also S. D. Goitein, "'Meeting in Jerusalem,' Messianic Expectations in the Letters of the Cairo Geniza," *AJS Review* 4 (1979), 47ff. Other sources simply state that the Temple will be rebuilt in messianic times: Babylonian Talmud, *Pesachim* 5a and *Targum* to Song of Songs 1:17. Cf. H. J. Schoeps, *Aus frühchristliche Zeit, Religionsgeschichtliche Untersuchungen* (Tübingen, 1950), 180ff.

The identification of a Temple-like structure on Jewish coins of the Second Revolt during the reign of Emperor Hadrian is very problematic. See the vast, contradictory literature on this subject cited in Gutmann, *op. cit.*, 133, n. 2. See also the Vatican gold glass, supposedly giving a "bird's eye view of the Temple . . . of Solomon with the two pillars, *Jachin* and *Boaz*, on either side." B. Narkiss, "A Scheme of the Sanctuary from the Time of Herod the Great," *Journal of Jewish Art* 1 (1974), 13. See also I. Schüler, "A Note on Jewish Gold Glasses," *Journal of Glass Studies* 8 (1966), 56, 59. R. Hachlili convincingly suggests that the "steps, columns and gables [of our gold glass, fig. 978] . . . are the usual components of the [Torah] niche." Cf. R. Hachlili, "The Niche and the Ark in Ancient Synagogues," *American Schools of Oriental Research Bulletin* 223 (1976), 50.

    6. Maimonides, Book 8, Treatise 1, 1:17 and Treatise 2, 2:7.

    7. Kimchi, Commentary to Ezekiel 37:12, tells us that the righteous dead will be resurrected in the land of Israel after having rolled there by means of underground caverns. Cf. Rashi's Commentary to Gen. 47:29; Babylonian Talmud, *Ketubot* 111a; *Avodat ha-Kodesh* 40, 108; *Yalkut Shimoni*, Isaiah 49, par. 469 and *Pesikta Rabbati* 31, 147a add that the righteous dead will roll underneath the earth until they come to the Mount of Olives. *Targum* to Song of Songs 8:5 states that when the dead are resurrected, the Mount of Olives will split itself and the dead, having rolled in underground caverns, will emerge from it. *Ma'aseh Daniel* in *Bet ha-Midrash*, V (ed. A. Jellinek), 128 makes clear that the Messiah, standing on the Mount of Olives, will command Elijah to blow the shofar, and the dead will arise and view the rebuilt Temple, as prophesied. Cf. Maimonides, Book 8, Treatise 1, 6:5; I. Gafni, "Reinterment in the Land of Israel: Notes on the Origin and Development of the Custom," *The Jerusalem Cathedra* 1 (1981), 102; J. Fleming, "The Undiscovered Gate underneath the Golden Gate," *Biblical Archaeology Review* 9 (1983), 24ff.; Gutmann, *Temple of Solomon* 143–44, n. 30.

    8. Gutmann, *Temple of Solomon*, 131–32.

    9. Cf. H. Riesenfeld, "The Resurrection in Ezekiel XXXVII and in the Dura-Europos Paintings," *No Graven Images: Studies in Art and the Hebrew Bible*, ed. J. Gutmann (New York, 1971), 144ff.

    10. Maimonides, Book 8, Treatise 1, 4:1. Cf. Babylonian Talmud, *Yoma*, 52b; *Horayot* 12a; *Keritot* 5b; Jerusalem Talmud, *Shekalim* VI:2; Abravanel, Commentary to II Kings 23:3. Kimchi, Commentary to I Kings 6:19; and II Chron. 35:3; Abravanel, Commentary to I Kings 6:19, state that the Ark was hidden in a secret place under the *devir*. Cf. *Mishnah, Shekalim* 6:1–2. Some sources claim that God had hidden and would restore the sacred vessels (ark, *menorah*, cherubim, etc.). *Numbers Rabbah* 15:10; *Tanchuma Beha'aloteka* 6; *Seder Elihu Rabbah* 23, p. 129. Other sources state that it is King Messiah (and/or Elijah) who will reveal the hidden cultic implements. *Pirkei Mashiach, Bet ha-Midrash*, III (ed. A. Jellinek), 72; *Mekhilta Wa-Yassa'* 5, 51b (on Exodus 33–34)—ark, jar of manna, budding rod of Aaron. Cf. also *Massekhet Kelim, Bet ha-Midrash*, II, 88–91 (*menorah*, ark, cherubim, jar of manna, altar of burnt offering, and incense offering). Cf. *Pirkei Mashiach, Bet ha-Midrash*, III, 72 and *Pirkei R. Yoshiyyahu, Bet ha-Midrash*, VI, 115, and *Abot d'Rabbi Nathan* 41, fol. 34b (ark, tablets, jar of manna, staff of Aaron,

Moses' rod, the table of showbread, *menorah*, etc.). Cf. also L. Ginzberg, *The Legends of the Jews* (Philadelphia, 1947), III, 48, 161; IV, 234, 282, 320–21, 350; VI, 19, n. 112; 66, n. 341; 340, n. 114; 377, n. 118; and P. R. Ackroyd, "The Temple Vessels—A Continuity Theme," *Supplements to Vetus Testamentum* 23 (1972), 180ff. According to Samaritan tradition, the sacred vessels were buried by Moses on Mt. Gerizim; cf. M. F. Collins, "The Hidden Vessels in Samaritan Tradition," *Journal for the Study of Judaism* 3 (1972), 101ff. Rabbinic tradition does not link the hidden vessels with Jeremiah; only the apocryphal tradition does. Cf. II Maccabees 2:4–8 and II Baruch 6:7–10 and 4:6–7; Ginzberg, *op. cit.*, VI, 410, n. 61, and 411, n. 64. While the rabbis emphasized the physical appearance of the Temple vessels in the messianic Temple, Christians underscored the allegorical and antitypal meaning of the cult objects. Such implements as the *menorah*, the rod of Aaron, the jar of manna were seen as types or prefigurations of Christ and/or the Virgin (Hebrews 9:11); Gutmann, *Temple of Solomon*, 141–42. Cf. also B. Z. Wacholder, *Eupolemus. A Study of Judeo-Greek Literature* (Cincinnati, 1976), 247f.

11. See J. Gutmann, "*Masorah Figurata*: The Origins and Development of a Jewish Art Form," *Estudios Masoreticos*, ed. E. F. Tejero (Madrid, 1983), 59, n. 18; also Gutmann, *Temple of Solomon*, 132 and 144, n. 33. The Bible, called *mikdashyah* (Hebr. 4°780), in the Jewish National and University Library, Jerusalem, is dated 1322 in C. Sirat and M. Beit-Arié, *Manuscrits médiévaux en caractères hebraïques*, I (Jerusalem-Paris, 1972), I.31.

12. See, for instance, Babylonian Talmud, *Yoma* 9b, 21b; *Taanit* 29a; *Berakhot* 3a; *Pesachim* 57a; Rashi, Commentary on Gen. 9:27 and T. S. Ross, "The Attitude of the Rabbis toward the Destruction of the Second Temple," (Unpublished D.H.L. diss., Hebrew Union College, Cincinnati, 1943), 67ff. According to rabbinic tradition, the Solomonic Temple had five things that were missing in the Second Temple —the sacred fire, the ark, the urim and thummim, the oil for anointment, and the Holy Spirit (of prophecy). Cf. S. J. D. Cohen, "The Temple and the Synagogue," in *The Temple in Antiquity*, ed. T. G. Madsen (Provo, Utah, 1984), 158, and E. Rivkin "The Meaning of Messiah in Jewish Thought," *Union Seminary Quarterly Review* 26, (1971), 394ff. Cf. also J. Neusner, "Emergent Rabbinic Judaism in a Time of Crisis: Four Responses to the Destruction of the Second Temple," *Early Rabbinic Judaism* (Leiden, 1975), 34–49; B. Z. Wacholder, *Messianism and Mishnah: Time and Place in the Early Halakhah* (Cincinnati, 1979), 26ff.; S. D. Cohen, "The Destruction: From Scripture to Midrash," *Prooftexts* 2 (1982), 18–39; R. Goldenberg, "Early Rabbinic Explanations of the Destruction of Jerusalem," *Journal of Jewish Studies* 33 (1982), 517–25.

13. Babylonian Talmud, *Megillah* 17b, *Avodat ha-Kodesh* 40, 53. Cf. also J. Heinemann, *Prayer in the Talmud* (Berlin, 1977), 70ff.

14. On the synagogue as a *mikdash me'at*, see Babylonian Talmud, *Megillah* 29a: "Yet I have been to them as a little sanctuary"; *Leket Yosher* I, 31: "our synagogues are called *mikdash me'at*"; cf. *Yalkut Shimoni*, Psalms 12, par. 659; Abraham ben Nathan Hayarchi, *Sefer ha-Manhig*, end, par. 148; Isaac Lampronti, *Pachad Yitz-*

chak (s.v. *Ner Tamid*), II, fol. 90v. Cf. also *Targum*, Ezekiel 11:16; Rashi, Commentary to Ezekiel 11:16; S. Krauss, *Synagogale Altertümer* (Vienna, 1922), 17–18, 80; O. Böcher, "Die alte Synagoge zu Worms," *Festschrift zur Wiedereinweihung der Alten Synagoge zu Worms*, ed. E. Roth (Frankfurt, 1961), 97–the 1034 inscription reads: "they beautified the *mikdash me'at.*" See also B. Blumenkranz, "Les synagogues," in *Art et archéologie des juifs en France médiévale*, ed. B. Blumenkranz (Toulouse, 1980), 40f. for the Molsheim and Haguenau synagogues, which are called *mikdash me'at.*

15. *Mishnah, Berakhot* 4:6; Babylonian Talmud, *Berakhot* 30a; Maimonides, Book 2, 11:2; Isserles to *Orach Chayyim* 150:5. Cf. F. Landsberger, "The Sacred Direction in Synagogue and Church," *The Synagogue: Studies in Origins, Archaeology and Architecture*, ed. J. Gutmann (New York, 1975), xix, xxvii, 239ff.; S. Freehof, *Reform Jewish Practice and its Rabbinic Background*, II (Cincinnati, 1952), 12–16; Krauss, *op. cit.*, 317ff. Eighteenth-century Central Europe knew the custom of hanging special tablets in Jewish homes to indicate the direction of prayer. Called *mizrach* (the east, i.e. Jerusalem), they frequently carried Hebrew inscriptions and were gaily decorated with biblical scenes, depictions of holiday observances and ceremonial objects, or simply ornamental motifs. M. W. Christiani in *Bet ha-Knesset, oder kurtze Beschreibungen einer wohleingerichteten Synagog* (Regensburg, 1723), 47 writes: "Eine Tafel worauf das *Mizrach* mit seiner sonderbahren Bedeutung geschrieben. Diese wird von den Juden in ihre Stuben gegen Morgen an die Wand gehangen zu wissen wohin sie sich in ihrem Gebeth richten müssen." C. Antons, *Kurtzer Entwurf der Erklärung jüdischer Gebräuche* (Helmstadt, 1751), 98, comments: "Die Juden pflegen auch in ihren Stuben an die Morgenwand einen Bogen Papier zu schlagen und darauf das Wort *mizrach*, Mizrach, Morgen, mit grossen Buchstaben zu malen, damit ein jeder, der in die Stube kommt, sogleich die Morgenwand erblicken mögte. Denn wenn sie im Hause ihre Morgen und Nachmittagsgebeten verrichten, so müssen sie ihr Angesicht gegen Morgen wenden." Cf. K. Schilling, ed., *Monumenta Judaica, 2000 Jahre Geschichte und Kultur der Juden am Rhein* (Cologne, 1964), E26-35. R. D. Barnett, ed., *Catalogue of the Permanent and Loan Collection of the Jewish Museum* (London, 1974), 5; I. Shachar, ed. *The Feuchtwanger Collection: Jewish Tradition and Art* (Jerusalem, 1971), 50–58 (in Hebrew); J. Doleželová, "Mizrahs from the Collections of the State Jewish Museum in Prague," *Judaica Bohemiae* 11 (1975), 14–28. These interesting tablets have yet to be studied. E. R. Goodenough, *Jewish Symbols in the Greco-Roman Period*, IV (New York, 1954), 124–26 discusses *mizrach* tablets. It should be noted that the oldest *mizrach* is dated 1720 (Shachar, *op. cit.*, 55), and not eighth century as Goodenough claimed. Goodenough's description of a *mizrach* (see illustration in *The Jewish Encyclopedia*, VIII, 629) should be corrected. His claim that "the acrostic which no one . . . could identify" actually reads: "You are mighty forever, O Lord. Praised be His name, whose glorious kingdom is forever and ever." The top inscription is taken from Exodus 29:45: "I will abide among the Israelites." Goodenough's translation on p. 126 is unacceptable: "I will be the Shekinah among the sons of Israel." The leg-

end at the bottom of the *mizrach* is taken from Psalms 113:3: "From the rising of the sun to its setting the name of the Lord is praised"—not as Goodenough would have it: "The sun, until its setting, praises the name of Yahweh." The so-called "most mysterious scene" within the central conch is not a "representation of God himself," but is a poor copy of a well-known nineteenth-century painting by Eduard Bendemann showing Jeremiah surrounded by mourning Jews. Cf. *Synagoga*, Catalog, Städtische Kunsthalle, Recklinghausen (Nov.–Jan., 1961), D 11.

16. Recitation of prayers is equal to sacrifices: Babylonian Talmud, *Berakhot* 15a, 17a, 26a–b; Jerusalem Talmud, *Berakhot* V: 1; *Leviticus Rabbah* 7:3. Torah reading or study is equal to sacrifices: Babylonian Talmud, *Taanit* 27b, *Megillah* 31b, *Menachot* 110a. Cf. J. Gutmann, "Programmatic Painting in the Dura Synagogue," *The Dura-Europos Synagogue: A Re-evaluation*, ed. J. Gutmann (Religion and the Arts 1, Missoula, 1973), 154. For other synagogal observances, set up because they were formerly practiced in the Jerusalem Temple, such as praying three times daily, reciting sacrificial portions from the Torah, sounding the shofar on the Sabbath, etc., see Krauss, *op. cit.*, 95ff. See also R. S. Sarason, "Religion and Worship: The Case of Judaism," in J. Neusner, ed., *Take Judaism for Example: Studies toward the Comparison of Religions* (Chicago, 1982), 49–65; Cohen, "The Temple," 151–74 and B. M. Bokser, "Rabbinic Responses to Catastrophe: From Continuity to Discontinuity," *Proceedings of the American Academy for Jewish Research*, 50 (1983), 37–61 on deeds of loving kindness and charity as substitutes for sacrifices.

17. See also the capital of a column in the Worms synagogue, 1174–75, which has a verse chiseled in the stone, which refers to the Solomonic Temple columns, *Jakhin* and *Boaz* (I Kings 7:41f.). Cf. W. Cahn, "Solomonic Elements in Romanesque Art," *Temple of Solomon*, 63, n. 14. Portuguese synagogue buildings in seventeenth-century Holland were at times inspired by contemporary reconstructions of Solomon's Temple. See R. Wischnitzer, *The Architecture of the European Synagogue* (Philadelphia, 1964), 94–95. Nineteenth-century Reform synagogues are sometimes referred to as new Solomonic Temples. Often they utilize contemporary reconstructions of Solomon's Temple and incorporate into the synagogue such Solomonic elements as the two columns; the synagogue, moreover, is generally called a Temple. See Gutmann, *No Graven Images*, xxii and H. Hammer-Schenk, *Untersuchungen zum Synagogenbauten in Deutschland von der ersten Emanzipation bis zur gesetzlichen Gleichberechtigung der Juden (1800–1871)* (Bamberg, 1974), 106f., 110f., 126, 497. Cf. also Moses Sofer, *Chatam Sofer, Orach Chayyim* 28, who states that we must make our synagogues as much as possible like the Temple of Jerusalem. Cf. H. Rosenau, *Vision of the Temple: The Image of the Temple of Jerusalem in Judaism and Christianity* (London, 1979), 134ff.

18. II Chron. 35:3. *Sefer Chasidim* (ed. Margoliot), par. 934, which draws a parallel between the Temple and the synagogue ark. "Just as the tablets [of stone] and also the broken tablets [of stone] were placed in the ark [aron of the Temple], so [pasul] Torah scrolls with their torn and pierced sections may be put with [kasher]

Torah scrolls in the ark [aron of the synagogue]." I am indebted to Dr. Solomon B. Freehof for calling this reference to my attention. Cf. also Sefer Chasidim (ed. Wistinetzki), par. 1625. Cf. J. Gutmann, "The History of the Ark," Zeitschrift für die Alttestamentliche Wissenschaft 83 (1971), 22ff.; Jacob ben Moses ha-Levi Möllin, Sefer Maharil, Hilkhot Shavuot 14b; Mordecai Jaffe in Levush, Orach Chayyim 150:5.

19. Cf. Joseph Caro, Avkat Rokhel, No. 66; S. B. Freehof, A Treasury of Reform Responsa (Philadelphia, 1963), 108ff. A. Margaritha, Der gantz jüdisch Glaub (Augsburg, 1530) Sib; J. Buxtorf, Jüden Schül (Frankfurt, 1728), 327: "They like to have beautiful birds embroidered upon them [curtains], because birds hovered over the Ark of the Covenant in the Old Testament." Cf. also F. Landsberger, "Old-Time Torah Curtains," Beauty in Holiness: Studies in Jewish Customs and Ceremonial Art, ed. J. Gutmann (New York, 1970), xvi, 125–63. When a curtain was used in Sefardic synagogues, it was usually placed behind the ark doors, see J. Gutmann, Jewish Ceremonial Art (New York, 1964), 18.

20. O. Muneles, ed., Prague Ghetto in the Renaissance Period (Prague, 1965), 108, figs. 56–57 and J. Gutmann, The Jewish Sanctuary (Leiden, 1983), 12, pl. 33.

21. S. S. Kayser, ed., Jewish Ceremonial Art (Philadelphia, 1959), 25, 27, No. 6: Embroidered by Simchah, wife of Menachem Levi Meshullam, 1680/1681. Cf. colorplate 1 in Fabric of Jewish Life: Textiles from the Jewish Museum Collection, eds. B. Kirshenblatt-Gimblett and C. Grossman (New York, 1977), 131.

22. A. Piattelli, ed. Jewish Art Treasures from Venice (Venice, n.d.), 93, No. 22: Embroidered by Stella, wife of Isaac Perugia, seventeenth century. A. Piattelli, "Un arrazo veneziano dell XVII secolo," Rassegna Mensile di Israel 36 (1970), 315–22.

23. Cf. U. Nahon, Holy Arks and Ritual Appurtenances from Italy (Tel Aviv, 1970), 26, 51, 63, 71, 101, 105, 106, 110, 126 (Hebrew with English and Italian Summaries). The earliest surviving examples are perhaps an ark from Mantua-Sermide, 1543, Nahon, op. cit., 51 and an ark donated to the synagogue of Urbino, Kayser, op. cit., 22. The 1551 date given in the catalog needs re-examination; the Torah ark may be earlier. Cf. also R. Mellinkoff, "The Round-Topped Tablets of the Law: Sacred Symbol and Emblem of Evil," Journal of Jewish Art 1 (1974), 28–43; Gutmann, No Graven Images, xxxi–xxxii.

24. Margaritha, op. cit., Sib: "Thuet darnach das thürlin auff des sie Kapores nennen das ist der gnadenstuel un nimpt also die zehenn gepot herauss." Cf. J. Bodenschatz, Kirchliche Verfassung der heutigen Juden, II (Erlangen, 1748), 67. On the biblical kapporet, cf. M. Görg, "Eine neue Deutung für kapporaet," Zeitschrift für die Alttestamentliche Wissenschaft 89 (1977), 115–18; J. M. de Tarragon, "La kapporet, est-elle une fiction ou un element du culte tartif?" Revue biblique 88 (1981), 5–11.

25. Krauss, op. cit., 376: "kapporet . . . in dem opferlosen Bethaus der nach-biblischen Zeit mit Recht keinen Platz erhielt."

26. The inscription of this kapporet reads: "Gift of the esteemed Ber (may God protect him), son of the esteemed Hersch Scheftels (of blessed memory) and

his wife Rikele, daughter of Wolf Reich, 1763/64." Originally donated to the Klaus synagogue, this valance is now in the State Jewish Museum, Prague, No. 117.216. Baroque valances were of course known in the secular environment and were popular in the seventeenth and eighteenth centuries for canopies, window draperies, etc. In Bohemia, the valances are often donated separately; in Germany, they are usually donated along with the curtain. The Temple appurtenances are no doubt based on models of 17th/18th-century engravings of Temple vessels found in such works as C. Semler, *Tempel Salomonis* (Halle, 1718). The whole subject merits study. Cf. Landsberger, *Beauty in Holiness*, 152f.; L. Freehof and B. King, *Embroideries and Fabrics for Synagogue and Home* (New York, 1966), 72–73; I. Posen, "Die Mainzer Toraschrein Vorhänge," *Notizblatt der Gesellschaft zur Erforschung jüdischer Kunstdenkmäler* 29 (1932); 2–12. J. Gutmann, *The Jewish Sanctuary* (Leiden, 1983), 13, 32, plate 39.

    27. S. Z. Schück, *Takkanot u-tefillot* (Muncacs, 1890), 41 writes: "to kindle the *ner tamid* in remembrance of the Temple (*mikdash*)." Cf. G. Morosini, *Via della fede* (Rome, 1683), 245: "la lampada, *Tamid,* che sempre arde avanti all' Hechal." Isaac Lampronti, *Pachad Yitzchak,* II (s.v. *tamid*), fol. 90v. "the *ner tamid* which we have in the synagogue. . . ." Yedidya Samuel Tarika, *Ben Yedid* 7: "It is just like ours [church lamp] which we hang before the ark and which we call 'eternal' (*t'midim*)." Yair Chayyim Bacharach, *Chavot Yair,* par. 68 speaks of eternal lights, hanging before Torah arks made of silver and polished brass. Cf. J. Gutmann, "How Traditional are our Traditions?" *Beauty in Holiness,* 417f.; S. Freehof, *Current Reform Responsa* (Cincinnati, 1969), 8ff.; L. Loeb-Larocque, "Ewig-Licht-Ampel (jüdisch)," *Reallexikon zur deutschen Kunstgeschichte* 6, 639–48. Bacharach does not speak of golden eternal lights as Loeb-Larocque claims. Cf. H. M. Orlinsky, *Notes on the New Translation of the Torah* (Philadelphia, 1969), 190, n. 20. *Ner-tamid* sometimes referred to the large candle lit during the circumcision ceremony in medieval Germany (cf. *Sefer Maharil, Hilkhot Brit-Milah*); it could also refer to the memorial candle (*neshamah Licht*) lit in the medieval German synagogue on *Yom Kippur* [A. Margaritha, *Der gantze jüdische Glaube* (Leipzig, 1705), 72]. Cf. also J. Gutmann, "Christian Influences on Jewish Customs," in *Spirituality and Prayer: Jewish and Christian Understandings,* eds. L. Klenicki and G. Huck (New York, 1983), 136 n. 10.

    28. Isaac Tyrnau, *Sefer Minhagim* 52b.

    29. Israel Isserlein, *Terumat ha-Deshen* 48a. Cf. Yuspa Hahn, *Sefer Yosif Ometz,* 69, par. 327; Christiani, *op. cit.* 16. Cf. also Abraham ben Nathan Hayarchi, *Sefer ha-Manhig* 105a (end of par. 148), and Isaac bar Sheshet, Responsa No. 111. The custom of placing the *menorah* in the synagogue is also recorded from the thirteenth century on in Sephardic literature. According to Abudraham, it was placed in the center of the synagogue. See S. Freehof, "Home Rituals and the Spanish Synagogue," *Beauty in Holiness,* 510. Literary references give no clue as to what the *Chanukah menorah* looked like. Only one miniature from late fifteenth-century Italy survives—it does not yet show the familiar nine-branched "Temple" *menorah.*

F. Landsberger, "Old Hanukkah Lamps," *Beauty in Holiness*, 306, fig. 12. The bronze *menorah* from the Padua synagogue, *ibid.*, 306, fig. 13, is not from the fifteenth century, as Landsberger maintained; it is much later.

30. Böcher, *op. cit.*, 87; Gutmann, *Beauty in Holiness*, 418–19; Landsberger, *op. cit.*, xx, 299ff., 307.

31. The placement of the ancient Sanctuary vessels in the medieval Ashkenazic synagogue may also have been prompted by the Christian placement of such Solomonic Temple objects as the *menorah* and the molten sea in the medieval church, which was sometimes called the "New Solomonic Temple." To counter the Christian claim that the church was the "New Temple of Solomon," Ashkenazic Jews may have wanted to emphasize that the synagogue was simply a *mikdash me'at* — a surrogate for the messianic Solomonic Temple of the future. Cf. the bibliography cited in Gutmann, *Temple of Solomon*, 142, n. 22.

32. J. Gutmann, "Thirteen Manuscripts in Search of an Author: Joel ben Simeon, 15th-Century Scribe-Artist," *Studies in Bibliography and Booklore* 9 (1970), 93.

33. *Sefer Yosif Ometz* 172, par. 788. Cf. J. Gutmann, "The Messiah at the Seder: A Fifteenth-Century Motif in Jewish Art," *Raphael Mahler Jubilee Volume: Studies in Jewish History*, ed. S. Yeivin (Tel Aviv, 1974), 29–38. The list of Haggadah manuscripts on ibid., 30–31, n. 3 needs revision. The Haggadah in a Siddur (12) is now in Oxford, Bodleian Library, Lyell 99 and should be dated Germany (?), ca. 1460–1470. Cf. T. and M. Metzger, *Jewish Life in the Middle Ages: Illuminated Hebrew Manuscripts of the Thirteenth to the Sixteenth Centuries* (New York, 1982), 306, No. 160. If the date of Sassoon, Ms. No. 511 (formerly private collection of Rabbi S. D. Sassoon) is to be read as 1462 (rather than 1502) as Metzger indicates, then Darmstadt, Cod. Or. 28 (11) should also be dated in the last quarter of the fifteenth century. Cf. M. Metzger, "L'aide et les risques qu'offrent le décor et illustration pour dater and localiser les manuscrits hébreux médiévaux," *La Paléographie hébraïque médiévale* (Paris, 1974), 121. The "Washington Haggadah" (2) may have been executed in Germany (?), cf. M. Beit Arié, "Joel ben Simeon's Manuscripts: A Codicologer's View," *Journal of Jewish Art* 3/4 (1977), 29ff. and S. Edmunds "The Place of the London *Haggadah* in the Work of Joel ben Simeon," *Journal of Jewish Art* 7 (1980), 25–34. Cf. also M. Metzger, *La Haggada enluminée* (Leiden, 1973), 319–28.

34. Cf. Z. Vilnay, *The Holy Land in Old Prints and Maps* (Jerusalem, 1963), 31ff. It should be noted that the rebuilt Temple of Solomon looks like the seventh-century Dome of the Rock, still extant in Jerusalem. Artists from the fifteenth century on usually label the Muslim Dome of the Rock the Temple of Solomon. Cf. J. Comay, *The Temple of Jerusalem* (New York, 1975), 80, 154. Cf. also illustrations of the Temple and the walls surrounding Jerusalem in 17th/18th-century Italian marriage contracts and earlier printed books; H. Lazar, "Raffigurazioni di Gerusalemme in Ketubboth italiane," *Rassegna Mensile di Israel* (Nov.–Dec., 1980), 354–

62 and I. Fishof, "'Jerusalem above my chief Joy': Depictions of Jerusalem in Italian Ketubot," *Journal of Jewish Art* 9 (1982), 61ff. In Italy, Psalm 128 was included in the marriage benedictions. Along with depictions of Jerusalem, we therefore frequently find the verse from Ps. 128:5—"May the Lord bless you from Zion; may you share the prosperity of Jerusalem"—written in large letters on Italian *ketubot*, cf. ibid., 64. Cf. also M. A. Friedman, *Jewish Marriage Contracts in Palestine: A Cairo Genizah Study*, II (Tel Aviv and New York, 1981), 6, 61–62, 193, 454, where we find *genizah ketubot* from the eleventh century on, sometimes include a passage expressing the hope for a rebuilt Temple—"May it be rebuilt in our days and in the days of all Israel." The Temple is sometimes painted on the walls of some Ashkenazic wooden synagogue interiors in Horb, Unterlimpurg and Kirchheim; see Vilnay, *op. cit.*, 33ff. D. Davidowicz, *Wandmalereien in alten Synagogen* (Hameln-Hannover, 1969), 16ff., 46, 50, 54. Rosenau, *op. cit.*, 66.

35. C. Roth, "Itineraries of Erez Israel," *Encyclopaedia Judaica*, IX (Jerusalem, 1971), 1148–49; R. Barnett, "A Group of Embroidered Cloths from Jerusalem," *Journal of Jewish Art* 2 (1975), 39ff.; Vilnay, *op. cit.*, xxivff. Cf. also *Fabric of Jewish Life*, 241, Nos. 230–231 for two additional Sabbath cloths.

36. L. Brieger, *E. M. Lilien* (Berlin-Vienna, 1922), 77; J. Gutmann, *Jerusalem by Ephraim Moses Lilien* (New York, 1976), 10; and M. Heyd, "Lilien and Beardsley," *Journal of Jewish Art* 7 (1980), 62.

PART IV

The Land of Israel in the Modern Period

Off Center:
The Concept of the Land of Israel
in Modern Jewish Thought

ARNOLD M. EISEN

[Editor's note: Dr. Arnold Eisen serves as Senior Lecturer in Jewish Thought at
the University of Tel Aviv. His essay here traces the role of the Land of Israel in
modern thought back to the formative influences of Spinoza and Mendelssohn,
who, he says, set the stage for successive thinkers on the subject by defining a
three-fold process of demystification, resymbolization, and politicization. The
Land has been stripped of its traditional "many-layered dress of imagery and significance" (demystification); once a distinct locus of God's unique dwelling place,
the particularity of Land has reemerged as "a universal symbol of human brotherhood and peace, located wherever those dreams of all mankind attain fulfillment"
(resymbolization); and "the Jewish polity has become a nation among nations, its
territory one among many others," dependent now on normal modes of political
action (politicization). In his remarkably comprehensive tracing of these trends,
Eisen moves from their founding fathers (Spinoza and Mendelssohn) to both Zionist and non-Zionist reactions to them: thinkers as diverse as Franz Rosenzweig and
Hermann Cohen (religionists but not Zionists) and Leo Pinsker and Theodor
Herzl (Zionists but anti-religious). He then deals extensively with the range of
Zionist thinkers, particularly Moses Hess, whose "synthesis of matter and spirit,
resymbolization and politicization" was to "re-echo in several Zionist thinkers of
immense influence"; Ahad Haam, who advocated a spiritual center in the Land,
in contrast to Herzl's politicized entity; and A. D. Gordon, who applied Tolstoyan notions of the "redemptive power of labor" but used traditional language
drawn from Kabbalah. He concludes with a consideration of "the dilemmas of
Orthodox Zionism," first in a consideration of the legacy of Abraham Isaac Kook,
but then, by examining the contemporary debate between Zvi Yehudah Kook and
Yeshayahu Leibowitz. He sums up his remarks by showing us what the Land means
today for those inside and those outside of it, in a situation that has essentially
remained unchanged from that perceived by Spinoza and Mendelssohn at the dawn
of modernity.]

In the two works which set the agenda for Jewish thought in the modern period and fixed the terms in which the principal issues of Jewish reflection would subsequently be addressed, the Land of Israel is a subject of decidedly peripheral concern. Spinoza's *Tractatus* considers the "strip of territory" once inhabited by the "Hebrews" only to deny contemporary Jews and their erstwhile homeland all relevance in the political order he seeks to describe. Moses Mendelssohn's counter-essay *On Religious Power and Judaism* attempts to secure the Jews and their religion a legitimate place within the modern order, but it too, despite the honorific title *Jerusalem*, makes reference to the Land only marginally. The reason is obvious: while the Jewish role in the emerging European order was a matter of immediate concern, the possibility of return to the Land of Israel (mentioned in passing by Spinoza) could safely be left in the realm of fantasy. Not surprisingly, the political and spiritual centers of discussion in both treatises lie elsewhere.

What *is* surprising is that little changed in the treatment of the issue in succeeding centuries, even though the age-old fantasy of return to Zion has, to a degree, come true. My claim here is twofold. I will argue, first, that the Land of Israel has remained a marginal concern at best to Jewish religious thought throughout the modern era. The issue has loomed large —with a very few exceptions to be noted—only in the political writings of the Zionists. That generalization holds true even after the creation of the State of Israel, and even within that State. Second, conceptualization of the Land in Jewish religious and political thought has continued to follow the lines laid down by Spinoza and Mendelssohn at the beginning of our period. Through a brief sketch of how the Land figures in the corpus of modern Jewish reflection (paying special attention to those thinkers who have paid the Land most attention), I hope to show that the three principal elements of the "founders'" conceptualization have remained predominant in the thought of their successors. Almost all have continued to *demystify, resymbolize*, and *politicize* the idea of *Eretz Yisra'el*. The Land, that is, has been stripped of the many-layered dress of imagery and significance which had draped it through generations of Jewish tradition (demystification). The particular soil prepared for God's chosen people, the unique dwelling place of His glory, has become the universal symbol of human brotherhood and peace, located wherever those dreams of all mankind attain fulfillment (resymbolization). Finally, the Jewish polity has become a nation among the nations, its territory one among many others, to be secured through the real-world instruments of political action (politicization). Jewish reflection before Spinoza and Mendelssohn had treated the idea of *Eretz Yisra'el* very differently indeed.

I. The Founding Reconceptions

The demystification of both the Land and its Scriptural "constitution" undertaken by Spinoza was essential to the larger twofold ambition informing his *Tractatus*. He wished, first, to demonstrate that freedom of thought could safely be granted in the modern state, once religion had been rendered effectively subservient to the reigning political authority. Second, as part of that larger effort, Spinoza sought to show that the Jews and their faith were entirely dispensable in the new order which he correctly saw emerging. In order to accomplish the first objective, prophecy is dethroned at the very outset of the treatise. Necessarily so: if reason and its practitioners (the philosophers) are to serve as sole arbiters of the truth concerning God, world, and humanity, the claims of the competition (who invoke divine revelation) must be dismissed. Spinoza then passes immediately to the claim of Jewish prophets to the effect that Israel was and had remained God's chosen people, a doctrine here reformulated, significantly, as "the vocation of the Hebrews." Again the logic is straightforward. If particular religions are to be dissolved (except for inconsequential outward forms) in a universal and rational creed, the pretension of the Jews to a special blessing must be exploded. Once that has been accomplished, Spinoza can rest confident that all similar claims by successor "chosen peoples" will stand exposed as well.

God's "kingdom of priests and holy nation" becomes, in Spinoza's rereading, a mere rabble of unruly slaves to whose lowly desires and childlike understanding of the truth Scripture must constantly stoop. The "Hebrews" chosenness for a uniquely blessed Land and a uniquely central role in the divine plan for creation is reduced to election to the "social organization and the good fortune with which [the Hebrew nation] obtained supremacy and kept it so many years."[2] This reinterpretation is also mandated by Spinoza's understanding of divinity. Denied purpose or personality, Spinoza's God cannot possibly perform in any literal way the feats which Scripture regularly ascribes to him. The "help of God" can only mean "the fixed and unchangeable order of nature or the chain of natural events."[3] No special animus against the Jews is needed, therefore, to motivate deflation of their claims to divine chosenness. The concept simply does not make sense,

except if it means that the Hebrews had been destined to live in the land
of Canaan, under the sway of such laws as had governed them there—
destined by the same natural laws which had established every other people
in every other land by every other set of laws. When Israel's ability to maintain its sovereignty against foreign incursions had lapsed, so had its chosenness. Every other people's "vocation" had come, and gone, in precisely the
same way. Once this conceptual groundwork is in place, Spinoza's subsequent treatments of "divine law," "ceremonial law," and "miracles" are entirely predictable.

The Land, then, has been demystified: stripped of the many-layered
dress of imagery and significance which had draped it through generations
of Jewish tradition.[4] The Land of Israel is not uniquely cared-for by the
earth's Creator, as Deuteronomy would have it. No special holiness attaches
to its soil. Indeed, the laws which had once instituted that holiness are criticized and/or historicized. In some cases they are explained away as a device
meant to obtain the obedience of a rebellious populace. Jerusalem is no
longer the idealized center of rabbinic geography, the city by which an entire people in dispersion had located itself on the map of existence. Its tem-
poral centrality has vanished as well, for no vision of a messianic age,
whether it be the Kabbalists' myth of cosmic renewal or Maimonides' tempered enumeration of the elements of redemption, could possibly persuade
a citizen of Spinoza's universal kingdom of the mind. One need not have
recourse to supernatural intervention in order to explain Israel's survival
among the nations, Spinoza argued. Distinguishing marks like circumcision,
and the "universal" hatred which Jewish separateness had provoked, were
explanation enough. Finally, he speculated, "If the foundations of their religion have not emasculated their minds they may even, if occasion offers,
so changeable are human affairs, raise up their empire afresh, and . . . God
may a second time elect them."[5] The preconditions of what Jews called messianic redemption, boldly stated in that "if" clause, would not be lost on
Zionist readers centuries later.

Mendelssohn, defending the Jews against Spinoza's attack,[6] began by
accepting many of his adversary's premises—not least the disjunction between religion (which was necessarily rational and universal) and the unique
system of "divine legislation" binding only upon the Jews.[7] His redefinition
of Jewish faith, seminal in the intellectual history of modern Judaism, has
by now become familiar. The relevant point for us is Mendelssohn's attempt
to reconcile his own contention that religious authorities have no right to
employ coercion with the clearly opposite view of Scripture. To that end,

he was forced to concede that the "mosaic constitution" that had united state and religion in the past was no longer applicable. Once upon a time, crimes such as sabbath-breaking had been proscribed as "offenses against the majesty of the Lawgiver, insolent violations of fundamental laws and the civil constitution." Judaism "as religion," however, "knows no punishment."[8] To the reader who, acquainted with Spinoza and Machiavelli, was "quite aware of the presumptions which such a constitution permits itself," ripe for imitation by any despot, Mendelssohn immediately added that Israel's "priestly state" or "ecclesiastical government" or "theocracy, if you will" had been unique. It had existed only once, and had disappeared. "Only the Almighty knows among what people and in which century something similar may appear once again."[9]

The words "among what people" jar us even more than Mendelssohn's relegation of the mosaic constitution to the distant past. Is he seriously suggesting that God might once again choose a people as He had chosen Israel, *another* people? Might the messianic kingdom be centered elsewhere than in Jerusalem? The reference to Plato which follows at once in the essay[10] calls to mind the similar passage in the Republic where Socrates asserts that his vision of the perfect state is not impossible. Whether it be in the infinity of past time, or in the future, or even at the present "in some foreign country beyond our horizons," the state of the philosopher-king "either exists or existed or will exist."[11] Mendelssohn may well have had that Platonic parallel to Deuteronomy (cf. 30:11–14) in mind here. More likely, he was cleverly—in a parenthesis, as it were—responding to opponents of Jewish emancipation, who argued that belief in the messianic ingathering of exiles constituted grounds for suspicion of Jewish loyalties to the nations in which they resided. Jews might continue to pray for a return to Jerusalem, but Mendelssohn's essay, indeed its very title, has rendered Jerusalem a universal symbol for a messianic redemption which could, perhaps, take place elsewhere—or anywhere. The entire essay, after all, is a polemic written, in the context of the struggle for emancipation, to counter the anonymous "Searcher for Light and Right." Indeed, an injunction to the Jews to "adopt the mores and constitution of the country" in which they found themselves, while remaining steadfast in upholding their religion, follows the passage at hand almost at once.[12] The universalization of messianic hope accomplished in that passage lays the groundwork for the entire conclusion of the essay.

Whatever Mendelssohn's motive, the message articulated is decisive. How much more striking, then, that this essay which seeks the integration of the Jews in modern European society, and as part of that effort univer-salizes both religion and belief in the messiah, is called *Jerusalem*. To a de-gree, Mendelssohn only followed rabbinic precedent in this regard. The Rab-bis too had stressed the centrality of Jerusalem and its Temple at the very moment that they severed Jewish faith and practice from dependence on the Land and Temple. Every table became an altar, every Israelite a priest,[13] in a diaspora for which Jerusalem became an idealized though nonexistent center. In Mendelssohn's modern exilic order, Jerusalem could assume a mean-ing derived from that "heavenly Jerusalem" of the Rabbis, its very name help-ing to distance Jews — and Gentiles! — from the Rabbis' expectation that the earthly Jerusalem would be rebuilt "speedily and in their days." Mendels-sohn, writes Alexander Altmann, "chose the name in order to indicate that Jerusalem, though destroyed and bereft of power, was still the symbol of the true worship of God."[14] Symbolization at rabbinic hands in the second century, however, was one thing. Mendelssohn's own re-symbolization in the context of the eighteenth-century struggle for Emancipation was quite another. The move would later prove crucial, for Zionists and non-Zionists alike.

We will survey those nineteenth- and twentieth-century developments momentarily. Here I wish to note only that the effect of Spinoza's and Men-delssohn's reconceptions, considered jointly, was what we might call the politicization of the idea of the Land of Israel. Mendelssohn, no less than Spinoza, had severed the Jewish polity from its unique religious legitima-tion, and rendered it a nation among the nations. True, his own reference to "the Almighty" in the passage cited above is quite literal. He has in mind a real and personal divine providence who takes special care of Israel, whereas the God of Spinoza who "may a second time elect them" does not really exist for Spinoza as such. The phrase may even be a cynical thrust at belief in such a God and his promised messiah. Despite that difference, the two statements work to the same effect. Mendelssohn too has enabled his mod-ern readers, bent on acceptance by enlightened Europeans, to conceive of their ancient state as long gone and never to return. The messiah could now represent *either* a mere hope for the indefinite future, *or* a real opportunity, available equally to all peoples, that had to be seized through the real-world instruments of political action. Mendelssohn's essay no less than Spinoza's has opened the space for such action, despite and because of the fact that it directs Jewish political energies away from the traditional messianic cen-ter, and channels them instead toward Emancipation in the diaspora.

In sum, Mendelssohn contributed, perhaps unintentionally, to the "normalization" of Jewish political thought, by politicizing consideration of the Jews' ancient homeland—and of their very survival. He showed how Spinoza's lessons could be used for ends that Spinoza opposed. Soon his own "Jewish politics," like his understanding of the Jewish religion, would be invoked by others to support positions which he had not conceived and would likely have opposed.

II. Zionist & Non-Zionist Developments

In the religious context, Mendelssohn's emphasis upon Jerusalem (and, by extension, the Jews) as a symbol, albeit "bereft of power," of "the true worship of God," soon developed into notions of a Jewish "mission unto the nations." Orthodox thinkers who shared Mendelssohn's conviction that the "divine legislation" was still binding upon Jews preached the doctrine of a Jewish mission no less than Reform thinkers for whom, in the wake of Kant, one's religious duty toward the Creator had been reduced to moral obligation toward one's fellow creatures. The Reform thinker Abraham Geiger (1810–74) trumpeted the notion of mission and made it the centerpiece of both his history of Israel and his theology. However, Samson Raphael Hirsch (1808–88), Heinrich Graetz (1817–91) and Nachman Krochmal (1785–1840)—all far from the Reform camp—adopted the notion as well, if somewhat more discreetly. Along with it, they accepted to varying degrees the understanding of Judaism as religion (rather than nationality) which the motif of Israel's mission in Reform thought was meant to serve.[15]

Hirsch, for example, recounting the *Heilsgeschichte* of the Jews in his *Nineteen Letters,* dwells at length on the patriarchs and the generation of the wilderness. He then touches briefly on occupation of the Land as a means to fulfillment of the demands of Torah, only to rush on to a prolonged peroration on the meaning of exile, complete with the "suffering servant" passages from Isaiah, quoted in full. The Land of Israel, and the Jewish state once established there, are clearly of minor importance.[16] Krochmal's schematic history is designed to show that the Jewish people, uniquely connected to the Spiritual Absolute, had survived the cycle of birth, maturity, and destruction undergone by all nations—and would continue to survive it, forever. Possession of the Land is of peripheral importance in his chronological division of Jewish history into cycles of youth, maturity, and decline. The period from Joshua to Solomon, for example, occurs in the "maturity" phase of the first cycle, whereas the period from the Hasmoneans to the fall of

Betar is located in the "decline" phase of cycle two. That cycle in fact established the non-dependence of the national spirit upon residence in the national homeland. On the pinnacle of the third cycle, philosophy, and not sovereignty, stands triumphant.[17] In Geiger's own periodization, the era of Israel's "compact nationality" and "united community" is seen as a short but necessary prelude to the performance, in exile, of Israel's world-historical mission. "The world-reforming and world-moving Idea of Judaism naturally required for its practical introduction a ready host bearing its arms." Once the idea had matured, it could break through those narrow national bounds and go forth to conquer all humanity.[18]

Only Graetz provides an exception to this pattern. Insisting that "the totality of Judaism is discernible only in its history," he affirms that political sovereignty was an integral part of that history and so belonged to the essence of Judaism. It could not be sloughed off as a mere relic of a bygone past: "The revealed idea of God exists not for itself, in order to be known merely in a theoretical fashion, but seeks, at the same time, to be a holy institution which furthers earthly happiness. The concept of God must immediately become a concept of the state."[19] Sovereignty was the distinguishing mark of the first phase of Jewish history, as the second phase—much of which was also spent in the Land—was characterized by an "overriding religious stamp." The religious and the political "constitute the twin axes around which Jewish life revolves."[20] Following the third phase, marked by martyrdom and intellectual advances, "the task of Judaism's God idea" would be to realize all the potential stored up in itself from the beginning. This could only be accomplished, Graetz concludes, with the foundation of a "religious state which is conscious of its activity, purpose, and connection with the world."[21]

Underneath these variations on a theme by Hegel, we can hear the chords first sounded within the Jewish world by Mendelssohn, in part echoing Spinoza. All four nineteenth-century thinkers sought to legitimate some form of Jewish life within the European social and political order. To that end, all removed Jewish life in the present and foreseeable future from any necessary connection with the actual Land of Israel. Diaspora existence was positively essential to the mission given prominence by Geiger and Hirsch. It was perfectly sufficient to the view of Judaism-cum-spirituality articulated by Krochmal; no messianic return was needed. Graetz too was quite content with the possibilities of exile, even if he deplored attempts to reduce Judaism to a credal or ethical "essence," and insisted that political sovereignty would be an integral part of the phase of Jewish fulfillment yet to come.

Eretz Yisra'el does not need to be demystified in these works, for demystification is presumed. The Land's holy garb has already been removed. Traditional notions of cosmic centrality and messianic return are absent, except as history. In their stead, we have the resymbolizations introduced by Mendelssohn and Spinoza. Geiger's Jerusalem too could one day rise, like Blake's, in "England's green and pleasant land." Politicization, finally, is absent in these works, a latent possibility which would be grasped later on, by others, once the project of integration furthered by these four thinkers had run its course and been declared by some a failure.

Leo Pinsker (1821–91), moving after the pogroms of 1881 to grasp that possibility firmly, could safely dispense with resymbolization and demystification, because even the Land itself was no longer essential to the "auto-emancipation" of Jewry, so successfully had the threefold reconception of Zion been carried out. Exile, for Pinsker, was all too real, a series of terrors which even Enlightenment would not end, because anti-Semitism was a disease that did not admit of cure. "Among the living nations of the earth the Jews occupy the position of a nation long since dead," Pinsker argued. They therefore aroused the same anxieties as any other ghosts.[22] The natives of any land treated aliens decently only so that their own nationals, on alien soil, would be treated with equal courtesy. Jews, however, were a ghost people of guests who could never assume the role of host, and so aroused only a "natural antagonism" that resulted in their own "degrading dependence."[23] There was only one solution: a homeland in which the Jews could play host to others, attained by a national organization and suitable for provision of the needed "single refuge—politically assured."[24] Though Pinsker was soon catapulted to leadership of the fledgling "Lovers of Zion" society, he himself did not much care where the "single refuge" was, so long as it could serve the Jewish people's purposes. It did not have to be the Land of Israel.[25] God's expressed preference in the matter, as it were, was of little import now that the redemption of the Jews had been placed in other hands.

Herzl's attitude was similar, witness his willingness to entertain the option of establishing the *Judenstaat* in Uganda, if need be. His hopes for that state, expressed in the fantasy of a bourgeois European technological paradise titled *Altneuland*, drew only anger and scorn from Jews such as Ahad Ha'am (1856–1927) who were more rooted than Herzl (1860–1905) in the "old land" they sought to renew.[26] It is certainly no coincidence that the two founding theorists of political Zionism, as it came to be called, were content to settle for any piece of earth as a solution to the pressing problem of the Jews, and regarded the religio-cultural problem of Judaism as a separate issue that could take care of itself. The Land of Israel was in their eyes an instrumentality to another goal, a means to another end, rather than an end in itself, much less an object of either obligation or piety. It was a symbol of unique power but only that, and, precisely because of its modern symbolic meaning, not limited to any *particular* piece of earth.

Such was the possibility opened up by the threefold reconception that we have examined. The Land of Israel had been demystified, and so could now be surveyed dispassionately in order to determine if it suited requirements of redemption set independently. Its resymbolization as the land of salvation through progress, the place where modern messianic ideals of peace and justice could be realized by the application of reason, endowed the modern project of return — even to Uganda, a place Jews had never been! — with ancient messianic energies. Traditional longings could combine with contemporary ideals. The *shtetl* Jew, and the English Protestant, could both rally to a cause championed by a bourgeois Viennese atheist, particularly when the Uganda proposal was abandoned, and Herzl invoked the universalist symbolization of Zion to speed the Jews' return to the particular, *actual* Land of Israel and no other. That cause, finally, was political through and through, despite the secondary meanings attached to it by religious or cultural Zionists. The movement negotiated with kings, purchased land from effendi, engaged geographers and geologists, practiced reclamation and reforestation — all without prayers for divine intervention. In the end, it resorted to the supremely political means of securing desired goals: violence.[27] The Land had come to mean, above all else, the "certain strip of territory" first described by Spinoza, rather than the Land of Israel imagined by Deuteronomy or the Rabbis or Yehudah Halevi. Only as such could the Zionists have conceived it. This political reconception of the Land, moreover, is assumed by all parties to the twentieth-century debate on the future of Jewry and Judaism — Zionists and non-Zionists, "political Zionists" and "cultural Zionists" alike.

Opposition to the Zionist enterprise was largely based on — or at least couched in — the refusal to abandon the resymbolization first carried out by Mendelssohn. Kaufmann Kohler (1843–1926), the heir to German Reform thought and head of the Reform Movement in America, gave the doctrine of a universalist Jewish mission its most extreme formulation. When a traditional Jewish fast recalling the destruction of the Temple fell at the same time as the fourth of July in 1885, Kohler asked his American congregants if they wished to "wail over past political power and glory" or instead thank "the sublime Ruler of History for the new terms and prospects opened on this free soil for the realization of our messianic expectations."[28] Some forty years later, in Kohler's *Jewish Theology, Systematically and Historically Considered,* Israel's mission was still the centerpiece. This time the target was Zionism, which, having "lost faith in the religious mission of Israel," sought to reduce Judaism to a species of nationalism. Simon Dubnow (1860–1941), who opposed the Zionists and favored the establishment of autonomous Jewish polities in the diaspora, was accused along with Ahad Ha'am "and the rest of the nationalists" of underrating "the religious power of the Jew's soul, which forms the essence of his character and the motive power of all his aspirations and hopes, as well as of all his achievements in history."[29] For Kohler, Jerusalem symbolized the "messianic goal" of One and holy God and one, undivided humanity"—and only that.[30] He dismissed the Jewish state of the past as a mere preparation of Israel's mission as the "servant of the Lord, Martyr and Messiah of the Nations"—a role he treated lovingly and at great length.

More sophisticated non-Zionist positions do not differ from Kohler's in substance. For Hermann Cohen (1842–1918), the Jews' "stateless isolation" was itself a symbol for the unity of the confederation of mankind which constituted the "ultimate value" of world history.[31] Indeed, Deuteronomy had taught that Israel's national history was but an idealization from the point of view of its historic task, an opportunity to depict the people's sin in repeatedly relinquishing the true God.[32] Realization of the "idea of messianic mankind" was the task of the Jewish people. The Zionists, by contrast, believed that Judaism could be preserved only by an "all-encompassing nationalism." Their writings "abounded in frivolous derisions of [the] supreme idea of the Jewish religion," and charged that liberal Jews such as Cohen himself were "deluded for feeling at home in the civilized countries in which we are living." Cohen's reply is twofold. First, "no restriction of civil rights must be allowed to make us waver in our sense of obligation and total commitment to the country we claim as our own." On the other hand, "we regard the moral world as it unfolds throughout history as our Promised Land."[33] This was the only land of any consequence to Cohen beside his own—Germany.

In the thought of Franz Rosenzweig (1886–1929), theoretical antagonism to the Zionists' understanding of Jewish history and Jewish faith is tempered by the realization that the nationalists' attempt to save world Jewry was both vital and necessary. "There are better Jews among the Zionists than among us—regardless of theory," he wrote.[34] Rosenzweig took particular exception to the writings of Jacob Klatzkin, a political Zionist especially scornful of diaspora existence. However, Zionism, like other movements, should be judged not by its theory but by its earthbound practical activity — and that activity in the case of Zionism should be supported, powerful theoretical objections notwithstanding. "According to the words of a philosopher whom I regard as an authority even greater than Hermann Cohen, what is not to come save in eternity will not come in all eternity."[35]

All of that having been noted, we are struck nonetheless by the illegitimacy of the Zionist project according to Rosenzweig's own theoretical masterpiece, the *Star of Redemption*. A Jewish state is simply inconceivable according to the view of God, world, and humanity set forth in the work. The "eternal people," unlike all others, had forsaken attachment to the "night of earth," — that is, to homelands inevitably "watered by the blood of their sons." Only by virtue of that renunciation had Israel remained eternal, trusting in its community of blood, and maintaining the self-awareness of a stranger and a sojourner never permitted to "while away time in any home."[36] The Jews also lacked the native language possessed by every other people, for language too, like all things mortal, would in time disappear. Finally, Jews lacked an "outwardly visible life" such as all other nations lived "in accordance with their own customs and laws."[37]

Land, language, sovereignty — the three pillars of Zionist renewal — are all declared inconsistent with Israel's status as the eternal people, and so impossible, given the divine order which had fixed that status. Israel already stood, in Rosenzweig's conception, at the goal which all other peoples strove restlessly to achieve — unity of faith and life:

> But just because it has that unity, the Jewish people is bound to be outside the world that does not yet have it. Through living in a state of eternal peace, it is outside of time agitated by wars . . . therefore the true eternity of the eternal people must always be alien and vexing to the state, and to the history of the world.[38]

Land and landlessness are *both* symbolic of a larger order, in this magisterial survey of the human condition conducted *sub specie aeternitatis*. Had Rosenzweig lived to see the actual Land of Israel reclaimed and the actual State of Israel reborn to fight repeated wars, he would presumably have declared both Land and state aberrations from the cosmic order engraved (so he believed) on a six-pointed star. More likely, he would have abandoned theory and gravitated back to earth, recalling that "if a symbol is to be more than an arbitrary appendage, then it must somewhere and somehow exist as an entirely asymbolical reality."[39]

There were of course religious thinkers who embraced the Land-of-Israel-centered conceptualization of the Zionist project, seeking to unite what Pinsker and Herzl (anti-religious Zionists) on the one hand, and Rosenzweig and Cohen (religious non- or anti-Zionists) on the other, had torn asunder. Demystification in their view did not have to be carried to Herzl's extreme. Politicization of the idea of the Land did not have to come at the expense of symbolizations, old or new. Two traditions of such Zionist thought especially merit our attention, because they comprise the lineage of the two ideological streams competing in our own day for the loyalty of all Zionist Jews, particularly Israelis. The first stream began with the socialist "forerunner"[40] of Zionism, Moses Hess, continued through one of the founding fathers, Ahad Ha'am, and gained hold over contemporary thought via Martin Buber and A. D. Gordon. Its aim was to endow the Jews' political return to the Land with cultural and religious significance derived from the language, if not the substance, of Jewish tradition. The second pattern, religiously Orthodox, had its origins in the religious Zionist "forerunners" Yehudah Alkalai and Zvi Hirsch Kalischer, and reached fruition in the writings of the first Ashkenazi chief rabbi of Palestine, Abraham Isaac Kook. A brief survey of both streams should help us to understand how and why the reconception of the Land of Israel by Spinoza and Mendelssohn continues to reverberate in much of the Jewish thought of our own time—even within the Land of Israel itself.

III. Attempts at Synthesis

Rome and Jerusalem, published in 1862, contrasted sharply with the universalism that Hess (1812–75) had articulated a quarter-century earlier in *The Holy History of Mankind, by a Young Spinozist*. The older Hess, still a Spinozist, had not renounced the master's vision of the unity of all things, nor had he surrendered his own conviction that human history is a sacred process: "a unified, organic development which has its origin in the love of the family."[41] However, the universalist ethical socialism that had led Hess to join with and then break from Karl Marx was now tempered by an appreciation of the importance of national sentiment—including Hess's own powerful national feelings as a Jew. The "pure human nature" preached by the Germans, he wrote caustically, was "in reality the nature of the pure German race, which can rise to the concept of humanity in theory only."[42] In practice the Jews would never be at home among the Germans, who would never cease to despise them. Realizing this, Hess "after twenty years of estrangement" had "returned to my people," raising to the forefront of consciousness those sentiments of nationality that he had once thought "suppressed beyond recall."[43] *Rome and Jerusalem* was the inevitable result of that reawakening, because "the thought of my nationality . . . is inseparably connected with my ancestral heritage, with the Holy Land and the Eternal City, the birthplace of the belief in the divine unity of life and of the hope for the ultimate brotherhood of all men."[44] As the Italians would soon found a state centered in their own Eternal City, so, too, should the Jews.

There are two aspects to Hess's vision, and their combination enables him to synthesize commitments which in Herzl or Cohen are never unified. First, Hess had a keen understanding of "the Jewish question," not least because he knew so well the man who had done so much to pose it. (Hess collaborated with Marx on the *Rheinische Zeitung* and like him was active in the German revolution of 1848, but could not accept Marx's materialist "scientific socialism," and was therefore ridiculed by Marx as a utopian in the Communist Manifesto.) Unlike Marx, Hess believed that national aspirations were an elemental fact of being which would not disappear, least of all among the Germans. Therefore Jewish attempts to disguise their distinctiveness through religious reform would not avail. The Germans "hate the peculiar faith of the Jews less than their peculiar noses," and, indeed, Jewish noses could not be reformed, since "the Jewish race is one of the primary races of mankind . . . the Jewish type has conserved its purity through the centuries."[45] Jews, in a word, were in exile, and they could escape persecution only when they escaped exile. That day would soon be at hand, Hess believed, and this messianic faith comprised the second element of his vision. The various national awakenings in Europe furnished proof that the realization of the messianic era first promised by Isaiah was imminent. In the meantime, Hess urged his readers to "keep alive the hope of the political rebirth of our people, and, next, to reawaken that hope where it slumbers." The first step recommended was the founding of Jewish colonies in the Jewish homeland.[46]

We note that the Land is essential both to Hess's nationalism and to his messianism. In a variant of the mission theory that he attacked, Hess assigns to "bearers of history and civilization" such as the Jews the task of inaugurating universal redemption, by means of individual national revivals.[47] The latter could take place only if each nation were reunified upon its own land. "Jerusalem," therefore, is not only the symbol of the larger process but one of its preconditions. Moreover, its "heavenly" and "earthly" aspects are equally important. Hess's Zion could be rebuilt only as part of a complete national renaissance encompassing all of the people's life, spirit as well as body. In the Jewish case, return to the Land would permit a healthy relation between Jewish capital and labor, providing the "wide, free soil" without which "the social Man," lacking growth and development, sinks inevitably to the status of "a parasite which feeds at the expense of others." Productive labor, precluded to Jews by diaspora conditions, would flourish. Equally important, return would promote spiritual creativity that could not occur so long as any Jewish adjustment to modernity came only at the price of a break with the Jews' "national religion and tradition." Hess argued that Orthodoxy had become "rigid" over the centuries of exile as a necessary defense against encroachment by the Gentile world.[48] It could be revitalized without damage to the "innermost essence of Judaism, its historical national religion,"[49] only when such a renaissance was protected by the borders of a native soil. "The Jewish people will participate in the great historical movement of present-day humanity only when it will have its own fatherland."[50]

Hess is not linked in any direct way to those who began the realization of his vision. He remains a "forerunner" rather than a "founder." Nevertheless, his synthesis of matter and spirit, resymbolization and politicization, did re-echo in several Zionist theorists of immense influence, particularly in the lucid prose, sober criticism, and romantic dogmas of Ahad Ha'am. I will focus on two conceptions of Ahad Ha'am's "cultural Zionism" that follow directly on Hess's concerns and still figure as shibboleths of Zionist debate: the "spiritual center" to be built in Palestine, and the "negation of the diaspora" on its periphery.

Writing a generation after Hess, with return to the Land already underway, Ahad Ha'am took a far more sober view of its possibilities. Like Hess, he called for a union of body and spirit, but stressed from the start that reclamation of the Land, upon which national revival depended, had itself to be preceded by a change in the national spirit of the Jewish people. The essay which launched his career in 1889, "This is Not the Way," argued that too much had already been attempted in the Land too quickly. The wrong people had gone to Palestine, for the wrong reasons, with the wrong assumptions about what was needed if they were to succeed. "The heart of the nation is the foundation on which the Land will be rebuilt—and the nation is fragmented and undisciplined."[51] The message never changed. Over and over Ahad Ha'am urged that Jewish settlers do gradually and well what little could be done, while admitting that much which was desirable and even necessary lay outside their grasp—salvation of the Eastern European masses first of all.

It was because he saw no immediate solution to the Jewish problem that Ahad Ha'am insisted so relentlessly that attention be focused on the problem of Judaism or Jewish culture. The Land was unsuitable as a "safe haven" for the millions of Jews suffering persecution, but it could serve as a safe refuge for Judaism, a "national spiritual center" that could renew the spirit of Jews throughout their dispersions.[52] Ridiculing the idea of the Jewish mission to the nations, Ahad Ha'am wrote that the natural mission of every organism lay in creating the conditions suitable to its character, development of its "latent power and attitudes," its own "form of life"—in short, "in obedience to the demands of its nature." This was no less true for national "organisms."[53] A home of refuge for the Jewish spirit was therefore "not less imperatively necessary than a home of refuge for our homeless wanderers."[54] The latter end was not possible in the short term, and in any event was only a means to the more important goal of spiritual revival; neither could occur until a nucleus was in place.

Herzl's purely political vision was therefore attacked without mercy. Ahad Ha'am had only scorn for those to whom the Hebrew language and Jewish tradition were irrelevant. There was nothing *Jewish* about Herzl's *Judenstaat*, he complained. *Altneuland* should better have been called *al-t'na'i-land* or "land on condition"—on condition that Herzl's entire vision came to fruition within twenty years.[55] Ahad Ha'am's reply to proponents of the Uganda option was simple: he would leave "metaphysical" questions "to others." The Jewish people recognized Zion as its place. The best of them, in whose hearts the "national sense" still truly lived, knew better than to consider any alternative to Zion.[56]

Politicization is present in this vision but not central. Ahad Ha'am assumed—mistakenly, as it turns out—that Herzl's hopes for a political solution to the Jewish problem were bootless in the short term. Political Zionism could thus add nothing to the older Zionism that Ahad Ha'am represented, because "Zionism has always been, in its hopes for the distant future, essentially 'political,'" seeking to attain in Palestine "absolute independence in the conduct of the national life" at "some distant date."[57] Ahad Ha'am therefore could not understand the criticism repeatedly levelled at the primacy which he afforded to the "spiritual center." Would the center's achievement preclude material settlement of the Land? Certainly not; it could not possibly occur without such settlement. In the foreseeable future, no more was possible than a nucleus of settlement which would provide a "fixed cen-

ter for the national spirit and its culture," a picture in "miniature of the people of Israel as it should be."[58]

In reality, of course, the differences separating this cultural Zionism
from the political approach taken by Herzl and others were fundamental
and not the result of either the latter's misreading of the former or the former's misreading of historical practicality. Herzl had been driven to seek
Jewish sovereignty because he stood convinced that anti-Semitism would
not go away and that assimilation was impossible for all but a few. Ahad
Ha'am shared Herzl's pessimism about overcoming anti-Semitism. It therefore took no special insight, in his view, to "negate the diaspora." All Jews
hated the status of a lamb among wolves, he wrote, except for "weak-kneed
optimists" who saw it as a heavenly dispensation, i.e., advocates of the Jewish mission. However, while Ahad Ha'am shared this "subjective negation"
of the diaspora with Herzl, his "objective negation" (the terms are his) was
motivated by more than Herzl's fear that Jews could not survive in exile.
For Ahad Ha'am, the point was the Jews' inability to survive in exile *as Jews,*
now that spiritual isolation once maintained by *halakhah* had ended and
left the Jews defenseless against an "ocean of foreign culture."[59] Herzl would
have seen no point to this question, even if he had stood convinced that
physical Jewish survival in the diaspora were a possibility. Ahad Ha'am, realizing that most Jews would not emigrate to Zion even were that a possibility, sought a way of ensuring their *spiritual* survival in the lands which,
for the foreseeable future, would be home.[60] Given that commitment to
save Judaism as well as Jews, the idea of the spiritual center was not only
logical but well-nigh inevitable. The only available historical model for such
a relation of diaspora to homeland, that of the Second Temple period, needed
to be secularized in keeping with Ahad Ha'am's conviction that the time
of religion had passed. A diaspora people centered in a Temple to which
it made physical pilgrimage and paid tangible tribute would now give way
to a new diaspora linked to its center by the bond which held all peoples
together: spirit, culture. Moreover, it was unrealistic to expect diaspora Jews
to relate to a living Jewish society in Zion in any other way. Economic and
political life were unexportable; culture was not.[61] The very emphasis upon
"Judaism" rather than the Jews proceeded from the premise that the periphery would not disappear into its center, even gradually, but rather—precisely
the opposite—be served by it.

Ahad Ha'am's confidence that Judaism could be saved, and was worth
saving, may have derived from the instinctive will to live that he, like every
other "organism," possessed. Its articulation, however, came in terms of a

romantic Idealist vision of national spirits that infused and were reflected in every aspect of a people's life. In order to answer Hegel's charge that the Jewish spirit had long outlived its usefulness, and the temptation of assimilation facing Western Jews, Ahad Ha'am was forced to accord the Jewish national spirit a supremacy over all others. He had recourse to an idea very similar to the Jewish mission which he ridiculed. Not only did every people's moral code reflect its own particular spirit; the Jews had long been recognized to have a unique "genius" for, or commitment to, moral excellence. True, that moral sense had been bound up in the past with religious forms — necessarily so. The famous dictum that the Sabbath had preserved the Jews more than vice versa only expressed Ahad Ha'am's larger conviction that religion had been the "spiritual center" of Jewish life, and love of Torah the "spiritual homeland" which had kept Jews alive during their exile.[62] Moral excellence could and would be severed from its religious vessel, however, once the Jews had returned to their homeland,[63] exactly as Hess had argued. In this sense and in this sense only could that center save "Judaism" — implicitly understood not as religion but — as Mordecai Kaplan (1881–1983), an American student of his, would later phrase it — as the "civilization of the Jewish people." Ahad Ha'am's conception of Zion, however politicized, thus serves a purpose defined by the Land's modern resymbolization.

Two later attempts at a synthesis between politicized and resymbolized conceptions of the Land edged closer to the religious tradition which Ahad Ha'am was unable to embrace. A. D. Gordon (1856–1922), who arrived in Palestine rather late in life to work the land of Israel, began his writings on the subject with a critique of the "spiritual center." The idea lacked all content, Gordon charged; the spiritual revival which Ahad Ha'am urged had not occurred. "Flesh" and "Spirit" both remained "sick" in the Land of Israel, in large part because even Zionists like Ahad Ha'am who had claimed to favor a synthesis between the two had concentrated on Jewish culture rather than on real physical labor upon the land.[64] Gordon's criticism of all Zionists not committed to the centrality of physical labor was unremitting and untempered. Exile (*galut*) was slavery, sickness, alienation, darkness, estrangement, and death. It was, in a favorite term, the existence of parasites.[65] However, an abyss separated that existence from national renewal and the divide had not yet been crossed. Halfway measures such as those adopted thus far only brought parasitism — and *galut* — into the borders of Eretz Yisra'el. Instead of urging work and more work, the "Satan of *galut*" had infused the *Yishuv*'s society with "galut wisdom" and divisiveness.[66]

The Tolstoyan origins of Gordon's belief in the redemptive power of

labor have long been noted. His perennial opposition of *Gemeinschaft* (organic life rooted in the land) to *Gesellschaft* (urban cosmopolitanism) was
likewise, of course, a mere echo of themes first sounded elsewhere by others.
Gordon's uniqueness lay in marrying these general conceptions to the historical situation of the Jews in the Land of Israel, and articulating them
in language associated with the Land in Jewish tradition. Like Deuteronomy, Gordon believed that Jewish fulfillment could come only through work
upon the *adamah* (soil) in one's national *eretz* (land). Such work brought
the Jew into contact with the earth as a whole—and so with Heaven. Lacking such contact, Gordon argued, Jews were *avud*—lost, orphans, wanderers, at the mercy of foreigners and their cultures—precisely as Deuteronomy
had proclaimed, using precisely the same word, *avod* (see, for example, Deut.
4:26, 7:24, 9:3, 26:5). Adopting the Rabbis' term for idolatry, *avodah zarah*
(literally, foreign work or servitude), Gordon inveighed against the use of
Arab labor on the one hand and the imitation of European culture on the
other. Invoking kabbalah, he called for a "shattering of the vessels" which
would make way for a new creation.[67]

Such traditional language, combined with a worldview in which Jewish national life took on a cosmic importance parallel to that ascribed it
by the tradition, lent added power to Gordon's special pleading on behalf
of one Zionist vision among others. His mystical faith in the significance
of labor upon God's earth, his conviction that religiosity was a matter of
connection to the unity of all things and not a set of beliefs or practices,
lent fury to a pen that did not spare even the socialist "kibbutznikim" so
close to Gordon's heart. Only nature and nature's nationalism could guide
a people correctly. A European import such as socialism could encourage
only rancor and divisiveness.[68]

Gordon, then, had a foot in each of the Zionist camps, political and
spiritual. On the one hand, the speakers for political Zionism, Herzl and
Klatzkin, could not hold a candle to his passionate negation of the diaspora.
The Gentiles "pollute your daughters, judge you all day long, scheme to
do you evil," he wrote to Jews in the *golah* (diaspora). In Israel too Jews
had problems, but their sufferings were not in vain, for the fruit of their
dedication remained behind to inspire others. In exile—including exile within
the Land—Jews did not engage in productive labor, but instead became merchants, members of the stock exchange—parasites.[69] But work upon the land
could overcome that exile, and once the Jewish people had been led by dis-
gust at its predicament to attain self-awareness, even the diaspora would no
longer be exile. Diaspora Jews would simply be aliens abroad, like the na-

tionals of other lands. The key, then, was activity and influence versus passivity and subjection to the influence of others. Indeed, the Jewish people could be healthy even if only a minority of Jews lived on the land[70]—a notion akin to Ahad Ha'am's spiritual Zionism. For Gordon, as for others, the analogy of nation to organism proved decisive. Labor performed by a part of the people would benefit the nation as a whole, just as the exercise of a single limb stimulated the flow of blood to all the organs of the body. In the end, then, the cogency of Gordon's viewpoint does not rest on the larger coherence of political or spiritual Zionism. It depends rather on the appeal of his own eclectic borrowings from Tolstoy and Schleiermacher, Fichte and Toennies.

Martin Buber's (1878–1965) attempt to accomplish a synthesis between politicization and resymbolization was far more sophisticated, but rested on many of the same presuppositions. Especially in Buber's early Zionist writings, dating from the opening years of the center, we find the same ideal of organic wholeness, combined with the same belief in national spirits and/or racial types that underlie the thought of both Gordon and Ahad Ha'am. Those ideas are invoked, furthermore, to attack a diaspora existence described variously as poor, distorted, sickly, sterile, sunken, abysmal, fragmented, tortured, tormented, lacking in unity, and characterized by a barren intellectuality.[71] The Jews, for Buber, were the very picture of the homeless world. Their need to create a home for the spirit, out of their own soul and on their own soil, would overcome the rationality and alienation from nature afflicting all the modern world—and so pave the way for a larger human fulfillment.[72] Echoes of successive modern resymbolizations of the Land, including Gordon's, are evident. Jerusalem is not so much a real earthly city or the goal of Jewish pilgrimage as the route to spirit, soul, unity, nature, and humanity.

In Buber's later work such rhetoric is muted, and his vision becomes tempered by political realism. The mature Buberian philosophy adumbrated in *I and Thou* diagnoses the sickness of modern society as the result of excessive growth in impersonal "I-It" relationships, with the consequence that "I-Thou" relationships between whole human beings had withered. People unable to relate to each other as "Thou's" not surprisingly found it difficult to relate to the Being eternally a Thou—God. The task facing mankind, then, was the creation of communities and institutions which would facilitate I-Thou relations rather than preclude them. It is in that conceptual context that Buber places the Jews' return to Zion and particularly the founding of kibbutzim. The Bible, more than any other book, had articulated God's demand that human beings live in justice and wholeness, and the Jews more than any other people had therefore come to know the indivisibility of the national and religious dimensions of existence.[73]

Return to Israel meant a renewed possibility to achieve personal wholeness impossible in the urban diaspora. *Gesellschaft* could be supplanted by a revived *Gemeinschaft*. Moreover, it provided the opportunity to live within institutions shaped by Jewish commitments and hence capable of carrying out the biblical demand. Buber did not urge a renunciation of force and realpolitik, only a recognition of the compromises forced upon moral actors by the facts, and awareness that some compromises were morally unacceptable.[74] He did not laud the kibbutz as the sole pattern for Jewish I-Thou living but more modestly proclaimed it the one experiment in human community which had not yet failed.

In a sense, and to a degree, of course, I-Thou relations were possible at any time in any place and facilitated by any true community. Jews could come to know their fellows and their God no matter where they lived, as any mystic anywhere could experience the divine regardless of material circumstances. Homeland, Buber wrote, was "unarbitrary life in the face of God."[75] Consequently, discussion of the Land occupies but a small part of Buber's work, most of which is devoted to a Jewish spirituality and ethics applicable anywhere.

However, unlike Rosenzweig, Buber found homelands of the spirit insufficient. Modernity had set a trap for spirit, Jewish or Gentile, which could be avoided only with the establishment of true communities. Jews could create such institutions only in Zion, while in the diaspora they were condemned to practice Judaism as a mere religion—and religion, Buber wrote, was "the exile of man," which "wills precisely to cease being religion" and to become "all of life."[76] Unlike Cohen and Rosenzweig, then, Buber did see ultimate religious meaning in the Jewish return to Zion. Unlike the political Zionists, he saw no point to a return unaccompanied by the biblical commitments which he titled "Hebrew Humanism." Unlike Ahad Ha'am, he held fast to the belief in a real and personal God who comes forth to encounter human beings in the world. Yet Buber's conception of the Land is nonetheless demystified and utterly resymbolized, because, unlike the Orthodox, he could not believe in the God of Torah revealed by Jewish tradition; Buber rather maintained, to the end of his life, that the forms of revealed religion were fatal to the true religiosity to which God called us.

IV. The Dilemmas of Orthodox Zionism

For a traditional religious conception of the Land in the modern period one must turn to the Orthodox, who have, for the most part, clung until recently to a *non*-demystified and *non*-resymbolized conception of the Land that precluded acceptance of the Zionist movement. Our interest here lies in the exceptions to that rule, a stream of thought which begins with the Zionist "forerunners" Yehudah Alkalai (1798–1878) and Zvi Hirsch Kalischer (1795–1879). Return to the Land on a small scale was not an infringement on divine prerogatives, they insisted, rather a first step towards God's gift of redemption. The purchase of parcels of *Eretz Yisra'el* from the Turks did not represent a denial of the Land's unique holiness but rather a redemption of the Land that would permit fulfillment of commandments tied to its possession.[77] Despite the two rabbis' prescient call for organized funding and settlement, then, their *concept* of the Land remained unpoliticized. No demystification is evident, and the symbols associated with the Land are strictly traditional.

This pattern of thought changed somewhat with the rise of the orthodox religious Zionist movement known as Mizrachi, but the synthesis of a traditional, mystical conception of the Land with modern symbols and politicization received its full expression only in the copious writings of Abraham Isaac Kook (1865–1935). This chief rabbi's all-comprehending perspective on history and the cosmos reconciled elements far more disparate than the views of Theodore Herzl and Rabbi Akiba. It is no wonder, then, that a reunification between political and cultural Zionism soon fell into place as well. Kook's larger perspective on the workings of Divine Spirit enabled him to hail modern atheists as unknowing purifiers of the faith who cleansed religion of superstition and rigidity.[78] His Kabbalistic commitment to the redemption of "sparks" trapped in evil "husks" likewise permitted him to embrace secular Zionists — profaners of the Sabbath, professors of disbelief — as God's unwitting agents in the "flowering of our redemption."[79] Such was the cunning of Spirit — and it made possible a synthesis inconceivable to other minds.

That synthesis is immediately evident in Kook's remarkably fluid and lyrical language. Exile is described as bitter, hard, dark, the sleep of death, sick, a time of neglect for the body and deracination for the spirit[80] — stock images in a vocabulary shared by Klatzkin and Gordon, Buber and Ahad Ha'am. However, Kook even more than Gordon invokes another vocabulary, largely Kabbalist, which renders common critique of exile and praise of the

Land infinitely sharper and more compelling. Return to the Land, for example, assumes added significance when joined explicitly to the concept of *teshuvah* (return or repentance). Failure to seize the opportunity of return is a more serious offense when it is called *chilul ha-shem*: "profanation of the name"—of the *Land* of Israel![81] Even flourishes such as these are superfluous, however, given Kook's reliance on another theme, reiterated on countless occasions, to motivate and legitimate the Zionist renewal—the Land's unique and transcendent holiness.

Eretz Yisra'el, Kook wrote, was the spatial center of holiness in the world, radiating holiness vertically to the Jews who lived upon the Land as well as horizontally to other portions and peoples of the earth. The spirit of the Land was entirely pure and clean, while spirit elsewhere was mired in *kelipot* or "husks" of impurity.[82] The air of the Land really did "make one wise," as the Rabbis had said. In a typical elevation of sociology to theology, Kook argued that the Jewish imagination outside the Land had become stunted and even deformed. The cause was not merely assimilation to Gentile cultures possessed of far less light and holiness than Israel. In addition, the Jews had depleted over two millennia the store of creativity carried away with them into exile. During their absence, the flow of spirit had ceased; its gradual diminishing was responsible for the character of *galut* life; realizing these facts, the Jews had grasped the urgency of return.[83] Moreover, since the entire world was poor in holiness and sunk in wickedness, it was utterly dependent upon the Jews for a renewal of light and spirit. Israel's return to the Land would thus mark the end of a worldwide era of darkness, and initiate the redemption of all humanity.[84]

It is astounding to read such claims in a twentieth-century work. Instead of engaging in apologetic, Kook merely notes that the unique qualities of the holy Land cannot be comprehended by reason.[85] Once his assumptions have been granted, however, they legitimate a powerful critique of *galut* life and *galut* Judaism, and sanctify political activities and conceptions that would otherwise have been unacceptable. We have already noted that the Jewish spirit meant to guide the rest of creation had sunk to imitation of "uncircumcised" Gentiles, while the Jewish body, sorely neglected in exile, had suffered a comparable impoverishment. The full and varied character of Jewish life could not achieve expression, given oppression and exposure to foreign winds.[86] For Kook, this low estate explained a phenomenon which, rightly understood, was a contradiction in terms: Jewish atheism. Many Jews of thoughtful and moral character had cast off their inherited faith, only because that Jewish faith had degenerated to the point where superstition passed for true belief, and Jewish practice had become frozen in old forms. However, the people of Israel was inseparable in its very essence from God. Many Jewish souls had expressed their rebellion, therefore, precisely by returning to the Land of Israel where God's spirit most reposed—thereby releasing the light trapped in exilic husks, and facilitating the renewal of Jewish religion. Both thought and practice would return to their original purity once the nation had returned to full life upon its holy soil. Atheism and rejection of the "yoke of the commandments" would gradually disappear.[87]

Kook could therefore embrace the Zionist project even though he, no less than other rabbis, knew it to be essentially secular. Qualms about the legitimacy of a movement led by professed atheists and characterized by public disregard of the commandments were silenced by the confidence that in God's good time, soon to be upon us, such deviance would be seen as the "arrogance" that tradition had said would accompany the first footsteps of the Messiah.[88] Kook criticized departures from *halakhah* but at the same time asserted that "every labor and activity, spiritual or material, that contributes directly or indirectly to the ingathering of our exile and the return of our people to our Land is embraced by me with an affection of soul that knows no bounds."[89] Even more important, Kook could explain away the clear inapplicability of *halakhah* as it had taken shape over two millennia of exile to the actual conditions of the Land and society which he wished that *halakhah* to govern. The law's insufficiencies were the result of exilic darkness, and needed correction. The profane indecencies of the *Yishuv* were a necessary stage to be endured and transcended. Thesis and antithesis would give way to synthesis; so worked the God of Spirit.

In our terms: politicization and resymbolization could be harmonized with a non-demystified tradition, as part of a larger cosmic order, a more inclusive divine plan. Kook's synthesis leads, through the figure of his son Zvi Yehudah Kook, to a messianic stream of religious Zionism which gained prominence in Israeli society in the years following the victory of 1967.[90] [Ed. note: for Zvi Yehudah Kook and other contemporary views, see discussion below by Uriel Tal, pp. 319–25.] Other Orthodox thinkers, however, have been unable to share in Kook's messianic confidence that the contradictions would soon be overcome, and so have remained unwilling to combine a traditional symbolic conception of the Land with the politicization which their role in the State would seem to demand. By living within the polity of the State, they have chosen to act out in practice a course which their theory can neither sanction nor explain. To understand why, we will turn briefly to the trenchant writings of the man who, since the State's establishment, has offered the most perceptive analysis and the most persistent criticism of religious Zionism: Yeshayahu Leibowitz (b. 1903).

Religion, Leibowitz argues, must conceive of itself as an end in itself; it must reject any view which makes its existence a means to other ends such as the morality of society or the authority of the state. It must rather be "totalitarian in the realm of values," regarding all else in life as a means to its one end: knowing and cleaving to God.[91] Given this irrefragable assumption, can the State of Israel have any religious significance? Jewish tradition, Leibowitz suggests, offers two answers. The first, represented by Bahya ibn Pakuda (11th cent.) and Moses Chaim Luzzatto (1707–1746), holds that religiosity is not dependent upon or influenced by any social situation. Even the people of Israel qua national-political entity is not needed for the Jew's religious life, let alone the apparatus of a modern state. A second stream of thought, however, believes that perfection of the social and political orders is a divine demand, and so an essential part of Jewish religious life. Certainly the biblical prophets held this view, and so did Maimonides. The problem, Leibowitz continues, is that no specific political program for a contemporary state can be derived from such traditional sources. In fact, they presume precisely opposite conditions to those which apply in a sovereign Jewish state in the Land of Israel.[92]

His argument is twofold. Neither Scripture nor Mishnah nor Talmud nor Maimonides knew of any Jewish state in the historical present. There was the state of the distant past, ruled by David and Solomon, and there would be the state of "King Messiah," in some far-distant future. A state created without direct divine intervention, in the space of time between Destruction and Messiah, was simply not conceived. Such a state thus represents a daring attempt to draw legitimacy from a tradition which never even considers the possibility of its existence.[93] Moreover, the *halakhah* reflects that lack of consideration utterly and completely, presuming on every page of text either life among the nations in exile or submission to a Gentile authority in power within Eretz Yisra'el. The Jew is commanded to say the *Shema* when he gets up in the morning, told what words to say and when to say them. However, the conditions necessary if he is to wake up in the first place—police, fire department, an army, etc.—are passed over in silence. Previous generations of Jews could trust in Gentile rulers to provide them; contemporary Orthodox Israelis relied on other Jews. Thus, at the very same moment that such Jews demanded that the state be governed according to the letter of *halakhah*, they acquiesced in an arrangement whereby Orthodoxy remained a sect within a larger secular state—and then depended on that state for the preconditions of its own religious observance.[94]

This, Leibowitz charges, is hypocritical, and damages both religion and the state. Jews should rather face the challenge posed to their faith by the state which they have created and confront the following choice. Either the Torah's legislation was intended *lekhatchilah*, a priori, and so contained a model to which any Jewish state at any time must conform, or it represented a code enacted *bedi'avad*, ex post facto, in accord with particular circumstances prevailing at one time but no longer. If the former, Neturei Karta in Israel and non-Zionists abroad such as the Satmar Hasidim are correct.[95] Zionism is illegitimate; the Jewish state can have no religious meaning, and in fact violates God's laws. (In our terms: politicization and resymbolization are incompatible with Jewish tradition.) If the latter, a revision of *halakhah* is needed, commensurate with the revision of Jewish history accomplished by Zionism. This the Orthodox community in Israel and its supporters abroad have so far refused to undertake.[96] Leibowitz can neither approve of their "hypocrisy," nor endorse the non-Zionists' position, nor embrace Kook's messianism. He has, moreover, repeatedly opposed the political positions taken by those who have invoked messianism as their justification. Leibowitz thus remains a critic rather than the leader of a movement, caught in the rifts that have opened up in the modern period between the reconceptions of Eretz Yisra'el that we have examined.

V. Conclusion: The Present Situation

Even today, then, and even within the Land, the lines of thought set at the start of the modern period remain relevant, and even decisive. That is so, first of all, because the situation which Spinoza and Mendelssohn analyzed, or at least foresaw, has (outside of the Land) remained a constant. Jewish thinkers are still seeking above all to integrate Jews and their faith within a modern social, political, and intellectual order. In such an effort the Jews' religious rather than their national identity is necessarily paramount, and Jewish religious thought has focused on the adjustment of beliefs and practices to changed circumstances and modes of thought. National sentiment has been accommodated within, and lent transcendent meaning by, that essentially religious context. The existence of a Jewish state, ironically, has only strengthened the religious focus, providing a sort of lightning rod for the national energies of diaspora Jews, which ensures that they come down to earth only *elsewhere*. Jewish nationality, in other words, can be focused on Israel, while outside it Jews can participate in their various diaspora nationalities as a group differentiated primarily by its religion. Inside the Land, political thought derived largely from the West continues to regard separation of state and church—politicization and religious symbolization—as a prerequisite of democracy and modernity.

Not surprisingly, the Land has figured directly in *diaspora* Jewish thought only as part of an idealized past, a symbolic present, and a messianic future. It has remained the place of which one's ancestors dreamed, and become, in addition, the Land one's cousins have recently reclaimed. Out of the ashes of the Holocaust, Jews have brought a desert, and themselves, to life. Diaspora Jewry moves with the pulse of that inspiration. Its religious thought has been unaffected, however. Only one of the thinkers represented in a 1963 symposium in *Midstream* magazine agreed that the concept of *galut* was at all applicable to American Jewry.[97] The influences most often cited in a 1966 symposium in *Commentary* were for similar reasons not Ahad Ha'am, or Kook, or Gordon, but Rosenzweig and Buber.[98] Demystification and resymbolization had been very successful indeed. Politicization had created a reality cherished and supported but kept separate from one's religious identity as a Jew. The meaning of Jewish life for many diaspora Jews might well depend, to some degree, on the existence of the Jewish state, but the meaning of diaspora religious thought does not. This is not surprising; Israel is not of central importance to those who do not live there, and diaspora religious thought reflects that. Questions of life and death, sickness and pain, law and covenant, and, most recently, the theological implications of the Holocaust, take precedence over a Land and State which are far from everyday experience.[99]

Inside *Eretz Yisra'el*, the situation is of course somewhat different. Orthodox thinkers as a rule have interpreted the return to Zion, and particular events in the history of the State, as acts of divine providence. The commandments dependent upon settlement in the Land are regularly cited. The State of Israel is proclaimed weekly in Sabbath prayers to be "the beginning of the flowering of our redemption," even if further stages in the process are not imminently expected. However, the State's existence has substantially affected the religious thought only of those who, like Zvi Yehudah Kook, have believed the messianic redemption to be at hand. Such thinkers, as a study by Uriel Tal demonstrates [see below, pp. 319–21], have tended to conceive of current history in apocalyptic terms, identifying Israel's contemporary foes with biblical prototypes. The messianic political movement

Gush Emunim has drawn on their work for legitimation.¹⁰⁰ Other thinkers, recoiling from such political and moral implications, have tended to
bifurcate their political and symbolic conceptions. The Land might or might
not be inherently sacred, the return to it was surely an act of divine blessing, but more than this can not be said. *Halakhah* should in principle come
to govern Israeli society, but not *halakhah* as it currently exists, and not in
the foreseeable future. Is Israel the "beginning of the flowering of our redemption?" Might it only be so.

Even within the State, then, politicization has exacted its price in resymbolization and demystification. Those most reluctant to perform the
latter reconceptions, such as Neturei Karta, are not by chance those who
have remained most aloof from the former. Leibowitz's critique cannot be
answered by any except the political messianists, and their response is not
one which he wishes to hear. The thoroughgoing changes for which he calls
are unlikely, if only because they would reveal the enormous extent of the
innovation already acceded to by virtue of the three reconceptions examined here. Such a development would open a gap between the State and
the tradition used to legitimate it which might in turn place the effective-
ness of that legitimacy in doubt.

Secular or semi-religious circles, finally, have been served until now by
an eclectic synthesis of their forebears. Herzl and Ahad Ha'am alike turned
out to be both correct and mistaken. The State became a reality within
the outer limit of the period predicted by Herzl, and yet the diaspora per-
sists, looking to the State as its "spiritual center" and importing from it the
various artifacts of a national culture. Gordon remains of interest to "kibbutznikim" in a way Israelis not working the Land in small communities cannot
share.¹⁰¹ In a similar fashion, Israelis as a whole find in Gordon's lyrical
hymns to the Land, or those of poets such as Saul Tschernichowsky, a meaning
that is lost on the ears of Jews outside the Land. Negation of the diaspora
continues, particularly among those who see no transcendent purpose in
the State and are not linked to diaspora Jewry by the unifying force of
religion.¹⁰² Thoroughgoing "normalization," however, has usually been tempered by recourse to some variant of an Israeli "mission." Given the demystification of the Land and people of Israel on which secular Zionism depends, resymbolization has thus proven an indispensable aid to politicization.

The tensions born of such a fragmented conception of the Land—
both within Israel, and between Israel and its diaspora—will likely continue,
unless the conditions which gave rise to that conception at the start of the
modern era are themselves appreciably altered. In the absence of a new po-

litical order that replaces the current system of nation-states, a new religious revelation that puts an end to the current predominance of pluralism and doubt, and a new scientific and/or mystical worldview in which humanity's relationship to nature is differently understood, the reconceptions of Spinoza and Mendelssohn will likely stand. Jews will wait for the Messiah, inside and outside the Land, and in the meantime go about their business—"regardless of theory," as Rosenzweig said, or of its manifold contradictions.

Notes

1. Benedict de Spinoza, *A Theologico-Political Treatise*, trans. R. H. M. Elwes (New York: Dover, 1951), p. 6. My reading of the work generally follows that of Leo Strauss in *Spinoza's Critique of Religion* (New York: Schocken, 1982). See especially Strauss's preface.

2. Spinoza, p. 46.

3. Ibid., p. 44.

4. The examples which follow are of course intended to be illustrative rather than exhaustive.

5. Spinoza, p. 56.

6. On Mendelssohn's *Jerusalem*, see Alexander Altmann's magisterial *Moses Mendelssohn: A Biographical Study* (Philadelphia: Jewish Publication Society, 1973), pp. 514–52; and Julius Guttmann, "Mendelssohn's *Jerusalem* and Spinoza's *Theologico-Political Treatise*," in Alfred Jospe, ed., *Studies in Jewish Thought* (Detroit: Wayne State University Press, 1981), pp. 361–86.

7. Moses Mendelssohn, *Jerusalem* (New York: Schocken Books, 1969), p. 61.

8. Ibid., pp. 101–02.

9. Ibid., p. 102.

10. Ibid.: "Just as Plato spoke of an earthly and a heavenly love, one might also speak of earthly and heavenly politics."

11. Plato, *The Republic*, trans. Desmond Lee (New York: Penguin, 1974), l. 499c, p. 296.

12. Mendelssohn, p. 104.

13. For this reading of the rabbinic project see especially Jacob Neusner, *Method and Meaning in Ancient Judaism* (Missoula: Scholars Press, 1979) and his more recent *Judaism: The Evidence of the Mishnah* (Chicago: University of Chicago Press, 1981).

14. Altmann, p. 514.

15. For more on the development of the mission theme, see my *The Chosen People in America* (Bloomington: Indiana University Press, 1983), pp. 13–21.

16. Samson Raphael Hirsch, *The Nineteen Letters on Judaism*, trans. Bernard Drachman (New York: Feldheim, 1969).

17. Nachman Krochmal, *Guide for the Perplexed of the Time* in *The Writings of Nachman Krochmal*, ed. Simon Rawidowicz (Hebrew; Waltham: Ararat Publishing Society, 1961), chapters 8–9; see especially pp. 50–51.

18. Abraham Geiger, *Judaism and its History*, trans. Charles Newburgh (New York: Bloch, 1911), p. 68. See Geiger's tracing of the mission in chapters 1–6, and, for a periodization of Jewish history, "A General Introduction to the Science of Judaism" in Max Wiener, ed., *Abraham Geiger and Liberal Judaism* (Philadelphia: Jewish Publication Society, 1962), pp. 149–54.

19. Heinrich Graetz, "The Structure of Jewish History," in *The Structure of Jewish History and Other Essays*, ed. and trans. Ismar Schorsch (New York: Jewish Theological Seminary of America, 1975), pp. 65, 69.

20. Ibid., pp. 71–72.

21. Ibid., p. 124.

22. Leo Pinsker, "Auto-Emancipation," in Arthur Hertzberg, ed., *The Zionist Idea* (New York: Harper Torchbooks, 1966), pp. 182–86.

23. Ibid., pp. 186–88.

24. Ibid., pp. 188–97.

25. Ibid., pp. 194, 197–98.

26. Ahad Ha'am, "Altneuland," in *Complete Writings* (Hebrew; Jerusalem: Jewish Publishing House, Ltd., 1965), pp. 313–20.

27. On violence as the means specific to politics, compare Max Weber, "Politics as a Vocation," in Hans Gerth and C. Wright Mills, eds., *From Max Weber* (New York: Oxford University Press, 1969), pp. 77–78. It is interesting to note that what is said here about Herzl's political Zionism applies with equal force to such theorists of socialist Zionism as Nachman Syrkin. In their works, too, politicization is combined with resymbolization in secular, universalist terms.

28. Kaufman Kohler, *Backwards or Forwards? A Series of Discourses on Reform Judaism* (New York: Congregation Beth-El, 1885), pp. 34–35.

29. Kaufman Kohler, *Jewish Theology: Systematically and Historically Considered* (New York: Macmillan, 1928), pp. 7–8.

30. Ibid. See also his *Hebrew Union College and Other Addresses* (Cincinnati: Ark Publishing Company, 1916), p. 24 ("The Jew has at all times been the true cosmopolitan"), p. 196 (on America as the "God-blessed land of liberty") and p. 204 (on America as Zion).

31. Hermann Cohen, *Religion of Reason out of the Sources of Judaism*, trans. Simon Kaplan (New York: Frederick Ungar, 1972) p. 254.

32. Ibid., p. 263.

33. Hermann Cohen, "A Reply to Dr. Martin Buber's Open Letter to Hermann Cohen," in Alfred Jospe, ed. *Reason and Hope* (New York: W. W. Norton, 1971), pp. 164–70.

34. *Franz Rosenzweig: His Life and Thought,* ed. Nahum N. Glatzer (New York: Schocken Books, 1976), pp. 354–56.

35. Ibid., p. 358.

36. Franz Rosenzweig, *The Star of Redemption,* trans. William W. Hallo (Notre Dame, Ind.: University of Notre Dame Press, 1985), pp. 298–301.

37. Ibid., pp. 301–03.

38. Ibid., pp. 331–32. The Eng. trans. erroneously reads, "*Though* living in a state . . ."

39. Glatzer, *Franz Rosenzweig,* pp. 358, 354.

40. Cf. Hertzberg, p. 117.

41. Moses Hess, "Rome and Jerusalem," in Hertzberg, p. 129.

42. Ibid., p. 120.

43. Ibid., pp. 119–20.

44. Ibid., p. 119.

45. Ibid., pp. 120–21.

46. Ibid., p. 133.

47. Ibid., pp. 122–23.

48. Ibid., pp. 136–37.

49. Ibid., p. 123.

50. Ibid., p. 137.

51. Ahad Ha'am, *Complete Writings,* pp. 11–14.

52. Ibid., p. 45.

53. Ahad Ha'am, "Slavery in Freedom," in *Selected Essays of Ahad Ha'am,* ed. and trans. Leon Simon (Philadelphia: Jewish Publication Society, 1962), p. 192.

54. Ahad Ha'am, "The Spiritual Revival," ibid., p. 287.

55. *Complete Writings,* p. 313.

56. Ibid., p. 187.

57. "The Spiritual Revival," p. 254.

58. *Complete Writings,* p. 421.

59. Ahad Ha'am, "The Negation of the Diaspora," in Hertzberg, p. 270.

60. *Complete Writings,* p. 136.

61. Ibid., p. 313. On the transition from sacred to secular see the discussion of whether one could be a "good, atheist Jew": Ibid., pp. 151, 292. On p. 278, Ahad Ha'am even employs the term *kedushat ha'aretz*—"the holiness of the land"— and notes that a Gentile writer whom he cites feels that holiness more than many Jewish Zionists.

62. Ibid., p. 266.

63. See "The National Morality" in ibid., pp. 159–64.

64. A. D. Gordon, *The Nation and Labor* (Hebrew; Jerusalem: World Zionist Organization, 1952), pp. 140–42, 168, 173; see also 108, 134.

65. For example see ibid., p. 282: "Here, before us, today, life has revealed the disease of parasitism in all its ugliness and rot. All our strength devoted to heal-

ing the nation must be centered in this labor of cure, of surgery, of cleansing of the air. . . ." The image, of course, comes from Nietzsche, transmitted by Jewish Nietzscheans such as Micah Joseph Berdichevsky.

66. Ibid., pp. 91, 104, 127, 198, and (the quote on "*galut* wisdom") p. 257. The *Yishuv* is the Jewish community in the Land of Israel.

67. Ibid., pp. 144, 185, 140, 208.

68. Ibid., pp. 189, 215–31.

69. Ibid., pp. 493–503, 517–21.

70. Ibid., pp. 261–65.

71. See especially the "Three Addresses on Judaism" included in Martin Buber, *On Judaism*, ed. Nahum Glatzer (New York: Schocken Books, 1972), pp. 11–55. Buber's strongest denunciations of exile can be found on pp. 29–31.

72. *On Judaism*, pp. 53, 85, 128–34.

73. In particular, see Martin Buber, *I and Thou*, trans. Walter Kaufmann (New York: Scribner's, 1970); the collection *Israel and the World: Essays in a Time of Crisis* (New York: Schocken Books, 1963); and *Paths in Utopia* (Boston: Beacon Press, 1958).

74. See, for example, "The Man of Today and the Jewish Bible" and "Hebrew Humanism" in *Israel*, pp. 89–102, 240–52; and the recent collection *A Land of Two Peoples: Martin Buber on Jews and Arabs*, ed. Paul R. Mendes-Flohr (New York: Oxford University Press, 1983), particularly the writings from 1947–1949.

75. Martin Buber, "Religion and Philosophy," in *Eclipse of God*, trans. Maurice Friedman et al. (New York: Harper Torchbooks, 1957), p. 34.

76. Ibid.

77. Hertzberg, pp. 103–14.

78. See, for example, Abraham Isaac Kook, *Orot* ("Lights") (Jerusalem: Mossad Harav Kook, 1975), pp. 126–27.

79. See, for example, Abraham Isaac Kook, *Chazon Hage'ullah* ("The Vision of Redemption") (Jerusalem: Association for Publishing the Works of the Chief Rabbi A. I. Kook, 1941), p. 275.

80. Ibid., pp. 35, 56, 61, 74, 87, 169—but a few examples.

81. Ibid., pp. 231, 233.

82. See, for example, *Orot*, pp. 9, 20, 77, 88–89, 100–04, 151; *Chazon*, pp. 69–70, 78, 85. On pp. 261–62 Kook's routine use of the word "holy" is apparent in the phrases "It is a holy duty to propose . . ." and "the holy connection" (between the *Yishuv* and Orthodox party in Europe, Agudat Israel).

83. *Orot*, pp. 9–12, 20, 62, 84.

84. *Orot*, pp. 22, 34, 59, 100.

85. *Orot*, p. 9.

86. *Chazon*, pp. 87–90.

87. *Chazon*, pp. 70–72, 76–78, 85; *Orot*, pp. 45–47, 49, 66.

88. *Orot*, p. 82.

89. *Chazon*, p. 278. For a general collection of Kook's writings in English, see *The Lights of Penitence* (and other works) ed. and trans. Ben Zion Bokser (New York: Paulist Press, 1978).

90. Zvi Yehudah Kook, *Linetivot Yisra'el* ("In the Pathways of Israel") (Jerusalem: Menorah Publishing Co., 1963). Israel's current chief rabbi, Shlomo Goren, takes a moderate messianist position in his *Torat Hamo'adim* ("Laws of the Festivals") (Tel Aviv: Avraham Zioni Publishing Co., 1964), concluding (p. 565) that we stand in an intermediate period in which the preparatory tasks of conquering the Land, ingathering the exiles, and making barren soil bloom are being accomplished. The essay dates from before 1967, however; Israel's salvation from apparent danger, its military victory, and its conquest of more of the Land that year have fueled messianic speculation and politics. The elder Rabbi Kook himself lays the groundwork for both that speculation and that politics in passages such as those in *Chazon*, pp. 37–38 and 85 which correlate Israel's increased power with increased holiness.

91. Yeshayahu Leibowitz, *Judaism, the Jewish People, and the State of Israel* (Hebrew; Jerusalem: Schocken Books, 1976), pp. 122–23.

92. Ibid., pp. 125–28.

93. Ibid., pp. 131–32, 137.

94. Ibid., pp. 129–31, 139–42, 151–52.

95. Ibid., p. 138. On the Satmar rebbe, Yoel Teitelbaum, see Allen L. Nadler, "Piety and Politics: The Case of the Satmar Rebbe," *Judaism*, Spring 1982, pp. 135–51.

96. Leibowitz, pp. 139–42. Although the essays cited date from 1952–1953, Leibowitz's views have not changed in the interim, as he testifies in his preface, p. 11.

97. "The Meaning of *Galut* in America Today: A Symposium," *Midstream*, March 1963, pp. 3–45. The exception to the rule was Ben Halpern, a secular labor Zionist.

98. "The State of Jewish Belief," *Commentary*, August 1966, pp. 71–160.

99. For an excellent discussion of these issues see Jacob Neusner, *Stranger at Home* (Chicago: University of Chicago Press, 1981). The Land is represented in Abraham Heschel's thought primarily in the work *Israel: An Echo of Eternity* (New York: Farrar, Straus and Giroux, 1973) where the creation of the State is said to be an event "in accord with the hidden Presence in Jewish history" (p. 139). That event is not central to Heschel's philosophy of Judaism. Joseph Soloveitchik treats the issue primarily in his essay "*Kol Dodi Dofek*" ("The Sound of My Beloved Knocking"), where the State's creation is likewise said to be a sign of God's renewed presence after the Holocaust. The traditional symbols are invoked; messianism, however, is eschewed. See the collection *Besod Hayachid Vehayachad* ("In Aloneness, In Togetherness"), ed. Pinchas Peli (Jerusalem: Orot, 1976), pp. 354–67. In the works of other contemporary diaspora thinkers, the Land is even more peripheral.

100. Remarks at a conference dedicated to the memory of Jacob Talmon,

Jerusalem, 1982. See below, pp. 000–000, and Tal's "The Land and the State of Israel in Comtemporary Israeli Hebrew Writing: A Selected Bibliography," in *Proceedings of the Rabbinical Assembly of America*, 1976, pp. 23–40.

101. For one expression of this view, see Muky Tsur, *Lelo Ketonet Pasim* ("Without a Coat of Many Colors") (Tel Aviv: Am Oved, 1976). Tsur, one of the intellectual leaders of the kibbutz movement, looks for inspiration to Gordon, Berl Katznelson, and Y. H. Brenner.

102. For example, the Israeli thinker Eliezer Schweid. See his debate with Mordecai Bar-On (who takes a more positive stance towards the diaspora) in *Kivvunim* (Hebrew), May and August 1981. An even more extreme "negation of the diaspora" is put forth in A. B. Yehoshua, *Bizkhut Hanormaliyut* ("In Defense of Normality") (Jerusalem: Schocken Books, 1980). Finally, for a related survey of classical and twentieth-century concepts of Eretz Israel, see Eliezer Schweid, *Homeland and a Land of Promise* (Hebrew; Tel Aviv: Am Oved, 1979).

The Jews of North Africa and the Land of Israel in the Eighteenth and Nineteenth Centuries: The Reversal in Attitude toward *Aliyah* (Immigration to the Land) from 1770 to 1860

[Editor's note: Dr. Shalom Bar Asher, a Senior Lecturer at the Hebrew University in Jerusalem, is a prominent exponent of Sephardic history and thought, particularly as it is found in documents bequeathed to us from Jews in North Africa, or the Maghreb, as it is customarily called. In this essay, he looks at the marked change in attitude toward *aliyah* that occurred, particularly in Morocco, from 1770 to 1860, a reversal of approach that is evident in the sheer number of people who opted to leave the Maghreb for the Land of Israel, as well as in the reasons for their return, and in the social makeup of the migrants themselves, who more and more became representative of all ages and socio-economic classes, rather than being composed predominantly of elderly Jews bent on dying in the Holy Land, or religious visionaries, moved only by the hope that they might serve God to the fullest there. Bar Asher traces the change, first, to internal decay in the Maghreb: the persistent failure of the authorities to curb Berber incursions, for example, the tyrannical rule of Sultan Yazid (1790–1792), the severe famine that plagued the area from 1776 to 1882, and the rise of religious zealotry attendant upon the French conquest of Algeria in 1830; but he notes also the effect of external factors, both socio-economic and ideological: improved communications with Jews already in the Land, who were well represented by formal agents (*shelichim*) pressing Maghrebian Jewry to emigrate, and the increasing popularity of Lurianic Kabbalah which emphasized themes supportive of *aliyah*. Of particular interest is Bar Asher's treatment of rabbinic responsa in which the traditional literature on *aliyah*—in large part, the same body of opinions analyzed earlier in this book by Saperstein—was again scrutinized, this time with appropriately novel results for these eighteenth and nineteenth-century would-be migrants. Bar Asher has given us a case study in which many of the themes discussed elsewhere in these pages coalesce in a single example of a particular Jewish community, for whom the Jewish attachment to the Land of Israel became a mass movement of enormous historic consequence.]

297

The Beginning of the Reversal: 1777–1830

In the second half of the eighteenth century, Jews living in the Maghreb[1] [a general term meaning "The West," and corresponding to North Africa, but emanating originally from usage by Arabic geographers who applied it to people of North Africa and Spain as well] and particularly in Morocco, demonstrated a change in attitude toward *aliyah*—that is, toward return to the Land of Israel. To be sure, in earlier ages also, and practically without interruption, North African Jewry supported *aliyah*, but now new circumstances gave the movement an added impetus. To begin with, there was the sheer number of emigrants: whereas for the earlier periods it was possible to measure those who moved to the Land in waves of tens, the numbers in this new era reached into the hundreds. From 1809 to 1839, for example, North African emigrants to Safed alone amounted to 307 souls.[2] The stream of individuals and even of whole families grew steadily, such that (for example) in approximately fifty years (1780–1830), one small town in Morocco, Sefrou, produced fifty emigrants; and this is only according to those documents that have been preserved, so that we may assume that the actual number was larger still.[3]

Another change occurred with regard to the age of those who left, in that a greater proportion were now of working age, whereas beforehand, most of the people were elderly:[4] in 1827, for example, adult emigrants varied between 18 and 60 years of age, with the majority being between 30 and 50.[5] But the most significant novelty was to be found in the motivations of the emigrants. Most people, of course, still moved to the Holy Land out of a sense of serving God[6] or so as to hasten the day of redemption;[7] or, if they were elderly, because they wanted to live out the remainder of their lives in the Land of their ancestors. But gradually, the number was growing of those in search of new economic opportunity. The greater part of this latter group were Jews from the middle or lower social strata. Typical of the occupational composition of the majority of those making *aliyah* in the nineteenth century were peddlers, artisans, petty merchants, and a recognizable segment of the indigent,[8] a structure that corresponded to the occupational stratification of the lands whence they hailed, the Maghreb, particularly its inland regions. Among the Moroccan emigrants, for example, a considerable proportion came from the foothills of the Middle Atlas mountain range (the regions of Fez and Meknes) and the Tafilalt district, in which a relatively large percentage of people earned their livelihoods in these ways, in contrast to the coastal cities where a prominent proportion of people were middle class merchants, business brokers, suppliers, wholesalers, and even a few large-scale merchants.[9]

Sources for the Attitude toward Aliyah of the North African Rabbis

An important source that will help us, in general, to explicate these changes, and in particular, to investigate the position taken by the North African rabbis toward *aliyah* during the period in question, is rabbinic literature itself: legal decisions, enactments [*takkanot*], responsa literature, sermons, and compendia of customs. This source is particularly significant since as late as the end of the nineteenth century—and in Morocco and the southern districts of the Maghreb even until recently—the rabbis still dominated the ruling class among Maghrebian Jewry. Even though legal decisions and responsa on *aliyah* had been a subject of rabbinic discussion in the Maghreb already at the beginning of the eighteenth century—for example, by R. Judah Ayash who functioned as Av Bet Din in Algiers during the first half of the eighteenth century[10]—they became more frequent and more detailed (particularly in rabbinic literature from Morocco) from the end of the eighteenth century on, thus constituting a literary and social index of the changes in question.

One portion of the responsa, relatively restricted in scope, illustrates the phenomenon of individuals who seek to make *aliyah*, sell their land or other possessions, and embark on the way, but because of certain difficulties, dangers *en route* in particular, subsequently change their minds and attempt to annul the business relationships which they have entered into as part of their preparations to depart.[11] At a time predating the changes in question, the rabbis decide in favor of the sellers, thus indicating their general "traditional" or pre-change perspective of deemphasizing migration to the Land.[12] The question of *aliyah* became particularly acute on account of wives who refused to make *aliyah* with their husbands, reclaiming for themselves their rightful portion of the capital that they had brought into their marriage.[13] The question was far from new; the greatest of medieval rabbis had dealt with it in considerable quantity and detail. [Ed note: see above, pp. 190–95, where the history of this question in responsum literature is treated by Marc Saperstein.] But the issue arose with new intensity now.

Changes in Attitude in the Law Courts of Morocco

Such questions surfaced again in Morocco (and to a lesser extent, in Algeria) in the eighteenth century, indicating that the issues represented by them were becoming particularly pressing. But until the final quarter of the century, Moroccan courts maintained what we have called the "traditional" approach. In a legal decision of 1732, for example, a court in Fez ruled in favor of the wife, without, however, indicating its reasons for doing so.[14] Rabbi Jacob ben Tsur, also a judge in Fez, who ruled likewise in a similar case, based his decision principally on the notion that according to the conditions then contained in the *ketubah* (the marriage contract that stipulates the conditions under which a wife may request the court to force her husband to grant her a divorce, and to pay her a stipulated indemnity) a husband may not remove himself from one city to another without his wife's consent.[15] The decisor did not exempt the Land of Israel as unique, but included its cities in the terms covered by the condition in question.

Petachiah Berdugo (1764–1820), the Dayyan (judge) in Meknes, ruled similarly, claiming that because of the dangers on the routes to the Land of Israel, and because the matter was in any case under dispute, one ought to follow existing tradition.[16] A similar opinion was registered by Rabbi Joseph Toledano (d. 1782), another rabbinic scholar in Meknes. Here, the question was raised in connection with another matter (not a conflict between spouses): someone who vows to make *aliyah* but then reneges. One should take the lenient position of retroactively annuling the oath, he reasons, and he cites arguments similar to those of Rabbi Petachiah.[17] But in the course of his remarks, he inserts wording that reveals his own personal opinion that is at odds with the prevailing "tradition," and foreshadows the change in attitude that was to become dominant: "Even if he had the wherewithal to have gone [on *aliyah*] but he does not go, remaining [instead] in secure quarters [at home], there is no remedy; but God knows that if there were any possibility that I might go, even alone, I would travel day and night without stop or surcease until I arrived at that final destination of rest, the Land of my inheritance."[18] R. Toledano does not reveal what prevented his going, but perhaps his motives approximated those of R. Judah Ayash who regularly postponed his own *aliyah* because his congregation in Algiers asked that he not abandon them without spiritual leadership.[19]

A new approach is expressed by R. Saul Joshua Abitbul of Sefrou (1739–1808).[20] In a clear and comprehensive opinion, he examines the question and expresses his own perspective on it.[21] His words reflect the spiritual world of the rabbis of North Africa (and the east), as well as the straits in which the Jewish community of Morocco found itself in the second half of the eighteenth century. The defendant before the court was someone "whose spirit moved him, whose soul greatly yearned to make *aliyah* and to appear in the House of the Lord, in the courtyard of God";[22] that is, he wanted to make *aliyah* to the Holy Land, but his wife, who would not leave her relatives, claimed her *Get* (her bill of divorce, along with the freedom to remarry) including, naturally, financial compensation (the monetary penalty called for by the marriage contract—the *ketubah*—if the husband fails to fulfill his obligations to her), which seems to have been a serious sum of money in this case; particularly, inasmuch as "all the travel routes are to be considered under the legal presumption of being hazardous."[23] Despite this, however, the Mishnaic authorities had obviously established the general principle that a man can force his wife to make *aliyah* with him.[24] To put it another way, in the time of the Mishnaic and Talmudic authorities the routes were also dangerous, but even so, Jewish law laid down its principle, obligating the wife to accompany her husband regardless of presumptive dangers along the way. By way of explanation he adds, "This law was not made just for miracle workers [*ba'alei shem*] who can skip through the air instantly to get to the Land [*kefitsat haderekh*] but for all Israel."[25] The concepts of "miracle worker" and the miraculous ability of saintly miracle workers to traverse great distances in an instant resonated with the world of the rabbis, including those of North Africa.

It would appear that the rabbi is not altogether consistent with his earlier words, however, for he adds: "Nevertheless [that is, despite his prior reasoning that would imply that all Jews, not just miracle workers, have the right to force their wives to accompany them on *aliyah*], there is room to argue that the threat of danger overrides the fear of disobeying a commandment [in this case, consideration of danger on the travel routes takes precedence over consideration arising out of one's failure to obey the command to make *aliyah*]. Why, therefore, should we *not* worry [about the dangers en route]?"[26] Perhaps he made this claim because there was a definite and real danger in North Africa, as compared to the possibility that the Mishnaic sages dealt only with a theoretical threat. Thus he posits what he calls a *ta'ama raba*, "a great reason," rooted in the mystical tradition. He borrows the literary expression of the Sifre[27] and of Nachmanides,[28] in seeing the commandment to settle the Land of Israel not simply as one of the 613 commandments of the Torah, but as being itself equal to all of the others taken together and concludes, "In cases where a commandment is at

stake, and the would-be keeper of the commandment does not recognize
a danger [lying on the way to fulfilling that commandment], and those sent
to perform the commandment [i.e. *aliyah*] do not recognize the danger,"[29]
then special divine protection accompanies that person intent on fulfilling
the commandment of *aliyah*. But the rabbi remains dissatisfied even with
this explanation, since in a case of certain danger, such as the clear knowledge
that on a particular road most people meet up with highway robbers, one
should not depend on protection miraculously reserved for those who keep
commandments.[30] So he arrives at a novel distinction: only when the danger
is *certain* should one follow the traditional precedents to the effect that a
husband may not force his wife to make *aliyah* with him. But in a case
where danger is only *possible*, its potential may not serve as an excuse for
his wife to refuse to accompany him.[31]

It is this distinction that brings the decisor-judge to a third argument,
and from the way he constructs it, one may conclude that it is this that
he considers decisive. On the routes to the Land of Israel, he argues, there
is only the fear of possible danger, whereas in his city, Sefrou, there is *actual*
danger, in that it is open to attacks at the hand of rebellious bands and exposed to forays of Berber tribes from the Atlas Mountains; it suffers also
from famine, inflated prices for wheat, and debased coinage.[32] His description is anchored in reality: it emanates from the end of the eighth decade
of the eighteenth century (1779). Though the Sultan, Muhammad ben Ab-
dallah, had succeeded in improving security conditions in the large centers
of Morocco, he had failed to curb incursions of the Berber tribes against
the villages and towns on the borders of the Middle Atlas Mountains[33]
where Sefrou, among other places, was located. The period in question also
bears the imprint[34] of the severe famine which visited Morocco from 1776
to 1782, a famine whose economic consequences were devastating.[35] The
decisor, therefore, naturally found conducive the straightforward logic of
the Talmudic authorities (which favored forcing one's wife to go along with
aliyah); the religious faith in guaranteed protection for those who move to
the Land of Israel (because they are thereby fulfilling a great commandment); and the mere *uncertainty* of danger on the migration routes to the
Land of Israel compared to the dwindling security and real economic dis-
tress in Morocco—these led the rabbi to a completely novel decision.

By no means limited to Sefrou alone, this halakhic about-face in favor
of *aliyah* became general opinion among rabbis in the great urban centers,
such as Meknes.[36] From the onset of the nineteenth century, legal emphasis
was placed on the removal of dangers of the trip to the Land of Israel.[37]
The change stands out clearly in the decisions of Rabbi Petachiah Berdugo

who, as we said, had previously proved negative regarding *aliyah*, but now opined that, "Since it is a known fact that these days, the road to the Land is open (without hazards), so that nothing prevents [one's successful journey], as we see from [the accounts of] so many travellers," the legal position deserves to be reversed.[38]

An extension of the central discussion regarding the turn-about in *halakhah* can be found in two works by R. Raphael Berdugo (Meknes, 1747–1822), one of the greatest Moroccan scholars of the last four centuries. In one work, a sermon for Shabbat Hagadol [the Sabbath preceding Passover], he speaks out strongly against those who build grandiose homes, presumably indicating (in the rabbi's eyes) their attachment to life in the Diaspora.[39] The specific pictures he draws, such as, "Let them not even imagine that they might settle outside the Land, building elaborate homes with upper storeys,"[40] lead us to believe that he is addressing the wealthy of his age. The second source of information is a custom cited in a collection of laws and customs of Rabbi Raphael. He notes the existence of a custom among the people to sell a Torah scroll in order to finance *aliyah*.[41] But, as we know, the Halakhah permits the sale of a Torah scroll only for the purposes of Torah study, marriage, and the redemption of captives. So we can infer with near certainty from the sermon and from the custom regarding the sale of a Torah scroll that these are inescapable symptoms of a reversal in attitude toward *aliyah* to the Land of Israel.

Affinity for the Land as Integral Part of Consciousness among Maghreb Jewry

Factors both internal and external coalesced in the changing attitude toward *aliyah*.

Links between the Jewish communities of the Maghreb and the *Yishuv* [the name given to pre-state settlements in the Land of Israel] had already been forged in geonic times [ca. 7th–11th cents.][42] and these continued to grow until the time in question.[43] The very existence of a separate community of "Westerners"[44] — as those who left the Maghreb, coming from the west to the Land of Israel were called — is an irrefutable witness to the steady stream (albeit generally of individuals) finding its way from North Africa to the Land.[45] The connection to the Land received yet an additional basis at the beginning of the seventeenth century when the community of Fez became one of the first in the Diaspora to pass an ordinance (in the year 1603) favoring fixed economic support of the Land.[46] Toward that end, it appointed a special treasurer in every synagogue in the community.[47] In this period bonds existed above all else through *shelichim*, agents, who arrived in the Maghreb (according to documents in our possession) from the beginning of the seventeenth century. The agents came to collect donations or to instigate organized drives for money and to establish funds for the collection of monies to support the *Yishuv* in the Land.[48] In the very nature of things, these conditions and this relationship became stronger and better still as events unfolded at the end of the eighteenth century.

An additional factor in the strengthening of the connection to the Land was the spread of Safed Kabbalah [ed. note: on the Land of Israel in Kabbalistic thought, see comments by Moshe Idel above, pp. 170–81], particularly in its Lurianic form. By the end of the seventeenth century, the Kabbalah had become an important branch of knowledge for most North African rabbis,[49] and, since it dealt so extensively with subjects like exile and redemption or the coming of the Messiah and calculations of the end of history, it naturally strengthened the bond with the Land. Moreover, in the literature that is typical of Maghreb Jewry of this period, poetry in the style of the Golden Age of Spain emphasized the place of the Land of Israel. [Ed. note: for the Land of Israel in the poetry of Judah Halevi see comments by Shalom Rosenberg, above, p. 159.] R. Aaron Perez (Djerba, eighteenth century)[50] and R. David Hasin (Meknes, 1730–ca. 1792)[51] are only two examples. Poets of the period dedicated special poetry to the representatives (i.e., the *shelichim*) sent by those in the Land to their communities in North Africa.[52] Folk custom too, like the tradition in Djerba to put a black stripe on the cuffs of one's trousers in memory of the Temple's destruction, drew the bond to the Land even tighter.[53]

In sum, a long historical affinity, the organization of the Maghrebian community to sustain the *Yishuv* economically, and the Land of Israel in Kabbalah and poetry—as well as the prayers and the messianic hope (which they held in common with other communities as well)—all combined to make the Land of Israel an inseparable part of the consciousness of the Jews of North Africa.

Changes in the Legal and Political Status of Moroccan and Algerian Jewry: A Cause of the Change in Aliyah

Aside from communal and spiritual factors, at the end of the eighteenth and the beginning of the nineteenth centuries there were also alterations in the legal and political situation of the Jews in Morocco and Algeria; these too presented a basis for change in attitude toward *aliyah*.

As we know, Moroccan Jewry suffered drastically during the reign of the tyrannical sultan Yazid (1790–92).[54] Jewish anguish was expressed in elegies which conclude with expressions of fervent yearning for redemption.[55] More than that, there was awakened anew the messianic tension that had subsided since the time of Sabbetai Zevi, so that many of the scholars were engaged in "calculations of the end."[56] In one place it is explicitly stated that as a result of the events of Yazid, "again a movement to go up to the Land was awakened; and many of the town's inhabitants [Meknes] scattered in all directions, some to the Land, and others to the cities of Tunisia and Algeria."[57] One of the city's sages, Rabbi Mordecai Messas, intended to emigrate to the Land but was pressed to remain in Morocco to lead his people.[58]

Even though Yazid's successor Mulay Suleiman (1792–1822) annulled his predecessor's decrees, and even reestablished stability in the kingdom, still, inasmuch as he was given to being influenced by radical religious thinking, he decreed in 1807 that Jews be expelled from the centers of cities and forced to build separate quarters of their own, the *Mellahs*.[59] This legal demarcation carried extensive consequences for the conditions of Jewish life in Morocco throughout the nineteenth century: overcrowding and constrained living conditions in the Jewish quarters. At the same time, migration from the villages to the great cities, both inland and on the coast, was increasing so that crowding in these quarters was exacerbated even further. This situation pressed hundreds of Jews into migrating from the land of their birth to other countries, the Land of Israel among them.[60]

In Algeria too, the end of the eighteenth century brought about the undermining of Jewish status on account of the rise of religious zealotry, particularly in the wake of the controversies between Algeria and France regarding the sizable financial obligations of the Algerians, who included among their ranks great Jewish merchants, these being also leaders of the Algerian community. By 1805, the animosity shown by the Janissaries against the Dey and his Jewish advisor Naphtali Busnach led to persecutions in which tens of Jews were killed (according to other estimates, the numbers reached into the hundreds). At the end of the eighteenth century and as late as 1815, there were sharp conflicts with those in power which ended in eight of the community's leaders being executed.[61] This development further frightened Algerian Jews. European travellers in Algeria at the time testified that there were Jews who had witnessed the persecutions of 1805 and the execution of communal leaders, and saw in these events a divine omen that they should make *aliyah.*[62] In the years after the conquest (1830) about two hundred Jews left for the Land.[63]

The French conquest of Algeria in 1830 promised a change in social and economic conditions of Algerian Jewry, and of North African Jewry in general. It evoked hope not only in Algerian Jewish circles, but in Morocco and in Tunisia too, where Jews looked to better their social and economic status.[64] Some actually moved to Algeria, and it is to be assumed that among them, there were those who changed their mind and turned in the direction of the Land of Israel. (It is also to be expected that there were some Jews who suspected the reforms in community and religious standing that accompanied the French conquest of Algeria.)[65]

Changes in the Routes to the Land, and the Settlements Therein

Meanwhile, sea travel was becoming safer, particularly with the demise of the Corsair pirates, whose power had already dwindled at the end of the eighteenth century (when the European powers had outlawed naval brigandage) but who were now finally overthrown by the French.

The change regarding *aliyah* owes its existence also to modifications in the situation of the Jewish *Yishuv* in the Land, especially after the Egyptian conquest of 1830, and to the legal and social reforms throughout the Ottoman Empire, including the Land of Israel.[66] There was also the fact that activities initiated by the European powers and the Jews of Europe regarding the Land were becoming known in North Africa. In the forties of the nineteenth century, travellers' rumours were widespread throughout the Maghreb to the effect that wealthy Jews, chief among them, Rothschild and Montefiore, were on the verge of buying the Land from the Turks.[67]

The influence of the stream of immigrants who arrived in the Land from the Maghreb at the end of the eighteenth and at the beginning of the nineteenth centuries is readily recognizable. Its first expressions are to be found in letters from the Moroccan communities to the Sephardic community in the *Yishuv* pleading with the latter not to cut short the rightful portion that the "Western" Jews, particularly the Yeshivah students from North Africa, deserved out of the North African charitable contribution.[68] However, by the beginning of the nineteenth century, in Galilee, particularly in Tiberias and in Safed, Jews from the Maghreb had attained to a position of ascendancy over those from other Islamic lands. Among the segment of Moroccan and Algerian Jewry that grew up in Galilee,[69] were to be found those who had reached the very heights of leadership: the families of Toledano, Berdugo, Bahlul, and Ben-Yuli.[70] A sign of this ascendancy is the designation of Tiberias, found in many documents, as "The little Meknes," a reference to the great city in Morocco whence a respectable proportion of its immigrants had come.[71] Similarly, in the Galilean settlements, more and more Judaeo-Arabic (in Maghrebi dialect) was heard, and less Ladino.[72] Contributing to their status was the diplomatic protection, especially from France, to which some of the immigrants—the Abus, one of the leading families in Safed, for example—had a right.

Demographic and political changes in the Land of Israel left their mark on the preferred destinations of North African Jewry in this period. They turned more and more to Jerusalem, and played an important role (often a decisive one) in the renewal of the Jewish *Yishuv* in Jaffa, Haifa, western Galilee, and later still, in Gaza and Shechem. Contributing to the acculturation of Maghrebian Jews in the Land was the fact that so many of them were middle-aged people who worked at small businesses, artisanry, and peddling, so were able to sink roots not only in the midst of the Jewish *Yishuv* but also to establish economic ties with the Arab community as well. Their knowledge of Arabic and a way of life similar to the Arabs' made matters simpler still.[73]

Typical also of the changing situation in the Land was the drastic alteration in the number of Jews emigrating from the Maghreb. As common as it had been in the preceding period for many of the new immigrants to return to their land of origin, now, in the nineteenth century, not only did the majority of them remain in the Land, but frequently, they drew their friends and relatives after them.[74] It is difficult to estimate the exact number of Maghrebian Jews in the nineteenth century, since it was a time when census takers were inexact, but according to one survey, the decades that represent the apex of Maghrebian immigration (1830–1860) saw hundreds of people make *aliyah.*[75] All in all, the Jewish *Yishuv* in the Land during the reign of Muhammad Ali [that is, the period of Egyptian rule] for example, amounted to about 10,000 people.[76] Because of (1) the important foundation laid in this period, (2) the great mortality that followed (about half the Jewish population in the second third of the century died from sickness and plague),[77] and to some extent, (3) as mentioned above, the new commerce and industry that began to develop as part of the cycle of creativity, this *aliyah* is credited with the renewal of the Jewish *Yishuv*.

There is more to the story as well. The gradual increase in numbers from the beginning of the nineteenth century (as much as a quarter of the

Sephardic community in Jerusalem at the end of the century) constituted a central factor in the realization of the aspiration of Jews from North Africa to establish a separate organization to manage their own affairs. In 1860, a compromise was reached by which there was instituted a separation between Sephardic and "western," that is, Maghrebian, communities, by means of the establishment of reciprocal arrangements between them in certain areas.[78] (That year, however, represents the beginning of a further chapter in the history of Maghrebian Jewry and the Land of Israel—see below, "Afterward.")

Although the essence of their affinity for the Land was expressed in *aliyah*, at the same time, the Jews of North Africa continued just as before to extend secondary support to the Land. Visitations of *shelichim* from the Land reached its all time high in the nineteenth century, so that not a year went by without some *shaliach* or other coming through the Maghreb.[79] Several of them reached as far as the communities in the distant Sahara.[80] The enactments established in Fez in the seventeenth to eighteenth centuries for the support of progress in the *Yishuv*[81] extended also to other communities in the eighteenth to the nineteenth centuries.[82] These contributions, we know, were made on two principal kinds of occasion. In addition to donations that were volunteered on the Festivals, people also contributed on the occasion of family festivities, such as a *bar mitzvah* or a *brit milah*.[83] In a document from the end of the eighteenth century, we find a beautiful custom from Sefrou: if a bridegroom did not remember to make a donation to the Land, the congregation present in the synagogue protested until he was reminded of his duty.[84]

In literary sources too, which developed apace, the Land of Israel continued to hold its position as a favored theme, for example, in the poems of redemption by R. Chaim Pinto of Mogador,[85] or in the kabbalistic and ethical tracts of R. Jacob Avi-Hasira (from the Tafilalt area on the Algerian-Moroccan border).[86]

Afterword: Aliyah of Maghrebian Jews to the Land, 1800–1860, as an Integral Part of Communal Life

In the period under discussion, development was rapid and significant. It began as a stream of individuals in the second half of the eighteenth century. But the reaction of the rabbis, the leaders of the community, was conditioned by their spiritual approach to things known already from the late seventeenth century with regard to other social problems.[87]

There are still questions that require answers before we can estimate with absolute certainty the causes of the change. Did the spread of internal conservative tendencies and the rejection of Europe, both so typical of the Moslem world in the period under discussion, play a role in influencing also the Jews—as strangers, now, in the Arab milieu, and, therefore, identified with Europeans—to adopt the strategy of making *aliyah?* In a fragment of an account of a journey through Libya, from the fifth decade of the nineteenth century, an Anglican priest describes the messianic faith of the Jews in the region of Misrata, and of people caught up in the spirit of eschatology—according to a report passed on to him via a Moslem religious sage. According to a Moslem vision of the end of days, the appointed time of the Dajal—the Jewish enemy of the redeemer (according to Moslem tradition)—to rule the world, had come and gone. After that, the Christian messiah would make his appearance and kill the Dajal. And the final stage would be when the Wahabites, a puritanical dynasty which had begun to rule around the end of the eighteenth century, would destroy the Jewish community.[88] These feelings, which must have influenced the Moslem masses in the Maghreb (as well as the ruling circles, such as the sultan of Morocco, Mulay Suleiman [1792–1822], who was greatly influenced by the wahabiyya), created a more turbulent climate for Jews. In the course of the nineteenth century, the Jewish position, which could never be described as particularly stable, deteriorated even more, and, naturally, served as an additional spur toward *aliyah*.

As yet, evaluation of the change in attitude cannot be complete, since our data on the subject under discussion is still lacking (and not always substantiated). *Aliyah* from Tunisia, the third great Jewish center in the Maghreb in the nineteenth century (besides Morocco and Algeria) is practically undocumented. It would seem that *aliyah* from there was somewhat less than it was from the other countries. But perhaps this tentative conclusion depends on an argument from silence regarding the paucity of sources from that area. According to information appearing in *Hator*, the newspaper of the Land at the turn of the twentieth century, in 1777 (a year of large-scale *aliyah* from eastern Europe) a group of 130 Jews arrived from Tunis.[89] To be sure, a very active *shaliach* was making his rounds in Tunis at the time, and he may have played a role in instigating the *aliyah*.[90] And this is to be added to the echoes from the Maghreb, the Mediterranean, and the Land itself, that must have been heard in Tunisia, in Tunis, and in Djerba and elsewhere.

Whatever the nature of our knowledge in these matters, one conclusion is crystal-clear: *aliyah* from North Africa to the Land of Israel became a regularized matter in the first half of the nineteenth century. The documents that were examined in the last stages of preparing this essay (they are located in Alberta in western Canada!) provide additional support for this conclusion. Communal scholars and "secular" authorities (*Negidim*) in the west thought and spoke of the Land as if it were an intimate part of their daily experience. In a document from 1841, the general *shaliach*, Rabbi Raphael Halevi, praises the fervent attachment of the people in *hama'arav hapenimi*, the inland regions of the west, that is, Morocco, for the Land.[91] *Shelichim* from the Land were such regular visitors to that country, that the *Nagid* of Fez at the time issued a regular directive on the itineraries of *shelichim* in the hope that they would succeed.[92] From 1860 to 1917, the bonds connecting Jews of the Maghreb and those in the Land of Israel were solidified even further, in that they were extended to the inhabitants of the entire area, particularly in the many new communities which had arisen in Algeria in the period.

Thus, throughout the entire Maghreb, the tie to the Land of Israel, always present, sometimes somewhat dormant, grew to the point where it became a major factor in Jewish self-identity.

Notes

*The author wishes to thank the Memorial Foundation for Jewish Culture for the research grant which aided in the study for and writing of this essay. I also want to thank Prof. Y. Dan for his encouragement to apply to the foundation, and to my teachers and mentors, Profs. H. Beinart and S. Ettinger, for their recommendations.

1. Main sources for this summary essay dating from the end of the fifteenth cent. throughout the period under discussion were collected and published in S. Bar Asher, ed., *Yehudei Artsot Ha'islam Ve'erets Yisra'el Beme'ot Ha 17–19* pt. 1 "North Africa and Egypt," (Jerusalem, 1980); a prior survey of some of the sources in this collection can be found in S. Ettinger, ed., *Toldot Hayehudim Be'artsot Ha'islam* (Jerusalem, 1982), pp. 191–94. Similarly, see the collection edited by this author with A. Maman, *Yehudei Tsefon Africa Ve'erets Yisra'el* (Jerusalem, 1981). Also very important are two works by Eliezer Bashan — see below, notes 16 and 62. My essay here and these two complement each other.

2. See J. Meisel, *Reshimat Yehudei Tsfat Usevivoteha Mishnat 5599*, a demographic-statistical study compiled on the basis of the census organized under the direction of Moses Montefiore, *Sefunot* 6 (1962), p. 445.

3. See D. Obadiah, *Kehilot Sefrou* (Jerusalem, 1975), vols. I, II, Indices.

4. See N. 1, above.

5. See M. D. Gaon, "Moshe Montefiore Ved'agato Legoral Benei Adat Hayehudim Hama'aravi'im Birushalayim," in *Minchah Le'avraham: Jubilee Volume Presented to Abraham Elmaleh on the Occasion of His Seventieth Birthday* (Jerusalem, 1959), pp. 179–80.

6. This was the goal of several great scholars, such as Rabbi Yehudah Ayyash, the leader of the Jews in Algeria in the first half of the eighteenth cent. See his essay, *She'elot Uteshuvot Benei Yehudah* (Leghorn, 1758), p. 204a.

7. Such was the impetus for the *aliyah* of Rabbi Chaim Ben Atar from Morocco. See what is included of his writings in B. Ts. Dinur, ed., *Sefer Hatsionut* (Tel Aviv, 1939), vol. 1, pt. 1, p. 51.

8. See n. 5, above.

9. The Sefrou document typifies this type of composition. See D. Obadiah, *op. cit.*, vol. I, pp. 163–64. On the economic structure of North African Jewry, see my chapter on the economy in Ettinger, note 1 above.

10. See his book *She'elot Uteshuvot Beit Yehudah* (Leghorn, 1758), sec. 54, p. 40a–b.

11. For example, see P. Berdugo, *Nofet Tsofim* (Casablanca, 1939), "Chosen Mishpat," par. 22, pp. 85b–86b; par. 131, p. 116; par. 132, pp. 116b–117b.

12. Typical is the sage cited in ibid., par. 133, p. 117b.

13. The basis of the halachic discussion can be found in the Mishnah, M. Ket. 13:11: "All may be compelled to go up to the Land of Israel but none may be compelled to leave it. All may be compelled to go up to Jerusalem but none may be compelled to leave it, whether they be men or women" (H. Danby, *The Mishnah* [Oxford, 1933], p. 263).

The Talmud cites an additional source, this baraita (Ket. 111b: "If [the husband] desires to go up [to the Land of Israel] and his wife refuses she must be pressed to go up; and if [she does] not [consent] she may be divorced without payment of the ketubah. [Conversely, she may force him to go up to the Land of Israel.]" Through their discussion of this and other questions, the sages expressed their position on the primary obligation in their day to move to the Land of Israel. By the twelfth and thirteenth centuries, two positions on the issue had emerged. Nachmanides is prominent amongst the *rishonim* who held that the obligation to settle in the Land of Israel was a continuing affirmative commandment deriving from the Torah, within the general category of "conquest of the Land" and therefore constituted a continuing obligation throughout all generations. See Ch. D. Chavel, ed., *Sefer Hamitsvot Larambam* and *Hasagot Haramban* (Jerusalem, 1981), 244–46. Opposed to them was the position expressed primarily by the sages of France and Germany in the eleventh and twelfth centuries, among them, Rabbi Chaim ben Hananel Hacohen (one of the Tosaphists). They ruled that the law in M. Ket. 11:13 was not in force in their day. They based this ruling on two different grounds: 1) the danger of travel; 2) the status of the other commandments which are dependent on residence in the Land of Israel (e.g. the Sabbatical year) – after hundreds of years in exile during which Jews were not involved in agriculture, there were no authorities in the application of these laws – (commentary to Ket. 111a). Through the Middle Ages, the sages of North Africa limited themselves primarily to the question of whether it was dangerous to travel to the Land of Israel by land or by sea in order to avoid the commandment of settlement. Rabbi Shlomo ben Shimeon Duran, who served in Algiers in the fifteenth century, saw in *aliyah* an elementary mitsvah in Judaism and leveled criticism at the medieval philosophers who held that *aliyah* neither adds to nor detracts from the perfection of man. See "Shlomo ben Shimeon Duran" *Ha'Entsiklopedia Ha'ivrit* vol. 2, pp. 244–45. Nonetheless, he set a legitimate geographical standard regarding the dangers of travel (*She'elot Uteshuvot* [Leghorn, 1741] Sec. A, p. 2b, cols. 3–4): "At this time [i.e. in the 15th century] in the Western lands that is, I intend, all who dwell from the extreme West [Morocco] to No'amon [Alexandria] do not compel [the spouse] to go up [to the Land of Israel]; and from No'amon upward, they do compel [the spouse to move in order to fulfill the commandment] to dwell [in the Land of Israel], and they also go by way of the sea during the dry season, if there are no thieves on the sea." (Pirates preyed on ships in the Mediterranean; the major center of piracy was in Algiers.) There are no sources from the *maghreb* on this question from the sixteenth and seventeenth centuries. Apparently, interest in the problem waxed and waned.

14. Rabbi Ya'akov ben-Tsur. *Mishpat Utsedakah Beya'akov* (Alexandria, 1892), vol. I, sec. 159, p. 100a.

15. Ibid., sec. 28, pp. 44a–45a.

16. Berdugo, *op. cit.*, sec. 25, p. 41a. A. Bashan. "Yachasam shel Chokhmei Moroko Bema'ot Ha-18-19 Lechovat Ha'aliyah Le'erets Yisra'el," *Vatikin* 1 (1974), pp. 39–40. He shows that Rabbi Petachia ruled as he did because he feared the problems involved with the fulfillment of the commandments contingent on settlement in the Land of Israel; see note 13 above. Besides the additions on this point, he does not raise those commandments contingent on the settlement of the land as a reason, but rather, the two topics I noted. Compare Berdugo, *op. cit.*, sec. 133, where he says that when he changed his opinion it was because the dangers had disappeared.

17. Rabbi Moshe Toledano, *Hashamayim Hachadashim* (Casablanca, 1937), pp. 30b–31b. Bashan. *op. cit.*, p. 38. He is not accurate and notes that the authority is Rabbi Moshe Toledano. While the work in which Rabbi Joseph's words are cited is that of his grandfather, Rabbi Moshe, this responsum is signed by Rabbi Joseph.

18. *Hashamayim Hachadashim*, p. 31a, col. b.

19. Y. Ayash, *op. cit.*, p. 40a–b.

20. This sage had a large part in the development of his community and its transformation into an important spiritual center in Morocco.

21. Rabbi Saul Abitbol, *Avnei Shai'ish* (Jerusalem, 1933), sec. 94, pp. 67b–68a.

22. Ibid., p. 67b.

23. Ibid.

24. Ibid. Compare a similar matter: Y. Berdugo, *Shufreh Deya'akov* (Jerusalem, 1909), sec. 61; p. 42a, col 1. "V'ha'ech titkayem hamishnah . . ."

25. Abitbol, *loc. cit.*

26. Ibid.

27. A. Finkelstein, ed. *Sifrei al Devarim* (Berlin, 1839), p. 146.

28. Chavel, *loc. cit.*

29. Abitbol, *op. cit.*, p. 67a, col. 1.

30. Ibid., col. 2.

31. Ibid., p. 68a, col. 1.

32. Ibid.

33. See R. Laurido-Diaz, *Marruecos en la Segunda Mitad del Siglo XVIII* (Madrid, 1978), pp. 201–13.

34. See, for example, the historian of the period, A. K. al-Zayyani, *Al-Khabar min Awal Dawlat min al-Ashraf al-'Alawiyyin min Awlad Mawlana al-Sharif bin-'Ali* (Paris, 1903), pp. 72–73.

35. Laurido-Diaz; see n. 33, above.

36. Like R. Petachiah Berdugo, or R. Jacob Berdugo. See his book, *Shufreh Deya'akov*, p. 52b, col. 4.

37. See above.

38. See n. 12, above.

39. *Rav Penimim*, in the Passover Haggadah *Peh Yesharim Hamurchav* (Tel Aviv, 1975), pp. 74–75.

40. Ibid.

41. See R. Raphael Berdugo, *Torot Emet* (Meknes, 1939), p. 38, col. 1.

42. H. Z. Hirschberg, "Hakesharim ben Yehudei Hamagrebh uven Eretz Yisra'el Bitekufat Hageonim," in *Eretz Yisra'el* 5 (1959): 213–19.

43. See, for example, the essay on Algeria: M. Weinstein, "Hakesharim ben Yehudei Algeria uven Eretz Yisra'el Mishenat 1391 ad Kibush Hatsorfati (1830)," in *Vatikin* 1 (1975): 10–14.

44. Y. Ben Tzvi, *Eretz Yisra'el Veyishuvah Bimei Hashilton Ha'otomani* (Jerusalem, 1968), pp. 143, 147.

45. See n. 43, above.

46. *Sefer Hatakkanot* in *Takkanot Yehudei Morocco* (Jerusalem, 1977), *Takkanah* 48:34; cf. A. Ya'ari, *Sheluchei Eretz Yisra'el* (Jerusalem, 1977), pp. 226–30.

47. Ibid., 46.

48. The book by Ya'ari, mentioned in n. 46 is a lexicon of these ties. See the index of entries for Morocco, Algeria, Tunisia, and Tripoli.

49. See Bar Asher in the middle collection listed in n. 1, above, pp. 176–78.

50. M. Saraf, "R. Aaron Perets—Payyetan of Djerba in the 18th Century" (Hebrew), *Pe'amim* 6 (1981): 112–14.

51. One of the 14 sections in his Divan is *Zimrat Ha'aretz Tehillah Ledavid* (Casablanca, 1931), 17, pp. 17a–18b.

52. See, for example, R. Jacob Berdugo, *Kol Ya'akov* (London, 1844), 85–86.

53. *Sefer Djerba Yehudit* (Jerusalem, n.d.), 67.

54. For a summary of this period, see S. Bar Asher, *Hakehillah Hayehudit Bemorocco Bemeiah Hashemonah Esrei*, doctoral dissertation, Hebrew University, Jerusalem, pp. 6–7.

55. For example, see the elegy published by D. Kaufman, "Une Elégie de David ben Aron Ibn Houssein (=Hassin) sur les souffrances des Juifs au Maroc en 1790," *REJ*, 37 (1898), pp. 120–26.

56. For example, see R. S.J. Abitbol, *Avnei Kodesh* in *Avnei Shayish*, vol. 2 (Jerusalem, 1934), p. 38b.

57. See Joseph Meshash, *Otsar Hamichtavim* (Jerusalem, 1968), 1, Introduction, 13.

58. Ibid., and cf. above regarding R. Judah Ayash.

59. D. Corcos, *Studies in the History of the Jews of Morocco* (Jerusalem, 1976), pp. 92ff.

60. See M. Abitbol, *Mishpachat Corcos Vehahistoriyah shel Morocco Bizmanenu* (Jerusalem, 1978), pp. 13–18.

61. This development is described extensively by Hirschberg, *Toldot Hayehudim Be'africa Hatsefonit* (Jerusalem, 1968), pp. 66–74.

62. Bashan, "Zikatam shel Yehudei Hamaghreb Le'eretz Yisra'el," *Bar Ilan Yearbook* 14–15 (1977), p. 173. See also p. 174, the words of the American consul to Algeria to the effect that 1816 elderly Jews "hired a boat to the Land."

63. See S. Schwartzfuchs, *Hayehudim Vehashilton Hatzorfati (1830–1855)* (Jerusalem, 1981).

64. M. Eisnebeth, *Les Juifs d'Afrique du Nord, demographie et onomastique* (Algiers, 1936), p. 13.

65. See M. Aliav, *Erets Yisra'el Veyishuvah Bemeiah Hateshah Esrei: 1777–1917* (Jerusalem, 1978), pp. 42–47.

66. See the essay by Y. Bernay, in the collection mentioned last in note 1, above, p. 94.

67. See Y. M. Toledano, *Otsar Genazim* (Jerusalem, 1960), pp. 164–68.

68. Ibid., p. 164.

69. Ibid., p. 169.

70. See Abishar, ed., *Sefer Teveriah* (Jerusalem, 1973), p. 120.

71. Toledano, *Otsar Genazim*, p. 165.

72. Ibid., p. 165.

73. See A. Ya'ari, *Sinai* 25 (1950), pp. 336, 344–45.

74. See the essay by Z. Vilnay, "Hayehudim Hama'araviyim Bechalutsei Hayishuv Ba'aretz," in the collection mentioned in n. 1, above, pp. 86–90.

75. See n. 63, above; cf. the Introduction to *Otsar Hamichtavim*, p. 14, to the effect that in one month alone, in the year 1843–1844, 70 immigrants left Meknes alone; "and from all the cities [in the rest of Morocco], tremendous caravans made *aliyah*." Similarly, individual *aliyot* left Meknes in 1853 and in 1855.

76. For an explanation, see Y. Ben-Aryeh, "Hitpatchut He'arim Be'eretz Yisra'el," in *Habistoriyah shel Eretz Yisra'el, Shilahei Hatekufah Ha'otmanit – 1799–1917*, vol. 8 (Jerusalem, 1983), pp. 67–109.

77. See A. Schmeltz, *Perakim Betoldot Hayishuv Hayehudi Birushalayim*, vol. 2 (Jerusalem, 1976), pp. 65–72; and the entire essay there, pp. 52–76.

78. See Y. Bernay's essay, "Ha'eidah Hama'aravit Birushalayim Bamei'ah Hatesha Esrei," in the anthology edited by S. Bar Asher and A. Maman, cited in n. 1, pp. 97–100.

79. See n. 48, above, with its sources for the 19th cent.

80. See S. Ziv (Agini), in *Shevet Va'am* (Jerusalem, 2nd series, 1 (1971), p. 190, the first document on the page.

81. See the source cited in n. 46, above; and also, there, Takkanah #145, pp. 74–75.

82. See, for example, the congregation of Sefrou, the source cited in n. 9, pp. 85–86; and *Otsar Genazim*, pp. 128–29.

83. Cf. the 1st source cited in n. 81, and those in the note prior to it.

84. *Otsar Genazim*, p. 87.

85. See, for example, the poem *Enkat Asir-*, in R. Chaim Attar, ed., *Shir Yedidot* (Jerusalem, 1961), pp. 156–57.

86. See D. Manor, *Kabbalah Umusar Bemorocco, Darko shel Rabbi Yaakov Abichatsira* (Jerusalem, 1982).

87. On this, see Bar Asher in the composition cited in n. 54, above, pp. 54–62, 82–90. I have expanded this issue in the first lecture of "Halakhah and History: On Certain Aspects of Jewish Communal Life in Morocco in the 18th Century," The Conference on Jews in the 18th Century, Harvard University, April, 1984.

88. J. Richardson, *Travels in the Great Desert of Sahara in the Years 1845–1846*, vol. 1 (London, 1970), pp. 256–57.

89. 15 (1924), 8.

90. The Bension Collection of Sephardic Manuscripts and Texts, the University of Alberta (Canada) Library, Special Collections Department, B.C.Y.R. Ms. 283; and cf. mss. 278–79, 284, 288.

91. Ibid., 178.

92. Ibid., 44.

Contemporary Hermeneutics and Self-Views on the Relationship between State and Land

URIEL TAL, *z"l*

[Editor's note: The premature death of Dr. Uriel Tal was a tragic loss to the scholarly community, and to the larger world of men and women committed to humanitarian concerns of which the author was a prominent champion; he insisted throughout his lifetime on concerning himself with the things that matter most, the monumental ideas which, he believed, imprint history with their train of consequences. Of late, the Land of Israel loomed ever larger as such an idea, so Tal trained his scholarly sights on how it was becoming a formative factor in the contemporary range of ideologies that motivate Israel's intellectuals as well as its politics. He reported his findings in several arenas of public debate, both written and oral, including the chapter that follows, which was prepared originally in 1982 as part of the International Colloquium in Memory of the Late Professor Jacob L. Talmon. Shortly before he died, he gave permission to have it reproduced here. We gladly include it, despite some lacunae in the manuscript which the author left with us before he died.

Taking as his starting point Peter Berger's sociology of societal crisis, which posits the decisive role of "religious symbolizations" that direct mass movements at such times, Tal surveys contemporary treatises that center on the critical question of whether "our era is one of eschatological fulfillment or even apocalyptic salvation, or are we in the realm of historical time?" His essay provides a guide to the ideological debate underlying the headlines of today's newspapers, as he surveys the essays, bulletins, tracts, and speeches of representatives of the State of Israel's various parties, from Gush Emunim (on the one hand) to Oz Veshalom (on the other), for both of whom the sacrality of the Land is still an issue that commands political action in one way or another. His findings lead him to survey the relationship between theology and politics, and to conclude with a statement of "the dilemma of political theology" by which categories of history are transformed into political mythology, with consequences—either destructive or redemptive, depending on one's perspective—for actual societies engaged in the historical process.]

I. Introduction

The texts which are dealt with in this treatise reflect two divergent trends in Jewish religious nationalism in Israel—one of political messianism and one of the politics of religious restraint. Both revolve about different assumptions regarding the way in which the fact of a now-existent State of Israel alters the Jew's historical relationship with the Land of Israel.

The first group of texts is characterized by the collection of essays entitled *Eretz Nachalah* ("Land Possessed as an Inheritance"), written, among others, by leading teachers and members of the Gush Emunim movement.[1] They postulate that the Six Day War brought about radical changes in both our physical and metaphysical status; that the military victory was an astonishing and divine miracle; that the end of days—the eschatological era of redemption—has already begun and is being realized here and now. Using mystical terminology it is said that through the conquest of the Land Eretz Yisra'el has been redeemed from oppression by the *Sitra Achra* (literally, the "other side," or the "side of evil") and has entered the realm of all-embracing sanctity. Through the war, the *Shekhinah*, the Divine Presence dwelling among us, was elevated from the dust, for it too had been in exile. Hence, if we were to return one single strip of Land to the Nations, we would give control back to the forces of evil.[2] In this same strain, some of the leading participants in *Nekudah* (the journal of the settlements in the West Bank), interpret the latest campaign, the Shalom Hagalil War, as another sanctified war, another religious duty,[3] while Israel's military presence in Southern Lebanon is interpreted as evidence of the divine promise to the holy congregation of Israel to own ". . . every place whereon the soles of your feet shall tread . . . from the wilderness and Lebanon, from the river, the river Euphrates, even unto the uttermost sea shall your coast be. . . ."[4]

The second group of texts expresses the attitude of religious Zionists, such as the members of the Oz Veshalom movement, who oppose the stand of the Gush Emunim, yet also accept the *Halakhah* as the unquestionable binding authority in Judaism. They conceive the religious law as liberating the Jew from excesses of piety, zeal, and ecstasy. They argue that, ultimately, the mystification of social and political reality, as propounded by the Gush Emunim, is likely to retard the rational character of religious, social, and intellectual life, as well as the growth of an open society and of a democratic state. They are apprehensive of the possibility of a totalitarian political authority which could easily arise from fanaticism, and they warn of danger to the moral character of the society, and of the loss of political realism and civil responsibility should politics be mystically consecrated.[5]

The methodological point of departure used herein is similar to that used by Peter L. Berger in his studies of the social aspects of a theory of religion. He points out that one of the social functions of religion is the legitimization of "situations in terms of all-encompassing sacred reality."[6] Accordingly, situations of crisis, of tension, of threat to realities previously taken for granted and to the stability of one's existence, are often characterized by the experience of spiritual ecstasy. While ecstasy is usually thought of in terms of an individual phenomenon, in times of crisis entire societies have been known to experience it. When crises, such as natural catastrophes, social upheavals, or wars, give rise to the use of violence, it is frequently "accompanied by religious symbolizations" interpreted in mystic, ecstatic, and often (as Thomas Luckmann would have it), self-imposed totalitarian forms of political culture.

At this point, Berger emphasizes that these observations do not imply a sociologically deterministic theory of religion; nor do they constitute a behavioristic oversimplification claiming that any religious system applied to social and political institutions is nothing but the reflection of socio-political needs. Rather, if religion functions as a consecrating agent for social and political structures, those structures turn into totalities, into nondemocratic or antidemocratic forms of political behavior. Berger points out that the interrelationship of society and politics, on the one hand, and of consecrating religion, on the other, is a dialectical one. Accordingly, in a particular historical development, a social process is the effect of religious ideation, while in another situation, the reverse may be the case.

This last point is of great significance in the study of the two different and opposing trends in religious Zionism—that of political messianism, which conceives of the State of Israel as a metahistorical phenomenon realized in concrete history, and that of political democracy, which conceives of the State of Israel as a historical phenomenon symbolizing, inter alia, metahistorical values. If human activity and the individual within the larger social reality are conceived not merely in terms of reacting functions, but also as acting factors—initiating, forming, conditioning their concrete "Lebenswelt" as the social phenomenologist Alfred Schutz emphasized[7]—we may assume that the dichotomy, if not schism, between these trends cannot be reduced to a function of social background only. Indeed, the social background— ethnic origin, social stratification, age group, economic status, professions, education, and cultural milieu—of the members of both trends is practically identical. Hence, one of the major factors creating the split between these two camps may be what Berger calls "religious ideation." Or, it may be defined as the hermeneutical interpretation of the same religious norms according to different, sometimes opposing, interpretations, which are chosen, applied, and accepted by the believer. The ability to develop alternative explications of the same source and then to accept the yoke or consequences thereof, is perhaps one of the major strengths of Halakhic Judaism. A significant example is the drastic difference of positions taken by Rabbi Shaul Yisraeli and the late Rabbi Zvi Yehudah Kook.[8]

What, then, is the historical meaning of the State of Israel as understood by religious Zionists; what is the function of time and space in political realities? Is our time—our era—one of eschatological fulfillment or even of apocalyptical salvation, or are we in the realm of historical time? As far as the Land itself is concerned, is the sanctity of space, the domain in which the State of Israel expands, dependent on politically fixed boundaries, or are territorial boundaries conceived in terms of historical, hence changing, space?[9]

II. Political Messianism

By its own self-definition, the messianic trend is radical and uncompromising. It can be found in the Gush Emunim, among large sections of the religious Zionist youth movements, in public schools, high school *yeshivot*, student bodies, military units of *yeshivot*, settlers in the territories, and members and supporters of movements such as Greater Eretz Yisra'el, the *Techiyah* political party, and others.[10]

This trend interprets time in terms of a metaphysical fulfillment. This meaning of time is explicated in rabbinic interpretations of the difference between this world and the messianic age. The Babylonian sage, Samuel, asserts (Ber. 34b) that the only distinction between this world and the messianic age is "political subjugation," or the "subjugation of the exiles," meaning that the messianic age is a historical and political concept which lends itself to embodiment in concrete reality. It is not primarily a cosmic concept. As Maimonides emphasized, in the era of political redemption the King Messiah should not be expected to perform wonders (*Hilkhot Melakhim* 20:3). It follows that cosmic, drastic changes in the order of creation, the universe, and nature, which are prophesied for the final stage of redemption do not refer to the messianic age, and should not be expected at the current stage of political messianism, for they are related to a distant, unknown future in the world to come (cf. San. 99a).

Therefore, according to Rabbi Shlomo Goren's *Torat Hamo'adim*[11] — which seems to be a major source for this trend's orthodox political philosophy — such prophecies of cosmic redemption are not yet relevant to our time; rather, our political, military, concrete, worldly situation constitutes the beginning of the messianic age. Hence, according to Rabbi Shlomo Aviner, we are already in the era of the Revealed End, and "we affirm the absolute certitude of the appearance of the redemption now. Nothing here is in the realm of the secret or hidden." Ezekiel's prophecy, "O mountains of Israel ye shall shoot forth your branches and yield your fruit to My people of Israel, for they are at hand to come," renewed and reaffirmed in the eschatological yearnings of talmudic sages (as in Sanhedrin 98a), is — according to Rabbi Aviner and a growing number of political believers — being realized before our eyes. For indeed the agricultural settlement in our Land is generously bearing fruit.[12]

The thrust of this approach is that the mystique of the redemption has become tangible, concrete, and actual rather than covert. The commencement of the messianic age is revealed in the conquest of the Land, political sovereignty, and the ingathering of the exiles; only later will eschatological changes take place on a cosmic scale. Hence, our days should be understood in light of the Exodus from Egypt and the conquest by Joshua, for then too the events took place in a natural way, inaugurating the times of redemption through victorious warfare.[13]

A similar interpretation of redemptive time is related to the talmudic sage Rabbi Hiyya bar Abba who said in the name of Rabbi Johanan, "All the prophets prophesized only concerning the messianic age." This concept is now interpreted as a significant step forward in political messianism, as it claims that all prophecies, including those about changes of a cosmic nature, relate to concrete redemptive times — at which we have allegedly arrived. Indeed, Zvi Yehudah Kook and an ever-expanding number of disciples claim that since we are already in the New Era, in the era of personal salvation and national redemption, an existential political situation of totality, rather than of tolerance, has been inaugurated. This totality of holiness which now engulfs all aspects of reality was expounded in a symptomatic collection of sermons called *Hama'alot Mima'amakim* (published after the 1973 Yom Kippur War by Yeshivat Har Etzion): "We have to see the greatness of this hour in its biblical dimension, and it can be seen only through the messianic perspective . . . only in the light of the Messiah. . . . Why did the war of Gog and Magog come?. . . . After the establishment of the Kingdom of Israel the war can have only one significance: the purification, refining, and cleansing of the congregation of Israel."[14]

The second category of historical self-understanding is space. Space undergoes an exegetical reformulation similar to that of time. It assumes the form of and encompasses sanctified localities and neighborhoods and venerated sites such as burial grounds, gravestones, walls, and trees. It is the setting for events that took place or are believed to have taken place in the holy, promised, Land.

In recent years, the interpretation of the holiness of space has transcended the original halakhic meaning. According to the original meaning (stated for example in M. Kelim 1:6), the Land is holy because only there is it possible to fulfill the *mitzvot hateluyot ba'aretz,* i.e. to observe the religious and ritual laws concerning agriculture, socio-economic customs and ways of life related to rural economy. Now, however, following ancient or medieval folklore and folkways, the Land itself becomes holy rather than merely pointing to a metaspace; the space has actually become the incarnation of metahistorical holiness.

Among the sources of inspiration and political justification for this concept are biblical traditions related to the patriarchs. We read in Genesis of Abraham passing through the Land to Shechem, or Moreh; Sarah dying in Kiryat Arba ("the same is Hebron") and being buried in the cave of Machpelah. Eventually the land, the fields, the caves, the trees, the rocks and "all the borders round about" were "made sure unto Abraham for a possession," and promised by the Lord "unto thy seed." According to this perception, those places have become a metahistorical reality. Once these primordial roots are uncovered, the sanctification of place becomes a practical, political, not simply a theological, necessity.[15]

A systematic and dogmatic point of departure in this matter is found in Nachmanides' notes to the fourth positive commandment of Maimonides' *Sefer Hamitzvot,* the code enumerating the commandments, and his commentary to Numbers 33:53, 54: "And you shall take possession of the Land and settle in it, for I have given the Land to you to possess it." Nachmanides teaches that "we are commanded to take possession of the Land . . . we should not leave it in the hands of any other people or allow it to lie in waste." The essence of this commandment, in the words of Nachmanides, is "that we are commanded to enter the Land, to conquer its cities, and to settle our tribes there . . . for this is the commandment of conquest. . . ."

This source is cited as a binding normative authority in many studies, sermons, and treatises, including the Independence Day prayer book widely used by observant and nonobservant Jews and, recently, in a most significant ruling of the Council of the Chief Rabbinate headed by Rabbi Shlomo Goren and endorsed by Prime Minister Begin. Here, the oft-debated prohibition against withdrawing from the territories and surrendering parts of the Holy Land once they are conquered is strongly emphasized. In its session of March 1979, the Council ruled that this prohibition rests on the biblical commandment ". . . show them no mercy" *lo techonnem.* Deuteronomy 7:2 teaches that when the children of Israel were to have conquered the Land and dispossessed its inhabitants, they were commanded "thou shalt make no covenant with them, nor show mercy unto them" *(velo techonnem).* The Talmud *(AZ* 20 aff.) as well as Maimonides *(Hilkhot Akkum* 10:3–6, the rules concerning relations with gentiles or idolaters) interpret this phrase in several ways, among them the one emphasized by the Council: "You shall not give them a place of settlement on the soil." Here, *techonnem* is derived from *chnh,* "to encamp," rather than from *chnn,* "to show mercy." Referring to the "Covenant Between the Pieces" (Gen. 15) and subsequent talmudic interpretations *(BB* 191ab, and *AZ* 53b), the Council, led by Chief Rabbi Shlomo Goren and opposed by Chief Rabbi Ovadiah Yosef, added that the prohibition against ceding any of the occupied territories is derived from the fact that the possession of the Land is a divinely ordained inheritance. Hence Rabbi Goren and the Council overruled the opinion that even according to the Bible, parts of the Land could be surrendered to non-Jewish political powers, as with Solomon's gift of twenty Galilean cities to Hiram (I Kings), for in II Chronicles we learn the contrary—"that the cities which Hiram had restored to Solomon, Solomon built them and caused the children of Israel to dwell there."[16]

Thus, according to this trend, a total and uncompromising sanctity rests upon the current boundaries; we are in the era of messianic redemption, with the splendor and the glory and the total normative authority of eschatological salvation realized in our political situation.

III. Politics of Religious Restraint

The opposing trend in religious Zionism argues that contemporary political reality should be understood by applying rational and socio-ethical self-restraint, and that this approach is precisely what the *Halakhah,* the rabbinic law in its historical unfolding, requires.

The proponents of this second trend tend to be moderate and to urge compromise, as far as politics are concerned, for the sake of a historical rather than a metahistorical self-understanding. They are found in the Oz Veshalom movement, among members of the renewed Torah Ve'avodah which hopes to revive the religious Labor Zionist tradition, in the religious kibbutz movement, among members of the recently founded Netivot Shalom ("Paths of Peace") movement, and also within circles mentioned in connection with the first trend.

A systematic point of departure, as Ephraim E. Urbach pointed out years ago,[17] is the interpretation of the *Halakhah* as a factor which throughout history has freed Judaism from an excess of ecstasy or asceticism, from political romanticism, from the totality of time and space structured as myths. Accordingly, it is now argued that a mystification of political circumstances cannot but disrupt the peace process in the Middle East. While the sanctity of the Land is firmly maintained, territorial boundaries are to be conceived as historical phenomena, as results of political and strategic as well as moral considerations, and hence, if necessary, subject to change.

From these primary assumptions, a restraining policy condemning extremism as being contrary to the spirit of true Judaism is derived. The Oz Veshalom movement—in its published *Principles*, and according to its leading members such as Moshe Unna, Uriel Simon, Yosef Walk—advocates territorial and political concessions rather than fanaticism and radicalism.[18] Ethical rather than militant criteria are emphasized, due to the belief that prolonged imposed rule over ethnic or religious minorities such as the Arab population of the Land of Israel cannot but distort the democratic and ethical foundations of Jewish society. The personal and moral integrity of the rulers themselves, as of our youth, is at stake. Hence compromise, strongly commended in items 3 and 4 of the *Principles*, is understood as a religious value, as kibbutz member D. Elazar has shown referring to the Talmudic explication (San. 6b) of Zechariah's saying, "Execute the judgment of truth and peace in your gates." Precedent for compromise as a peaceful solution to conflicts of interest is adduced in several halakhically strict juridical matters (*Hilkhot Sanhedrin* 2:7 and the *Shulhan Arukh's* Ch. M. 12:2). As Uriel Simon points out, Abraham practiced compromise in order to make peace between his shepherds and those of Lot. The adoption of this policy for the sake of peace was rewarded by God's reconfirmation, in Genesis, of Abraham's right to the whole of the Land.[19]

Also, as Mordecai Breuer has pointed out,[20] from a strict halakhic point of view, there is no justification for the argument against territorial compromise if such compromise would indeed seriously enhance the peace process in the Middle East and thus the prospect of saving lives. Building his hermeneutical elaboration on authorities such as Rabbi Abraham Isaac Kook and Rabbi Abraham Yeshaya Karelitz, Breuer shows that the *lo techon-nem* clause, the prohibition from giving or selling land in Eretz Yisra'el to non-Jews, does not necessarily extend to the question of territorial surrender, especially if political and military experts are convinced that such an act may help avoid bloodshed. Moreover, in contrast to the late Rabbi Zvi Yehudah Kook, and to Rabbis Abraham Kahana-Shapira and Ya'akov Ariel Stiglitz who ruled that the conflict between Jews and Arabs is subsumed under the category of "religious persecution," which categorically calls for martyrdom, Breuer warns against the abuse of that motive. He says that inciting true believers to undertake unnecessary hazards simply out of zealous passion and ecstasy should be avoided. Referring to major halakhic authorities such as Maimonides (*Hilkhot Avodah Zarah* 5:2, 3, 4), Breuer argues, as does Rabbi Yishai Yovel,[21] that the Jewish-Arab conflict is hardly motivated by what the *Halakhah* calls "religious persecution," the attempt of non-Jews (in this case, Moslems) to force Jews to transgress their law and/or to apostatize (here to Islam). Hence from the *Shulchan Arukh*, (*Y.D.* 157), we infer that what is required in this conflict is not blind martyrdom but a readiness to compromise, albeit with a firm stand on the Jews' right to the Land of Israel.

It is this understanding of the calling to fulfill the *Halakhah* in a socio-ethical way which leads these religious Zionists to a historical rather than a metahistorical concept of time and space. Time is interpreted in the spirit of Maimonides' restraining teachings about the messianic era. Accordingly, the sages and the prophets await the days of the Messiah (*Hilkhot Melakhim* 12:3) not that they might rule over the world, nor that they might lord it over other nations, but "that they might be free to engage in the study of the Torah and its wisdom," thus establishing a better society firmly built on the Law. This means that moral and intellectual achievements, not the exercise of military might over a huge non-Jewish population, will eventually inaugurate messianic time.

The same criteria, and more, are applied to space. Nachmanides' frequently quoted critical comment on Maimonides—"we shall not leave it in the hand of others . . ."—is not necessarily and exclusively to be applied to maximal boundaries. As Rabbi Yishai Yovel points out, Scripture records a variety of boundaries for Eretz Yisra'el, the Promised Land, thus teaching us that it is not the changing political boundaries but the Land itself which is holy.[22] For example, the boundaries of Canaan at the time of the sons of Noah and their generations are not those promised to Abraham and his descendants at the "Covenant Between the Pieces" (Gen. 10:19; 15:18–21), and both of these differ from the boundaries promised to the children of Israel in the desert (Ex. 23:31); or prior to entering the Land (Deut. 1:7; 33:2–4). There is a further discrepancy between the various promises in the Pentateuch and those for the End of Days provided in Ezekiel (47:13). None of these boundaries coincides with those the tribes were to inherit by lot according to Numbers (34:2–12); nor are they the same as those of the inheritance and settlement found in Joshua (12) or Judges (3, 4). And none of these boundaries even compare with those of the second inheritance at the time of Ezra and Nehemiah or in the days of King Jannai and Agrippa I. Rabbi Yishai Yovel agrees with others, some of whom support policies quite different from his in matters of religion and state relations, that according to Maimonides (*Hilkhot Terumot* 1:5) the second inheritance is legally binding rather than the first; and if so, he concludes, Samaria, for instance, would not be included in the halakhically fixed boundaries, since it was not conquered by those who returned from Babylonia and was only briefly held by the Hasmoneans.

These religious Zionists are not alone in opposing the essential features of political extremism.[23] They oppose the attribution of absolute sanctity to phenomena that they see as historical rather than metahistorical, and, thus, subject to temporary change in matters such as territorial boundaries. They are against the blurring of rational and critical thought by an excess of political romanticism and pious sermonizing. They are against taking a personal mystical experience—no matter how rich and elevating it may be—and transferring it to political events, as this may lead to undemocratic and totalitarian policies, confusing coercion with freedom, indoctrination with education, and radical nationalism (both secular and religious) with democratic national policy.

IV. Forms of Political Messianic Experience: The Conceptual Framework

Texts such as we have seen expressing political messianic attitudes and policies reflect a relatively new phase in the development of Zionism and, therefore, deserve special focus in the last section of this treatise.

First, it is necessary to keep in mind that the authors of texts like these —the members of religious Zionist movements and of the Gush Emunim, the religious members of the Techiyah party and of the Greater Palestine Movement, the religious settlers in Judea and Samaria, teachers in religious schools and *yeshivah* high schools—do not constitute a monolithic block. Among them can be found a number of approaches to the Land and to the State of Israel; some may even be changing their minds, especially when confronting the problems of their relationship to the Arab population or when pondering the latest war.[24]

Also, it is important to keep in mind, when studying their writings, that some believers tend to be reluctant to reveal their innermost creeds, convictions, and feelings to the general public or to the noninitiated. This reluctance is found not only among believers with romantic or mystical inclinations, as one would expect, but also in the realm of halakhic discourse, especially where religious motivations have political implications.[25]

Thus, some of the spiritual leaders of the Gush Emunim advocate deemphasizing—for the time being—their conviction that Southern Lebanon is actually the patrimony of the tribes of Naphtali and Asher, and therefore belongs to greater Palestine no less than any other place in Israel.[26] They also play down, at this time, their contention that, in the light of the organic union of Israel the Land, and Israel the People, the liberal idea of equal rights, independent of ethnic or religious affiliation, can hardly be applied in a Jewish state. Civil rights, it would follow, should be granted to non-Jews only if and when they acknowledge the Noahide Laws according to their Judaic source. [Ed. note: i.e., the covenant said to be made between God and Noah, entailing certain universalistic precepts, such as the establishment of justice and the ban on murder.] Also, they suggest that the non-Jew should be entitled to civil rights only as a *Ger Toshav,* that is, a sojourner, a stranger in the Land who has renounced paganism and observes the seven Noahide Laws, and provided only that the non-Jew wishes to be an Israeli citizen "because of a tremendous admiration for the greatness and holiness of our nation," or if he or she demonstrates "acknowledgement of the great mission of the people of Israel." The non-Jew should not be granted the status of a *Ger Tzedek* who is a "proselyte of righteousness" and who would therefore be entitled to rights and duties equal to the Israeli Jew.[27]

And, finally, there are those who hint at a further position: their conviction that "the continuation of our existence in the Land is dependent upon the emigration of the Arabs," for we read, "They have no place here." Hence, in wartime one should not differentiate between warrior and civilian, for both are Israel's enemy.[28] In short, the people of Israel are commanded to be holy—but not necessarily to be moral or humane according to ordinary criteria. The moral teachings which have been accepted by mankind, in principle at least, do not commit the Jew, who was chosen to be beyond them.[29]

In order to discern some of the emotive and noetic forms in which hermeneutics like these are made possible, it should be kept in mind that political messianism is not limited to the realm of personal, communal, or sectarian salvation. Rather, we are facing a historical process called by Jacob Talmon "the new dispensation" amidst a modern society. In this divine order of worldly affairs, religion and society are totally interdependent so that politics, like religion, tends "to embrace all walks of life." Therefore, the secular state is capable of restoring theocracy to its ancient glory, to its total authority.[30] We are presently facing the emergence of highly articulated and consciously conceptualized forms of consecration of the Land, the Nation, the State, the Wars—in fact of everything and everybody Jewish. A total and all-embracing sacredness of reality—a "mystical realism"—has become a growing factor in Israeli life, education, and politics. This development has a dualistic structure for, while the Gush Emunim trend bestows mystic meaning upon reality, it is not entirely devoid of practical rationality; while it enflames emotions, it is not entirely devoid of sobriety; though it incites to enthusiasm, it does not ignore the tactical need for temporary restraint. It bestows a sense of holiness upon everything and hence embraces even secularism, not on its own merits but as an integral part of God's creation, to be redeemed and converted once the true light is seen and acknowledged by all secularists.

Mystical realism, then, constitutes an organic union unfolding in the process of redemption, here and now. The mystical component of the union is said to be experienced in reality, while reality is said to be experienced in the mystique of being. Both are to be sensed in living action, in the joy of the *mitzvah*—of the devotional fulfillment of a total normative commitment; in the daily renewed experience of the miracle of creation, but equally in the harshness of fear, suffering, pain, sorrow and death; in the devastation —yet also the splendor—of the sanctified wars of Israel.

One of the major expressions of the duality of "mystical realism" is found in the intertwining of the need for personal growth with the commitment to national expansionism. Both reflect a deeply felt urge to escape from a sense of confinement; both are seen as a means to achieving a closer, truer, more authentic participation in the cosmic dimensions of one's concrete existence; both embody the act of the purgation of the soul

and of the purification of the Land; both symbolize the union of time—
the messianic future realized now—and of space—the political sovereignty
over greater Palestine realized here. Eternity is reflected in current time
while cosmology is reflected in the settled Land. The conquest of wider
borders transcends the limitations of time, while the bestowal of eternal
holiness upon the present confirms the absolute consecration of historical
sites, soil, trees, stones, walls, waters, tombstones and burial plots.

The individual, the pious, the devoted, is seized by rapturous zeal,
yet also by a sense of bliss, joy, happiness, or overflowing light and radiance;
one's entire being longs to fuse in glorious communion with peers, congregation, community, settlement, movement, people, and nation. At the same
time, divine inspiration emanates from the Land. The Land embodies God's
sublime presence with overpowering clarity, with beauty and glory. At the
same time, one is neither stricken dumb with amazement, nor overwhelmed
by awe and rapture. Rather, this is an activating, invigorating, and exciting
ecstasy, an exaltation and rapture of ultimate union with the Land, the Nation, and Jewish statehood.

Thus, the realm of secularism is by no means neglected. On the contrary, it is only through natural vitality, through the enjoyment of exuberant
health, through the participation in the cosmic energy that pulsates in all corners of the world—everywhere—but most of all, in the holiness of the Land,
that the divine purpose can be realized. Profane action and divine creation,
physical power and divine might, warfare and waging the war of the Lord,
have now become forms of worship and sacrifice not less than the ordinary
ritual ceremonies. It is at this point that the term "possession" also acquires
its dual meaning; the devotional settler on recently conquered land is possessed by his messianic zeal, while his zeal transforms the conquest into redemption, and temporary borders into eternal horizons, thus realizing the
notion of *eretz nachalah*, of possessing the Holy Land by inheritance.

Like Jacob Talmon's perceptive statement about the language typical
of "Messianic Nationalism," the articulation of this kind of mystical realism
constitutes a "social slant" of theological modes of thinking. Accordingly,
political messianism functions as "a system of social and moral truths expressing God's thinking . . . and when embodied in institutions, constitutes
the Kingdom of God."[31]

Indeed, the cognitive form of Zionistic political messianism is structured quite similarly; it constitutes a duality of intuitive knowledge and practical rationality. While the main source of knowledge, belief and intuition,
is above pragmatic reasoning, its realization requires the use of pragmatism

and, to some extent, discursive thinking. Thus, the cognitive dualism is expressed in the immediacy of experience, the illumination of insight, the intimacy of participation in divine creation, the confidence in revelatory apprehension, on the one hand; and in the bestowal of total holiness upon all aspects of statehood, including power, violence, warfare, and the rule over non-Jewish populations, on the other.

For the political messianists, the knowledge of divine purpose, revealed to the initiated and manifested in all worldly affairs, is accepted as the primary mode of political consciousness. This source of knowledge conditions — or controls, or if necessary, substitutes, for — all other sources such as logical discourse, factual, experiential knowledge, and even a priori transcendental and critical cognition; hence the total superiority and indisputable normative authority this trend claims.

As a result, a process of meaning reversal has taken place. The symbol has been transformed into substance and the substance has been elevated to the realm of the sacred. Political hermeneutics interprets symbolic as well as prophetic texts literally, and is uncompromising in the meaning it derives not only from halakhic texts but even from literary, legendary, poetic, and edifying texts that have not previously enjoyed legally binding authority.

Moreover, the symbol participates in the concrete object to which it previously referred so that the difference between matter and form, material and spirit, sign and signified, past and future, intrinsic and extrinsic, perception and imagination, mundane and spiritual, essential and accidental, is dissolved; the hidden meaning is revealed and the apparent revelation is concealed in everything. This entire framework embodies the new position in which political messianists find themselves.

Pious, devotional believers no longer stand at a distance in respect to themselves, to the Land, to the Nation or to the State; they cease to accept the multiplicity of meanings and the complexity of existence. An all-inclusive totality reduces every phenomenon to its singular level of signification, creating a feeling of absolute certainty, of divine justification, of joy and of peace amidst an agonizing historical reality of antagonism, conflict, and warfare.

V. Closing Remarks—on the Contextual Framework

In contemporary historical, political and religious thought, there is a growing tendency to link social reality and theology. A significant current

in this development, especially in recent years, has been "political theology,"
which in itself includes a variety of trends. Semantically all are derived from
one root, from the original expression as voiced by Terentius Varro, which
is discussed in Augustine's *City of God*. Structurally, political theology takes
mythic forms, contrary to the forms of critical rationalism, on the one hand,
or of sheer metaphysics, on the other. Both language and form create a
framework for the interpretation of the political community in terms of
a divinized polis, even though its functions as such are secular, earthly, and
concrete. Thus a dialectic structure evolves whereby secular socio-political
needs are sacralized, while sacral, religious values are incorporated in secular, this-worldly affairs.

On this basis, political theology in our days has developed several systematic and dogmatic teachings.[32] Some theologians consider the renewed
term "political theology" a suitable framework for the awakening Third
World and the protest movements against racial, ethnic, economic, or sexual discrimination. This trend is sometimes called "revolutionary theology,"
for it accords political theology the character of a liberation movement. For
example, according to Paul Lehmann's *The Transfiguration of Politics*, religion
should not be confined to the individual or to society, nor to intellectual
historicism or critical demythologization, but should be politically involving, expressing civic and socio-ethical responsibility.

Others, such as Herbert W. Richardson and M. Darrol Bryant, consider political theology as a dialectical context for the constitutional separation of church and state, as opposed to the accepted historical interrelationship of religion and society. These dialectics have brought about a "civil
religion" which enables a democracy to function in the light of sacred, social
values, rooted in what Jonathan Edwards, back in the first half of the eighteenth century, called "America as God's Kingdom."

Still another trend—elaborated by Jürgen Moltmann and Johann B.
Metz—considers political theology, in addition to its liberating function,
as expressing a lesson to be learned from the historical experience of the
Third Reich, an experience that was critically termed by Eric Voegelin, on
the eve of World War II, "political religion."[33] As Jacob Talmon has shown,
this entire development in the modern era is rooted in historical movements
which at one and the same time prepared the ground for rationalism and
irrationalism, political self-restraint and political messianism—that is, the
Enlightenment, national Romanticism, and social Utopianism.

In the light of the interdisciplinary symposia on Religion and Political
Society, held in Europe in 1970 and in Canada in 1974, which dealt with

"the Enlightenment conceptions of rationalism and freedom . . . as principles for guiding political philosophy and theology today,"[34] the dilemma of political theology may be summed up as follows: if religion is to be conscientiously relevant, it must be involved in socio-political life. Since the authority of religion is divine, and thus absolute, introducing religion into socio-political affairs frequently brings about the absolute sacralization of those affairs. As a result, political religions emerge which transform the categories of history—time and space—into categories of political myth. Thus, time and space transcend history with its concrete, empirical past and present, projecting politics into a future structured as the fulfillment of the past and as the realization of primordial, archaic myth. History is now understood as time and space reborn—hence, as metahistory.

Notes

1. *Eretz-Nachalah-Zechutenu al Eretz Yisra'el* (*Land . . . as an Inheritance— Our Right on the Land of Israel*), Judah Shaviv, ed., (Youth Dept. of the Mafdal, Jerusalem, 1976), 143 pp.

2. Ibid., pp. 111–12, the late Rabbi E. Hadaya, "Is it Permissible to Return Conquered Territory—All or part of it?" (from his article in *No'am I*); see also *Gedolei Hatorah al Hachzarat Hashetachim* (*Rabbinical Authorities on Return of the Territories*), (Bnei-Brak: 1980), p. 126. This pamphlet, published without name of editor or publisher, includes the expressions of rabbis, Chasidic leaders, leaders of Agudat Israel, et sim., on the prohibition of returning territories to non-Jews; some of the extracts seem to have been taken out of their context.

3. *Nekudah*, Journal of the Settlements in Judea, Samaria and the Gaza Strip, published by the Association for Furthering the Colonization and Absorption in Judea, Samaria and Gaza Strip; Ofra, Doar Na Hills of Jerusalem. See, for example, Joel bin Nun, "Yesh gam Milchamah Musarit" ("There is also a Moral War"), *Nekudah* 47 (September 3, 1982), pp. 4, 5, 14. Also see Hagai Segal's interview of Rabbi Shlomo Aviner: "Leromem et Haruach" ("To Lift the Spirit"), *Nekudah* 48 (1982), pp. 4, 5. Cf. Shmaryahu Arieli, *Mishpat Hamilchamah* (*The Rules of War*) (Jerusalem: Reuven Mass Pub., 1971), esp. the chapter: "The Wars of the State of Israel," pp. 107ff.

4. Deuteronomy 11:24; Joel Elitzur, "Hagam Levanon Hi Eretz-Yisra'el?" ("Is Lebanon also the Land of Israel?"), *Nekudah* 48, (the High Holidays' Issue of 1982), p. 12. A systematic and dogmatic definition of "the holiness of conquered areas according to Jewish Law," according to this trend is offered by Rabbi Shlomo Goren in the light of the Six Day War. He isolates the category of all areas and territories which were sanctified by the returnees from the Babylonian Exile, spe-

cifically with a view to the commandments that can be observed in the Land of
Israel alone. The sanctity of such areas and territories continues to be valid and
binding for our days and the days to come. This approach is based on Maimonides'
Hilkhot Terumot, Chapter 1, Rule 5 and also on Chapter 1, Rule 2: " . . . the Land
of Israel . . . [denotes] each place conquered by the King of Israel or a prophet with
the approval of the majority of Israelites, and this is called conquest by majority. . . ."
Cf. Rabbi S. Goren, *Torat Hamo'adim* (*The Teachings of the Festivals*), (Tel-Aviv:
Abraham Zioni, 1964), p. 614. In the light of this approach see the detailed treatise
by Rabbi Yigal Ariel on Trans-Jordan and the Golan in the Halakhah, *Eretz Yarden
Vehermonim* (*Land of Jordan and the Hermons*), (Chaspit, Golan-Heights: The Golan
Academy, 1979), 42 pp., especially: ". . . the second sanctity—the conquest by Ezra
and the generations that followed," pp. 24ff.; also see there the map on the areas
settled by the returnees from Babylon, p. 26.

5. Platform of Oz Veshalom (9 paragraphs); also see selected paragraphs
of the "Platform" in *Oz Veshalom* 3, pp. 15, 16. Moshe Unna "Mi Kove'a Adifuyot
Le'umiot" ("Who determines National Priorities"), in *Yedion Hachug Hara'yoni-Medini
Letsionut Datit* (Bulletin of Oz Veshalom—Religious Zionists for Strength and Peace;
henceforth: *Yedion*) 9 (November, 1977), p. 9 (reprinted from *Hatsofeh*, October
11, 1977); Uriel Simon, "Hahitnachalut Bihudah Uveshomron: Bechinah Musarit-
Datit: ("The Settlement in Judea and Samaria—a Moral-religious Examination"),
in *Yedion* 10, (1978), p. 4; Mordecai Breuer, "Hama'avak Leshalom Vehamachaneh
Hadatit" ("The Struggle for Peace and the Religious Camp"), in *Yedion* 16 (1978),
pp. 8–12. On the impact of these issues on parents of members of the religious
Zionist youth movement "Bnei Akiva," see for example: *Yedion* 19 (June–August,
1979), pp. 4–15, and 21 (November–December 1979), pp. 3, 4; also *Amudim*, the
Journal of The Religious Kibbutz, Vol. 27, No. 402 (1979), pp. 223–26. Cf. J. O'dea-
Aviad, "The Messianic Problem," reprinted from the *Jerusalem Post*, in *Yedion* 16
(September–October, 1978), pp. 18–19. See also Z. Yaron, "A Criticism of 'Mes-
sianic Policy,'" in *Immanuel* 4 (1974), pp. 105–08.

6. P. L. Berger, *The Sacred Canopy—Elements of a Sociological Theory of Reli-
gion*, (Garden City, N.Y., 1967), pp. 44–47. See also P. Berger & T. Luckmann,
The Social Construction of Reality—A Treatise in the Sociology of Knowledge, (Norwich,
Penguin ed., 1979), pp. 122ff.

7. A. Schutz, "Some Structures of the 'Life World,'" in *Collected Papers* III,
(The Hague, 1966), pp. 118–139. See also M. Natanson: "Alfred Schutz Symposium: The Pregivenness of Sociality," in D. Ihde & R. M. Zaner, eds., *Interdisciplinary Phenomenology: Selected Studies in Phenomenology and Existential Philosophy*,
No. 6, (The Hague, 1977), pp. 109ff.

8. H. G. Gadamer, *Wahrheit und Methode* (Tübingen, 1965), II, 1, a, pp.
290ff.

9. U. Tal, "The Land and the State of Israel in Israeli Religious Life," in
Proceedings of the Rabbinical Assembly, 76th Annual Convention, 38 (1976); pp. 1–

40. See also idem, "Historical and Metahistorical Self-Views in Religious Zionism," in *Self-Views in Historical Perspective in Egypt and Israel*, S. Shamir, ed., (Tel Aviv, 1980), pp. 89–99.

      10. *Morashah (Heritage)* 9 (Jerusalem: Youth Department of the Mafdal, together with the Department for Religious Education and Culture in the Diaspora of the World Zionist Federation, Winter 1975), especially the part, "The Redemption of the People and the Land," pp. 8–65. The following are examples of self-expression typical to this movement. Rabbi Shlomo Aviner, "Sha'ar ha-Aretz" ("Section: The Land") in *Artzi (My Land)*, Journal for the Study of the Living Relationship between Israel and its Land in our Generation, 1, Jehudah Baharav, ed., (Jerusalem: Committee for the Deepening of the Land of Israel Consciousness, 1982), pp. 7–34. Also see *Gush Emunim: Tokhnit-Av Lehityashvut Bihudah Uveshomron, (Gush-Emunim: Basic Plan for the Settlement in Judea and Samaria)*, n.d., p. 41; and *Gush-Emunim: Hatza'ah Letokhnit Hityashvutit Bihudah Uveshomron (Gush-Emunim: A Proposal for a Settlement Plan in Judea and Samaria)*, Jerusalem: Summer, 1979, p. 6. On Gush-Emunim in its beginnings see: Benny Gal, ed., *Al-Emunim* (Jerusalem, 1976), pp. 3–38; also *Sefer Eretz Yisra'el Hashelemah (The Greater Palestine Book)*, Ahron Ben Ami, ed., published by the Movement for Greater Palestine (Tel Aviv: S. Friedman Pub., 1977), Part one: "Israel's Right on its Land," pp. 38ff.; Part Two, "Security and Foreign Policy," pp. 155ff.; Part Three, "Demography and Zionist Revolution," pp. 308ff. See the following most helpful studies on the Gush-Emunim Movement: Tsvi Ra'anan, *Gush Emunim* (Hebrew), pub. by the kibbutz Artzi, the Shomer Ha-Tzair (Tel-Aviv, 1980), 229 pp. with supplements; Amnon Rubinstein, *Miherzl ad Gush-Emunim Uvechazarah (From Herzl till Gush Emunim and Back)*, (Tel-Aviv: Schocken, 1980), 180 pp., Danny Rubinstein, *Mi Ladonai Elai – Gush Emunim (On the Lord's Side: Gush Emunim)*, (Tel-Aviv: Hakibbutz Hame'uchad, 1982), 197 pp.

      11. Shlomo Goren, *The Teachings of the Festivals*, pp. 542–551.

      12. Rabbi Shlomo Aviner, "Harealism Hameshikhi" ("The Messianic Realism"), in *Morashah* 9, p. 63; also see his essays in *Artzi* 1 – see above note 10. Here, as elsewhere, Aviner reflects the attitudes of Rabbi Zvi Yehudah Kook who said: ". . . People speak of the beginning of the redemption. In my opinion this is already the *middle* of the redemption . . ." According to Zvi Yehudah, the return to Zion, its conquest and settlement and the ". . . Kingdom of Israel being rebuilt anew . . . this is the revelation of the Kingdom of Heaven. . . ." Reprinted in the collection of essays *Torah Umelukhah – al Mekom Hamedinah Beyahadut (Law and Kingdom – on the Position of the State in Judaism)*, ed. by Shimon Federbusch (Jerusalem: Mosad Harav Kook, 1961), pp. 102–3. In the same spirit, Yehudah Chazani too quotes Zvi Yehudah Kook's *Lintivot Yisra'el (On the Ways of Israel)*, Part Two, p. 159; accordingly the State of Israel in our days is indeed the State foretold by the Prophets, among other reasons precisely because of the prominent place secularism fulfils in the process of salvation; see *Nekudah* 37 (December 18, 1981), p. 8.

13. *Torat Hamo'adim*, p. 551; also see a parallel source: in "Torah Uge'ullah" ("Law and Redemption"), in the above mentioned collection of essays *Torah Umelukhah*, p. 108, Rabbi Israel Shchepansky asserts that indeed all the wars, whether of the time of the Exodus from Egypt or in our own day, are part of the overall program for redemption, the character of which is yet natural, ". . . that they conquer the Land in a natural way, with weapons, so as to lift the people from dejection of slavery and subjugation, the result of which was the habit of stretching one's neck out for one's annihilators. . . . So as to breathe in him the spirit of courage and an 'elevated soul'. . . ."

14. Yehudah Amital, *Hama'alot Mima'amakim Devarim Besugiot Hador al Hateshuot ve'al Hamilchamot* (*The Ascents out of the Depths — Issues of our Generation on the Deliverances and on the Wars*), pub. by the Association of the Har-Etzion Talmudic Academy, Allon-Shevut, (Jerusalem, 1974), p. 21 (also cf. p. 22) and p. 28. Rabbi Amital seems to have changed his mind recently: see Yehudah Amital, "Messer Politi o Messer Chinukhi" ("A Political or an Educational Message"), in *Torah, Zionut, Shalom — Kovetz Ma'amarim*, pub. by Tenuat Netivot Shalom (The Paths of Peace Movement), (Jerusalem, 1983), pp. 3–8. See especially Rabbi Yehudah Amital's more detailed deliberations in *Allon Shevut*, ed. by Jossi Eliav, Har-Etzion Talmudic Academy, 1983, pp. 34–52.

15. *Kiryat-Arba hi Hebron* (*Kiryat-Arba indeed is Hebron*), Collection of Articles and Pictures on the Occasion of the Ten Year Anniversary since the Renewal of the Jewish Settlement in Hebron, Passover 1968–Passover 1978, ed. by Moshe Ozri, (Beer-Sheva: Mor, n.d.), p. 98. Also see *Alon Moreh-Chidush Hayishuv Hayehudi Beshomron* (*Alon Moreh — The Renewal of the Jewish Settlement in Samaria*), (Jerusalem, n.d.). Also, see the reports on discussions and polemics among members of The Religious Kibbutz such as in the aftermath of the conference entitled "Settlement — Foundation of Sovereignty," organized by the action-committee of the Hebron Hill Settlements, together with the Secretariat of The Religious Kibbutz, in *Amudim*, No. 388 (1978), pp. 155ff; also see Moshe Unna, "Settlement — Not Conquest," in *Amudim*, No. 390 (1978), pp. 221–23; and the response by Moshe Yogev of Kfar Etzion to Danny Lazar, "Shilo is Holier than Sa'ad," in *Amudim* No. 403 (1979), pp. 264ff.

16. "Communiqué to the Press," by Chief Rabbi Shlomo Goren of April 1, 1979 (No. 213/79); "Communiqué to the Press" by the Council of the Chief Rabbinate on the decision of March 28, 1979; "Communiqué by the Council of the Chief Rabbinate" presided by Chief Rabbi Goren, of May 23, 1979 (No. 612). See the declaration by Chief Rabbi the Rishon Lezion Yosef Ovadia on "Hachzarat Shetachim lema'an Hashalom le'or Hahalakhah" ("Returning territories for the sake of Peace in the Light of the Jewish Law"), of August 27, 1979; Cf. *Jerusalem Post*, August 22, 1979; August 23, 1979; September 5, 1979; and Rabbi Yosef's Radio Declaration according to *Ha'aretz*, September 15, 1978. A most informative source is the list of Rabbinic declarations, decisions and rulings on: "Our Right on the

Temple Site," on the absolute sanctity of "Holy Places"; on the "Prohibition against Returning Territories of the Land of Israel to non-Jews," on the belongingness of Judea and Samaria to the Land of Israel; on "Prayer for the Wholeness of the Land of Israel," in *Me'orot,* Quarterly of the Israel Chief Rabbinate on Issues of Jewish Law, Legend, Ethics and Judaism 1:1 (1979/80), Jerusalem, pp. 122ff. Also see an instructive example of political exegesis of the prohibition *lo techonnem* ("and show no mercy to them" or "do not allow them encampment"): Joseph Mizrahi of Kiryat Arba Yeshiva, "Israeli Sovereignty over the Land of Israel," in the pamphlet *Kiryat-Arba hi Hebron (Kiryat-Arba indeed is Hebron)*, p. 13.

17. Ephraim E. Urbach, "Mashma'utah Hadatit shel Hahalakhah" ("The Religious Significance of the Jewish Law"), in *Al Yahadut Vechinukh (On Judaism and Education)*, pub. by the School of Education of Hebrew University, (Jerusalem, 1967), pp. 127ff. This essay has been reprinted in a number of publications such as *Erkei Hayahadut (Values of Judaism)*, a collection of lectures, pub. by Makhbarot Lesifrut (Tel-Aviv, 1963), pp. 24ff. Also see Ephraim E. Urbach, "Who is a Hero— The One Who Turns his Enemy into his Friend," a paper delivered at a Symposium on the Israel-Arab conflict, Van Leer Institute, (Jerusalem, January 1970), in *Petachim*, No. 3 (13) 1970, pp. 5ff. Also see one of the educational attempts at teaching constructive social values in the framework of Jewish Law: *Torah Ve'avodah— Leket Mekorot Uma'amarim (Judaism and Labor—A Collection of Sources and Essays)*, pub. by the B'nai Akiba Youth Movement in Israel, collected and edited by Jochanan ben Yaakov, (Kfar-Etzion, Spring 1979), (The 50th Anniversary Year: 1929–1979), pp. 129ff. The volume includes essays critical of the *Torah Ve'avodah* policies as well, such as by Rabbi Ya'akov Ariel Stiglitz, pp. 124ff. Also see Mordecai Breuer, "Hama'avak Leshalom Vehamakhaneh Hadati" ("The Struggle for Peace and the Religious Camp"), in *Yedion* 16 (September–October 1978), pp. 8–12.

18. See above note 5, and also principles 3, 4. One of the earlier expressions of this attitude has been given by Pinchas Rosenblüth: "Lemahutah shel Medinah Datit" ("On the Nature of a Religious State"), *Gevilin— lemachshavah Datit Le'umit (Leaves—for Religious National Thought)*, No. 1 (Tel-Aviv, May 1957), pp. 13–16.

19. Uriel Simon, "Religion, Morality and Politics," in *Forum*, (Jerusalem, Winter 1978), pp. 102–10. See also Simon's warning against ". . . the danger of false Messianism"; "Biblical Calling—Conditional Promises," in *Petachim*, No. 2 (32), Jerusalem, 1975, p. 24.

20. *Af Sha'al—Mitzvah Min Hatorah (Not an Inch—According to the Law)*, pub. by Oz Veshalom (Jerusalem, 1978); the booklet includes questions by Moshe Unna and responses by Rabbis Shaul Yisraeli, Haim David Halevy, and an essay by Dr. Mordecai Breuer, pp. 10–16. Also see Rabbi Ahron Lichtenstein, "Reaffirming National and Israeli Pride—An Open Letter to the Prime Minister," in: *Torah-Zionut-Shalom*, pub. by the Tenuat Netivot-Shalom ("The Ways of Peace Movement"), (Jerusalem, 1983), pp. 9–12. Cf. the polemics between Abraham Abba Weingurt and Mordecai Breuer on the issue of returning territories of the Land

of Israel to non-Jews, in: *Hama'ayan* 18:4 (1977–78), pp. 1–29, pub. by the Isaac Breuer Institute of the Po'alei Agudat–Israel Movement, Jerusalem.

21. Rabbi Yishai Yovel, "Hitnachalut–Ya'avor Ve'al Yehareg" ("Settlement– Let one transgress [the law] and not be Killed," in *Morashah* 9, p. 29 (cf. pp. 26–30).

22. Ibid., pp. 28, 29. On the entire issue of the borders of the Land of Israel, their religious significance, and their historical and political development, see two significant publications published by the Israel Defence Forces: a) "Al Eretz Yisra'el Ligvuloteha" ("On the Land of Israel According to its Borders") in *Machanayim*, No. 127 (1972), pub. by the Chief Rabbinate of I.D.F.; b) "Eretz Yisra'el Beyahadut" ("The Land of Israel in Judaism"), in *Sekirah Chodshit* (Monthly Survey for the officers' corps of I.D.F.), No. 4–5, April–May 1979, pub. by the Chief of Staff, Chief Education Officer, pp. 1ff; pp. 37ff.; pp. 43ff. On the position of the Gush Emunim trend see Yoel Elitzur, "Hagam Levanon Hi Eretz-Yisra'el?" ("Is Lebanon also the Land of Israel?"), in *Nekudah* 48, The High Holy Days Edition, 1982/3, pp. 10ff.

23. Cf. Joshua Arieli, "Historical Attachment and Historical Right," in *Forum* 28–29 (Jerusalem, Winter 1979), pp. 90–101, and Nathan Rotenstreich, "Tizkoret al Ribonut" ("A Reminder on Sovereignty"), in the Literary Supplement of *Yediot Acharonot* (November 8, 1974); as to the critical and phenomenological approach of the author to the entire issue see Rotenstreich's significant study: *Otzma Udemutah* (*Power and its Mould*), (Jerusalem: Bialik Inst., 1963), pp. 94–123. Also see *Sipuach O Shalom* (*Annexation or Peace*), a collection of articles on the future of the administered territories, (Tel-Aviv, December 1967), pub. by the Movement for Israel-Palestine Federation, 40 pp.; see especially the contributions by S. Yizhar, Shulamit Har-Even, Boaz Evron, Amos Elon, Moshe Unna. Cf. A. Plascov, "A Palestinian State? Examining the Alternatives," *Adelphi Papers*, No. 163 (London: The International Institute for Strategic Studies, 1981), pp. 13–59.

24. See note 14; also cf. Chanan Porat's criticism of Rabbi Yehudah Amital: "Matai ein Cholkim Kavod Lerav" ("When does one not show Honor to a Rabbi-Teacher"), in *Nekudah* 50 (November 22, 1982), pp. 6, 7. On the varieties of opinions among Gush Emunim members, see for example: Rabbi Moshe Levinger, "We and the Arabs," in *Nekudah* 36 (November 27, 1981), pp. 8–11, 15; Illan Tor, "A Remedy for a National Mental Disease," in *Nekudah* 39 (February 5, 1982), pp. 8, 9; also, Eli Sadan, "To Establish Once Again the Jewish State," in *Nekudah* 35 (October 30, 1981), pp. 6, 7, 11; Yehuda Chazani, "The Jewish State was Established in 1948," in *Nekudah* 37 (December 18, 1981); Rabbi Shlomo Aviner, "Under Certain Circumstances it is Necessary to Act Forcefully," in *Nekudah* 38 (January 15, 1982), pp. 6/7. A significant example of differences of opinion among Gush Emunim members is the following group of articles: Rabbi Yehuda Shaviv (the name of Gideon Erlich was erroneously ascribed to the author), "Go, Turn to the Jewish Law" (in Hebrew, the words "go" and "Halakhah," i.e. Jewish Law, share the same root), in *Nekudah* 45 (July 16, 1982), pp. 16, 17; Yedidya Segal, "Indeed, Do Go to the Jewish Law," in *Nekudah* 47 (September 3, 1982), p. 7; Uri Dasberg,

"There is No Moral War," in *Nekudah* 49 (October 22, 1982), pp. 19, 20, 21. A voice against hatred and contempt towards the Arabs was raised by Miriam Shilo, "Thou shalt not Hate," in *Nekudah* 34 (September 8, 1981), pp. 16, 17. As to the varieties of opinion among the Religious Kibbutz members, see the polemics following the talk of Rabbi Shlomo Aviner to I.D.F. officers, the summary of which appeared in *Artzi* 2 (Summer, 1982), pp. 4–13; cf. especially the contributions by Amnon Shapira in *Amudim*, the Journal of the Religious Kibbutz Movement, No. 443 (1982), pp. 48–49, and "Reacting to Rabbi Aviner," in *Amudim*, No. 444, pp. 89–93, and "The People of Israel and the Land of Israel," in *Amudim*, No. 445, pp. 131–39. Amnon Shapira disagrees with Shlomo Aviner's assertion that ". . . even if there is peace we ought to initiate a war of redemption in order to conquer it [the Land]. . . ." Also see the source selection by Uriel Simon entitled "On Jewish Ethics of War," in his essay, *Shedding of Blood—Legal-Ethical Perspectives*, Oz Veshalom Publication Series, No. 2, pp. 10–16.

25. Rabbi Shlomo Aviner, ". . . That They May Not Understand One Another's Speech . . ." in *Nekudah* 27 (April 17, 1981), pp. 6, 7. Rabbi Shlomo Aviner, interviewed by Chaggai Segal, stated: "Let us, by no means, delete verses from the Torah which show that Lebanon is nothing but part of the Land of Israel, and that he who was killed in the latest war died on Israeli soil, kissing sacred ground. But, as we said, one should not say things that are unacceptable. A call for the annexation of Judea and Samaria, on the other hand, is indeed acceptable . . . ," in *Nekudah* 48, the High Holy Days issue, 1982, pp. 4, 5. On the necessity not to reveal openly, in public, all that the Jewish Law commands in matters such as the conquest of the Land, its borders, etc., according to Gush-Emunim interpretation, see especially Rabbi Yehuda Herzl Henkin, "Halakhot Shelo Lefirsum" ("Jewish Laws not to be Publicized"), in *Nekudah* 50 (November 12, 1982), pp. 14, 15.

26. See above, *Nekudah* 48, pp. 4, 5; also, see the detailed argumentation according to which the holiness of the Land of Israel embraces also the territories of Transjordan, Lebanon and probably even more: Yoel Elitzur, "Is Lebanon also the Land of Israel?," in *Nekudah* 48, pp. 10–13.

27. Illan Tor, "A Remedy for a National Mental Disease," in *Nekudah* 39 (February 5, 1982), pp. 8, 9; cf. Rabbi Moshe Levinger, "We and the Arabs," in *Nekudah* 36 (November 27, 1981), pp. 8, 9, 11, 15.

28. As above, the essay by Illan Tor; also see Yoel bin Nun, "There is Also a Moral War," in *Nekudah* 47 (September 3, 1982), p. 14. An entirely different religious Zionist approach to the Arab population is shown by Rabbi Shilo Raphael, "The Rights of the Minorities in Israel According to Jewish Law," reproduced with some omissions in the booklet *Hachzarat Shetachim, Zekhuyot Miyutim (The Return of Territories, Minorities' Rights)*, Oz Veshalom Publications, No. 3, pp. 11–14.

29. Yehoshua Zuckerman, "The Realization Ambushes the Faith," in *Nekudah* 43 (May 21, 1982), pp. 18–22. The metaphysical interpretation of the holiness of the Jewish people in the teachings of Rabbi Abraham Isaac Kook has been

transformed into a political strategy by his son, Rabbi Zvi Yehudah, and his disciples. Accordingly, the State of Israel is exempted from ordinary, moral commitments, for the Jews' ethics are bound by a unique and exclusive relationship to God, totally different from universal ethics. See, for example, *Nekudah* 47 (September 3, 1982), pp. 4, 5.

30. J. L. Talmon, *Political Messianism—The Romantic Phase* (London, 1960), pp. 65ff.

31. Ibid., p. 233.

32. S. Wiedenhofer, *Politische Theologie*, (Stuttgart-Berlin-Köln-Mainz, 1976), pp. 31–68; H. Peukert, ed., *Diskussion Zur "politischen Theologie,"* (Mainz, 1969); A. Kee, ed., *The Scope of Political Theology* (London 1978), Chaps. 1, 2.

33. J. Moltmann, et. al., *Religion and Political Society* (New York, Evanston, San Francisco, London, 1970), pp. 49ff.; 95ff.

34. Ibid., Preface.